ELIZABETHAN WOMEN AND THE POETRY OF COURTSHIP

This book offers an original study of lyric form and social custom in the Elizabethan age. Ilona Bell explores the tendency of Elizabethan love poems not only to represent an amorous thought, but to conduct the courtship itself. Where recent studies have focused on courtiership, patronage and preferment at court, her focus is on love poetry, amorous courtship, and relations between Elizabethan men and women. The book examines the ways in which the tropes and rhetoric of love poetry were used to court Elizabethan women (not only at court and in the great houses, but in society at large) and how the women responded to being wooed, in prose, poetry and speech. Bringing together canonical male poets and recently discovered women writers, Ilona Bell investigates a range of texts addressed to, written by, read, heard or transformed by Elizabethan women, and charts the beginnings of an early modern female lyric tradition.

Ilona Bell is Professor of English Literature at Williams College in Massachusetts. She has held a number of research fellowships, and published essays and reviews on Renaissance literature in a wide range of periodicals.

A Marriage Feast at Bermondsey by Joris Hoefnagel, 1570.

ELIZABETHAN WOMEN AND THE POETRY OF COURTSHIP

ILONA BELL

CAMBRIDGE
UNIVERSITY PRESS

PUBLISHED BY THE PRESS SYNDICATE OF THE UNIVERSITY OF CAMBRIDGE
The Pitt Building, Trumpington Street, Cambridge, United Kingdom

CAMBRIDGE UNIVERSITY PRESS
The Edinburgh Building, Cambridge CB2 2RU, UK
40 West 20th Street, New York, NY 10011–4211, USA
10 Stamford Road, Oakleigh, VIC 3166, Australia
Ruiz de Alarcón 13, 28014 Madrid, Spain
Dock House, The Waterfront, Cape Town 8001, South Africa

http://www.cambridge.org

First published 1998
Reprinted 2000

Printed in the United Kingdom at the University Press, Cambridge

Typeset in Baskerville MT 11/12½ [SE]

A catalogue record for this book is available from the British Library

Library of Congress Cataloguing in Publication data
Bell, Ilona
Elizabethan women and the poetry of courtship / by Ilona Bell.
p.   cm.
Includes bibliographical references pp. 230–57 and index.
ISBN 0 521 63007 x hardback
1. English poetry – Early modern, 1500–1700 – History and criticism.
2. Love poetry, English – History and criticism.   3. Women and
literature – England – History – 16th century.   4. English poetry –
Women authors – History and criticism.   5. Man–woman relationships
in literature.   6. Authorship – Sex differences.   7. Courtship in
literature.   I. Title.
PR535.L7B45   1998
821'.3093543–dc21   98-3857   CIP

ISBN 0 521 63007 x hardback

To Bob –
Let us love nobly, and live, and add again
Years and years unto years, till we attain
To write threescore.

John Donne, "The Anniversarie"

But if – fie of such a but! – you be born so near the dull-making cataract of Nilus, that you cannot hear the planet-like music of poetry; if you have so earth-creeping a mind that it cannot lift itself up to look to the sky of poetry . . . thus much curse I must send you in behalf of all poets: that while you live you live in love, and never get favour, for lacking skill of a sonnet. Sidney, *Defence of Poesy*

Contents

Illustrations

Acknowledgments

I am indebted to the National Endowment for the Humanities, the Francis C. Oakley Center for the Humanities and Social Sciences, the Williams College Faculty Research Fund, the Mary Ingraham Bunting Institute, and D. L. Smith for their generous support. Numerous colleagues and friends, Lynda Bundtzen, Teresa Cader, Lawrence Graver, Suzanne Graver, John Kleiner, Carole Levin, Carol Ockman, Christopher Pye, Lawrence Raab, John Reichert, Shawn Rosenheim, Stephen Tifft, and Anita Sokolsky, have read various chapters and offered invaluable advice.

My debts to other scholars of Renaissance poetry, Elizabethan women, and early modern England – are only barely indicated by the footnotes. I am especially thankful to Anne Davidson Ferry for teaching me to respect and love better the elegant intricacies of Renaissance poetry, and to Barbara Lewalski for asking me questions about Elizabethan women that I had no idea how to answer. Heather Dubrow not only taught me a great deal by her own writing on Renaissance poetry but also helped clarify mine. Clark Hulse's careful reading of the entire manuscript and astute suggestions were an unexpected boon. Darra Goldstein ran many miles with me and this book, and offered wise counsel and unflagging support all the way. My daughters, Kaitlin Jessica Bell and Amanda Dana Bell, provided a continuing source of inspiration, and Amanda supplied the title. I hope their view of the project ("I HATE Mom's book!") is not widespread. Above all, I am grateful to Robert Bell for the rich and witty conversations which helped me appreciate the poetry and playfulness of courtship, and for commenting so sensibly on the seemingly endless drafts of this manuscript.

I want to thank the librarians at Sawyer Library and Chapin Library who could not have been more unstinting with their help, and Josie Dixon, my editor, whose continuing support of this project is much appreciated. My students at Smith College, the Massachusetts Institute of Technology, and Williams College shared my education in Renaissance women, and my conversations with them remain a vital part of my own dialogues with Renaissance love poems. Brian Boucher, Elizabeth Geren, Christopher Kavanaugh, Anne Mallory, Tanya Stanciu, Nancy Vorsanger, and Margaret Wildrick, provided helpful editorial and research assistance. Anne Just edited and scrupulously checked an earlier draft of the manuscript. Any remaining blunders, oversimplifications, or over-complications are entirely my own doing.

This project began as an essay on the role of the lady in Donne's *Songs and Sonnets*, and a fascination with Elizabeth I's love language. Trying to understand the lives not only of Anne More Donne and Elizabeth Tudor but of all Elizabethan women proved so arduous and extensive an undertaking that Donne's poetry and Elizabeth's politics were relegated to the margins. And so I conclude this book haunted by the feeling that "Thou has not done."

Abbreviations

AS   *Astrophil and Stella*   Philip Sidney in *Poems*, William A. Ringler, Jr, (ed.) (Oxford: Clarendon Press, 1962)

SS   *Shakespeare's Sonnets*   *The Riverside Shakespeare*, G. Blakemore Evans *et al.* (eds.) (Boston: Houghton Mifflin, 1974)

Am   *Amoretti*   Edmund Spenser, *The Amoretti*, Edwin Greenlaw *et al.* (eds.) *The Works of Edmund Spenser: A Variorum Edition*. 10 volumes (Baltimore: Johns Hopkins Press, 1932–49), vol. VIII pp. 193–232.

Rom.   *Romeo and Juliet*   *The Riverside Shakespeare*, G. Blakemore Evans *et al.* (eds.) (Boston: Houghton Mifflin, 1974)

AYL   *As You Like It*   *The Riverside Shakespeare*, G. Blakemore Evans *et al.* (eds.) (Boston: Houghton Mifflin, 1974)

TT   *The Temple*   Herbert George, *The Works of George Herbert*, F. E. Hutchinson (ed.) (Oxford: Clarendon Press, 1970)

RS   *Rime Sparse*   Francesco Petrarch, *Petrarch's Lyric Poems: The Rime Sparse and Other Lyrics*, Robert Durling (trans. and ed.) (Cambridge: Harvard University Press, 1976)

DP   Sidney's *Defence of Poesie*   From *The Countesse Pembrokes Arcadia* (London, 1598)

AEP   *The Arte of English Poesie*   George Puttenham, *The Arte of English Poesie*, Gladys Doidge Willcock and Alice Walker (eds.) (Cambridge University Press, 1936)

PS   Poems and Sonnets   Sidney, Sir Philip, 'Poems and Sonnets of Sundrie Other Noble men and Gentlemen.' Syr P. S. his Astrophel and Stella. To the end of wh. are added Sundry other rare sonnets of divers gentlemen. J3v–L2v.

An introduction to Elizabethan courtship

Love's not so pure, and abstract, as they use
To say, which have no Mistresse but their Muse,
But as all else, being elemented too,
Love sometimes would contemplate, sometimes do
                    Donne, "Love's growth"[1]

A QUESTION TO BE ASKED

The fall I was on sabbatical, beginning this book, I found myself looking around to see if I could recognize a familiar face behind the faces that you meet at Halloween parties. A ghoul walked over and announced that he was on his way to Siberia to buy a gold mine. Great line, I thought, wondering what he really did for a living. I said I was working down the street at the Bunting Institute, writing a book about the poetry and prac-tice of courtship in Elizabethan England. To my surprise, he became visibly excited and said, "You absolutely must make your students mem-orize lots of Sidney, Shakespeare, and Donne. It's the most useful thing I did at college."

I was wondering just what he meant by "useful," thinking he was probably the kind of person who intones lofty poems at weddings and funerals, when he took off his mask and said, "When, in disgrace with Fortune and men's eyes, I all alone beweep my outcast state . . ."[2] Moved by his tone, but still skeptical about his poetics – not to mention that gold mine – I asked whether he had turned to Shakespeare for solace over the plummeting stock market. "Yes," he replied, "but that's not the main reason Renaissance poetry has been so helpful. I've used Shakespeare and Donne to woo all my lovers. It's uncanny how often their poems communicate what I want to say – better than I could say it myself. Unfortunately, there are a few problems that even Shakespeare can't resolve." Then he told me the story behind the story of the gold mine.

He was on his way to Siberia, hoping to win back the love of his life, a gorgeous opera singer who left him when his lust for venture consumed his first fortune and he began eyeing hers. I could actually see him reciting that sonnet, still hoping his "bootless cries" (*SS* 29:3) would "pitie winne, and pitie grace obtaine" (*AS* 1:4) as she walked out the door, carrying her bankbook and their CD player, leaving him to "look upon [him]self and curse [his] fate" (*SS* 29:4).[3] Perhaps in Siberia he would find some newly enfranchised Russian capitalist, eager to hook up with a Shakespeare-speaking venture capitalist. "It used to be enough to be cultured and witty," he concluded, "but after fifty, you also need to be rich."

He ceased, as if he had uttered the final couplet and was awaiting my professorial commentary, so I told him I was writing this book to demonstrate that the Elizabethans use poems for many of the same reasons: to luxuriate in "lovely enchanting language" (Herbert, "The Forerunners"); to woo a lover and "grace obtaine" (*AS* 1:4); to enjoy the license that an artfully chosen mask provides; finally, if all goes well, to improve their stature and fortune in men's eyes by writing or marrying well.[4] I had just started to explain why it is so important to listen to the woman's side of the conversation when he interrupted me. "Why," he asked, "do you need to write a book to prove that?"

A question to be asked . . .

AMOROUS COURTSHIP

During Elizabeth I's reign from 1558 to 1603 love poetry acquires a remarkable popularity and brilliance, unparalleled in English literary history. It is also during this period that the word courtship enters the English language, acquiring a telling concatenation of meanings: (1) behavior, action, or state befitting a court or courtier (2) the practice of the arts of a courtier; diplomacy, flattery (3) the paying of courteous and ceremonial attentions, especially to a dignitary (4) the process of courting or wooing a woman with a view to sex or marriage.[5] When a society denotes courtly behavior, diplomacy, and ceremonies of state by the very same neologism it also uses to signify wooing a woman with a view to marriage, it seems reasonable to surmise that amorous and political courtship are intricately interconnected; that politics and courtiership are feminized; and that wooing a woman involves not only flattery and courteous attentions but also art.[6]

Most studies of Elizabethan poetry and courtship focus on courtiership – on social and literary exchanges between men, or patronage and preferment at court.[7] When, for example, Astrophil describes his wooing of Stella as "this great cause, which needs both use and art" (*AS* 107:8), critics and editors generally assume that the lines must be referring to something else, something of great moment such as court politics or Sidney's own professional advancement.[8] This study maintains that love poetry and amorous courtship are themselves matters of "great" import for the Elizabethans.

Elizabethan Women and the Poetry of Courtship focuses on English Renaissance poetry, Elizabethan amorous courtship, and relations between early modern Englishwomen and Englishmen. It seeks above all to recover the ways in which the Elizabethans write, read, and hear love poetry. It investigates the ways in which the tropes and rhetoric of Renaissance love poetry are used to court Elizabethan women, not only at court and in the great houses but also in Elizabethan society at large.[9] It also examines the ways in which Elizabethan women respond – in prose, in poetry, and in speech.[10] Analogous developments are occurring in European poetry as well as in Elizabethan drama, epic, and romance, even as they were already stirring in medieval English literature. But one genre, one society, one historical era, and two sexes offer more than enough complications for a single volume.[11]

The literature of Renaissance courtship is so vast that any choice of material is necessarily selective. This study focuses on texts that are addressed to or written by Elizabethan women, as well as texts that are transformed by Elizabethan women. The great continental love poems such as Petrarch's *Rime Sparse* or Du Bellay's *Olive* concern us not for their own evident poetic merits but insofar as they can help us understand Elizabethan rewritings of conventional Petrarchan tropes – especially those that transform the self-reflexive, idolatrous relationship between the Petrarchan poet and the Petrarchan lady into Elizabethan poetry of courtship.[12] Native English songs, Ovidean complaints, and Neoplatonism are all important aspects of English Renaissance love poetry. Still, it is difficult for an Elizabethan to compose love poetry, or for that matter to write or speak about love at all, without also using the conventions of European Petrarchism.[13]

Petrarchism is the richest vocabulary available to analyze subjectivity and to express desire. As such, it serves many of the same functions for the Renaissance that psychoanalytic terminology serves for the twentieth century. Elizabethan love poems are rarely aPetrarchan, but they are often either anti-Petrarchan or what I call pseudo-Petrarchan. If we define poetry of courtship as poetry written to or for a loved one – or poetry written to look as if it is written for a loved one – then pseudo-Petrarchan poetry is the subset that uses the conventional tropes of Petrarchan idolatry to conceal an underlying persuasive or seductive purpose. Anti-Petrarchan poems, written for the amusement of a male coterie, have been widely discussed by twentieth-century critics; however, pseudo-Petrarchan poems, which range from brief posies or poem-and-answer sets to some of the period's most intricate and brilliant lyrics, have not been recognized as a vital category of Elizabethan verse.

Petrarchism, like Freudianism, defines subjectivity and desire as masculine, which is why twentieth-century critics often describe the Petrarchan lady as the object or reflection of male desire – the veil or slate upon which male subjectivity and male imagination inscribes itself. Yet Elizabethan women are not only objects of male desire or tropes for the male imagination; they are also writers, readers, and interlocutors, actively engaged in dialogue with men and other women.

To understand the full import of Elizabethan love poets, I believe we need to hear their voices not only confined to a male literary tradition where they can too easily seem only self-fashioning and self-advertising, but also embedded in a social and lyric dialogue with Elizabethan women – not only "in isolation, but as the *answer* or *rejoinder* to assertions current in the situation in which it arose."[14] To understand the full import of Elizabethan women, I believe we also need to hear their voices, not only isolated in a female literary tradition where they can too easily be marginalized and ignored, but also in dialogue with male writers and male interlocutors.

In trying to develop a paradigm for the poetics and practice of Elizabethan courtship, this book usually refers to the poet/lover as male and the reader/listener as female, not only because it is difficult to write expository English prose without using gendered pronouns but also because, more often than not, the Elizabethan poet/lover is male while the private lyric audience is female. Of course, Shakespeare's most intensely persuasive and notoriously intricate sonnets eternize and berate a beautiful young man. And later in the seventeenth century, Katherine Philips' poems to Mary Aubrey turn the literary conversation between men into a lyric conversation between women. There are currently only a few poems of courtship known to be written by Elizabethan women, though more will undoubtedly be identified. Yet precisely because the female poet/lover is the exception to the rule, she offers an exceptionally illuminating view of the genre.

Elizabethan love poems are often unsigned, or assigned by different manuscripts to different authors. ("Thoughe I seeme straunge," which is examined in chapter 5, is a case in point.) Since the lyric "I" is neither male nor female, it is often difficult, as Thomas Whythorne notes in his autobiography, to "judge whether [the poems] were written by a man or a woman."[15] The lyric dialogue of courtship, by its very nature, involves a continual fluctuation from male subject and female object to female subject and male object. When an Elizabethan woman reads a first person poem aloud, the lyric "I" undergoes a sex change, from male to female. Just as gender-bending is part of the fun in Shakespearean comedy, puns, syntactical ambiguities, and duplicitous figures of speech that turn traditional gender roles upside down and inside out are part of the private recreation of poetry-making and love-making in Elizabethan England. Whether my readers prefer feminist theory, gender theory, queer theory, or straight theory of one bent or another, I hope they will bear in mind that the lyric dialogue of courtship is constantly flirting with gender inversions that call conventional sex/gender roles into question.

Early modern women writers deserve greater consideration in their own right, for their writings provide an invaluable addition or corrective to the much more abundant and well-known male accounts of love and courtship. So, too, do women readers and listeners, for their numbers are far greater.[16] Most studies of the English Renaissance lyric written during the last half century emphasize the literary exchange "between men," between the male poet and the male lyric audience, whether a peer, a patron, a coterie, the reading public, or the literary profession.[17] As my title suggests, *Elizabethan Women and the Poetry of Courtship* focuses on the collaborative role female writers, readers, and interlocutors play in the Elizabethan socio-literary conversation. It begins with the premise that, for Elizabethan poetry of courtship, the female lyric audience is the primary, though by no means the only, lyric audience.

Modern critics tend to assume that Elizabethan love poems could not actually have been written to or for "real" women since few early modern women are literate. Yet if we are to understand the full extent of women's involvement with and access to Elizabethan culture in general and English Renaissance lyrics in particular, we need to consider not only writing literacy but also reading literacy and listening literacy. As the large list of printed books written for and addressed to women in the middling and upper ranks of early modern English society demonstrates, reading literacy is more common than writing literacy.[18] Indeed,

Figure 1 Portrait of an Unknown Girl with a Book, attributed to
Steven van der Meulen, 1567.

portraits of Elizabethan women holding books – and the sitters range from Elizabeth I, to Dorothy Wadham, to an unknown Elizabethan woman – show that female literacy is a matter of great pride.[19] Listening literacy is even more prevalent than reading literacy.

In the sixteenth century the printing press is a technological marvel that is revolutionizing the dissemination of knowledge. Yet most Elizabethans still prefer the familiar, old-fashioned experience of hearing literature recited or read aloud, just as many readers today still prefer to curl up with a good book rather than to download text onto a computer monitor. Silent reading is a relatively modern development. Sixteenth-century reading typically takes place not in solitude and silence, but orally, in the presence of others.[20]

Anne Clifford is an exceptionally literate early modern woman who keeps a diary and loves books. Yet, instead of reading to herself, she listens to Montaigne's essays and plays, the *Faerie Queene*, the Bible, and various religious texts. Margaret Hoby keeps a journal, but she too spends a great deal of time listening to literature read aloud to her by both men and women. The chaplain reads frequently, but others read as well: "one of the men," "one of my women," "one of my maids," "little Kate."[21] Gascoigne's Lady Elynor has a private secretary who reads to her and writes for her until F. J. appears and begins reciting poetic persuasions directly to her. (While trying to reconstruct the circumstances in which Elizabethan men and women court each other in songs and sonnets, I could not help but imagine how my extremely literary but not yet literate five-year-old daughter might respond at the age of sixteen or twenty – assuming she had *not* been taught to read but had continued listening hungrily to stories and poems – if a dashing young man appeared and, perish the thought, began to woo her with witty, passionate poems written expressly for her.)

Elizabethan architecture provides limited privacy; therefore, a person reading aloud is likely to be overheard by other members of the household. In families or social circles where men read, women can acquire listening literacy by attending to what is being read in their midst. In *The Instruction of a Christian Woman* Vives declares that women should not be permitted to read or even hear love literature of any kind: "It were better for them nat only to haue no lernynge at all; but also to lese theyr eies, that they shulde nat rede: and theyr eares, that they shulde nat here." It is tempting to equate Vives' prohibitions with actual reading practices, but to do so is to confuse prescription with description. While liberal in its defense of women's education, the *Instruction* is reactionary in its prohibition of love poetry; i.e., it reacts against and tries to suppress the popular songs and sonnets that are widely used to court and seduce Renaissance women. Vives censures the literature of love because, to his horror, there are so "many, in whom there is no good mynde all redy, [who] reden those bokes to kepe them self in the thoughtes of loue."[22]

Before the seventeenth century, there are relatively few women writing autobiographical prose, lyric poetry, romances, or secular literature of any kind, not only because of the low rates of female literacy but also because the Elizabethan code of ethics equates chastity with silence. Yet even the most dominant cultural codes are rarely as unremitting as they may appear centuries later, and the force of repression oftentimes reflects the pressure for change. In 1578, Margaret Tyler translates and publishes the French Romance, *The Mirrour of Knighthood*, in order to make continental literature of love more readily available to English-speaking women. Tyler's ground-breaking preface addresses the allegation "that women may not at al discourse in learning, for men lay in their claim to be sole possessioners of knowledge." Recognizing that her action is bound to provoke disapproval – "amongst al my il willers, some I hope are not so straight [that] they would enforce me necessarily either not to write or to write of diuinitie" – Tyler claims she was "forced" to do it "by the importunity of my friends." Clearly, Tyler and her friends believe that Elizabethan women have not only a right but also a responsibility to add their voices to the cultural store of learning so that other women can become "possessioners of knowledge."[23]

The sheer profusion of Elizabethan literature from all genres examining courtship, marriage, and relations between the sexes suggests that *both* poetry *and* courtship are grappling with dilemmas larger and murkier than one man's love for a woman. Poetry and poetics are not merely a reflection of social norms and generic codes; they are also symbolic acts that are continually reconfiguring sex and gender: "literature does more than transmit ideology: it actually creates it."[24] Elizabethan poets and their lyric audiences are formed by ideological structures they may not consciously perceive; yet, their writings and actions also alter those structures in ways they may or may not recognize, which is why sex/gender roles involve not only a set of rules for practice but also a gender unconscious.[25]

Despite its conservative roots and traditional forms, Elizabethan poetry is a living language, interacting with a wide range of literary and social forces. Elizabethan love poetry cannot be understood without paying careful attention both to poetic convention and to poetic form – to diction, metaphor, rhyme, scansion, ambiguity, tone, and point of view. At the same time, however, Elizabethan courtship and the use of poetry in courtship cannot be understood without paying careful attention to Elizabethan social mores, Elizabethan social practices, and Elizabethan poetics.

Mapping the largely unexplored terrain where the poetry and practice of amorous courtship converge places us in the paradoxical position of trying to understand literary and social conventions simultaneously. (1) What kind of poetry is best suited to the lyric dialogue of courtship? (2) What kind of culture and, specifically, what kind of relations between the sexes produce such brilliant love poetry? (3) What kind of culture and sexual relationships does the complex, multivious lyric dialogue of Elizabethan courtship produce?[26] As the word multivious (which means having many ways, or going in many directions) suggests, the most brilliant poems of courtship are those in which the complexities of poetry and the complexities of history interact and magically coalesce. Chapter 3, "The Practice of Elizabethan Courtship," and chapter 4, "The Lyric Dialogue of Elizabethan Courtship," examine both literary and non-literary texts in order to construct a brief history of Elizabethan courtship and to document the use of poetry in courtship. The surrounding chapters read history as part of poetry, even as they read poetry as part of history.

Courtship involves both material questions of law, finance, and social practice, and murkier questions of genre, ethics, and ideology – both the quotidian and the unspoken.[27] Many studies of early modern women rely heavily on male-authored instructional and prescriptive texts such as conduct books or marriage manuals – texts that describe how women ought to behave.[28] To understand not only what Elizabethan women are told they *ought* to say and do but also what they *actually* say and do when they are courted in poetry and in deed, we need to examine poetry and prescriptive literature along with other kinds of data: legal records, medical documents, statistics, diaries, letters, memoirs, autobiographies, annotated private manuscripts, and practical, instructional materials.[29]

The reasons for Elizabethan marriages are as mixed as they are vexed; it can therefore be difficult to know whether a suitor is professing love and desire in order to marry wealth and status, or falsely proposing marriage in order to obtain sexual favors. Sometimes the participants themselves may not know whether their aim is social and material advancement, amorous courtship, or extra-marital seduction. The various facets of courtship come together in the Elizabethan word, "mistress": a woman who is courted by a man, a woman who has power, a female teacher, a woman who illicitly occupies the place of wife.[30] If, on the one hand, to be wooed by a man means to risk being lured or tricked into occupying the place of a wife illicitly, on the other hand, the freedom to say no gives a mistress power to influence a suitor who grievously wants her to say yes.

What many Elizabethan poems of courtship imply, though sometimes unwillingly or even unwittingly, is what many Elizabethans (and many modern critics) would rather not face: the wooing of women threatens the exchange of women, transferring authority from fathers to sons and daughters. Courtship encourages men to rout female silence – to seek female responses and to heed female objections. It also creates a discursive space for female subjects to speak out and write back – to "Answer [him] fair with yea or nay."[31] Only the female interlocutor can decide whether or not to say, I take thee to be my favorite, my lover, my lawfully wedded husband. By inviting or enabling a mistress to say, as Rosalind does in *As You Like It*, "To thee, I give myself" (*AYL* 5.4.117), the poetry and practice of courtship produce mistresses and wives who have grown accustomed to speaking and acting according to their own wit, will, and liking.

For courtship to work in poetry as in practice, women as well as men must have at least some freedom to act and to choose. The persuasive strategies of rhetoric give the poet/lover power to persuade a mistress. At the same time, the pressure to elicit a desired response places the poet and the poem in danger of being undone by his mistress. If her critique induces him to see his own words in a new light, he may revise the poem or write another poem with a more capacious point of view or a more compelling rhetorical strategy. If Petrarchan poetry and patronage poetry emphasize the poet's undoing, poetry of amorous courtship is at least as likely to explore his response. Of course, there is nothing to prevent a poet from constructing a fictional poem or sonnet sequence that represents female autonomy in order to explore male subjection.

Both Elizabethan courtiers and Elizabethan poets/lovers succeed not by declaring their power, but by beseeching their private female readers, "Make what you read the better for your reading." The male poet/lover is always in the position of as*king*, may "Your gracious reading grac[e] my verse the better," as Harington's epigram, "To the Queens Majestie," wittily remarks. That is why poems of amorous courtship, originally written to woo Elizabethan women outside the court and noble households, can be readily readdressed to powerful patrons. Conversely, poems of courtship addressed to a female employer, patron, or monarch – to a mistress who has material or professional power over the poet – can also at the same time be addressed to a beloved. Male patrons are more numerous, but female patrons, such as Mary Sidney, Mary Wroth, and Elizabeth Tudor are highly sought after by Elizabethan love poets such as Daniel, Donne, and Spenser because, as women, they seem especially likely to appreciate the poet/lover's attentiveness to the female point of view.[32]

PREGNANT WITH RESPONSES AND OBJECTIONS

Modern and post-modern literary criticism have developed countless ways to read English Renaissance poetry; many of these approaches have shaped the interpretations appearing in the following chapters, for one cannot help but read the past textually, through the lens of one's own particular cultural or critical perspective. Yet, the one approach that both modern and post-modern literary criticism avoid, whether deliberately or unwittingly, is the one an Elizabethan would be most likely to adopt: reading a love poem as if it were addressed to the poet's mistress. This book sets out to reconstruct an Elizabethan poetics of courtship which will in turn help us to reconstruct the lyric dialogue of Elizabethan courtship.

During the last few decades, developments in feminist theory and women's studies have prepared the groundwork for retrieving women's place in English Renaissance literary tradition. My own initial attempt to understand the role of the woman in Donne's *Songs and Sonnets* consisted of a close reading of the text that was inspired by a feminist poetics "in which the *hypothesis* of a female reader changes our apprehension of a given text, awakening us to the significance of its sexual codes," and that applied feminist "strategies for reading" which make women's "silences 'speak', and which allow the woman reader to read against the grain, and to resist the marginalization she is offered."[33]

Two decades have passed since Fetterley's *The Resisting Reader* first appeared. Yet, the Elizabethan lyric has still not received the comprehensive, revisionist reinterpretation that has produced in so many other areas – in early modern women's history, in Shakespearean criticism, in the feminization of American culture, in the woman question and Victorian fiction – what Elaine Showalter calls "a radical alteration of our vision, a demand that we see meaning in what has previously been empty space. The orthodox plot recedes, and another plot, hitherto submerged in the anonymity of the background, stands out."[34] In applying feminist approaches such as these, there is a temptation to fill the silences either with female voices which we, as twentieth-century readers, would like to hear or with the chaste, silent, and obedient Renaissance women we have been taught to expect.

In developing a model for an Elizabethan poetics of courtship, *Elizabethan Women and the Poetry of Courtship* uses feminist theory and scholarship along with other critical approaches that locate the poem in Elizabethan England. An American cultural poetics demonstrates that writing is a mode of action, not only socially produced but also socially productive. An Elizabethan poetics of courtship represents Elizabethan women not only as victims of patriarchy or pawns of ideology, but also as subjects of consciousness and initiators of action. A philosophy of literary form interprets the poem's structure "by thinking always of the poem's function." An Elizabethan poetics of courtship uses the philosophy of literary form to give the Renaissance lyric tradition a female form for female purposes, for Elizabethan women also need a comprehensive vocabulary for social purposes. A dialogic imagination makes us more attuned to the ways in which language "provokes an answer, anticipates it and structures itself in the answer's direction."[35] A dialogic poetics of courtship calls attention to the collaborative role female writers, readers, and interlocutors play in reshaping Renaissance lyric tradition. It provides a lyric analog to the theatrics of cross-dressing, giving the Renaissance male lyric tradition a female guise and a female voice, calling stereotypical notions of masculinity and femininity into question.

Genre theory reads changes in genre as signs of cultural change; the political unconscious explores the paradoxical, mutually constitutive relationship between the poem and the Real. (And the term, the Real, is used throughout in a Jamesonian rather than a Lacanian sense.) An Elizabethan poetics of courtship gives the political unconscious a gender unconscious, even as it gives the male text of Petrarchism a female subtext; it helps us to hear marginal or oppositional female responses which are simultaneously intrinsic to the poem's structure and outside the poet's control. In sum, an Elizabethan poetics reconstructs the lyric dialogue of courtship between "Ladies and young Gentlewomen, or idle Courtiers, desirous to become skilful in their owne mother tongue, and for their priuate recreation to make now and then ditties of pleasure."[36]

The lyric dialogue of Elizabethan courtship is not only the work of men but also the domain of women who are all hard at play, learning the intricacies of Renaissance rhetoric, renegotiating relations between the sexes, diverting themselves with figurative solutions to real social problems. Literary conventions and social paradigms flourish when they confront pressing questions that beg for creative solutions; "it is in country unfamiliar emotionally or topographically that one needs poems and road maps."[37] When Elizabethan female readers/listeners question, reject, and redefine the traditional Petrarchan lady's role, or when Elizabethan female poets reappropriate the traditionally male lyric genre, they challenge the cultural silencing of women and reformulate what it means to be an Elizabethan woman.

Almost thirty-five years have passed since C. L. Barber observed that "[d]istinctions between life and art . . . which are obvious for our epoch were not altogether settled for Elizabethans." Barber's path-breaking study, *Shakespeare's Festive Comedy: A Study of Dramatic Form and its Relation to Social Custom*, showed me "the tendency for Elizabethan comedy to *be* a saturnalia, rather than to *represent* a saturnalian experience."[38] Over the last quarter century, feminism, cultural poetics, and cultural materialism have broken the barriers between life and art in almost every area of English Renaissance literary production, especially epic and drama. Yet this is the first full-length study of lyric form and social custom to explore the tendency of Elizabethan love poems not only to represent an amorous thought but also to transact an amorous courtship. Reading poetry of courtship as the embodiment of an act of courtship is what Elizabethan poets, critics, and readers do.[39] It seems perverse to refuse on principle, or because of tradition, to explore the ramifications of such a fascinating and wide-spread cultural practice.

Even if we cannot hope to understand Elizabethan poetry, Elizabethan courtship, and relations between Elizabethan men and women exactly as they were experienced by the Elizabethans, in all their complexity and diversity, there is still much to be gained from trying. By discussing aesthetic questions of language, form, and genre along with sexual politics and social history, we can enrich our understanding of Elizabethan poetry and society, making it less monologic and more "pregnant with responses and objections;" less self-referentially male and more attuned to Elizabethan women – or at least more stressed by the sparks and conflicts between men and women.[40] At the same time, by discussing social conventions along with literary conventions, we can complicate our understanding of amorous courtship, recovering aspects of earlier women's lives and writings which have become invisible because they were unfathomable or unavailable to intervening generations. "Such an analysis, of course, does not offer us simple answers."[41]

To construct an alternative literary and social paradigm, we need a very different set of tools, and that is what the following chapters attempt to provide. To begin with, we need to know how Elizabethan courtships are conducted. In particular, we need to attend more closely to early modern women, for their side of the conversation is all too often mis-understood – or disregarded.

2

An Elizabethan poetics of courtship

He would cry out on life, that what it wants
Is not its own love back in copy speech,
But counter-love, original response.

Frost, "The Most of It"[1]

SEEK HER TO PLEASE

All language is bound by rules and conventions, but poetic language, with its conservative roots and traditional forms, is probably the most rule-bound of all. Convention is the means by which genres adjust to cultures, but it is also the writers' way of delimiting appropriate responses and proscribing anachronistic or undesirable ones. The conventions of the Elizabethan lyric genre are designed, while obscuring or veiling more sensitive aspects of the private lyric dialogue, to indicate that the customary and "right vse"[2] of Elizabethan love poetry is courtship and seduction.

The great Elizabethan lyric sequences typically begin by identifying the poet's mistress as the primary lyric audience. Sidney, Daniel, and Spenser all write introductory sonnets charging the sonnet sequence with carrying the poet's/lover's plea to his mistress. Daniel's apostrophe directs the poem to plead directly with his mistress: "Presse to her eyes, importune me some good, / Waken her sleeping crueltie with crying, / Knock at her hard hart: say . . ." (Daniel, prefatory sonnet: 11–13). *Amoretti* 1 invokes a particular female reader to whom and for whom the poems are written: "seeke her to please alone, / whom if ye please, I care for other none" (*Am* 1:13–14). The final couplet sums it all up: she is the *only one* whose favorable response the poems actively "seeke" to elicit.

Sidney's brilliant and widely imitated introductory sonnet explains the intricate play of persuasion and response. "Oft turning others' leaves," the poet/lover carries on a literary conversation with other

Renaissance poets. Yet, he is also conducting a lyric dialogue with "the deare She" to whom the sonnet sequence is primarily addressed:

> Loving in truth, and faine in verse my love to show,
> That the deare She might take some pleasure of my paine:
> Pleasure might cause her reade, reading might make her know,
> Knowledge might pitie winne, and pitie grace obtaine (*AS* 1:1–4)

The operative word is "might." No matter how assiduously the poet/lover tries to anticipate and accommodate his mistress's wishes, he can neither determine her actions nor control her responses. Reading "might" make her know, but then again, it might not.

To be sure, not all Elizabethan love poems are poems of courtship. Yet, not all male-authored poems of courtship address the female lyric audience directly. Elizabethan songs and sonnets typically contain a wide variety of poems which range from Neoplatonic poems representing female beauty as the ladder to heavenly perfection, to apostrophes to the sun, the moon, or the poem itself, to poems addressed to a male friend, a potential patron, and even, as in the *Amoretti*, the queen herself. Critics often cite these poems as evidence that "the real reader" is not the poet's mistress but "the male coterie," "the patron," "the ideal reader," or "posterity."

Upon closer inspection, however, many of these poems also contain traces of a private lyric dialogue between a male poet/lover and a private female reader/listener. For example, the love poem addressed to a male friend typically silences his objections – "Rudely thou wrongest my deare harts desire" (*Am* 5:1–2) – so that the poet/lover can lavish his attentions – and his poems – on his mistress: "For Godsake hold your tongue and let me love" (Donne, "The Canonization"). Apostrophes to the sun, the moon, or poem itself are conventional surrogates for the female lyric audience. As Sidney explains, "Fancy, drawne by imag'd things" (*AS* 45:9) gives the poet/lover "free scope" to pressure, criticize, appease, or console his mistress, or would-be-mistress.

Sidney's gorgeous meditation, "With how sad steps, o Moone" (*AS* 31:1) asks the moon to explain what the poet/lover dares not ask his mistress directly, "Do they above love to be lov'd, and yet / Those Lovers scorne whom that *Love* doth possesse?" (*AS* 31:12–13). In this poem, and countless others like it, courtship is the subtext, and the female reader/listener is the indirect but ultimate lyric audience. In "A Valediction of weeping" Donne's lyric dialogue with his mistress sounds all the more intimate and endearing because it exposes the ruse of the apostrophe: "O more then Moone, / Draw not up seas to drowne me in thy spheare . . ." (Donne: 19–20)

In Sonnets 38–40, Astrophil is alone in bed, fantasizing about Stella. The image of her, created "by Love's owne selfe," proves so powerful that for a moment he thinks she is right there, answering his verse with a lyric of her own: "That she, me thinks, not onely shines but sings. / I start, looke, hearke" (*AS* 38:8–9). To calm his insomnia, he composes an apostrophe to sleep – "Come sleepe, o sleepe" (*AS* 39:1) – still referring to Stella in the third person. In Sonnet 40, however, he overcomes his obsessive self-absorption and begins to woo Stella directly: "As good to write as for to lie and grone. / O *Stella* deare, how much thy power hath wrought" (*AS* 40:1–2). With this climactic avowal, the mini-sequence comes to an end. In Sonnet 41, day has arrived and Astrophil is fighting in a tournament where "*Stella* lookt on" (*AS* 41:13).

Most modern anthologies, including the widely used *Norton Anthology of English Literature*, reprint Sonnets 39 and 41 but not Sonnet 40, the only one of the three that identifies the female lyric audience.[3] The omission – and its effects – need to be confronted. Modern lyric criticism neglects "how much thy power" – the woman's power – "hath wrought" not merely by disregarding female writers such as Mary Sidney or Isabella Whitney, but also by discounting female readers, by determining which poems *should not* be anthologized, and by declaring which questions *should not* be asked.

THE PROPER LANGUAGE OF LOVE

For T. S. Eliot and the modernist literary tradition his poetry and criticism did so much to shape, the lyric is by definition, "the voice of the poet speaking to himself or nobody," "a short poem directly expressing the poet's own thoughts and sentiments." In "The Three Voices of Poetry," probably still the most influential twentieth-century English definition of the lyric voice and the lyric audience, Eliot argues that it makes no difference whether the lyric poet addresses "a spirit of nature, a Muse," "a personal friend, a lover, a god, a personified abstraction, or a natural object." The poet only "pretends to be talking to himself or to someone else."[4] But in many Elizabethan poems of courtship, the meaning changes utterly, depending on whether the lyric audience is a coterie or a mistress.

Citing the intriguing fact that the Brownings wrote love poems to each other, Eliot acknowledges that "there is a well-known form, not always

Figure 2 Woodcut of Lovers Wooing.

amatory in content, called The Epistle." Cognizant that some short poems contain "[t]he voice of the poet talking to other people," Eliot does "not deny that a poem may be addressed to one person." Eliot might have expanded his definition of the lyric voice to include poems such as these. Instead, he argues that a lover who wants to communicate something in particular to someone special ought to write prose: "Surely, the proper language of love – that is, of communication to the beloved and to no one else – is prose."[5]

Yet, surely the Elizabethans would respond, the proper language of love, of persuading a mistress that "in truth they feele those passions" (*DP* 516), is not prose but poetry. In *A Defence of Poesie*, the preeminent articulation of an Elizabethan poetics, Sidney assumes that Elizabethan poets write love lyrics – rather than epic, drama, narrative poetry, or occasional verse – because they wish to "persuade" a mistress. "[I]f I were a mistresse," Sidney declares, those plodding versifiers who mechanically echo their predecessors "would neuer perswade me they were in loue: so coldly they apply fiery speeches as men that had rather read louers writings . . . than that in truth they feele those passions, which easily, as I think, may be bewrayed by that same forcibleness or *Energia* (as the Greeks call it) of the writer. But let this be a sufficient, though short note, that we misse the right vse of the materiall point of *Poesie*" (*DP* 516).[6]

A Defence of Poesie hints at connections between the poetry and practice of courtship that it simultaneously skirts or veils. Sidney cannot simply come out and say that Elizabethan love poems are regularly written to woo Elizabethan women such as Penelope Rich or Anne More without legitimating the very charges he wishes to defuse. The subjunctive construction, "if I were a mistress," leaves open the possibility that a male love poet could write poetry capable of persuading a woman that in truth he feels those passions even if he has "no Mistresse but [his] Muse" (Donne, "Loves growth"). These politic evasions notwithstanding, Sidney confidently asserts that Elizabethan love poetry is written and should be read *as if* it is a courtship.[7] As Touchstone remarks, and as a poetics of courtship so often gives us reason to observe, there is "much virtue in If" (*AYL* 5.4.103).

For Sidney and his contemporaries, the lyric dialogue of courtship is potentially true – or hypothetically true. The witty play of fiction and reality, of life "as it was" and "as it should be" (*DP* 500), is at once a sophisticated literary posture and a powerful rhetorical strategy. When Stella, unmoved by "the verie face of wo / Painted in my beclowded stormie face," is moved to tears by "a fable . . . Of Lovers never knowne" (*AS* 45:1–2, 5–6), Astrophil, feeling stymied by reality "where new doubts honor brings," wittily claims the freedom of fiction: "I am not I, pitie the tale of me" (*AS* 45:11, 14). Elizabethan poetry of courtship asks to be read *as if* it is at once real and imagined; "the truest poetry is the most feigning," Touchstone quips (*AYL* 3.3.19–20).

"Our Sidney and our perfect man" (to borrow an epithet from Yeats' poem, "In Memory of Major Robert Gregory") does not reduce the woman to metaphor, trope, mirror, or idol. Instead he depicts the woman as *the primary and prototypical Elizabethan lyric audience*. By suggesting that anyone who wishes to comprehend the "forcibleness" of the best Elizabethan lyric poetry should read as "if I were a mistress," Sidney depicts the female reader as the standard by which to judge Elizabethan poetry.[8] Moreover, like late twentieth-century feminist criticism, Sidney "employs the hypothesis of a woman reader to provide leverage for displacing the dominant male critical vision and revealing its misprisions."[9]

When we read Elizabethan love poetry in a printed book, "the objective yet ever intensifying alienation of the printed book" creates "the illusion that the situation itself did not exist before it, that there is nothing but a text."[10] Eliot "dismissed as an illusion the voice of the poet talking to one person only," thereby creating a chimera that exists only because the text generates her in the form of a mirage. A poetics of courtship merges lyric and life until "she, methinks, not only shines but sings" (*AS* 39:1). Like the political unconscious, the gender unconscious allows the Real to permeate the subtext while at the same time allowing the literary text to constitute the Real: "[t]he whole paradox of what we have here called the subtext may be summed up in this, that the literary work or cultural object, as though for the first time, brings into being that very situation to which it is also, at one and the same time, a reaction."[11] Elizabethan poems of courtship are both fantastical and real, both cause and effect.

The complex interaction between artful rhetorical persuasion and implicit response makes reading poems of courtship that are written for – or written to look as if they are written for – a private female reader/listener a very different matter from reading a female complaint such as "Shore's Wife" or *England's Heroicall Epistles*. When a male poet writes a complaint in the voice of a female persona, her point of view, her values, and her words are all inflected by his. When a male poet writes a poem of courtship, the situation is almost the reverse: the male lyric voice is inflected by the expectation of the female reader's answering response. The poet/lover is always trying to anticipate or influence her response, but he neither writes her script nor directs her performance.

A male poet/lover may sometimes attempt to speak for a female reader/listener, but his words are only the catalyst. "Sittinge alone upon my thought" (which we shall examine more closely in chapter 5) begins as a male-authored female complaint; however, it becomes an archetypal poem of courtship when the male poet stops trying to express the woman's feelings and begins expressing his own. The female reader's/listener's side of the lyric dialogue is by definition elusive and, at least for a time, oppositional – at once intrinsic to the poem's meaning and outside the poem's margins.[12]

Elizabethan poets who "have no Mistresse but their Muse" can write fictional poetry of courtship that simulates a lyric dialogue.[13] The challenge is to leave gaps in the lyric sequence or contradictions in the poem's argument that reveal how much "thy power" – the woman's power – "hath wrought" (*AS* 40:2). Fictional poetry of courtship, constructed as if it were one side of a lyric dialogue, challenges its readers to reconstruct the mistress's side of the lyric dialogue. Of course, that is precisely what allegorical, autobiographical poetry of courtship does when it veils its private lyric dialogue in enigmatic, figurative language.

A close reading of the text, along with manuscript annotations, biographical information, and publication data, can help us make informed judgments about whether a particular poem of courtship or lyric sequence is the poet's half of a "real" courtship conversation, a corrected, bowdlerized version of an earlier private courtship, or pure fiction, artfully constructed to look as if were transacting a courtship even as we read.[14] More often than not, the fluidity of Elizabethan manuscripts, and the need to avoid discovery or scandal, combined with the various ways the lyric argument can be taken, make it difficult to know for certain whether a particular poem is autobiography disguised as poetry, fiction disguised as autobiography, or a complex mixture of the true and the feigned – which seems most often to be the case.

In most instances, we have little or no information about the private lyric situation or the private lyric audience other than what the poem itself proffers. Without additional documentation, it is neither easy to determine, nor at this point particularly fruitful to debate, what really happened, since "every document bequeathed us by history must be treated as a *strategy for encompassing a situation*." Finally, it is not the identity of the poet/lover or his mistress but the presumption of a private lyric dialogue and a private female lyric audience that turns the monologic male voice of the Petrarchan lyric into a lyric dialogue between the sexes.[15]

MOVING ONE WAY AND ANOTHER TO GREAT COMPASSION

Puttenham's *The Arte of English Poesie* contains a chapter on love poetry which describes:

the poore soules sometimes praying, beseeching, sometimes honouring, auancing, praising: an other while railing, reuiling, and cursing: then sorrowing, weeping, lamenting: in the ende laughing, reioysing and solacing the beloued againe, with a thousand delicate deuises, odes, songs, elegies, ballads, sonets and other ditties, moouing one way and another to great compassion.[16]

The glut of present participles says it all: Puttenham assumes that love poems are the means by which Elizabethans *do* their wooing. The very chapter title, "In what forme of Poesie the amorous affections and allurements were vttered," defines love poems as utterances to be sung, recited, or sent as surrogates, uttering persuasions to love.

Rhetoric is the theory and practice of persuasion: the art of "moouing" the audience "one way and another." The *Arcadian Rhetorike* (1588) begins with the following definition: "Rhetorike is an Art of speaking." The second part is devoted to "Vtterance" which "hath two parts, *Voyce* and *Gesture*, the one pertaining to the eare, the other belonging to the eye." Rhetoric makes speakers into writers, even as it makes writers into speakers. As Castiglione explains in *The Courtier*, "wrytyng is nothinge elles, but a maner of speache, that remaineth stil after a man hath spoken, or (as it were) an Image, or rather the life of the woordes." For Sidney, Castiglione, and Puttenham, as for Burke, poetry is "a comprehensive vocabulary for social purposes."[17]

Puttenham's love poets give vent to emotions and reveal hidden secrets (a secondary meaning of the verb, utter). They propose and retract, constantly shifting tone and changing direction. They use a "thousand delicate deuises," a variety of poetic forms, facial expressions, performative gestures, and tones of voice. An ill-chosen word or unwelcome gesture may leave the poet/lover "lamenting" or "cursing." Yet, an unexpected response may suddenly enable the poet/lover to see the poem through her eyes, discovering aspects of his own lyric persuasion that he had not recognized – at least not consciously. If his rhetoric dispels her objections – and if there are no insurmountable practical impediments – the lyric utterance may become a lyric dialogue, "moouing one way and another to great compassion," meaning both great sympathy and great common passion.

In classical times, lyrics were written to be sung to the accompaniment of a lyre. Many Elizabethan lyrics are still written to be sung or performed. *The Autobiography of Thomas Whythorne* explains that he "used to sing songs and sonnets, sometimes to the lute and sometimes the virginals, whereby I might tell my tale with my voice as well as by word or writing."[18] Elizabethan poems are also written as missives or tokens of love. The Elizabethans have a particular fondness for "short epigrams called posies" that are inscribed directly upon the social situation: "made as it were vpon a table, or in a windowe, or vpon the wall or mantell of a chimney in some place of common resort, where it was allowed euery man might come," though they can also be "put in paper and in bookes, and vsed as ordinarie missives" (*AEP* 68).

Posies began in classical times as "witty scoffes," or riddling displays of wit. By Elizabethan times, they are also used as personalized gifts or tokens of love: "We do call them Posies, and do paint them now a dayes vpon the backe sides of our fruite trenchers of wood, or vse them as deuises in rings and armes and about such courtly purposes."[19] Since posies (like valentines) are commonly unsigned, they place the reader in the position of trying to discover the poet's identity in order to decipher his meaning, or trying to solve the posie's riddle in order to discover the poet's identity.

As Puttenham explains over and over again, Elizabethan poetry is the preferred language of courtship and seduction precisely because both poetry and seduction are, by their very nature, enigmatic and ambiguous. *The Arte of English Poesie* teaches its readers to recognize and use an entire panoply of "Figures and figurative speaches" designed for "drawing" the mind "from plainnesse and simplicitie to a certaine doublenesse." Indeed, *The Arte of English Poesie* is, in large measure, an anatomy of rhetorical figures, designed, first, to help poets and courtiers veil their meaning and, second, to help readers and listeners decipher those veiled meanings.

Rhetorical figures particularly recommended for both courtiers and lovers include "*Enigma*, or the Riddle," when "[w]e dissemble againe vnder couert and darke speaches," *Amphibologia*, "the *ambiguous*, or figure of sence incertaine," and, above all, "the Courtly figure *Allegoria*, which is when we speake one thing and thinke another, and that our wordes and our meanings meete not." *Allegoria* is particularly useful for courtship, both political and amorous: whether the poet's mistress is the queen or a fair young lady, "the vse of this figure is so large, and his virtue of so great efficacie as it is supposed no man can pleasantly vtter and persuade without it."[20]

Allegoria, the "chief ringleader and captaine of all other figures," is the quintessential figure of courtship because, as Puttenham repeatedly explains, both poetry and courtship thrive on the unsaid – on enigmatic inferences and double meanings that make one set of meanings available to the poet's coterie while sending a secret, veiled message to a particular reader or listener. In any given lyric or lyric sequence the poet/lover may be using allegorical language to ascertain his beloved's interest or to test his mistress's wit. He may be unwittingly deceiving himself, or deliberately deceiving her. He may be using the veil of poetry to communicate one meaning to the coterie while secretly conveying another, veiled meaning to his mistress. Elizabethan poets/lovers write riddling verses to test the reader's wit, to mislead family and friends, to amuse a coterie of rakes and anti-feminists, or to deceive the graver sort of readers who are in a position either to block the courtship or to provide material, professional, and political support.

The more erotic the proposition, the more useful a cover witty, enigmatic rhetoric provides. Should the female reader fail to respond as the poet/lover hopes, or should he wish to seduce and abandon her, he can claim that *she* misread his meaning. In some sense, the more intricate the poetry and the more intimate the relationship, the more the male poet/lover and female listener/reader have to fear. The more covertly and enigmatically the poet/lover writes or speaks, the more difficult it is for both the poet's coterie and his mistress to know how to interpret the poem's meaning and purpose. Yet, the more lovingly the poet/lover addresses his mistress, the more he risks either being hurt by her or being mocked by his peers. As Sidney observes, "there are many mysteries contained in *Poetry* which of purpose were written darklie, least by prophane wits it should be abused."[21] Thus Donne tells his male confidant that the lyric act of courtship and concealment is "a braver thing / Then all the *Worthies* did. / And a braver thence will spring / Which is, to keepe that hid" ("The Undertaking" 25–28).

In some cases, an Elizabethan poet/lover may only show the lyric in the strictest of confidence to a lover or a trusted male friend. When a poet/lover is a poet as well as a lover, however, he (or she) will want the poem to reach a wider lyric audience: a literary coterie, a patron, and ultimately, posterity. For these other lyric audiences, the experience is rather like reading a letter and trying to imagine the other side of the correspondence, or like overhearing a telephone conversation and trying to figure out what the person on the other end of the line could be saying. Paradoxically, the more Elizabethan writers from Puttenham, Sidney, or Donne to Whythorne, Gascoigne, and Daniel alert their readers that private love poems "of purpose were written darkly," the more they advertise the fact that secrets remain. The real secret is that there is no end to secrets – or possible readings.

Donne keeps such strict control over his manuscripts that, with a few exceptions, the *Songs and Sonets* do not begin to circulate for roughly two decades. Once the process of manuscript circulation begins, however, the poems eventually reach an expanding and increasingly distant readership. When the manuscript moves beyond the writer's control and there is no longer any possibility of an actual dialogue between the poet and the lyric audience, the poem is for all intents and purposes "published" – and Elizabethan poems are generally published well before they are printed and sold to the public at large.[22]

Elizabethan poems are often printed for the first time in a pirated text, since the "right" to a text, obtained from the Stationer's Company, is more a question of censorship than ownership. Pirated texts are often the catalyst for a revised and authorized first edition which may be undertaken either by the author or posthumously, by a literary executor. When the unofficial publication of the poet's/lover's private affairs and secrets threatens to create a scandal, he may decide (as Gascoigne and Daniel both do) to print an authorized, bowdlerized edition, omitting any overly erotic or potentially scandalous poems. A poet can transform private poetry of courtship into idealized poetry of praise by turning the autobiographical lyric situation into a fictionalized dramatic situation.

Once Sidney's and Daniel's poems are pirated and Gascoigne's are threatened with censorship, subsequent writers such as Spenser and Donne have all the more reason to conceal their private affairs and secrets. As a result, Daniel and subsequent Elizabethan poets find more intricate and elaborate ways of insinuating the lyric situation and the woman's half of the lyric dialogue. Puttenham recommends "the Figure of false semblant." Donne writes his songs and sonnets, "in cypher writ, or new made Idiome" ("Valediction of the booke" 21), carefully hiding his private meaning "From prophane men . . . / Which will no faith on this bestow, / Or, if they doe, deride" ("The undertaking" 22–24). Spenser writes Neoplatonic poetry and Petrarchan complaints, using the courtly Figure, *Allegoria,* to conceal his boldest persuasions to love and sex.[23]

Elizabethan love poetry is not, as a rule, written for print. Indeed, many of the greatest poems remain unpublished for a decade or more. (The *Amoretti* is a notable exception.) After several centuries of reading poems in books, we tend to see the text as fixed or frozen by print. Elizabethan lyrics enjoy the adaptability of the oral tradition, the fluidity of manuscript circulation, and the reproducibility of print. Much as the word processor encourages today's writers to personalize a letter or memo, the process of continually re-citing and re-copying poems encourages the Elizabethan poet to change a word here or a line there either to improve the poetry or to alter the meaning to suit a new lyric situation or a different lyric audience. Many textual variants, once thought to be scribal errors, are now recognized as revisions, either by the author who anticipates and responds to the views of one or another reader/listener, or by the reader who copies the text, making further changes, some inadvertent and others deliberate. Whereas print freezes the text, manuscript circulation is interactive (like the Internet), allowing both the writer and the recipient to revise the text before sending it along to a new network of readers and writers.

Literati such as Sir John Harington collect manuscripts of poems, much as aficionados of art collect paintings and sculptures. Their manuscript collections are usually transcribed by a private secretary or professional scribe who may unwittingly alter the text. Poetry collectors also add their own emendations and annotations, correcting errors of transcription, recording the name of the poet or the parties involved, citing subsequent owners, readers, and users of the poem. As poems move from one manuscript to another, titles, annotations, and subscriptions appear and disappear, variously contributing and eliminating vital information about the sort of eventfulness the poem contains.

Whereas the great collectors see themselves as both connoisseurs and archivists, selecting and preserving the most valuable works of poetry for posterity, many Elizabethans have a more pragmatic view of the poem and a more casual attitude toward the text. Elizabethans often rewrite poems for their own uses, changing a word here or a line there, omitting a stanza, perhaps even devising a new conclusion. As Puttenham reminds his readers, there are already "a thousand delicate deuises, odes, songs, elegies, ballads, sonets and other ditties," just waiting to be imitated and used in courtship and seduction.[24] "But," as Sidney remarks, "let this be a sufficient, though short note, that we miss the right use of the material point of poesy."

WE ARE NOT SUPPOSED TO ASK

The difference between Eliot's modernist poetics and Sidney's or Puttenham's Elizabethan poetics could not be more striking. For Eliot and many modern literary critics, love poetry is *the* example that most forcefully demonstrates the overriding theoretical point: "the very fact that [the writer] puts this statement in metre" tells us "that we are not supposed to ask whether he actually had a lover" because "what is at stake is a *way of talking* about a woman, rather than any particular real-life woman."[25] For Elizabethan poets, critics, and readers, the fact that the lover puts his statement in verse tells the private female lyric audience, and anyone else who tries to overhear or over-read the poem, that he has gone to a great deal of trouble to win her favor.

Following Eliot's lead, modernist literary criticism separates the epistolary poem rooted in a specific social context and "addressed to one person" from the lyric, the "voice of the poet speaking to himself or nobody." The Elizabethans make no such generic distinctions. For them, the difference between Whythorne or Gascoigne on the one hand, and Sidney, Spenser, or Donne on the other is one of skill rather than kind. After finding "the right words, or anyhow, the least wrong words," Eliot says, "Go away! Find a place for yourself in a book – and don't expect *me* to take any further interest in you." By contrast, when an Elizabethan love poet finally arranges the words "in what he comes to accept as the best arrangement he can find," he says, "Presse to her eyes, importune me some good . . ."

Modernists generally define poetic language as " 'non-pragmatic' discourse" – as "a kind of *self-referential* language, a language which talks about itself" and "serves no immediate practical purpose."[26] Elizabethan literary and social critics, however, assume that songs and sonnets are being used to court and seduce Elizabethan women. Eliot's alienated modern poet "is going to all that trouble, not in order to communicate with anyone, but to gain relief from acute discomfort." The Elizabethan poet/lover is going to all that trouble to gain the love of the Elizabethan woman who alone has the power to relieve his acute discomfort.[27]

When twentieth-century critics analyze Elizabethan love poems in a printed book, "as the lady recedes out of sight and hearing, the lover comes into focus."[28] When the Elizabethans read "published" love poems such as "Sittinge alone upon my thought," the poet/lover comes into focus as the lady comes into sight and hearing. Eliot's famous dictum that the lyric is "the voice of the poet speaking to himself or nobody" is the logical outcome of modernist poetry and criticism in which art and experience, non-pragmatic and pragmatic discourse, are directly opposed. Sidney's equally famous dictum – "the poet, he nothing affirms, and therefore never lieth" – is the logical outcome of a culture which thinks of courting as of poesie. Before following Eliot's lead and saying, "Go away! Find a place for yourself in a book," it might be wise to remember what Sidney would say: "thus much curse I must send you in the behalfe of all *Poets*, that while you liue, you liue in loue, and neuer get fauour, for lacking skill of a Sonet."[29]

Literary theory and criticism have moved far beyond the principles enunciated by Eliot in 1953 when he first lectured on "The Three Voices of Poetry." Yet, to a surprising extent Eliot's alienated, modernist esthetic still delimits the ways in which Renaissance poems are read today.[30] Regardless of which theoretical approach twentieth-century criticism adopts – whether to assert the impersonality and alienation of the lyric poet (Eliot); to distance and disembody the lyric audience (Eliot and Frye); to delineate the masks that readers learn to wear from earlier writers, but *not* from daily life (Ong); to demonstrate the formal coherence of the poem by dismissing everything outside the poem (New Criticism); to apply a cultural poetics of self-fashioning and self-promoting to the careers but *not* the courtships and marriages of aspiring male poets (new historicism); to define the subject, the symbolic order, and sexual desire as male (Lacan); or to deconstruct poet and poem alike, linking male poets and critics in a self-referential intertextuality (Derrida) – the effect is much the same. The woman does not exist (Lacan). She is a shadowy figment of male imagination – "some anonymous figure at whom the flow of language is being directed" – who has no effect on the poet's self-advertising.

One way or another, "the woman (the medium or occasion of the argument)," is a trope, a rhetorical catalyst that sets the process of deconstruction in motion: "Or to put the matter another way, to understand how what Donne does not and cannot name – the arbitrary and precarious system of Elizabethan patronage – at once says and unsays Donne."[31] What the majority of modern critics do not and cannot name – what at once says and unsays the Elizabethan love poem – is the private female lyric audience.

During the last half century, the woman to whom the English Renaissance love poem is addressed has been repeatedly disembodied, idealized, and allegorized out of existence. She is "a metaphor for the poet's worldly aspirations," or "some anonymous figure of voicing." She is "faceless and bodiless;" the poet "cannot see her – does not apparently want to see her; for it is *not* of her that he writes." "*Although* she is described in many of the sonnets, it is the lover who is characterized by his own descriptions." The poem's "primary object of description was *not* the woman at all, *but* the poem's argument." She is not a woman but a Neoplatonic ideal – "a symbol around which were mustered a set of important emotions." She is "*not* a 'person' " but "a function," "an excuse for similes . . . meaningful *not* because they tell us what some particular lady, actual or idealized, looked like, *but* because their tone communicates to us some of the various emotions a lover may experience." The lyric audience is the male coterie; the woman to whom the poems seem to be addressed is not the "real reader" but "a gendered median third term – the female text – to be trafficked among [male] readers."[32]

All too often in twentieth-century criticism, the woman is that which we are *not supposed* to consider. "[W]e know by the very fact that he puts this statement in metre that we are *not* supposed to ask whether he actually had a lover." The poet "is going to all that trouble, *not* in order to communicate with anyone, *but* to gain relief from acute discomfort." "A great poet does *not* write to convey private sentiments to a friend, *but* to give realized form to his imaginative experience." "Donne is addressing *not* a mistress *but* an audience of male peers" – "an audience he has learned to know *not* from daily life *but* from earlier writers."[33]

These insistent and remarkably pervasive not/buts make me suspect that it is *not* the Elizabethan poet *but* the modern critic who "cannot see her – does not apparently want to see her." To counter the not/buts of a literary history and critical tradition which is all too male, *Elizabethan Women and the Poetry of Courtship* seeks the "both/ands" or "not onlys/but alsos" of an Elizabethan poetics which includes "*both* use *and* art" (*AS* 108); *both* male persuasion *and* female response; *not only* male desire and male agency *but also* female desire and female agency; *not only* male authority *but also* female critique.[34]

A FEMALE LYRIC AUDIENCE

Of course, literary tradition is rarely as monolithic as it may seem. During the last two decades, there has emerged a quiet but steady counter-tradition which allots women a more substantial role in Elizabethan lyric tradition. According to Hallett Smith, the woman in the *Amoretti* is "the real protagonist of the series." According to Martz, "her 'deep wit' (Sonnet 43), her 'gentle wit, and vertuous mind' (Sonnet 79), her 'words so wise,' 'the message of her gentle spright' (Sonnet 81) – it is clear that all these tributes to her mental powers are very well deserved." Together, Smith and Martz make a strong case for the woman's impact on the *Amoretti*; however (or should I say, therefore?), subsequent critics seem all the more determined to eviscerate her character and allegorize her meaning.

As one particularly unguarded Spenserian remarks without a trace of irony, "[m]aleness displays its forces and reveals the full range of the resources available to it in its attack on femininity." Instead of a "sage and serious lady, the poet's proper mate," the woman becomes an allegorized abstraction: "the Neoplatonic ideal," "Woman," "perfection," "true chastity," "a mythic cosmic dimension." Only in the late 1970s does a revisionist argument begin to emerge that "demonstrates the power of [Spenser's] poetry while exhibiting the lady's capacity to manipulate, transform, and modify his art."[35]

A similar trend prevails in Sidney and Donne criticism. Most critics have assumed that the poetry "is composed exclusively, even domineeringly, from the viewpoint of the man. The woman is the partner in the sexual dance, and that is all she is." Yet here too, oppositional points of view have begun to emerge. In "The Role of the Lady in Donne's *Songs and Sonets*," I argued that "Donne's poems are less dramatic self-assertions of the man speaking than dramatic discoveries of the speaker learning to recognize and accommodate the [woman's] power." In "The Politics of *Astrophil and Stella*," Jones and Stallybrass declared that "Stella controls the outcome of the sequence. Her judgment of Astrophil, her limited consent, her final rejection determine his responses." In "Struggling into Discourse," Waller recounted the experience of being "puzzled by one of my brightest women students asking what Stella might reply to Astrophel's earnest, but self-regarding, pleas for favor. Even if her response was not in the poem, what might she say? Was her silence the repression of the poet? Or the dominant male character?" As if in answer to Waller's questions, there appeared "The Emergence of Stella in *Astrophil and Stella*"; Fienberg's essay "not only shows a male poet objectifying the beloved in the ways Petrarchan sonneteers characteristically do, but also shows a poet departing from lyric conventions to allow a female figure some autonomy of voice and character." In "Stella's Wit: Penelope Rich as Reader of Sidney's Sonnets" Hulse goes so far as to argue that "Stella becomes the virtual coauthor of the sonnets."[36]

These revisionist essays were all capacitated by, even as they were constrained by, the feminist theory and historical data current at the time they were written. Looking back, what seems most telling to me is that all these essays (my own included) reexamined Elizabethan love poetry without reexamining the lives and writings of Elizabethan women. Consequently, whenever a sonnet lady seemed to have individuality or agency, that was deemed either uncharacteristic of Renaissance lyric tradition or unrepresentative of Elizabethan women's experiences.[37]

Martz offered a delightful tribute to Spenser's mistress, only to assert her singularity: "Most Petrarchan ladies, as Pope might say, 'have no characters at all'. But Spenser's lady has a very decided and a very attractive character." My 1983 essay ("The Role of the Lady in Donne's *Songs and Sonets*") stressed Donne's attentiveness to his mistress's thoughts and feelings, only to conclude with the conventional and, I now think, erroneous view that Donne's predecessors "scanted the woman's point of view." Jones and Stallybrass's 1984 essay ("The Politics of *Astrophil and*

Stella") began with a brilliantly modulated reading of Sidney's rhetorical strategies, but ended with Kelso's *Doctrine for the Lady of the Renaissance*, "Let a woman have chastity, she has all. Let her lack chastity and she is nothing." The essay concluded on a familiar note: "The more passive the lady, the more active [the poet] must be; as the lady recedes out of sight and hearing, the lover comes into focus. And it is possible that he finds in her mainly the necessary precondition for his own dazzling pyrotechnics."[38]

Guided by feminist theory of the early 1980s, Gary Waller taught his students that "Astrophil's Stella or Drayton's Idea" are "fixed as 'images,' objects of gaze and analysis, within language they did not invent and do not control." A year later, Hulse's wonderful tribute to "Stella's wit" culminated in a conventional and condescending view of Queen Elizabeth, "spewing out clouds of rhetoric about virtue and glory." Halley's 1990 essay, "Textual Intercourse: Anne Donne, John Donne, and the Sexual Poetics of Textual Exchange," provided "a case study in the feminist project of recovering lost and silent women – a case study that warned us to examine carefully the forms, and the limits, of our knowledge." For Halley, "Anne Donne's historical actuality" is "imperiled by efforts to discover her presence in her husband's literary product."[39]

The interdependent insights and constraints of feminism and historicism came together in Wall's 1994 *Imprint of Gender*. The "focus on textual exchange and erotic interchange" enabled Wall to explore the sonnet's "highly gendered and sexualized rhetoric." She acknowledged that "some women did participate in poetic game playing, and [that] poetry could be employed in the service of courtship," but only mentioned the fact briefly, in passing. She referred to, but did not explore, "the vast changes in familial organization, marriage, and gender ideology that took place in early modern England." Her own readings yielded abundant evidence that the poet's mistress is "the text's true reader" and that manuscript circulation gives the reader considerable collaborative power over the process of poetry making. Yet, so strong is the view of literature as an "exchange between men" that Wall placed her own most stunning observations under erasure, concluding that "the real reader" – i.e. the male coterie – "writes over and subsumes the mistress's place in the economy of exchanged poems." Wall's conclusion is not hard to predict: the woman is not the private lyric audience but a construction of the male poet: "the 'turn' or trope for the conversation of the Renaissance [male] coterie."[40]

"There is . . . no word for the audience of the lyric," Frye writes; "what is wanted is something analogous to 'chorus' which does not suggest simultaneous presence or dramatic context." What is wanted, it seems to me, is not another universalizing term such as "chorus" but a variety of terms that recognize the multiple private and public lyric audiences: not only "the male coterie" (Marotti, Wall), "the patron" (Lytle and Orgel), "the literary tradition" (Ong), but also "the female reader" (Hull), "the resisting reader" (Fetterley), the female lyric audience, the female listener/interlocutor/reader.[41] The Elizabethan female lyric audience does not displace or diminish the male coterie, the system of patronage, or the literary exchange between men, but it does give Elizabethan women a central role in the history of English Renaissance love poetry. It also redresses the imbalance created by fifty years of literary criticism which (with a few exceptions) either tacitly disregards the woman to whom Elizabethan love poems are addressed, or expressly denies that she could be the real reader of the poem.

3

The practice of Elizabethan courtship

> [H]ow much more may we refuse such olde doting fooles as som-
> times ar procured by our pare^{n}tes to be suters to us, & have a thou-
> sand worse impedimentes, and nothyng but their goods and money
> to mary them, no not so much as any one good propertie or quali-
> tie.
>
> *A Letter sent by the Maydens of London, to the vertuous Matrones & Mistresses*
> *of the same, in the defense of their lawfull Libertie*[1]

BUT WOO HER, GENTLE PARIS, GET HER HEART

Only a decade ago, most English professors assumed, on the basis of
Stone's *Family, Sex, and Marriage in England 1600 to 1800*, that the typical
marriage was arranged by parents for their children.[2] If arranged marriages were as prevalent and incontestable as English Renaissance literary critics have traditionally assumed – if wooing a woman with a view
to marriage was condoned in the illiterate, lower ranks but unusual in
the middling ranks and virtually non-existent in the upper ranks – poetry
of courtship could have little material or political significance. Yet " 'cultures' do not hold still for their portraits," and pictures of other cultures
often look most balanced and consistent when underlying tensions and
contradictions have been left outside the frame of investigation.[3]

Early modern English marriage is a complex business, involving ideological, social, and material forces. Elizabethan women's social and
financial liberty is severely limited by an ethical code that defines female
honor as chastity, a social code that insists "the ornament of a woman is
silence," and a legal system that subjects women first to their fathers and
then to their husbands.[4] Yet women's silence and subordination are
never as monolithic as the stricter prescriptive texts might wish to
suggest.[5] Oddly enough, English canon law gives females over twelve
and males over fourteen the right to marry without parental permission

or church ceremony. And according to the law, marriage is contingent not on parental consent, but on the woman's and the man's freely given assent.

Though restricted by social norms and material considerations, this liberty is preserved throughout Elizabeth I's reign, even as it is being circumscribed throughout Europe, in both Catholic and Protestant countries.[6] Why, one might well ask, would the English church support a law that condones premarital sexuality and encourages filial disobedience? Many Elizabethans argue that stricter laws are necessary to prevent moral degeneration and social disorder, and one of the first acts taken by the Jacobean Parliament is to limit conjugal freedom of choice.[7] Yet other Elizabethans maintain that further limitations would simply increase illegitimacy without curtailing premarital sexuality.

The average age of first marriage is twenty-three for women and twenty-eight for men, though eldest sons who stand to inherit a title or estate tend to marry earlier and at a higher rate. Marriage is "usually the critical point at which men and women leave [home] and are endowed." Yet in early modern England, as in modern day America, "[y]oung people ceased to be sons and daughters long before they even thought of becoming husbands and wives."[8] Adolescents from all ranks, prompted either by financial necessity or social convention, leave their parents' household before reaching the age of marriage.

Between early childhood and late marriage, 15 percent of the population lives as servants in a neighboring or distant town. As Ralph Josselin's diary reports, "all the girls had left home for good by the age of 14½."[9] The gentry leave home in large numbers to earn and save money towards a dowry; to receive an education or acquire professional training; to make social and marital contacts. Isabella Whitney, "a yonge Gentilwoman," writes a verse epistle "to two of her yonger Sisters seruinge in London." She advises them to "obserue the rules / which in the same I tell. / So shal you wealth posses, / and quietnesse of mynde."[10]

The ancient ideal of service undergoes considerable strain during the Elizabethan era, but young people from the upper social ranks are still placed as servant/companions in the great houses and at court where they are brought up, educated, given professional training as secretaries or assistants, and introduced to potential patrons and marriage partners.[11] Margaret Dakins leaves her parents' home in Yorkshire to live and study under the protection of the Countess of Huntingdon. When Ann More comes to live at York House, to be introduced to society, and to be educated under the aegis of her aunt, John Donne is also living there, serving as Sir Thomas Egerton's secretary.

Early modern England is a highly ordered society with well-recognized gradations of wealth and status. Most early modern marriages are homologous, like marrying like, and endogamous, that is, within the same social rank. "[I]n the alliance of matrimony," Lord Howard advises Queen Elizabeth, "there should be found no dissimilitude or, at the least, antipathy in the qualities of the mind, much less in the estates, of the persons contracting matrimony." Whately advises his less privileged readers to choose "an equall yoke-fellow . . . of due proportion in state, birth, age, education, and the like, not much vnder, not much ouer, but fit and correspondent." Elizabeth Grymeston urges her son Bernye to "Marrie in thine owne ranke, and seeke especially in it thy contentment and preferment."[12]

Marital alliances are expected to preserve the social order, but marriage also can lead to social advancement or decline. Though England is not yet a class society, social rank is established by birth and constantly adjusted, however slightly, through education, professional advancement, mercantile success, court favor, titles, and marriage. On the one hand, arranged marriages often exchange wealth for status, matching aristocratic second sons such as Walter Devereux or Robert Sidney with wealthy gentlewomen such as Margaret Dakins or Barbara Gamage. On the other hand, clandestine marriages frequently defy parental wishes in order to breach social rank, as in John Donne's notorious marriage to Ann More, or the "great many" that Thomas Whythorne "did know" who "achieved as great enterprises as that."[13]

Among the highest orders of society, marriage is the occasion for dividing family wealth in the form of goods, money, or land. Surviving records of matrimonial allotments are much more scanty than wills, but accounts of marriage negotiations suggest that parents feel both a duty and a desire to provide equitably for children of both sexes. Inheritance bequests are calculated according to prior marital allotments, and the marriage portion acquired by a first son's marriage often provides marriage portions for his sisters. *Tom of all Trades, or The plaine Path-way to Preferment*, a popular guidebook addressed to the upwardly mobile, advises fathers to raise marriage portions for their daughters "by the Marriage of your eldest Sonne, or out of that part of your personall estate which you may spare without prejudice of your selfe."[14]

Though eager to marry her son to Lady Cornwallis, Lady Bacon is careful not to shortchange her other children: "We have offered what we are abell, and what we can and will fayhtfully performe. If it be accepted, we shall rejoyse much therein; if not, we must be contented without grudging. . . . We must not laye out all our stocke upon one purchas, having so many others to provide for." When Thomas Howard and Anne Murray fall passionately in love, her mother refuses to approve the match because his father's "fortune was such as had need of a more considerable portion then my mother could give mee, or els it must ruine his younger children," even though, as Anne later writes, his "quality was above mine and therefor better then any [my mother] could expect for mee."[15]

Early modern England is a culture in which marriage, though legally available to all, is a luxury that many members of society simply cannot afford. Before the advent of mass production, furnishing a home is a laborious and costly undertaking. Some aristocratic young married couples move onto the family estate, but most couples postpone marriage until they have the resources to establish a nuclear household. The marriage agreement between Margaret Dakins and her first husband, Walter Devereux, the second son of the Earl of Essex, commits 3000*l.* from each family to buy the couple the estate of Hackness. The Earl of Huntingdon not only agrees to pay the remaining 500*l.* outright, but also loans money to complete Dakins' share. To be sure, not every couple's kin can provide that kind of support. Whately nonetheless advises his more general readers, "if it may be, liue of thy selfe with thy wife, in a family of thine owne."[16]

Until industrialization occurs, the household remains the center not only of reproduction but also of production. In all ranks, women's financial contributions, whether in the form of prenuptial wages set aside for marriage or a portion of the family estate received as dowry or inheritance, are essential: first, to set up the household; second, to help support the family after marriage; third, to provide financial resources for the next generation.[17] For Anne Murray, it is a point of honor not to marry Sir James Halkett until she discharges the debts accumulated while living as a single woman.

By postponing marriage until their mid or late twenties, three-quarters of the society at husbandman level and below can earn enough money to establish an independent household without the help of family or friends. Artisans who typically begin their apprenticeships in their early twenties are not free to set up shop and home until their late twenties. Some employers help to provide a marriage portion for their employees. Other couples wait to inherit property and/or household furnishings. Margaret Paston writes to her son Sir John Paston, "I wuld that ye shuld not be to hasty to be maried til ye wer su[re] of your [live-lihood] . . . labour that ye may have releses of the londs, and be in more su[rety] of your lond, [before] ye be maried."[18]

At any given moment, approximately one-third of the adult population of sixteenth and seventeenth-century England – compared to about half today – is unmarried.[19] Social custom serves as the principal, though perhaps unconscious, stay against the population explosion that is threatening the social order. Late marriage significantly limits sexual intercourse during a woman's most fertile child-bearing years. About 10 percent never marry. Both men and women continue to make first marriages during their thirties, and sometimes into their forties or even fifties, well after a woman's child-bearing years are over. Hence Elizabeth I's courtships, continuing into her thirties and forties, are less belated than they might seem today.

Since adult life expectancy is so much shorter, the early modern family is fundamentally unstable, and closer in this respect to the complex family groupings of recent years than to the American nuclear family of the 1950s. The average marriage lasts less than twenty years. As Margaret Hoby's and Martha Moulsworth's three successive marriages indicate, there is a high rate of remarriage. Households commonly include a step-parent as well as half-brothers and sisters. Between 1595 and 1620 one-third of the peerage is estranged from their wives, according to Stone's estimate. Divorce is illegal, but separations of bed and board do occur, both officially and unofficially, and geographical mobility facilitates illegal remarriages, as the case of Martin Guerre illustrates.[20] Some bigamists are brought to court when rumors of a former life catch up with them. Indeed bigamy becomes a significant enough social problem during Elizabeth's reign to prompt the 1604 Jacobean Parliament to institute a statutory death penalty.

Lack of reliable birth control or sterile birth procedures and an almost uninterrupted cycle of pregnancy, miscarriage, and birth means that approximately one woman in six dies in childbirth. Yet, then as now, many wives outlive their husbands. Widows with a good jointure or substantial property, like Jane Cornwallis or Margaret Dakins Devereux, make attractive candidates for remarriage.[21] Some enterprising widows, including the redoubtable Bess of Hardwick, amass substantial wealth through successive remarriages.

When Walter Devereux dies at the siege of Rouen, Lady Russell writes to urge her son, Thomas Posthumus Hoby, to woo Devereux's wealthy young widow. As is typical of the day, Lady Russell discusses the financial terms unabashedly: "Yf this prove a matche, I will be bownd to leave to yow that which shall be worth v C li. by yere, wherof iii C li. of it joynter to her after my death, and a howse presently furnished to bring her to." The offer of an annual income, a jointure, and a fully furnished house is calculated to outbid Hoby's principal rival, Thomas Sidney, the youngest brother of Philip, Mary, and Robert: "if by reason she be willing to be ledd to her owne good, yow will be fownd the better mache of bothe."[22]

Many early modern women have more freedom to choose a second husband than a first. The widowed Margaret Dakins Devereux "hath her father's consent to match where she list." Mary Tudor agrees to marry the sick and aged King of France on the condition that when he dies, she be allowed to marry Charles Brandon, the man she loved from the start. Of course, most widows are not independently wealthy, and many have no choice but to remarry. When Martha Prynne, later Martha Moulsworth, is first widowed, she is allowed a year of mourning before a second marriage is arranged for her: "then was a yeare sett on my mourninge score."[23]

Moulsworth's verse narrative of her three successive marriages acquires an unusual degree of autobiographical authenticity from the marginal notes, "apparently composed by Moulsworth," which "run alongside the manuscript version of the poem itself": "l Husband, Mr Nicolas Prynne, Aprill 18 1598"; "2d Mr Tho: Througood ffebruary 3 1604"; "3d Mr Beuill Moulswoorth June 15, 1619" (lines 49, 55, 58). It is only after being twice widowed that Martha acquires sufficient financial independence, first, to live alone for almost four years and then to attract a man whom she herself is eager to marry: "three years eight Months I kept a widowes ffast. / The third I tooke a louely man, & kind / such comlines in age we seldome ffind" (lines 56–58). As the active verbs suggest, she chooses the life of a widow until she meets Moulsworth who is not only "louely," "kind," and "comely," but also a knight, descended from the Mortimers: "their Arms he bore, not bought wth Heraulds fee" (line 60).

Jane Cornwallis makes remarriage contingent upon the right to "do with my own estate, besides my child's, what I would."[24] Similarly, Martha Moulsworth retains a remarkable degree of financial independence during her third marriage:

> was neuer man so Buxome to his wife
> wth him I led an easie darlings life.
> I had my will in house, in purse in Store
> what would a women old or yong haue more? lines 65–8

Moulsworth mourns for her beloved third husband: "Two years Almost outwearinge since he died / And yett, & yett my tears ffor him nott dried" (lines 69–70). Yet she also enjoys the easy, unconstrained life bequeathed her by her successive widowhoods, as the jaunty tone of her conclusion reveals: "whie should I / then putt my Widowehood in jeopardy? / the Virgins life is gold, as Clarks vs tell / the Widowes siluar, I loue siluar well" (lines 107–10). Having finally acquired sufficient financial independence and self-reliance to do as she pleases, Moulsworth would rather remain single: "this must be my care / of knittinge here a fourth knott to beware" (lines 103–4). As a wealthy widow, she is free to enjoy the life of poetry and learning she grew to love in her youth.

AN ANGEL'S FACE WITH FAIR LANDS

A successful early modern marriage simply *has* to be economically viable. As the Maydens of London protest, "we are not so wynching wood [insane] to choose boyes or lads that lacke experience and the trade to live." Yet marriage is also expected to be mutually loving and sexually fulfilling to both parties.[25] Marriage manuals such as Gouge's *Domesticall Dvties* regularly acknowledge that a "louing mutuall affection must passe betwixt husband and wife . . . this is the ground of all the rest." In *A Ryght Frutefull Epystle* Erasmus writes – without any sense of incongruity – "sythe your age is lusty and floryshynge, nor ye lacke nat the beautie of ye body, . . . ther is offered you a wyfe, so lusty a mayde, so well borne as may be, chaste, sobre, demure, godly, hauying an aungels face with fayre landes . . ." According to Martin Bucer, a true marriage begins with a "true assent of hearts between those who made the agreement" and is "fully confirmed" by a wedding feast and "plenty of carnal intercourse."[26] Here, we might say, is God's plenty.

Marriage contracts in the middling to upper ranks are typically negotiated by parents, guardians, and kinfolk. Yet even when a marriage is arranged, the man is expected to court the woman and to obtain her consent. Like Juliet and Paris, courting couples are allowed ample opportunities to see "if looking liking move" (*Rom.* 1.3). Elizabethans from all social ranks, probably the majority of the lower and middling ranks, many of the gentry, and some of the aristocracy, conduct their own courtships – and not only on stage. Courting couples find ample opportunities to meet alone or with a friend: in private homes and in public spaces; at church and outdoor sermons; in alehouses, shops, and

Figure 3 Weighing the dowry.

taverns; at popular festivals and village dances; in deserted fields or secluded, tree-lined walks of country estates; at balls and social gatherings; and, of course, at the theater. Suitors woo their mistresses in private conversations, familiar letters, and for the history of English Renaissance poetry most importantly, in poetry or poetic love language.

Courtship is seen as a time to test character, compatibility, and desire. The astrologer, Napier, records the fascinating case of Ann Winch. Having convinced her father that her suitor has the means to support her, Ann obtains her father's permission to move into her suitor's home in order to decide whether or not she wants to marry him: "Hath been five weeks with him and by fits careth much for him and sometimes will not have him."[27]

In the best of all possible courtships, children and parents concur, though of course that is not always the case. "For as our parentes advi[c]e is always to be asked in the choyce of our husbands, so is it not alwaies to be followed, namely when we can not frame our selves to love the partie that our parentes have provided for us." Parental influence is directly related both to the parents' ability to provide financial support and to the children's need for their support. Among the middling to lower ranks, freely chosen courtships are common. Among the gentry and aristocracy, the social groups most likely to write and exchange the love poetry we read today, arranged marriage is still probably the norm, though it can by no means be taken for granted. While advising his son Robert to "marry thy daughters in time, lest they marry themselves," Burghley himself refuses a proffered marriage contract between his under-age daughter and the young Philip Sidney. Whatever reservations he may have had about Sidney's wealth or status, the reason Burghley gives is that he believes his daughter should be allowed to select her own suitor when she comes of age.[28]

What early modern men and women desire is profoundly influenced by material considerations. In the upper ranks, where land, money, and patronage depend on kinship networks, family and friends generally help select an appropriate match and actively negotiate the terms of the contract. In the middling and lower ranks, couples generally find their own marriage partners, although they are strongly advised to obtain parental consent. Sons and daughters in all ranks can refuse a proposed match, while parents can either approve the child's choice or refuse their support – if they have the financial or social means to provide it.

Elizabethan men and women, from all social ranks, conduct their own courtships both with and without their parents' approval. Smith's *Preparatiue to Mariage* recommends a "time of longing for their affections to settle in, because the deferring of that which wee loue doth kindle the desire, which if it came easilie and speedilie to vs, would make vs set lesse by it." "[T]rye him well before," Isabella Whitney warns her female readers. Marriage manuals, parental letters of advice, and other pre-scriptive texts offer Elizabethans detailed, lengthy instructions about choosing a mate *before* concluding with a belated reminder that the couple should, of course, obtain their parents' consent.[29]

Many parents happily approve their children's choices; others arrange marriages that never take place because a son or daughter balks – and not just in *Romeo and Juliet* or *A Midsummer Night's Dream*. When Simond D'Ewes dislikes the bride chosen for him by his father, the matter is dropped: "I was motioned by my father to a match that liked mee not, which I with thankes for his love refusing, like a most loving father hee pressed mee noe further." When Ralph Josselin tries to persuade his daughter Mary to marry one Mr. Shirley, she refuses because he is "not loving." Her father accepts her decision, for he "could not desire it, when shee said it would make both their lives miserable." Lucy Hutchinson's diary reports that "her mother and friends had a greate desire she should marry, and were displeas'd that she refus'd many offers which they thought advantageous enough; she was obedient, loath to displease them, but more herselfe, in marrying such as she could find no inclination to."[30]

Chamberlain's letters describe an arranged match which comes to naught after "all articles were agreed, and the wedding clothes made" because the young woman makes secret plans of her own: "when it came to the upshot, the gentlewoman had no manner of liking, nor could by any means be perswaded, which so displeased her uncle, that he left her worse by ten thousand pound than he meant to have done, which doth no whit grieve her, in respect that she hath her choice."[31] Dorothy Osborne and William Temple carry on an epistolary courtship for a good two years before overcoming their families' resistance.

Patriarchal control of marriage is less omnipresent than we might imagine. Two-fifths to two-thirds of fathers die before their sons and daughters marry. In the late sixteenth century, wardship becomes less oppressive. Many children are free to choose their own marriage partners upon a father's death. Moreover, mothers and female relatives play an active role in marriage negotiations. When Nathaniel Bacon wants to marry the wealthy widow Lady Jane Cornwallis, his mother negotiates the financial terms through an intermediary, Mr. Parr, before writing directly to Lady Jane to find out whether she loves Nathaniel as he loves her: "yor La[dyship], who I knowe is lodged in the principall p[ar]t of his hart. But how you stande affected vnto hym I knowe not."[32] Thomas Hoby begins his courtship of Margaret Dakins Devereux by bringing a letter from his mother to Margaret's father-in-law, the Earl of Essex.

Female relatives take it upon themselves not only to facilitate a desirable match, but also to ease tensions between recalcitrant fathers and their children, as a letter written by the Countess of Bedford to her intimate friend, Lady Cornwallis, illustrates: "an offer being made me for [my niece] pleases me well, & I doubt not will take effect, if her unreasonable father can be brought to do what he ought, which if love will not make him, I hope fear will prevaile."[33]

Peers are also deeply involved in early modern courtships at all social ranks. They arrange secret meetings, and serve as witnesses to secret contracts and clandestine marriages. They act as confidants, chaperones, go-betweens, and wooers by proxy. They convey messages, letters, and love poems. As Lord Julian explains in *The Courtier*, the lover is much "aided by some lovinge and faithfull friende. For the signes that the lover himselfe maketh, give a farr greater susspition, then those that he maketh by them that go in message betwene." William Knollys writes repeatedly to Anne Fitton in the hopes that she will help him to win her sister Mary's hand in marriage. Lowe goes awooing with his friend James Naylor, and later visits Ann Barrow as Naylor's emissary. The Duke of Alençon sends the charming, courtly Simier to court Queen Elizabeth (much as Orsino sends Viola to woo Olivia, with an artfully constructed though stiffly conventional speech which he writes and she recites). "[H]aving never any opertunity of beeing alone with mee [Anne Murray] to speake himself," Lord Howard "imployed a young gentleman (whose confidentt hee was in an amour betwixt him and my Lady Anne, his cousin german) to tell mee how much hee had indeavored all this time to smother his passion which hee said began the first time that ever hee saw mee."[34]

Peers can also prevent courtships by criticizing a friend's choice or by conveying damaging information, whether true or false. After his clandestine marriage to Ann More, John Donne writes to his father-in-law, Sir George More, to defend himself against "those yll reports wch malice hath raysd of me."[35] Anne Murray affiances herself to Colonel Bampfield upon being assured by him that his wife had died. The engagement persists for four years until her friends discover, and promptly inform her, that Bampfield's wife is still very much alive. Towards the end of the *Amoretti* Spenser defends his impending marriage against malicious gossip of this kind: "Venemous toung tipt with vile adders sting" (*Amoretti* 86:1).

LOVE EQUALLY BESTOWED

Court cases, medical records, and familiar letters confirm the fact that love and sexual attraction can exert an important role in the marriage choices of women from the middling to the upper ranks of early modern society. In a 1565 court case Margaret Underwood testifies that she rejected Thomas Deynes' suit because he expressed a desire for her property, not her affection: "he said if he might enjoy the house and land in her mother's possession that he would be content to marry with her, wherefore for that he would have had her for her land's sake as she conjectured, she made him an answer that she would no more talk with him in any matrimony [sic] matter."[36]

For many aristocratic Elizabethans, wealth and family connections are essential prerequisites for choosing a spouse, but nonetheless secondary. In a letter of advice addressed to his first son, Henry Percy describes his own choice of a wife: "first, that my wife should neither be ugly in body nor mind; secondly, that she should bring with her meat in her mouth to maintain her expense; lastly, that her friends should be of that eminency that they might probably appear to be steps for you to better your fortune." Burghley's letter to his second son mentions wealth and social status first. Yet he clearly believes that sexual attraction and intelligent conversation are vital if the marriage is to thrive: "use great providence and circumspection in the choice of a wife; for from thence will spring all thy future good or evil . . . Let her not be poor, how generous soever; for a man can buy nothing in the market with gentility. Nor choose a base and uncomely creature, although for wealth; for it will cause contempt in others, and loathing in thee. Neither make choice of a dwarf or a fool: for by the one thou shalt beget a race of pigmies: the other will be thy daily disgrace, and it will irk thee to hear her talk."[37]

Letters of advice written by mothers on the brink of death show that even the most pious early modern women place considerable emphasis on love and physical attraction. In *The Mothers Blessing*, Dorothy Leigh expresses two concerns about her sons' marriages: first, they should choose a godly wife; second, they should choose someone whom they can love until death do them part. "Do not a woman that wrong as to take her from her friends that love her, and after a while to begin to hate her," Leigh writes. "Methinks my son could not offend me in anything if he served God, except he chose a wife that he could not love to the end."[38]

Autobiographical writings and familiar letters demonstrate that love and sexual attraction often exert a powerful though sometimes disorderly or detrimental effect upon early modern courtship. Jane Cornwallis threatens to reject Nathaniel Bacon's suit unless she receives compelling assurances that she is not being wooed for her wealth alone: "they have made it seeme other wayes to me, in asseuring me that it was myselfe, and not my fortune, which they desiered; but, I confess, by several circumstances I maye justly feare that I shall find my fortune to

be the chiefe motive . . . if I do, yet it will much discourage me for per-
severing any furder in it."[39]

Elizabeth Grymeston urges her son Bernye to marry while he is still
youthful and attractive enough to arouse his wife's desire and win her
love: "For seldome shalt thou see a woman out of hir owne loue to pull
a rose that is full blowen, deeming them alwaies sweetest at the first
opening of the budde." Grymeston adapts male rhetoric of *carpe diem*
poetry to her own female purposes in order to teach her son to imagine
the female point of view. Above all, she wants him to recognize the
importance of female desire. Mary Wroth's *Urania*, a fictionalized,
encoded romance based on the earlier, quasi-autobiographical sonnet
sequence, *Pamphilia to Amphilanthus*, shows that early modern women are
also beginning to express their desires in poetry and to analyze the
dynamics of courtship in prose. Pamphilia willingly risks rejection in the
hopes of gaining equality and reciprocity: "loue is onely to be gaind by
loue equally bestowed, the giuer, and receiuer reciprocally liberall, else
it is no loue; nor can this be, but where affections meete; and that we
must not all expect, nor can it reasonably be demanded," Pamphilia
observes, "some must and do suffer."[40]

The diary of Ralph Josselin describes an experience of love at first
sight worthy of a comedy or romance: "the first lords day being Oct. 6
my eye fixed with love upon a Mayd, & hers upon mee, who afterwards
proved my wife." Roger Lowe's diary uses the language of love to
describe courtship practices remarkably similar to those dramatized in
Elizabethan lyric sequences: "my effections ran out violently after her,
so as that I was never contented one day to an end unles I had seene
her."[41]

Anne Halkett's *Memoirs* recount a clandestine courtship in language
worthy of a sonneteer: " 'Madam', said hee, 'what I love in you may well
increase, butt I am sure itt can never decay'. . . 'Oh, madam,' said hee,
'can you imagine I love att that rate as to have itt shaken with any
storme?' "[42] Whether these are the actual words of her suitor or Anne's
own literary reconstruction of a more prosaic wooing, the tropes of
Elizabethan love poetry are all too familiar: the omnipresent Petrarchan
ship of love, lost in a storm at sea; the eternizing rhetoric and financial
diction that pervade Daniel's and Shakespeare's sonnets; the trope of
love's increase which Donne mocks so brilliantly in "Loves
infinitenesse."

When Thomas Hoby goes to woo the recently widowed Margaret
Sidney, he begins his suit like a conventional sonneteer, praising

Margaret's renowned beauty and virtue. As the posthumous son of Thomas Hoby, the translator of *The Courtier,* Hoby Jr. is well schooled in the art of courtship. Carefully avoiding any mention of Margaret's wealth, Hoby offers two reasons for pressing his suit so precipitately: "One, in desier his eyes to witnes that which publicke reporte had delivered him, that the guyftes of nature had in some sorte equalled her vertues. Thother, havinge bene longe drawne to affect her for thes guyftes, he was desirous to be made knowne to her, as the first that shoulde seeke her." When Hoby fails to win Margaret's love with this idealizing rhetoric, he tries a more ardent persuasion, "ledd," as he himself tells the story to Huntingdon, "contynually to exceed good manners in beynge more ruled by my love then reasone."[43] The rhythms are prosaic, but the fervid diction might have come straight out of *Astrophil and Stella* or *The Courtier*.

It is customary for men to court more than one woman at a time, and for women to entertain several suitors simultaneously. Sometimes multiple courtships are conducted openly, with the full knowledge of all parties involved. Yet, most courtships are carried on, at least at the outset, in secret. Isabella Whitney's *letter, lately written in meeter, by a yonge Gentilwoman: to her vnconstant Louer* is prompted by the discovery that her fiancé has made secret plans to marry another woman. Despite her own plight, Whitney continues to defend Elizabethan women's right to conduct their own clandestine courtships. Roger Lowe is already courting Ann Barrow when he also decides to court Ellin Marsh, "who had a house and liveinge." Accordingly, he hires "a private mediator to intercede for me, from whom and by whome I received answer that she would give me the meeteinge ere longe, onely I must be secret, to which I promisd I would." When parents oppose a match, secrecy is crucial. After receiving initial protestations of love, Anne Murray's mother is so opposed to Lord Howard's suit that she has her daughter watched day and night. Anne manages to slip away, having "left my mother and sister in the[ir] bed" in order to meet her desperate suitor "in the backe way into the cellar."[44]

The cryptic language of most autobiographical texts makes it difficult to know just how far physical intimacy progresses during courtship. When Lord Howard looks grief-stricken during their clandestine rendezvous at the entrance to the cellar, Anne Murray takes pity on him: "I must confese did so much move mee that, laying aside all former distance I had kept him att, I satt downe upon his knee, and laying my head neere his I suffred him to kisse mee, which was a liberty I never gave

before; nor had nott then had I nott seene him so overcome with greefe."
By the time of Colonel Bampfield's wooing, Anne's watchful mother is
deceased, and Anne herself makes frequent "private visitts" to
Bampfield in his quarters. Upon one occasion he receives her "lying
upon his bed." Indeed, Anne expresses such passion for Bampfield and
such intense guilt about her own subsequent engagement to Sir Halkett
– even though she has by then discovered that Bampfield's wife is not
dead, as he claimed – that the modern editor wonders, "Was Anne
Murray the mistress of Colonel Bampfield?"[45]

The relatively stable rate of bridal pregnancy, between 10 and 20
percent for the early modern period, suggests that premarital sexuality,
though strictly condemned by the preachers, is condoned by social
custom and widely practiced by the populace.[46] Men and women in the
lower ranks frequently begin sleeping together as soon as they are fast
betrothed.[47] Some women from the upper and middling ranks do so as
well. A promise to marry followed by coitus constitutes a legally binding
common law marriage. Yet, until a couple can afford to live together in
marriage, early modern women are wise to limit the odds of pregnancy
by avoiding repeated sexual encounters.

There is, of course, no reliable method of birth control, but rudi-
mentary condoms, stinging salves designed to inhibit an erection and
discourage penetration, and abortifacients are all known and used. Then
as now, some men and women are infertile. Some are simply lucky. Many
women conceive and quickly marry the father to be. Others abort the
fetus or miscarry. Others are seduced and deserted. Some pregnant
women and unwed mothers, including some from the upper ranks such
as Ann Vavasour, marry men who are not the father of their child. Upon
hearing rumors of Mary Fitton's illegitimate pregnancy, William
Knollys, who had been seeking a match with Mary ever since she arrived
at court, begs the family for permission to marry her and save her from
dishonor. Mary's mother writes to her, warning her – and thus covertly
advising her – that harsh physics can cause spontaneous abortions.[48]
Mary is abandoned by the Earl of Pembroke, and the child, whatever
the reason, is stillborn. Knollys' offer is rejected.

Clandestine courtships take place even in the upper ranks – even in
cases where powerful kinfolk and substantial fortunes are involved.
Robert Sidney's marriage to Barbara Gamage is full of secrecy and
intrigue, as is Thomas Sidney's marriage to Margaret Dakins Devereux.
Upon hearing news of Devereux's death, the Earl and Countess of
Huntingdon send Thomas Sidney (his ward and her nephew) to

Figure 4 Unknown Lady, visibly pregnant, attributed to Sir William Segar, c. 1595.

Yorkshire with letters to her father, urging him to let Margaret stay with them in London until they can arrange a marriage with Sidney. In the meantime, Lady Russell begins scheming with Margaret's sister-in-law, "My La. Perrott the wisest, surest, and fittest to your good, who, after she hath fownd her disposityon tooching Sidney, may, on some tyme of the gentlewoman's comming to visitt my La. Dorothie, let you understand of the tyme when yowrself may mete her there." The barely perceptible hint of conspiratorial urgency turns into a full-blown plot in the stunning postscript: "Let Anthony Cooke help to steale her away. She hath her father's consent to match where she list."[49]

The scheme fails because, as Hoby later writes, "at her fyrst comynge" to London, Margaret "was brought to her chamber, which she closly kept untyll she was maryed . . . whyther none wer suffered to come, withowte especiall admyttance." "Nowe what I coolde say farther is fytter for my L. to imagyne, then for me to relate, and therfore leavynge her close prysoner in her chamber, whyther none wer sufered to come, withowte especiall admyttance, I wyll retourne unto my sute."[50] Yet Hoby's account of Margaret's confinement should be treated with a grain of salt, not only because it is designed to placate the new Earl of Essex who is angry at Margaret for marrying too soon after his brother's death, but also because he tells the story with such obvious rhetorical embellishment.

Rather than being imprisoned and forced to marry Sidney against her will as Hoby implies, Margaret takes refuge with the Huntingdons because she prefers Sidney to Hoby. Despite his wealth and powerful connections, Hoby is extremely ugly and notoriously disagreeable. He is "described by his enemies as a 'scurvy urchen,' a 'spindle shanked ape' " and "ridiculed 'as the little knight that useth to draw up his Breeches with a Shooing-horn.' " His own mother complains bitterly about his "vnnaturall bad nature and insolency."[51]

Although it is difficult to know from Hoby's letters how Margaret Devereux/Sidney feels about him, we can infer her point of view by reading between the lines of Huntingdon's letter to her. Huntingdon agrees to acquaint Hoby "with the contents of your lettre, and at the laste I dyd geve hym the lettre to peruse, but yt moved him not to that purpose you desyred. . . He doth not beleeve that you wyll geve such a denyall as your lettre mentioneth." Hoby refuses to leave without obtaining a letter of support from Huntingdon who is already suffering from the sickness that kills him soon after. Having succumbed to Hoby's insistence, Huntingdon writes privately to Margaret, saying, "For God's cawse have care of all our credyts, and soe handle the matter as his commynge agayne may be neyther offensyve to you nor dyspleasynge to hymself. And so with wysh of all good and happynes to you." Huntingdon sounds both concerned for her welfare and respectful of her wishes; he signs the letter, "Your lovynge freynde, H. HUNTYNGDON."[52]

The story is recounted in the introduction to the *Fortescue Papers* which quotes all the principals – except Margaret. Gardiner fails to mention whether any of her letters survived, even though Huntingdon refers to a letter he received from her. Moreover, after he made his selections, the original documents were destroyed. That we must settle for inferences about Margaret's feelings, derived from the words of others, chosen by a scholar who deemed the documents pertaining to her courtship unworthy of "a place amongst the State Papers of the present volume," is a limitation worth noting.[53] Indeed, the absence of Margaret Dakins' side of the courtship dramatizes the very important point that most modern histories of early modern courtship and marriage, like most recent literary studies of poetry and courtship, are based on the testimony of men. That does not invalidate the information we have, but it does illustrate why it is so important – and difficult – to reconstruct the woman's side of the story.

If Thomas and Margaret Hoby's courtship illustrates the complexities surrounding the marriages of the socially prominent, educated elite, *The Autobiography of Thomas Whythorne*, the earliest extant English auto-biography, contains a wealth of information about Elizabethan poetry and courtship among the gentry and their serving men and women. Unpublished until 1961, the autobiography is still relatively unplumbed by literary critics and social historians alike.[54]

As a professional tutor and music master, Whythorne is in a position to know and woo a wide range of Elizabethan gentlewomen and serving women. In one particularly instructive incident, Whythorne becomes a tutor and music master to "a young gentlewoman" who makes him desire what he has not previously wished for: "to become a married man, with the rest of that holy estate." Since his "ability and wealth was so small in comparison of hers," Whythorne furnishes himself "with convenient apparel and jewels so well as I could (with the glorious show of the which, among other things, a young maiden must be wooed)." Hoping to parlay his literary and musical talent into wealth and status, Whythorne pro-ceeds to woo the gentlewoman with "pretty ditties made of love."

She encourages him to "sing them oftentimes unto her on the vir-ginals or lute," but then rejects him on the basis of finances alone: "For that possibility of living, which I have, is not so certain but that it depend-eth wholly upon the good will and pleasure of my parents. And there-fore, if I should not be ruled by them in giving my consent in marriage, I should have nothing of them to live by hereafter." Whythorne, a prag-matist above all, is willing to let the matter drop. The gentlewoman soon changes her mind, however, and the courtship is rekindled, only to be "detected and known to divers in the house where we were." At this point, the young woman's friends intervene, informing her that Whythorne "reported something of her, the which did sound very ill unto her." The lovers quarrel, and the courtship falters. Yet, discretion to the contrary, they are again reconciled.

If marriages were always perforce arranged by parents or guardians, if Whythorne had not been able to call "to mind a great many that I did know" who "achieved as great enterprises as that," the courtship would never have progressed. On the other hand, if the young woman had been willing to risk more, and her friends had not been able to instill perfectly reasonable suspicions about Whythorne's ulterior motives, the courtship might have ended in a clandestine but legal marriage. Instead, the gentlewoman's friends inform her parents, and "there was secret means wrought to bring an heir of great living to be a suitor unto her for marriage." When parents, fearing a clandestine marriage, resort to "secret means" of their own (like Lady Russell urging her son, Thomas Hoby, to "steal" Margaret Devereux away from Sidney), and a "rich heir" is instructed to act *as if* he were an amorous "suitor unto her for marriage," we can conclude that arranged marriage is not as incontestable as we might have thought.

To be sure, some couples choose a small, private marriage ceremony in order to avoid the considerable cost of a large public wedding. Yet many others marry by license to avoid posting banns, lest their families oppose the marriage. Some unscrupulous suitors arrange secret marriage ceremonies that are not legally binding. Some Elizabethan men, having deserted their wives, marry again secretly and illegally as Colonel Bampfield apparently intended to do with Anne Murray. Yet most couples from the middling and upper ranks who marry by license choose secrecy to evade parental disapproval.

The life stories we have been examining show Elizabethan sons and daughters conducting their own courtships, using poetry or the rhetorical strategies of poetry, even as Elizabethan parents are trying to influence their children's choices, using the rhetorical strategies available to them: language, wealth, and the power of kinship. The lawful liberty to marry is always constrained, at least to some extent, by parental authority and practical considerations. At the same time, however, parental authority is being challenged by Elizabethan men's and women's "defense of their lawfull libertie."[55] Thomas Whythorne's courtship fails because neither he nor the gentlewoman is willing to take the risk that a clandestine marriage, bridging social rank, would entail. John Donne secretly marries Anne More despite her father's prohibition. Margaret Devereux chooses Thomas Sidney over Thomas Hoby, material considerations notwithstanding. Yet Hoby's courtship finally succeeds when Sidney dies and Margaret encounters legal and financial difficulties which make his powerful kinship network indispensable.

The story of Hoby's successive courtships of Margaret Dakins/ Devereux/Sidney, complete with secret plots and assignations, with poetic battles between the forces of love and reason, with testimonies to Margaret's beauty and virtue and Hoby's not-to-be dissuaded ardor, sounds remarkably like the Elizabethan lyric sequences we shall be examining in the following chapters. Here, as is so often the case, we must weigh Hoby's rhetorical persuasion and Margaret's freedom to "match where she list" against financial and legal considerations that permit the young widow to marry Sidney – a "worthy gentleman . . . to whom she was wholly devoted"[56] – but later force her to marry where, it seems, she least list. In the end, Margaret Dakins/Devereux/Sidney becomes Margaret Hoby, but, the evidence suggests, not out of affection. Instead, it seems, she marries Hoby because she needs his influence with Burghley and Egerton to secure her estate against a lawsuit by the new, and much less loving, Earl of Huntingdon.

By encouraging marriageable women to entertain a number of suitors, by warning against the dangers of hasty marriage while permitting considerable emotional and physical intimacy during the months of courtship, by making marriage legally contingent upon the woman's and man's freely given consent but *not* their parents' consent, early modern English courtship enables couples to test their compatibility and to negotiate the terms of their relationship. At the same time, the prevalence of privy contracts and clandestine marriages, denounced by the preachers but condoned by social custom and recognized by the law, greatly increases the danger of deceit and the fear of betrayal.

4

The lyric dialogue of Elizabethan courtship

The characteristically Elizabethan texts examined in this chapter – *The Autobiography of Thomas Whythorne, A Hundreth Sundrie Flowres, The Arte of English Poesie,* and a number of letter-writing manuals – span the transition from private manuscript poetry to printed book. These texts combine poetry and prose commentary, and thus offer a wealth of information about the social history of poetry-making and the fine art of love-making. Whythorne, Gascoigne, Puttenham, and the authors of the letter-writing manuals enunciate what Daniel, Sidney, Spenser, Donne, and Shakespeare imply: first, that Elizabethan love poems are addressed primarily but not exclusively to a particular female reader; second, that the expectation of her answering response cannot help but affect the way in which the poet/lover formulates his lyric persuasion. Moreover, Whythorne, Gascoigne, Puttenham, and the letter-writing manuals either quote or describe a wide range of female responses. Thus they offer us a much more fully embodied account of the woman's side of the Elizabethan lyric dialogue than is typically available in a sonnet sequence or a discrete love poem.

The Autobiography of Thomas Whythorne is the epitome of a private manuscript. Not only does it remain unpublished until 1962, but it is also addressed to a specific reader: "My good friend, – Recalling to mind my promise made unto you, I have here sent you the copies of such songs and sonnets as I have made from time to time until the writing hereof." The manuscript is a generic hybrid: it begins as a series of private lyric poems that were primarily sent or sung to Elizabethan women. Whythorne also quotes a few poems that were written or sung to him by Elizabethan women. The accompanying prose narrative, written "when I did make these songs and sonnets" and lately "augmented," explains the poems' cause, purpose, and private meaning: "I do think it needful not only to show you the cause why I wrote them, but also to open my secret meaning in divers of them."[1]

A Hundreth Sundrie Flowres is a miscellany of poems accompanied by discursive titles describing the circumstances in which the poems were originally (or allegedly) written and read. Here too, the lyrics are mostly poems of courtship or seduction written to or for Elizabethan women and, in a few cases, by Elizabethan women. A remarkably large number are love letters – such as the one "He wrote unto a Skotish Dame whom he chose for his Mistresse in the french Court, as followeth" – addressed to a private female reader. There are poem-and-answer sets, exchanged between a male poet/lover and an Elizabethan woman, as well as poems written in the voice of a female speaker: "An absent Dame thus complayneth" or "A Lady being both wronged by false suspect, and also wounded by the durance of hir husband, doth thus bewray hir grief." Finally, there are poems written by Gascoigne for other men to use in wooing their mistresses: "He wrote (at his friend's request) in prayse of a Gentlewoman, whose name was Phillip." Typically, the poems are tied to a specific lyric situation, although some of the titles also imply that the poem could be appropriately re-used whenever, for example, "An absent lover doth thus encourage his Lady to continew constant."[2]

The Arte of English Poesie, as we have already observed, comprises a systematic poetics of courtship, both amorous and political. It is a private manuscript dedicated to the queen and circulated among a courtly coterie. Probably written in 1581–82 when Alençon is in England courting the queen, it is expanded circa 1585 and published anonymously in 1589.[3] The printed text offers the general reader the thrill of eavesdropping on a private conversation among the writer, the court, and the queen. Even more important, it makes the art of poetry and courtship available to the Elizabethan reading public.

The chapter concludes with letter-writing manuals which first appear during the 1580s and continue to sell in great numbers well into the seventeenth century. As the genre evolves, increasing prominence is given to amatory epistles, poetic love language, and specifically to poetry of courtship and seduction. Some amatory epistles printed in letter-writing manuals may originally have been private letters, later recycled for profit, much as private love poems, written to Whythorne's and Gascoigne's mistresses, are later circulated to a male coterie, a patron, or the public. Yet, regardless of their origin, the sample love letters in prose and verse are collected and sold to be copied, imitated, and used in courtship and seduction.

The production and marketing of imitated intimacies seems somewhat bizarre from a modern point of view, but it suggests that the Elizabethans are developing the rhetoric of courtship, beginning to grasp its complexities and to codify its methodology.

ABOUT SUCH COURTLY PURPOSES

One day towards the beginning of his career as a music master, Whythorne discovers a song left for him on his guitar: "Words that you have rehearsed / Hath my heart oppressed, / and causeth me to die, / Without remedy." The diction and imagery are thoroughly Petrarchan, but the enigmatic brevity, the means of transmission, and the provocative anonymity make this a classic posie. Whythorne wonders "who it should be that made it and did put it there . . . My mind then was so void of love matters, as I could not well judge whether it were written by a man or a woman; and doubting sometime on one thing, and sometime another, as whether it were done of a woman of purpose for love, or in mockage by some man."[4] As it turns out, the writer is "a young girl" living "in that house" who "seemed to bear me very much good will, the which, through maidenly shamefastness, was not by her uttered unto me in word and deed . . . but by writing." Under the guidance of "her counsellor and tutor in this matter," she "devised certain verses in English, writing them with her own hand; and did put them between the strings of [my] gittern."[5]

Thanks to the girl and her counsellor – the former like himself a novice in the ways of love and the latter "very skilful in such practices" – Whythorne learns how poetry of courtship works in practice. To begin with, he discovers that even the most conventional Petrarchan conceits can push the conversation of courtship into places where more straightforward speech cannot go. By composing a lyric for Whythorne to sing back to her, this aspiring female poet/lover seeks to make him the instrument of her amorous designs. When he reads the poem, however, he is the one who determines its meaning and purpose. If, on the one hand, he decides the verse was written "in mockage by some man," his imputed irony will transform her Petrarchan complaint into an exercise in anti-Petrarchan wit. If, on the other hand, he discovers that the song was written expressly for him "of purpose for love," he can either sing the words back to her so as to indicate that his heart is also oppressed by love, or he can spurn her advances, reducing her pseudo-Petrarchan persuasion to a conventional Petrarchan complaint.

Before he can respond, Whythorne learns to his dismay that the poet and reader are never fully in command of the lyric situation: "Shortly after this (by what mean I know not), this matter brake out and was known all about the house where we were, the which made me to blush, and she more so." As a result, Whythorne also learns that Elizabethan poetry can have serious practical consequences: "she was discharged out of that house and service."[6] But most important of all, he discovers the intrigue and interpretive excitement that enigmatic, private poetry can produce.

Before long, Whythorne finds an opportunity to put his new-found knowledge to use:

As one day, coming into my mistress' chamber and finding there a pen, ink and paper, I wrote in a piece of the paper as thus following:

> *When pain is pleasure and joy is care,*
> *Then shall good will in me wax rare.*[7]

When read in isolation, this posie could mean any number of different things. Whythorne might be offering to play the role of a Petrarchan lover so long as he can still hope to find joy and pleasure. Or conversely, he might be saying that his good intentions will never become more powerful than they are at this very moment, since he has no intention of spending his life mooning over a proud, inaccessible beauty. Then too, he could be saying that his good intentions will prevail when the prospect of pleasure turns to pain and his only joy is care – but until then, he would rather satisfy his not so "good will," or carnal desire. Whythorne's intentions are necessarily cryptic because the posie is addressed to his employer, a wealthy widow who enjoys being admired and wooed by attractive young serving men.

What makes this lyric situation particularly instructive is that it provokes a female lyric response:

This writing I left where I found the said implements to write withal; and coming the next day to her chamber, I found written as followeth:

> *For your good will look for no meed,*
> *Till that a proof you show by deed.*

Even as the pseudo-Petrarchan rhetoric allows Whythorne to make his interest known and to play it safe, it allows his female interlocutor to signal her interest while veiling her intentions. She might be saying that if he wishes to receive any favors from her, he had better show his "good will," or upright moral intentions, by honorably proposing marriage. Or she might be saying that if Whythorne wants something to happen, he had better make his wishes clear. One way or the other, her witty, no-nonsense response urges Whythorne to join her in defining their "situations with sufficient realistic accuracy to prepare an *image* for action"[8] – rather like Eliza's exhortation in *My Fair Lady*: "enough talk of love, show me."

To his surprise, Whythorne discovers that "the answer to my foresaid rhythm was not made by my mistress, but by a waiting gentlewoman of hers." Dismayed "because I like not to make love to two at once," he tries to make a graceful retreat – only to discover that the lyric dialogue has reconfigured the social situation: "For our affairs were not so closely handled but they were espied and much talked of in the house." As a result, his mistress begins to distrust his motives, and Whythorne does what Elizabethan poets/lovers are wont to do. He sends her another poem, even more urgent than the last: "Then, wishing to provoke and move her to the full, I did compose a long and full discourse, with much point and circumstance that had happened before this time between us, to the intent to urge and provoke her to show herself in deed what she meant towards me."[9]

Instead of making her intentions clear, his mistress seizes the enigmatic advantage, claiming the position of poet: "If you have any hope in me, / The suds of soap / Shall wash your hope." Worried that the courtship will prove a wash, but also unsure what to make of her soapy trope, Whythorne formulates an "answer" that is "as doubtful to be taken and understood now, as that [lyric] was which I wrote to her at the first; the which I did so make because I would see how she would take it."[10] The widow, it seems, is only toying with him in order to assert her power over him.

As this "long discourse" (meaning both a narrative tale and communication by speech or familiar intercourse) illustrates, Elizabethan lyric dialogues are poised between oral communication and written missive. The success or failure of a lyric courtship – though not, let me hasten to add, its artistic merit – is determined both by the poet's/lover's persuasiveness and by the reader's/listener's receptivity. The more artful the persuasion, the more likely the desired response. Yet the poem's power is conditional: greater pathos or desire may or may not translate into greater likelihood of rejoicing. Whythorne uses poetry and rhetoric to "urge," "provoke," and "move her to the full." Having done so, he, like every other poet/lover, can only wait for her to respond.

In *A Hundreth Sundrie Flowres*, a male poet/lover, identified only as G. G., uses a similar panoply of poetic forms and rhetorical strategies to much better effect. It all starts when G. G. meets a "Gentlewoman whom he liked very well, and yit had never any oportunity to discover his affection, being always brydled by jelouse lookes, which attended them both, and therfore gessing by hir looks, that she partly also liked him: he wrot in a booke of hirs" a posie. The incident perfectly illustrates Puttenham's assertion that Elizabethan posies are "put in paper and in bookes, and vsed as ordinarie missiues."[11]

G. G.'s posie ends by inviting the gentlewoman to "think it were thy part, / To looke again, and linke with me in hart." Much to his delight, she not only looks back but she also writes back, giving his pseudo-Petrarchan trope a witty turn of her own:

> With these verses you shall judge the quick capacity of
> the Lady: for she wrot therunder this short aunswer.
>   Looke as long as you list, but surely if I take you
>   looking, I will looke with you.
> And for a further profe of this Dames quick
> understanding, you shall now understand, that soone
> after this answer of hirs, the same Author chaunced to
> be at a supper in hir company . . .[12]

After dinner, a game of riddles provides the perfect occasion for G. G. and the woman to match wits and wills:

> I Cast myne eye and saw ten eies at once,
> All seemely set upon one lovely face:
> Two gaz'd, two glanc'd, two watched for the nonce,
> Two winked wyles, two fround with froward grace . . .
> And every eye for jelouse love did pine,
> And sigh'd and said, I would that eye were mine.[13]

G. G.'s riddle is not a great poem, but it provides a fine paradigm for a dialogic poetics. The Renaissance love lyric is always to some extent a composite design, comprised of all the male eyes/I's that have inscribed their vision onto the image of Woman. Yet, this quick-witted Elizabethan woman is no Petrarchan lady, forever inciting and frustrating male desire. Nor is she one of those Neoplatonic beauties, elevating love from carnal desire to heavenly perfection. Instead, she is a subject with a voice and a will of her own.

Upon first reading, it seems as if all ten eyes are admiring the lady, experiencing the voyeuristic pleasure or pain of seeing her reduced to the object of male desire. Yet, this all-too-familiar interpretation is belied by the prose commentary which explains the five pairs of eyes thus. First, G. G. is gazing at the lady because he "could none otherwise relieve his passion." Second, the lady herself "deigned (now and then) to requite the same with glancing at him." Third, the lady's brother "could not absteyne from winking" a warning to his sister. Fourth, her "old lover occupied his eyes with watching." As a result, her husband is "constreyned to play the fifth part in froward frowninge."[14] This Elizabethan lady is not simply the proprietary possession of her husband, or the guarantor of her brother's sense of family honor and propriety, or the plaything of her old lover, or the reflection of G. G.'s desire. Instead, she is a subject with two eyes and an I/dentity of her own.

The deliciousness of the epigrammatic turn depends on knowing that one pair of eyes belongs to the lady, for that means she is also saying, "I would that eye were mine." When G. G. writes, "I would that eye were mine," he is not only expressing his own desire. When she reads his posie, she tells G. G., her brother, her former lover, and her husband, 'I wish your eyes would see as mine do.'

Much as the Suds-of-Soap Widow appropriates Whythorne's position as poet, this quick-witted, quick-eyed Elizabethan woman uses "her quick capacity" to transform "His Riddle" into "Hir Question": "Sir, quod she, bicause your dark speech is much too curious for this simple companie, I wilbe so bold as to quit one question with an other."[15] The battle of wits continues, but suffice it to say that the syntax of gender reversal, the fluctuation from male subject and female object to female subject and male object – from male I/eye that strives to make her "mine" to female I/eye whose reading makes his words "mine" – calls traditional male and female roles into question.

A Hundreth Sundrie Flowres contains a fascinating lyric sequence that begins with two poems "Written by a Gentlewoman in court" and "An other Sonet written by the same Gentlewoman uppon the same occasion." As we read on, we learn that the poems are not written by a woman but by a male admirer who is moved to poetry when "the same Gentlewoman" passes by: "He began to write by a gentlewoman who passed by him." "Whiles he sat at the dore of his lodging, devysing these verses above rehearsed, the same Gentlewoman passed by agayne, and cast a longe looke towards him, wherby he left his former invention."[16]

Elizabethan poetry of courtship is constantly blurring the distinction between the male writer and the female reader because "[t]o some extent, primacy belongs to the response, as the activating principle"; it "prepares the ground for an active and engaged understanding."[17] Because posies, songs, and sonnets are typically unsigned, it is often difficult to "judge whether [they] were written by a man or a woman," as Whythorne discovers when he finds the posie on his guitar. On a symbolic level, the female reader's power to validate or undo the poet's persuasion turns the lyric I into a lyric dialogue between two I's. On the one hand, when a male poet/lover recites his lyric persuasion to an Elizabethan woman, she is bound to attribute meanings the poet had not consciously intended. On the other hand, when she reads the poem aloud in her own voice, her interpretation gives the male voice of Renaissance lyric tradition a female intonation and female perspective. The titles – Written by a Gentlewoman and An other Sonet written by the same Gentlewoman – fuse what is written *by* the poet/lover with what is said or done *by* the woman to whom the poem is written. Our initial misprision holds the key to a deeper truth, for even though, as it turns out, the woman is not the poet, she is the poem's collaborator, at once its provocation and its undoing.

DOUBTFULLY CONSTRUED, AND (THEREFORE) SCANDALOUS

Whythorne's autobiography is embedded in an epistolary frame that transforms the veiled lyric dialogue between Whythorne and his female interlocutors into a more prosaic exchange between men:

> And because that you did impart unto me at our last being together some of your private and secret affairs past, and also some of the secret purposes and intents the which have lain hid and been as it were entombed in your heart, I, to gratify your good opinion had of me, do now lay open unto you the most part of all my private affairs and secrets, not only to show you the cause why I wrote them but also to open my secret meaning in divers of them, as well in words and sentences, as in the whole of the same, lest you should think them to be made to smaller purpose than I did mean.[18]

The subject of this long, intricate sentence shifts almost imperceptibly from the antecedent "private affairs and secrets," to the songs and sonnets, to the prose commentary written "in words and sentences," to "the whole of the same." The eroding syntactical boundaries between poetry and prose recreate the earlier interfusion of lyric and life.

The prose narrative reproduces the enigmatic seduction the poems once enacted. Whythorne's "secret meaning" exists both within the lyrics, at the level of the subtext – for "a man cannot always speak in print" – and outside the manuscript, in the social situation that constitutes the poems' "cause" and "purpose." Together, the poems and prose do "now lay open unto you" just enough of their original "cause" and "purpose" to transform the reader from a critical outsider to an actively engaged insider. Consider yourself, "my good friend," part of the dialogue.[19]

This epistolary frame, addressed to Whythorne's male confidant, is, it turns out, the beginning of the autobiography itself. The manuscript also contains a prefatory lyric addressed to a male coterie: "Ye youthful imps, that like on shows to look, / As by strange sights, reports, or else in book . . ." It doesn't take a great deal of wit to figure out what kind of sights Whythorne is offering up for these youths' specular pleasure. An "imp" is not only a young man or a scion of a noble house but also a little devil, while a "strange" woman is common slang for a loose woman or a prostitute.

Renaissance literature is supposed to "teach and delight;" therefore, the prefatory lyric ends with a promise of edification: "wherein young youths are learned lessons large. / By which they may, if like chance to them charge / the better know to deal / Therein, and so it may be for their weal." Beneath the tone of high seriousness, however, the jocular innuendo continues. If these mischievous young imps are clever enough to detect Whythorne's secret meaning, they will not only enjoy some male banter about women but they will also learn how to use the enigmatic rhetoric of poetry to court and seduce the women who are the "guerdons" promised "those who play their part aright." "Ye youthful imps" and "my good friend," let us "return again to the feminine sex and their loves."[20]

The literary exchange between men falls out of the picture, often for pages on end, "when time served to be in company with women, to talk with them, to toy with them, to jibe and to jest with them, to discourse with them, and to be merry with them (all the which some do call courting)." Then, suddenly, Whythorne will interrupt the narrative with an apostrophe to his good friend: "Lo, sir, and if I had had then any mind of marriage, it was like that then I might have been sped of a wife." It is when the lyric dialogue is at its most erotic that Whythorne tends to interrupt the narrative to give the male reader directions for interpretation: "But and if it came to making of love by word, sign or deed, especially in deed," why "I had no more face to do that than had a sheep." On one occasion, an ague produces a more holy ejaculation: "Lo, sir, this cross or punishment of sickness aforesaid made me now to remember God a little."[21] But only a little!

Most of the apostrophes, "Sir," are respectful bows to that "good friend" Whythorne is so eager to impress. Now and then, he also seems mindful of those impish youths: "Also, whereas you and such other suspicious heads would think, peradventure, that so much friendship as I spake of in the foresaid song could not be, except a conjunction copulative had been made . . . to the which I must say, and say truly, that neither my hand, nor any other part of mine, did once touch that part of hers where the conjunction is made."[22] The exaggerated protestations of propriety make one wonder which body "part" Whythorne is thinking of using to "touch that part of hers where the conjunction is made." The witty play on words draws on the dual meanings of a "conjunction copulative": a linguistic term for a connecting conjunction and an idiomatic expression for copulation and marriage. As Wall explains, this kind of verbal play between men turns the female reader into a sexual part: "a gendered median third term – the female text – to be trafficked among [male] readers."[23]

Even at his most didactic, Whythorne sounds more pragmatic than high-minded: "Whereas before I spake *of* the quenching *of* fire, understand no otherwise there*of* but only the obtaining *of* my desire *of* the benefits that I received *at* her hands."[24] As one prepositional phrase turns into another, it becomes harder and harder to separate erotic desire from professional and material advancement. Whythorne's admonishment "against those who do mind no marriage at all, but woo altogether for lecherous lust" sounds less like high-minded edification than like sex education or career planning: "And also such as commonly do seek and use the company of brothels, ruffians, bawds and harlots, do not only become beggars in the end, but also be filled with the most horrible, filthy and incurable diseases."[25]

The apostrophes to the male reader interrupt the narrative, as if they were written later, once Whythorne and his original, largely female, lyric audience have completed their collaborative exercise in poetry-making and love-making. This implicit chronology is confirmed by Whythorne's own account: "Part of the which discourses I made and wrote when I did make these songs and sonnets, and now, as more matter hath come unto my remembrance, so have I augmented the same."[26] The literary dialogue between Whythorne and his male readers gives the autobiography an "augmented" purpose, but it is secondary and subsequent to the amorous courtships and seductions that were enacted in poetry and explicated in prose when Whythorne was himself an impish young man.

In sum, *The Autobiography of Thomas Whythorne* is a generic hybrid which has, as its center, poems addressed to Elizabethan women. The retrospective prose commentary is addressed primarily to a male friend (whom Whythorne is probably wooing as a potential patron), and secondarily to a coterie of young men interested in acquiring the arts of courting and poesie. The autobiography is the repository of these earlier songs and sonnets, its purpose being "not only to show you the cause why

I wrote them but also to open my secret meaning in divers of them." Thus the poems and "the cause why I wrote them" are prior to, and distinct from, the cause and purpose of the prose narrative. The poems set out to convey "my secret meaning" to the private female lyric audience; the prose sets out to explain the original lyric situation and the private female lyric audience to male readers who might otherwise fail to grasp the poems' "secret meaning."

Whythorne's autobiography is the quintessential Elizabethan private manuscript. Gascoigne's *A Hundreth Sundrie Flowres* stands on the cusp between this older, more intimate world of oral communication and manuscript transmission and the new, more distant world of print. The elaborate prefatory apparatus, so characteristic of early modern printed books, fosters the illusion that print is just one more stage in the ongoing process of manuscript circulation. "The Printer to the Reader," "H. W. to the Reader," and "The letter of G. T. to his very friend H. W. concerning this worke" describe the provenance of the manuscript which has supposedly passed from F. J. to his friend G. T. to his friend H. W. to the printer who "entreated my friend A. B. to emprint." It all sounds rather clubby: "For the case seemeth doubtful," the printer tells the reader, explaining that G. T.'s letter "doth with no lesse clerkly cunning seeke to perswade the readers, that he (also) woulde by no meanes have it published."[27] The prefatory epistle hints at what cannot be said: that the printer and the poet have collaborated to evade the censors and to maintain a *semblance* of intimacy with the reader.

Like Whythorne's epistolary frame, the prefatory letters and the discursive titles remind the public that the text is only one side of an earlier, private lovers' conversation. To read one poem "Wherin he bewrayeth both their names in cloudes," or another "(in ciphers) disciphering his name,"[28] is to become a voyeur, peering through the veil of enigma, allegory, and amphibology to the private lyric dialogue that the poems once enacted and now conceal. The title page conceals both the author and the publication date. Instead, it represents the poems as a hundred, sundry flowers – the "Invention out of our own fruitful orchardes in England," implying that the poems are the work of several Elizabethan writers and translators. It is only once we are safely inside the volume that some of the poems are attributed to George Gascoigne, or G. G. But the elaborate pretense that the volume is not the work of a single man fails because the public lyric audience is an extension of the manuscript audience which already knows that George Gascoigne is the translator, the poet, and in some cases, the poet/lover as well.

To counter the growing scandal and forestall the threat of censorship, Gascoigne publishes a revised edition in 1575, complete with a new title, an author, a date, and a *raison d'être*: *The Posies of George Gascoigne Esquire*. "Corrected, perfected, and augmented by the Authour." The volume begins with three new dedicatory epistles by the author and twenty-two commendatory verses in his praise. The first epistle from the author "To the Reverend Divines" explains that the poems are now being offered to the public, "gelded from all filthie phrases, corrected in all erronious places, and beautified with addition of many moral examples."[29] That makes me wonder just what was going on before Gascoigne decided to play the eunuch!

If poetry can be "beautified with addition of many moral examples," then its ideal beauty is merely a decorative façade, applied like a coat of fresh paint to a dirty old structure. The new edition attempts to make a bad situation better by coloring over the most "erronious" parts: "now at my returne, I find that some of them have not onely bene offensive for sundrie wanton speeches and lascivious phrases, but further I heare that the same have beene doubtfully construed, and (therefore) scandalous." This carefully worded disclaimer blames the more "doubtful" [meaning ambiguous, uncertain] interpretations on scandal-mongering readers. Yet, it does not deny that the original version, with its "sundrie wanton speeches and lascivious phrases," provided more than enough material for scandal.[30]

Omitted entirely are three readily identifiable, and thus all the more "scandalous" poems, including one that describes Gascoigne's affair with Elizabeth Bacon Bretton and Edward Boyes: "Written to a gentlewoman who had refused him and chosen a husband (as he thought) much inferior to himself, both in knowledge byrth and parsonage." Any overly erotic or biographical sequences of poems are dismantled. The remaining poems are rearranged and classified as Flowers, Herbs, and Weeds.[31] *The Adventures of Master F. J.* is uprooted, translated from England to Italy, and moved along with the accompanying prefatory letters from the beginning to the end of the volume. The label "Weeds" is presumably meant to placate any reader who thinks F. J.'s poetry of seduction should be yanked out and tossed away.

The revised version is represented as "a myrrour for unbrydled youth, to avoyde those perilles which I had passed." Discreetly passing over the fact that the majority of the poems still mirror his own "unbrydled youth," Gascoigne offers the authorized edition "to the ende all men might see the reformation of my minde." Yet, here too, the profession of pious atonement for earlier offenses – "that all suspitions may be suppressed and throughly satisfied" – is belied by a witty innuendo which hints that some readers' appetites will be "satisfied" by what the reverend divines would rather have "suppressed."[32]

The second epistle, "To al yong Gentlemen, and generally to the youth of England," explains that *A Hundreth Sundrie Flowres* has been threatened with censorship for two reasons: (1) it is too popular among "the yonger sort"; (2) rumor has it that "the greater part hath beene written in pursute of amorous enterpryses."[33] Once again, Gascoigne cites the charges, without denying the fact that the poems were written, and can still be used, "in pursuite of amorous enterpryses." That would presumably involve a female lyric audience, though there is still no mention of her.

To appease the censors and to demonstrate that neither he nor the poems are "woorthie of reproofe or condemnation," Gascoigne transfers the moral responsibility to the reader. To that end, he creates an elaborate allegory, describing the posies as herbs that can be either salutary or "unfruitfull" depending on whether they are used to control inflammation or to "more inflame the Impostume" [the swelling]. The subtext again implies that the poems can be used to inflame the passions: "To speake English it is your using (my lustie Gallants) or misusing of these Posies that may make me praysed or dispraysed for publishing of the same."[34] Yes, "my gallant Gentlemen, and lustie youthes," buy the book, and proceed at your own risk.

The third epistle, "To the Readers generally," balances the "grave judgementes" of the first letter with the lusty badinage of the second: "And as there are some ditties which may please and delight the godly and graver sort, so are there some which may allure the yonger sort unto fond attempts. But what for that?" Above all, Gascoigne wants the general reader to know that most of the poems are written for courtship and seduction: "the number of loving lynes exceedeth in the Superlative." To appease the censors, Gascoigne claims that a mere 10 percent were written for his own amorous pursuits: "And out of all doubt, if ever I wrote lyne for my selfe in causes of love, I have written tenne for other men in layes of lust."[35] Once again, much virtue in *if*!

While the "generall advertisement of the Authour" is at pains to defend Gascoigne's character and reputation, the bawdy pun on "layes" (meaning both songs and sexual acts) covertly advertises Gascoigne's skill as a writer of witty, pseudo-Petrarchan verse: "Even so (good Reader) I was a great while the man which dwelt at Billingsgate. For in wanton delightes I helped all men, though in sad earnest I never furthered my selfe any kinde of way."[36] Gascoigne claims that he himself profited neither financially nor sexually from the poems, but both claims are dubious: surely the man who "dwelt at Billingsgate," selling amorous verses, was dealing not "in sad earnest" but "in wanton delightes."

Among "the Readers generally," there are undoubtedly some women. At one point, it almost seems as if Gascoigne is on the verge of addressing the female reader directly: "Truely (gentle Reader) I protest that I have not ment heerein to displease any . . ." Yet, she is quickly displaced by Gascoigne's overriding need not to "displease any man, but my desire hath rather bene to content most men." Consequently, Wall concludes that "the real reader" is the male reader who "writes over and subsumes the mistress's place in the economy of exchanged poems."[37] I would argue instead that the female reader is not subsumed but "suppressed," hidden deep within the volume. In fact, readers of *The Posies* must make it past three dedicatory epistles and twenty-two commendatory verses in English and Latin before encountering the private female reader.

It is at this juncture in the history of the book – when the art of poetry is making its way from court and coterie to readers generally, and pressures from "the godly and graver sort" are growing – that the female reader becomes the subtext or gender unconscious: "the negative, absence, contradiction, repression, the *non-dit*, or the *impensé*"; "that which being before mistically covered, and commonly misconstrued, might be no lesse perillous in seducing you, [the male reader] than greevous evidence for to prove mee guiltie of condemnation."

Whythorne's and Gascoigne's prefatory letters hint at the women to whom the poems are primarily addressed. Puttenham also conceals the importance of the Elizabethan female lyric audience until we are well into *The Arte of English Poesie*: "our chiefe purpose herein is for the learning of Ladies and young Gentlewomen, or idle Courtiers, desirous to become skilful in their owne mother tongue, and for their priuate recreation to make now and then ditties of pleasure, thinking for our parte none other science so fit for them and the place as that which teacheth *beau* semblant, the chiefe profession as well of Courting as of poesie."[38]

Puttenham's figurative language contains seductive double entendres that are very similar to Whythorne's and Gascoigne's. When Elizabethan gentlewomen and courtiers get together "for their priuate recreation to make now and then ditties of pleasure," they are collaborators in poetry-making as in love-making. Sometimes, they entertain each other with poems that re-create the pleasures of their own earlier and even more private love-making. Sometimes sharing the pleasures of private poetry leads to the even more private pleasures of love-making.

Just as Gascoigne tries to placate the graver sort of reader before admitting that the posies were used "in causes of love," Puttenham begins with a disquisition on how the Courtly figure *Allegoria* is used by "euery common Courtier, but also the grauest counsellour, yea and the most noble and wisest Prince of them all are many times enforced to vse it." It is only *in medias res* that he cites a brief epigram or posie sent by an Elizabethan man to an Elizabethan woman: "Louely Lady I long full fore to heare, / If ye remaine the same, I left you the last yeare."[39] Is the writer inquiring about the lady's health, or seeking her patronage? Or is he a clandestine suitor, inquiring whether she has been betrothed to someone else during his absence? This posie is sufficiently enigmatic to be entrusted to a messenger: the writer's private meaning is covered with a veil, in case the posie should be read by someone other than the lovely lady.

Here, as in Whythorne's lyric exchange with the Suds-of-Soap widow or G. G.'s lyric battle with the quick-witted lady, it is impossible to know what the poet is trying to tell his private reader without being privy to the lyric situation. Of course, that is precisely why Puttenham chooses this posie to illustrate the Courtly figure *Allegoria*. It is also why Puttenham's prose explanation sounds remarkably like Whythorne's and Gascoigne's:

A noble man after a whole yeares absence from his ladie, sent to know how she did, and whether she remayned affected toward him as she was when he left her.

> Louely Lady I long full fore to heare,
> If ye remaine the same, I left you the last yeare.

Here as in *The Autobiography of Thomas Whythorne* or *A Hundreth Sundrie Flowres,* the prose occupies the place of the intervening events, providing an objective correlative for the "private affairs and secrets" that give the lyric dialogue its "secret Meaning."[40]

What makes this particular posie such an apt illustration of Elizabethan courtship is that it elicits a response:

To whom she answered in *allegorie* other two verses:

> My louing Lorde I will well that ye wist,
> The thred is spon, that neuer shall vntwist.

Meaning, that her loue was so stedfast and constant toward him as no time or occasion could alter it.[41]

Unlike the Suds-of-Soap widow, this Elizabethan lady responds in veiled poetry that makes her meaning clear to her "louing Lorde" – and no one else.

Elizabethan poetry is the preferred language of courtship, amorous no less than political, as Puttenham, Whythorne, and Gascoigne all explain, because its formal doubleness, its persuasive rhetoric, and enigmatic figures of speech simultaneously conduct and conceal the "private affairs and secrets" that are the "secret purpose and intent" of courting, as of poesy.

Puttenham codifies what Whythorne and Gascoigne enact: Elizabethan poetry of courtship may be overheard or overread by any number of readers, but it is written for a specific private reader/listener. Some Elizabethan love poems are written to be "vttered," but others are sent and "vsed as ordinarie missives."[42] *Pace* Eliot, that doesn't make them any the less poetic.

Even the most familiar letters are expected to follow a conventional, formal structure. They begin with an *Exordium*, or introduction to the matter to be written of, "wherein either for our selves, or the cause we write of, or in respect of him, for or to whom we write, wee studie to win fauor or allowance of the matter." Having solicited the reader's attention, the letter writer moves on to the *Narratio* or *Propositio*, "wherein is declared or proponed, in the one by plaine tearmes, in the other by inference, or comparison, the verie substance of the matter whatsoeuer to be handled."[43] While books of rhetoric teach Elizabethans the art of speech, letter-writing manuals teach their readers to perceive letters and poems as alternative forms of speech.

AMATORY EPISTLES AND EPISTOLARY VERSES

Marriage manuals, which have received a lot of scholarly attention, tell us how Elizabethan men and women are taught to behave. Letter-writing manuals, which have received considerably less scholarly attention, come much closer to what Elizabethan lovers are actually writing and saying to each other. Not only do model love letters provide an invaluable source of information about the use of poetry in courtship and seduction, but they also confirm and clarify what Sidney, Whythorne, Gascoigne, and Puttenham declare.[44]

These model love letters – clichéd versions of the dramatic situations and rhetorical strategies commonly found in the great English Renaissance love poems – represent the diverse roles amatory epistles

EMBLEMATA

133

Ciç.

LITTERIS ABSENTES VIDEMVS.

Viuis in extremis ignoti partibus orbis,
Et procul ex oculis dulcis amica meis.
At te præsentem, absentem licèt, esse putabo,
Si mihi sit verbis charta notata tuis.

Seneca.   Si imagines amantibus, etiam absentium, iucundę sunt, quòd
memoriam renouent, & desiderium absentiæ falso atque inani so-
latio leuent: quantò iucundiores sunt litteræ, quæ vera amantis
vestigia, veras notas afferunt.

Loues ioy is reuyued by letters.

When loue impatient growes through absence & delay,
And with his loue to bee no remedie can fynd,
Loue letters come to him & tell his louers mynd,
Whereby his ioy is kept from dying and decay.

Congiunto sempre.

Per lunga absenza Amore impatiente
Il modo ritrouò da giunger l'alme,
Benche sian sparte le corporee salme.
l'Amor lontan per lettere è presente.

.FLAM.

AMORVM.   133

R 3

Figure 5 An emblem poem depicting the use of love letters in courtship.

and epistolary verses play in Elizabethan courtship. *The Enimie of Idlenesse*, for example, offers a selection of love letters in prose, followed by seven highly imitable love letters in verse. There are conventional lover's complaints that (like *Astrophil and Stella* 1) describe the lover's misery in the hopes of evoking the woman's pity and love: "A louer sicke for verie loue, / To pittie doth his Laide moue"; "A faithfull Louer feeling smart, / doth nippe his Ladie false of heart." One frustrated letter writer "Thinkes [how to be] rid from woe." Another triumphant poet/lover celebrates his success: "A Louer hath his Ladies heart, / And writes to her, as is his part."[45]

The alternatives set forth in these model love letters, where social, political, personal, and economic considerations are all at work, inextricably intertwined, offer women a variety of rhetorical postures, ranging from outraged chastity, moral indignation, and daughterly submission on the one hand to demure encouragement, barely veiled ardor, and initiatives as bold as Shakespeare's cross-dressed heroines' on the other.

Epistolary courtships conventionally begin with a poetic apostrophe to the woman's beauty and virtue, followed by a request for permission to pay court. To assure a selection of letters, both useful and marketable, Angel Day's *The English Secretory* offers his readers/writers a range of choices, keyed to their rank, sex, and circumstance. A "first entreatie of good will" is written in the "superlative degree" for male suitors whose "birth, education, or other complements, maie sufficientlie answere the greatnesse and efficacie thereof." An alternative first entreaty, written in a comparatively plain style, is recommended for suitors "lesse enabled."[46]

In answering the first epistle, the woman of "superlative degree" modestly responds that the man's "eloquence is farre beyonde the reach of my poore witte." She proceeds, however, to question the sincerity of his conventional rhetoric, "fitter for a Poeticall Goddess" than for an "earthlie" woman. Indeed, her pointed female critique of her suitor's initial, highly conventional and overly idealized rhetoric sounds remarkably like the female responses described by Whythorne, Gascoigne, and Puttenham and dramatized by Daniel and Spenser.

When Day's letter writer continues his stylized rhetoric in his second epistle, the woman responds even more probingly. Having "bene taught, that of fairest speaches ensueth often the fowlest actions," she is understandably wary of the dangers described by instructional literature like *The Courtier*. "For surelye the provocations of lovers, the craftes that they use, the snares that they laye in waite are suche and so applyed, that it is a great wonder, that a tender girle should escape them."[47] Nonetheless hoping for "the best of your dealings," she suggests the possibility of a meeting, "when you shall by further notice sufficientlie make apparant that with modestie I may doe it."[48] By instructing the woman to raise the possibility of a meeting, Day appeals to male fantasies, but that is not all he does. He is also teaching Elizabethan men and women to imagine the written text as part of an ongoing private conversation.

Much as Whythorne's "long and full discourse" transforms persuasion poetry into oral communication, Day's sample love letters are "speaches" that will, if all goes well, lead to a more direct exchange of words. Whythorne and Gascoigne adjust their rhetorical strategies to the lyric situation and the private lyric audience; so, too, letter-writing manuals teach their readers/writers to adapt their diction, tone, and argumentation to the responses they seek to elicit – as well as to the responses they have already received.

Epistolary verse is especially useful for negotiating clandestine courtships or seductions. The first edition of Day's *The English Secretorie* contains a chapter devoted to amatory epistles that reads like an episode out of Whythorne's autobiography or Gascoigne's *Hundreth Sundrie Flowres*. The steamy clandestine courtship, narrated in prose, is carried out by letters and speeches, in both prose and poetry: "hee forgatte not as well in speeches as in writing many times to sollicite her forward conceipt towards him, sometimes by gratifying her with diuers sonettes, otherwise in admiring her prayses (to none so manifest, as to himselfe woonderfull). As occasion serued againe with letters."[49] First printed in 1586, the chapter was reprinted at least three times before being replaced in 1599 by five pairs of highly usable and much more proper "Epistles Amatorie," designed to commence a courtship.

Amatory epistles and epistolary love poems provide invaluable substitutes for oral communication not only during periods of physical separation, but also at watershed moments when particular delicacy of language is needed. As idealized praise turns to amorous persuasion, letters become increasingly dependent on the figurative speech and enigmatic diction of the lyric. For example, Fulwood's *The Enimie of Idlenesse* contains two verse letters of seduction. The ambiguous language of one is explicitly designed to offer the female reader a choice: "One writes in earnest, or in iest / As then shall like his Ladie best." Another – "A Secret Louer writes his will, / By storie of *Pigmalions* ill" – uses enigma, allegory, and myth (much as *Amoretti* 28 uses Daphne and Apollo) to urge the "blinde delights of burning love." As the cold, statuesque beauty is "laide in his bed," she is transformed into a living embodiment of the male letter writer's fantasy. The conventional catalogue of female beauty becomes increasingly erotic, moving down her body to "Her tender thighes, her beding knees . . ."[50]

Bending the language in the hope of bedding the lady, Fulwood, like Whythorne, Gascoigne, and Puttenham, teaches his readers how to use poetry's ambiguous, allegorical verbal wit to hint at sexual favors that cannot be mentioned directly.[51] The more erotic the proposition, the more veiled the language. Should the female recipient wish to continue the conversation, she can write back, adapting his trope to her wishes. Should she take offense, he can write a follow-up letter, claiming that she mistook the meaning.

Elizabethan and early seventeenth-century letter-writing manuals typically contain either a chapter devoted to "epistles amatorie" or a few scattered exchanges of love letters in prose and verse. By the mid-seventeenth century, there are entire books devoted largely or exclusively to courtship and seduction such as *The Academy of Complements* (1640) or *The Academy of Eloquence, Containing a Compleate English rhetorique Exemplified; common-places and Formulas digested into an easie and methodical way to speak and write fluently, according to the mode of the present Times with Letters both Amorous and Morall, upon emergent Occasions* (1656).

The Academy of Complements (1640) offers formulaic "compliments to the lady" as well as "a tender of service to ones soveraigne and the Queene." Sample texts teach potential suitors how to comport themselves in a variety of amorous situations: to entertain a gentlewoman in your chamber; to seduce a maid by jest; to contract oneself privately and tie the knot of marriage; to court a gentlewoman in the way of marriage; to offer service to a young maid; to confer with a widow in "an amorous wooing manner." The text also includes a variety of useful love letters *in verse*, including "a complementall and amorous letter to renew affection," a letter to a maid from one that expected no portion, and a letter to a sweet heart far absent in the country.[52]

The Mysteries of Love & Eloquence, Or, the ARTS of Wooing and complementing (P[hillips] 1685), designed both as a practical guide to wooing and as an entertaining parody of lovers' folly, contains a similar range of rhetorical devices: love letters to and from women; jests; mock letters and drolling letters; a rhyming dictionary; a list of appropriate adjectives; an alphabet of epithets; an alphabetical collection of similitudes; mock compliments; sample conversations including an address of courtship; dialogues suitable for a ball. Finally, the *pièce de résistance* – seventy pages of epistolary love poems!

By the seventeenth century, love letters in prose and verse are not only fashionable stratagems of courtship and seduction but well-established, marketable commodities. Packaged and reduced to alphabetized clichés, the love poem *cum* letter is essentially defunct as a literary genre, its "secrets and mysteries . . . made naked and manifestly revealed to the weakest Iudgement."[53] Before that happens, however, the enigmatic rhetoric of amatory epistles and epistolary verse engage large numbers of early modern English men and women. Conventional epistolary situations regularly appear as dramatic situations in Elizabethan love poems – and vice versa. Not only does this demonstrate that love poems are being written and sent as love letters, but it also reveals a remarkably close connection between social convention and poetic convention, popular culture and high art.

RAMIFICATIONS AND REVERBERATIONS

As Puttenham, Gascoigne, Whythorne, and the letter-writing manuals demonstrate, Elizabethans need not be writers to be poets/lovers. Just as Shakespeare freely reuses earlier stories and plays, Elizabethan readers readily recite and rewrite others' persuasions to love. Illiterate Elizabethans commission professional writers such as Gascoigne to write love letters and poems for them – at least until they receive the lady's permission to speak for themselves. More literate but prosaic Elizabethans, eager to woo a lover in prose or verse, can imitate or use the amatory epistles, epistolary verses, and rhetorical strategies of seduction from romances such as *A Discourse of the Adventures passed by Master F. J.* or *The Golden Aphroditis*, or letter-writing manuals such as *The English Secretorie*, poetry collections such as *A Hundreth Sundrie Flowres*, or poetry-writing manuals such as Puttenham's *Arte of English Poesie*. At the same time, more cultivated Elizabethans can use their poetic ability, when an occasion arises, to woo the person they want to marry or seduce. Elizabethan women are less likely to be literate, so they write amatory epistles and epistolary love poems in fewer numbers, though for many of the same reasons. More often, they receive and respond to love poems written for or addressed to them.

One could, but should not, describe the women who appear in these poems as "an excuse for similes" or "the thing which makes the poet experience the emotions about which he writes."[54] They are much more than "a metaphor for the poet's worldly aspirations"[55] or a trope "that authorized subject and author on the basis of gender."[56] They are the means to considerable material reward "because of the commodities that might be gotten by such a one as she, either by marriage or otherwise," as Whythorne puts it so indelicately.[57] Whether freely encouraging the lover's persuasion or artfully criticizing his rhetoric, these Elizabethan women are not only the narcissistic reflection of male desire or male subjectivity; they are also subjects whose female eye/I represents an alternative way of seeing the world and whose willing collaboration is essential to poetry-making and love-making.

5

Anne Vavasour and Henry Lee

But my position is this: That if we try to discover what the poem is doing for the poet, we may discover a set of generalizations as to what poems do for everybody. With these in mind, we have cues for analyzing the sort of eventfulness that the poem contains. And in analyzing this eventfulness, we shall make basic discoveries about the structure of the work itself . . . And I contend that the kind of observation about structure is more relevant when you approach the work as the functioning of a structure.[1]

THE SORT OF *EVENTFULNESS* THAT A POEM CONTAINS

This chapter examines two Elizabethan poems which circulate privately, surviving in a number of manuscripts before being rediscovered and printed by modern scholars. The first poem consists of a ventriloquized female voice, framed by the observations of a male speaker and answered by an echo. The second offers a rare example of a poem of courtship written from a female perspective in the voice of an Elizabethan woman and addressed to a male reader: "thou", "sweet freende," "he" who has "my harte."[2]

Thanks to E. K. Chambers, we know that both poems are somehow connected to the clandestine love affair between Anne Vavasour, a Gentlewoman of the Queen's Bedchamber, and Edward de Vere, the Earl of Oxford. The poems have received a fair amount of scholarly attention, but it is still not clear who wrote them or what rhetorical purpose they serve.

The unusual combination of so much information and so many fundamental, unanswered questions gives us a rare opportunity to see how an Elizabethan poetics of courtship can be applied as practical criticism. By analyzing the form, point of view, figures of speech, and rhetorical purpose, we can explore what the poems are doing for the poet and the manuscript audience. Moreover, by looking for cues to the

Figure 6 Portrait of Anne Vavasour, painted by Marcus Gheerhaerts
the Younger, after she had become Sir Henry Lee's mistress

sort of *eventfulness* the poems contain, we can make some basic discoveries about the *structure* of the works themselves. Finally, we may begin to discover a set of generalizations as to what poems of courtship do for everybody – for the poet/lover, the person to whom the poem is addressed, the poet's coterie, and us.

CUES FOR ANALYZING

In the first poem, the male speaker is sitting alone, lost in thought, when he espies a beautiful young lady:

Sittinge alone upon my thought in melancholye moode,
In sight of sea and at my backe an aunceyent horye woode,
I sawe a fayre yonge ladye come her secreate teares to wayle,
Clad all in colour of a vowe and covered with a vayle.
Yet for the daye was clere and calme, I might descerne her face,
As one mighte see a damaske rose thoughe hid with cristall glasse.
Three tymes with her softe hande full harde upon her heart she knockes,
And sighte soe sore as mighte have moved some mercy in the rocks;
From sighes and sheadinge amber teares into swete songe she brake,
And thus the eccho answered her to every woorde she spake.

O heavenes, quoth she, who was the firste that bred in me this fevere?   vere
Who was the firste that gave the wounde whose scarre I were forever?   vere
What tyrant, Cupid, to my harmes usurpes thy golden quivere?   vere
What wighte first caughte this hearte and can from bondage it delivere?   vere
Yet who dothe moste adore this wighte? O hollow caves tell true;   yowe
What nimphe deserves his likinge beste? yet doth in sorrowe rue?   yowe
What makes him not regarde good will with some remorse or ruthe?   youthe
What makes him shewe besides his birthe such pride and such
     untruthe?   youthe
May I his beautye matche with love if he my love will trye?   I
May I requite his birthe with faythe? then faythfull will I dye.   I
And I that knewe this ladye well said lorde, how great a myracle,
To heare the eccho tell her truthe as 'twere Apollo's oracle.   Vavaser.

The lady's veiled visage and secret tears seem to be the signs of a clandestine love affair gone awry. Yet, the narrator's description raises a number of questions.[3] What is her secret? What kind of vow has she taken? What is being hidden, first, by her veil and, second, by the indirection of the narrative frame? Is she a stranger to the narrator as the indefinite article ("a fayre yonge ladye") seems to suggest? Or does he have some prior knowledge of her plight as the allusion to "a vowe" – something that cannot be inferred from her physical appearance alone – might suggest?

The legal connotations of "sitting" in judgment "upon" associate the poem with the male-authored female complaint – a didactic genre that combines sympathy for the female complainant's fall from fortune with moral judgment of her sexual abandon or female weakness.[4] In Churchyard's complaint, for example, Shore's Wife recounts the story of her rape to teach other women to avoid her plight. In "Sittinge alone" the narrative frame presents the male speaker as an objective observer – "for the daye was clere and calme" – who remains at a distance from the lady. But the pretense of esthetic distance disappears when the speaker describes her as a "sighte soe sore as mighte have moved some mercy in the rocks." By the end of the narrator's description, it is all but impossible for any but the most stony-hearted reader to judge her harshly.

Having made the case for compassion and mercy, the male narrator withdraws. But first, since sixteenth-century punctuation does not include quotations marks, he pauses to inform the reader that the following lines are spoken by the lady: "And thus the eccho answered her to every woorde she spake."[5] The narrator interrupts the first line of her complaint – "O heavens, quoth she" – to make it absolutely clear that she is the speaker. The ensuing questions are full of first person pronouns, alerting us to the lady's point of view: "that bred in me this fevere," "the wounde whose scarre I w[ear]," "to my harmes."

The lady's questions and the echo's answers serve a dual purpose: they identify the young lady's inconstant lover, and they hold him accountable for her secret worry. Who bred in her this fever? Vere. Who gave the wound? Vere. Who caught her heart? Vere. To dispel any possible doubt that Vere is Edward de Vere, the Earl of Oxford, the poem specifically cites his ancient lineage: "What makes him shewe besides his birthe such pride and such untruthe? youthe." As the flattery and excuses reveal, it is not easy to bring charges against the country's preeminent earl, especially when he is a talented courtier poet, a generous patron of the arts, and, to top it all off, Burley's son-in-law.[6] The narrative frame, the female persona, and the echo all maintain the poet's anonymity, thereby protecting him from Vere's anger. The verdict is nonetheless definitive: "such pride and such untruthe"!

The poem ends as it began, with a narrative frame that converts judgment into mercy: "And I that knewe this ladye well said lorde, how great a myracle, / To heare the eccho tell her truthe as 'twere Apollo's oracle." The surprising revelation that the male narrator knows the lady well makes him appear all the more knowledgeable and trustworthy. The exclamatory syntax and elevated diction ("how great a myracle") give

Figure 7 Engraving of Edward de Vere, 17th Earl of Oxford by J. Brown after
G. P. Harding.

the echo miraculous or prophetic powers to reveal "her truth": first, to confirm the truth of her troth-plight to Vere; second, to reveal the truth of the words the poet attributes to her; finally, to tell her the "truth" the poet thinks she is too distraught to perceive.

The invocation to the "lord" above, combined with the references to miracle and oracle, recalls the sanctity of her "vowe," and reaffirms the male speaker's earlier attempt to absolve her guilt and alleviate her sorrow. Finally, the apostrophe, "lorde," fuses divine inspiration and worldly concern, suggesting that the poem is addressed not only to God who, in his omniscience, has the power to confirm the truth the poem tells, but also to a courtly coterie comprised of lords and courtiers who would otherwise not have access to the truth the poem reveals.

One can imagine the reaction at court as the echoing reverberations – "vere," "vere," "vere," "vere" – broadcast the news. You have to hear this! Vere has seduced a fair young lady. Who is she? No doubt, the secrecy surrounding the lady's identity feeds the gossip, increasing the poem's impact. As it turns out, there is no need for the poem or the oracle to reveal her name. Mother Nature and Father Time bespeak what the poet discreetly omits:

On Tuesday at night Anne Vavysor was brought to bed of a son in the maiden's chamber. The E. of Oxford is avowed to be the father, who hath withdrawn himself with intent, as it is thought, to pass the seas. The ports are laid for him and therefore if he have any such determination it is not likely that he will escape. The gentlewoman the selfsame night she was delivered was conveyed out of the house and the next day committed to the Tower. Others that have been found any ways party to the cause have also been committed. Her Majesty is greatly grieved with the accident.[7]

Contemporary manuscripts, replete with titles, annotations, and sub-scriptions, leave little doubt that the "fayre yonge ladye" is Anne Vavasour. The two best texts of the poem are both subscribed "vavaser," which suggests that Anne Vavasour is either the poet or the protagonist. In one manuscript, "her swete song" is prefaced by the subtitle "Anne Vavasour's echo," which implies that she is the principal speaker in a lyric dialogue written about her by someone else. The Arundel Harington Manuscript includes the subscription "ffinis q^d E. Veer. count d'Oxford" which seems to attribute the poem to Oxford. To further complicate matters, two manuscripts from a common source are entitled respectively, "Verses made by the earle of Oxford [and Mrs Anne Vauesor]" and "Verses made of ye Earle of Ox^enforde And Mrs. Ann vauesor."[8] As we have already observed in *A Hundreth Sundrie Flowres* and as we shall see again in the *Amoretti*, Elizabethan discursive titles conven-tionally use the preposition "by," not only to designate a poem written *by* a particular person but also to indicate a male-authored poem prompted by a woman's presence nearby. To summarize, the manuscript evidence suggests that the poet is either Vavasour, or Vere, or both of them working together, or some unidentified third party "that knewe this ladye well."

The idea of a female-authored female complaint, framed by a ventriloquized male voice, is intriguing to contemplate. Yet under the circumstances, it seems unlikely that Vavasour could have mustered the esthetic distance to describe herself through the eyes of an admiring male observer. If Vavasour had wished to write about Oxford's betrayal, she might have written a Petrarchan lyric, representing the situation from her own point of view, as Queen Elizabeth does in "On Monsieur's Departure." Or she might have written a persuasion poem, demonstrating her own worth and urging her unconstant lover to honor his secret lover's vow, as Isabella Whitney does in *The Copy of a letter to her Unconstant Lover*. Compared to the female-authored lyrics examined in the next chapter, "Sittinge alone" sounds less like a woman's lyric voice and viewpoint than like a male poet's female persona. Indeed, the female speaker is so blinded by the veil of her own misery – "O hollow caves tell true" – that she is incapable of perceiving the truth the poem reveals by means of the echo: "And I that knewe this ladye well said lorde, how great a myracle, / To heare the eccho tell her truthe as 'twere Apollo's oracle."

The allusion to the Delphic Oracle might imply that she could solve her problems if she were to assess her situation according to a pagan code of ethics. But even more important, it implies that the echo reveals "her truthe" in the same way that Apollo's oracle tells its petitioners the truth: in riddling prophesies. The Delphic oracle is the source of purification, healing, and enlightenment – but only if the auditor has the wherewithal and the courage to decipher the oracle's cryptic and potentially disturbing message.

In the Arundel Harington manuscript, "Sittinge alone" is prefaced by a note in Sir John Harington's handwriting, "The best verse that ever th'autor made." A subscription follows, also in Harington's hand: "ffinis q^d E. Veer. count d'Oxford." Hughey finds it difficult to reconcile the prefatory note with the fact that Harington's manuscript contains only one poem by Oxford. Yet she nonetheless concludes that "Harington assigns the poem only to Edward de Vere." May concurs, though he finds "the tone and point of view quite inappropriate for either of the principals."[9] Harington clearly knows who wrote the poem, but is it Oxford?

Oxford fled the country at the very moment Vavasour was laboring to bring their son into the world; it therefore seems unlikely that he would have gone out of his way to write a poem describing her as a "sighte soe sore as mighte have moved some mercy in the rocks." It is even harder to imagine a man as proud as Oxford writing and circulating such a scathing critique of his own character and behavior: "such pride and such untruthe."

The Paradise of Dainty Devices, first published in 1576 and already in its third printing by the time Vavasour becomes Oxford's lover, includes eight poems by Oxford. Seven of the poems contain the conventional abstractions of love, but one is an overtly autobiographical self defense: "I stayles[s] stand tabide the shocke of shame and infamy."[10] The self-pitying, bitterly defensive tone alludes to the shock waves reverberating through Elizabethan high society when Oxford accused his wife, Elizabeth Cecil de Vere, of bearing an illegitimate child. No one seems to have believed the accusations, not even Oxford, for he made no attempt to disown the child. Instead of justifying his desire to be rid of his wife, Oxford only managed to discredit himself. With his reputation plummeting, Oxford decided to publish the lyric. This was an unprecedented act for a man of his social stature, for print was still considered déclassé and suspiciously self-advertising. Publication only magnified Oxford's "shame and infamy," making the final apostrophe all the more pitifully ironic: "Helpe eccho that in ayre dooth flee, shril voyces to resound, / To waile this losse of my good name, as of these greefes the ground."

"Sittinge alone" answers Oxford's lyric. The echo, "vere," "vere," "vere," "vere," makes the loss of Vere's good name "resound" in the most literal sense, i.e., it repeats his tainted name in a loud and echoing manner. By alluding to Oxford's own account of this prior scandal, our anonymous poet reminds the court that Oxford is not a man of his word. He also implies that Oxford's infamy and shame are the ground or cause of Vavasour's grief: "as of these greefes the ground."

Many of the poems in the Arundel Harington manuscript are subscribed "ffinis," some with a name alongside. What distinguishes the subscription "ffinis q^d E. Veer. count d'Oxford," from the rest is the word "q^{d}" which refers back to line 11, "O heavenes quothe she." The subscription, added to the text of the poem in Harington's own handwriting, is not an indication of Oxford's authorship, as Hughey and May assume, but rather Harington's ironic commentary on the poem's impact. When Anne Vavasour gives birth to an illegitimate son in the maiden's chamber, "The E. of Oxeford is avowed to be the father" – thanks in considerable measure, I believe, to the information disseminated by "Sittinge alone."

As Walsingham reports – and as Harington is undoubtedly in a position to know – "Her Majesty is greatly grieved with the accident."[11]

Oxford tries to flee, but is apprehended and imprisoned. He is released not long after, only to be badly wounded in a duel with Anne's uncle, Thomas Knyvet (a detail which will crop up later in this chapter along with a surprising new piece of information). Queen Elizabeth banishes the earl from court, and refuses to relent, despite Burley's intercession, for two long years. Ralegh finally negotiates a truce, but Oxford never receives a position of any power, either in the government or in the military. Oxford's prospects are indeed "ffinis," as Harington's subscription puts it so bluntly.

Below the subscription is a line, comprised of five crossed-out words, that Hughey is "unable to decipher satisfactorily."[12] The next page, folio 131, is torn out. Clearly, Harington is trying to conceal something, but what? _____ _____ to _____ _____ is the most likely possibility, not only because manuscript subscriptions typically record who wrote the poem to whom, but also because Harington had good reason to remove the two crucial pieces of information that the poem itself is at pains to conceal: (1) the identity of the female speaker; (2) the name of the male poet who took it upon himself to inform the court that Oxford should be held accountable for Vavasour's plight.

WHAT THE POEM IS DOING FOR THE POET

The point of view is neither Oxford's nor Vavasour's. Rather it is the point of view of someone "that knewe this ladye well." A twentieth-century reader encountering this line in a book of poems would probably take it as a self-reflexive comment on the poetic fiction; however, a sixteenth-century reader, hearing the poem along with the latest court gossip, would be much more likely to see it as confirmation of the poem's biographical truth. If we assume, for the moment, that the poet really does know the lady well, how does that change the functioning of the structure? And what might the poet have hoped to accomplish by writing this "swete songe" for the fair young lady?

As long as we focus on the lady's voice and viewpoint, the lines seem to express her longing for Vere. But "if we try to discover what the poem is doing for the poet," as Burke advises us to do, we can also hear the poet's voice reverberating therein: "Yet who dothe moste adore this wighte? O hollowe caves tell true; Yowe." The lines not only express what the lady wants to tell Vere; they also express what the male poet wants to tell the fair young lady: I know you adore Vere most of all, but I nonetheless want you to know that I adore you most of all. The sexual ambiguity of "this wighte" makes it possible to attribute the lines both to the female speaker and to the male poet.

Indeed, if we reread the lady's questions and the echo's answers, looking for evidence of "the Courtly figure *Allegoria*, which is when we speake one thing and thinke another, and that our wordes and our meanings meete not," we can hear the poet's voice reverberating throughout, line by line, intimating what he cannot tell the lady directly: I know you find Vere irresistible, but I find you irresistible. I know Vere was "the firste that bred in [you] this fevere," and the "first [that] caughte this hearte," but you are the first that bred in me this fever, and the first that caught my heart.[13]

The poet/lover empathizes with the lady's sorrow and understands her love for Vere, but he wants her to know that, whatever the consequences of her sexual liaison, he admires and adores her as much as ever: "Yet who dothe moste adore this wighte? O hollow caves tell true; Yowe. / What nimphe deserves his likinge beste? yet doth in sorrowe rue? Yowe." He knows she "dothe moste adore" Vere. He even believes that she "deserves his likinge beste" which is no small matter, given the fact that Oxford is still legally married to Burley's daughter. The poet wants her to realize that there is no way, short of finding Cupid's golden arrow, to make Oxford faithful to her. The very qualities that make Vere so attractive to her – his birth, beauty, and self-assurance – make him incapable of feeling "remorse" for his wrongdoing or "ruthe" for her suffering.

Although many Elizabethans will see her as the archetypal female complainant – the fallen woman who is condemned to pay for her sexual abandon – the poet/lover appreciates her sexuality and defends "her truthe." He knows she is in love with Vere, but he is in love with her. And he cannot help but fantasize about being the next to arouse her passions by touching "her softe hande." To him, she is neither a delicate rosebud waiting to be plucked nor a faded blossom ready to be discarded: "I might descerne her face, / As one mighte see a damaske rose thoughe hid with cristall glasse." Instead she is a lush, aromatic, full-blown rose whose barely concealed, blushing passion he cherishes and wishes to preserve – but cannot touch. In so doing, he turns the moral teachings of the male-authored female complaint upside down – and even pauses *in medias res* to update the *carpe diem* tradition.

By going to such lengths to attribute the questions to the lady, the male narrator prevents the courtly lyric audience from detecting the private lyric dialogue between the unidentified poet/lover and the unidentified female speaker. The narrative frame is addressed to the court, but the questions and echoing answers are addressed directly to "Yowe" – to the fair young lady. If Anne Vavasour is not the poet but the private lyric audience, there is no need for the poet, knowing her as well as he does, to identify himself to her. If he utters the words to her when she is nearby, or if he gives her the poem to read to herself, she will surely hear his voice, reverberating within the questions and echoing answers the poem presents for her consideration.

Although it is not necessary for us to know the poet's name in order to discern his point of view, the dramatic revelation that he "knewe this ladye well" hints that his identity might provide some further "cues for analyzing the sort of *eventfulness* that the poem contains." Thanks to Chambers, we know that while Vavasour was at court, serving as a Gentlewoman of the Queen's Bedchamber, she captured the fancy not only of Edward de Vere (1550–1604) but also of Sir Henry Lee (1533–1611). Lee was already married, and thus no more at liberty to marry her than was Oxford. Although Chambers doesn't consider the possibility, the narrative frame, the ventriloquized questions, the drum-beat of echoing answers – Vere, you, youth, I – capture Henry Lee's point of view perfectly. While Vere and Vavasour were drawn together by beauty and passion, Lee was left "Sittinge alone upon my thought in melancholye moode."

May tries to attribute the poem to Vere or Vavasour, only to be stymied by inexplicable inconsistencies in tone and point of view. Yet, even the oddest details make perfect sense if the poem is a clandestine proposal of love written to Anne Vavasour by Henry Lee (or by someone with feelings similar to Lee's for Vavasour). Consider, for example, the defense of Vere's behavior on the grounds of youth which sounds so jarring, coming as it does immediately after the poem's harshest charges: "What makes him shewe besides his birthe such pride and such untruthe? youthe."[14] As May remarks, the poem flatters Oxford by emphasizing his beauty and youth. Yet, it also subjects him to a heavy dose of irony, for Oxford is no young imp. The echo implies what the poet dares not say: as a mature married man of thirty, Oxford is too old to get away with acting like an irresponsible young rake.[15]

Henry Lee dreams of being Anne Vavasour's champion; he even goes so far as to have one of his three sets of armor engraved with the initials A. V.[16] But he is forty-seven years old. Even if Anne Vavasour is his ideal of female beauty, he knows that he is not her ideal image of a knight in shining armor. Lee watches as Vavasour becomes more and more sexually involved with Oxford who represents the ideal courtier: beautiful, proud, aristocratic, and renowned at the tilt. I believe Henry Lee writes

Figure 8 The armor worn by Sir Henry Lee as Master of the Armoury when Anne
Vavasour was a Gentlewoman of the Queen's Bedchamber. The inset shows the
initials A. V. engraved into the pattern of the armor.

"Sittinge alone upon my thought" because he wants the queen, the
court, and, above all, Anne Vavasour to see Oxford as the villain of a
male-authored female complaint – as the powerful, high-born seducer
whose heartless behavior leaves the female complainant to face a life of
degradation and misery.

When we pause to hear Lee's voice reverberating within the ventriloquized voice of the female complainant, the questions and echoing
answers are not only more psychologically compelling but they are also
more rhetorically brilliant: "May I his beautye matche with love if he my
love will trye? I / May I requite his birthe with faythe? then faythfull will

I dye. I." If Vavasour were the poet, she would have no reason to praise Oxford's birth and beauty to her own detriment. But if Henry Lee is the poet/lover, he has every reason to want Vavasour to see that Vere is incapable of the compassion, understanding, and devotion which he, the poet/lover, demonstrates in such abundance.

To the courtly coterie, the echo reveals the secret of Oxford's paternity and betrayal. To Anne Vavasour, the private female lyric audience, the ventriloquized female voice poses the questions the male poet/lover wants her to consider. The echo speaks the truth he wants her to hear and recognize as "her truthe." Lee knows he is no match for Oxford's birth and youthful beauty, but he loves Vavasour and understands her point of view as Oxford does not. His love has already been put to the test by Oxford's inconstancy and Vavasour's pregnancy, and he is as enamored of her and as devoted to her as ever. He is prepared to do everything in his power to defend her character and behavior. Indeed, he – unlike Oxford – is prepared to remain her faithful admirer and protector as long as he lives.

SOME BASIC DISCOVERIES ABOUT THE *STRUCTURE* OF THE WORK ITSELF

The echo's final answers, "I," "I," are the subject of two discrete sentences that remain to be completed after the poem stops. "Sitting alone" has three central characters, the male speaker, the fair young lady, and Vere, but it has only two I's: the male "I" of the narrative frame and the ventriloquized female "I" that appears in lines 11–14 and 19–20. We know how Lee would finish lines 19–20 if it were only up to him, for his answer is the poem's subtext: I love you. I will honor and protect you and be faithful to you (even if I can't marry you) until I die. What we do not know, since the poem does not presume to say, is how Vavasour responds to his lyric proposal.

Putting the narrative frame aside for the moment, the body of the poem is divided into quatrains, each containing a single rhyme and reinforced by the echo's rhyming iteration. The first two quatrains establish the pattern, but the third quatrain breaks off *in medias res* when the persona preempts the echo's answer: "then faythfull will I dye. I." The two missing lines are easy to perceive in those manuscripts that set the concluding narrative frame apart – as four tetrameters capping the long, lugubrious seven-foot lines. Some manuscripts deal with the problem by combining the incomplete third quatrain with the closing narrative frame; however, that is structurally misleading, for the final couplet not only introduces a new rhyme but also adds an extra foot. The missing lines are intrinsic to the functioning of the poem's structure: they are the space left for the fair young lady to answer the poem's veiled proposal of love. No matter how artfully a poet/lover tries to anticipate or accommodate a female reader's point of view, he cannot prescribe her response without denying her liberty and will – the very qualities that a male poet/lover (as opposed to the male author of a conventional female complaint) needs to nourish.

Having been quiescent for eighteen lines, the male speaker suddenly reappears: "And I that knewe this ladye well said . . ." This "I" echoes the echo's two I's – as if to acknowledge that his intimate knowledge of the lady comprises a space outside the poem where the lyric dialogue of courtship will continue, should she choose to answer his proposal. The poem does not reach a conclusion; it simply stops, leaving Vavasour to choose between the two very different female roles and two genres the poem offers for her consideration. She can continue to weep her secret tears, uttering the female complainant's classic tale of woe, "then faythfull will I dye." Or she can join the poet/lover in a lyric dialogue of courtship, answering his offer of undying devotion with two I's of her own, saying, aye, I too say aye.

ANALYZING THIS EVENTFULNESS

In the life of Sir Henry Lee, Chambers prints a second poem that is also somehow connected to Anne Vavasour's love affair with Edward de Vere. Since conflicting manuscript annotations again raise questions about the poet's identity, let us put the question of authorship aside for the moment in order to consider what the poem is doing for the poet and what the poet is trying to convey to the private lyric audience. First of all, let us examine the poem, looking for cues to the lyric situation and the functioning of the lyric structure:

> Thoughe I seeme straunge sweete freende, be thou not so
>   do not accoy thy selfe with sullen will
> Myne harte hathe vo[wed] althoughe my tongue saye noe
>   To be thyne owne in freendly liking styll.
>
> Thou seeste me liue amongest the Lynxes eyes
> That pryes into the priuy thoughte of mynde
> Thou knowest ryghte well what sorrowes maye aryse
>   If once they chaunce my setled lookes to fynde

Contente thy selfe that once I made an othe
  To sheylde my selfe in shrowde of honest shame
And when thou lyste make tryall of my trouthe
  So that thou save the honoure of my name

And let me seme althoughe I be not coye
  To cloak my sadd conceyts wth smylinge cheere
Let not my iestures showe wherein I ioye
  Nor by my lookes lett not my loue apeere.

We seely dames that falles suspecte, do feare
  And liue within the moughte [mouthe] of enuyes lake
Muste in oure heartes a secrete meaning beare
  Far from the reste whiche outwardlye we make

So were I lyke, I lyste not vaunte my loue
  Where I desyre there moste I fayne debate
One hathe my hande an other hathe my gloue
  But he my harte whome I seeme moste to hate

Thus farwell freende I will continewe straunge
  Thou shalte not heere by worde or writing oughte
Let it suffice my vowe shall neuer chaunge
  As for the rest I leaue yt to thy thoughte.[17]

The speaker begins *in medias res*, with a dependent clause that sounds as if it is part of an ongoing, private conversation. Indeed, the speaker is so immersed in the lyric situation that it is difficult to figure out the literal meaning of many of the lines. It is not even clear until the sixth stanza that the poet/lover is a woman.

The first stanza ends with a promise "To be thyne owne in freendly liking styl," but what exactly does that mean? Is the speaker promising to remain "freendly" in the sense of amicable? Or is she accepting a proposal of marriage, agreeing to become his wife, "thyne owne" forever? Or is she promising to be his "friend," in the sense of paramour? Without being privy to what is understood between them, it is difficult to know whether this is a poem of idealized love, a written confirmation of a clandestine marriage contract, or an amatory epistle, sent to confirm an illicit tryst.

The poem is full of ambiguous phrases that could be taken as evidence for any one of these readings. It is extremely difficult to decide whether the oath, "To sheylde my selfe in shrowde of honest shame," refers to a vow of virginity (i.e., a shroud of maidenly shamefastness), to a secret marriage contract that will "shrowde" her "shame," or pregnancy, beneath the honorable veil of matrimony, or to a solemn pledge that shrouds their illicit love affair in the "honest shame" of fidelity to each other.

The tight-lipped final comment, "As for the rest I leaue yt to thy thoughte," provides little help. Is the poet bidding her male reader a polite farewell, urging him to sublimate his sexual desire? Or is she reminding him that it is up to him to carry out the plans for their clandestine marriage? Or is she coyly alluding to the illicit sexual pleasures that are awaiting him? It is difficult to choose among these various readings precisely because this a classic poem of courtship, constructed so as to mean different things to different readers. The female poet/lover admits as much when she mentions her "secret meaning far from the rest."

More often than not, the key to reading Elizabethan poetry of courtship lies in what the poem implies but does not say directly. In "Sittinge alone," for example, the echo declares that the young lady's inconstant lover is Vere, while the narrative frame carefully conceals the poet's/lover's proposal to the fair young lady. The secret meaning of the poem only begins to emerge if we pause to ask why the poet is so eager to keep her face and his name "covered with a vayle." In the case of "Thoughe I seeme straunge," the repeated and decidedly enigmatic references to a vow, a troth, and an oath suggest that this is not a Neoplatonic poem of idealized love but a pseudo-Petrarchan poem of clandestine courtship. The vow, the oath, and troth all allude to a private understanding between the female poet/lover and the male reader which they – and the poem – have carefully concealed from everyone else – especially from the "One" who "hathe my hand." Whether they are engaged in a premarital love affair, an extramarital love affair, or an elopement in the offing is still unclear.

A KIND OF OBSERVATION ABOUT STRUCTURE

Upon first reading, the extremely regular rhythms and rhyme scheme, the end-stopped lines and frequent caesurae, the terseness of the imagery, all seem to contain the lyric situation within the strict limits of line and stanza. Yet the more one tries to decipher the lyric situation, the more equivocal the language becomes, and the more the syntax pushes against the limits of the lyric structure.

The pressure reaches a climax when the female poet/lover tells the male reader/lover that he must fulfill one condition: "And when thou lyste make tryall of my trouthe / So that thou save the honoure of my name" (lines 11–12). These lines can be paraphrased: And you can test my troth (my truth or my oath) whenever you are ready, so long as you promise to protect the honor of my name. But what exactly does that imply? Is she asking him to make an honest woman of her by marrying her? Or does she want him to save the honor of her name by keeping their extra-marital love affair a secret?

If we read the lines without stopping to add a caesura – and both the Bodleian Rawlinson Manuscript and the Cornwallis Manuscript have marked pauses elsewhere but not here – the two subordinate clauses swallow up the main clause, and the words rush forward without a moment's pause, saying: and when you are ready to test my troth, as long as you promise to save the honor of my name, then . . . What then? Here the syntax trails off into the white space surrounding the lines – the marginal space where an expectant pause invites the private lyric audience to react.

Given all the vows, oaths, and troths, a privy contract seems like the most probable explanation. But that would mean the poem could not have been written by Anne Vavasour to either Edward de Vere or Henry Lee because both men were already married when she arrived at court. Upon closer inspection, however, it becomes clear that a secret marriage contract does not fit the lyric any better than it fits the life: "One hathe my hande an other hathe my gloue / But he my harte whome I seeme moste to hate." The syntax of these lines is particularly clotted – as if they were concealing important clues to the lyric situation. If one man has her hand, presumably she is either married or betrothed to be married. A second man has her glove, a token of her love, but she is neither married nor betrothed to him. The poem is addressed to the third man: he who has her heart; he whom she is forced to seem to hate.

Anne Vavasour is not married in 1580. If she is the poet, as two of the three extant manuscripts seem to suggest, she could be writing to Oxford after discovering she is pregnant, asking him to save her from having to go through with a pragmatic marriage to someone she does not love. Or she could be writing to someone else who is in the position to save the honor of her name by making her child legitimate, and thus saving her from having to marry the person to whom she has made a promise of marriage. Given Vavasour's predicament, both readings are tempting, but neither quite describes the poem's argument.

The female poet/lover is not trying to convince the male reader to remain true to *his* vow. Rather, she is trying to reassure him that she will remain true to *her* vow: "do not accoy thy selfe with sullen will";

"Myne harte hathe vo[wed] althoughe my tongue saye noe / To be thyne owne in freendly liking styll." Above all, the poetic rhetoric strives to convince the male realer not to be misled by words, looks, and gestures that might cause him to doubt her: "And let me seme," "Let not my iestures showe," "Nor by my lookes lett not my loue apeere."

The elusive syntax and ambiguous diction, the repeated hints of a private understanding between the poet and the reader, the tender tone and persuasive purpose, the hints that this is an amatory verse epistle bearing a secret message the writer cannot utter either in person or in writing – these are the signs of a private lyric dialogue between clandestine lovers. Even when "Thoughe I seeme straunge" is read intrinsically, as we have been doing, the poetry gestures towards a private subtext and begs to be explained by events that occupy the margins, the quasi-poetic, quasi-historical space where lyric meets life.

THE FUNCTIONING OF A STRUCTURE

In at least two different manuscripts "Thoughe I seeme straunge" is subscribed "vavaser," but scholars have been chary of attributing the poem to Anne Vavasour because a third extant manuscript is subscribed "La[dy] B to N." An annotation of this kind is a scholar's nightmare: Lady B. and N. could refer to any number of people. Indeed, one sixteenth-century diary represents Anne Vavasour herself as Lady B.: "My lord of Oxford fought with Master Knyvet about the quarrel of Bessie Bavisar."

It would certainly clarify matters if Lady B. proved to be none other than Anne Vavasour (especially if N. were a coded reference to Nry Lee). Yet, I myself would almost prefer to think that Lady B. is some other Elizabethan woman who, upon acquiring a copy of Vavasour's poem, sent it along to her own clandestine lover, Monsieur N., whoever he might be. The poem seems to have circulated among a female coterie, for in addition to Lady B.'s copy, it appears in "Anne Cornwallis's short collection of verse from the late Elizabethan period."[18]

To some extent, I find myself agreeing with Marotti: "the important thing is not the identification of the author, but the representativeness of the utterance: the poem occurs in at least five manuscripts." Yet I would have to add a qualification: we should not let the representativeness of the utterance prevent us from trying to understand the poem in all its particularity. If our goal is to understand the private lyric dialogue of courtship, the identity of the author might provide some important clues to the lyric situation. I would therefore temper Marotti's conclusions with Chambers': "The poem is a woman's and may be Anne's own. It would fit her position in 1580 well enough."[19] What neither Chambers nor Marotti seems to consider is that the poem fits Anne Vavasour's position in 1590 perfectly.

It is not clear when or why Anne Vavasour marries John Finch, but, thanks to Chambers, we know that she *is* married to him in 1590 – the year Henry Lee's wife dies. That is also the year that Lee resigns as Master of the Armoury and moves to the country. The female speaker of "Thoughe I seeme straunge" sounds less like the distraught, helpless Anne Vavasour depicted in "Sittinge alone" than like the considerably more experienced Anne Vavasour Finch who a full decade later makes a calculated decision to leave her husband in order to become the mistress of the recently widowed, fifty-seven-year-old Sir Henry Lee.

If Vavasour writes the poem to Lee in 1590, it is easy to understand why she is so anxious to conceal her plans from "the Lynxes eyes / That pryes into the priuy thoughte of mynde." The metaphor of the wildcat suggests that John Finch is a violently jealous man, furtively stalking his beautiful, worldly wife, prying into her thoughts, prepared to tear her apart should she betray him. The metaphor may also be an allusion to catty court gossips who are just waiting to pounce on any further proof that Vavasour is a "strange" woman – an idiomatic expression for a loose woman or a harlot.

What to my mind makes it all but certain that "Thoughe I seeme straunge" is a veiled poem of courtship, written by Anne Vavasour to Henry Lee in 1590 when she is planning to become his mistress and living companion, is the play on the word *rest*. The word occurs twice – in the two most blatantly cryptic moments of the poem: "a secrete meaning beare / Far from the reste whiche outwardlye we make"; "As for the rest I leaue yt to thy thoughte." At the risk of sounding like the *Oxford English Dictionary*, let me cite from the long list of available meanings those that are most apt: the others; a pause from speaking or reading; that which remains quiescent or undisturbed; the ar*rest* of persons or goods; a heraldic device fixed to the cuirass which prevents the lance from being driven back upon impact.

Rest in the sense of *arrest* recalls the beginning of our tale: Lee's attempt to convince the queen to treat Vavasour's case with mercy, and Vavasour's subsequent arrest and imprisonment in the Tower. Between 1580, when I believe Henry Lee wrote "Sittinge alone" to defend Anne Vavasour from the dishonor of bearing Oxford's illegitimate child, and

1590, when Vavasour leaves her husband to live with Lee, there has been a *rest* or *pause* in their lyric dialogue. During these years Vavasour was not at court, and their care for each other *remained quiescent*. Another meaning of the word "rest" – an armorial device on a knight's cuirass that holds the butt end of the lance and prevents it from being driven back upon impact – could be an allusion to Lee's position as Master of the Armoury. This time his charge – his endeavor to be her champion – will not be driven back.

In 1590, at the age of fifty-seven, Lee resigns as Master of the Armoury, and buys the residue of a lease of Abbots Wood in Charlbury where he builds a lodge named Little Rest, or Lee's Rest.[20] The name is a witty play on still more meanings of the word "rest": the others; a dwelling or residence; the repose obtained by ceasing to work; that which remains to be done; freedom from distress or aggression; the repose of death. Lee's *Rest* is a haven where Lee can find *rest* from his labors and where Vavasour can be safe from the *rest* of their world, both from her husband's jealousy and from society's condemnation.

It is hard to believe that a single word could so fully describe a love affair and a lyric dialogue as long and complicated as Anne Vavasour's and Henry Lee's. But what clinches the link between "Thoughe I seeme straunge," Henry Lee, and Lee's Rest is the fact that the word "rest" is also a play on Lee's name. Since the noun, lee, also means protection, shelter, or a *rest*ing place, the final line, "As for the rest I leaue yt to thy thoughte," contains a double pun on Lee/leave and lee/rest. To those in the know, the veiled but nonetheless insistent wordplay identifies the private lyric audience as Henry Lee – just as Sidney's puns on "rich" and Donne's puns on "more" identify their mistresses respectively as Penelope Rich and Anne More.

It is at this point in their long, complicated relationship, when their plans must still be kept secret from the *rest*, that, I believe, Anne Vavasour writes and sends "Thoughe I seeme straunge" to Henry Lee. The final line, "As for the rest I leaue yt to thy thoughte," alludes to Lee's earlier poem of courtship, "Sittinge alone upon [my] thought." For the moment, Vavasour leaves Lee alone to recall all that has happened since he first courted her in poetry, and to plan the *rest* of the work that remains to be done on Lee's *Rest* so that he can take Anne Vavasour there to be his mistress for the *rest* of his life, before being called to his final *rest*ing place.

The more closely we examine the diction, imagery, and rhetoric, the more successfully the functioning of the structure both conveys and

Figure 9 Portrait of Sir Henry Lee, painted by Marcus Gheerhaerts the Younger, in 1600 when he was living with Anne Vavasour.

conceals the "secrete meaning" that Anne Vavasour needs to find a way to communicate to Sir Henry Lee in 1590 when she is waiting to leave her husband and join Sir Henry Lee at Lee's Rest, "far from the reste" of the courtly coterie. Until Lee's Rest is ready for occupancy, Anne Vavasour must, as she warns him, continue to "seem straunge," i.e., she must act like a stranger. Yet, she has every reason to believe that Lee – the "sweete freende" whose "swete songe" defended her from calumny – will see her as "straunge" in a very different sense of the word: exceptional to a degree that excites wonder or astonishment.

It seems as if we now have sufficient information to conclude that "Thoughe I seeme straunge" is Anne Vavasour's secret answer to Henry Lee's veiled poem of courtship. If there are any remaining doubts, Lee has bequeathed us one more set of clues, *The Ditchley Entertainment*, in which he informs the queen, the court, and posterity that he courted Anne Vavasour in veiled poetry and that she accepted his suit in veiled poetry of her own.

AS FOR THE REST

Lee resigns his official duties at court on the occasion of the Accession Day Tilt – an annual ceremony, full of pomp and poetry, honoring the queen's accession to the throne. Lee masterminded the tilts which earned him the position of Master of the Armoury. "Characteristically he made his retirement the occasion for an elaborate *spectacle*."[21] Lee writes a poem for the occasion in which he humbly requests the queen's permission to retire to the country so that he can dedicate the rest of his life to her worship: "Goddesse, vouchsafe this aged man his right, / To be your Beadsman now, that was your Knight."

Concealed within Lee's tribute to the queen is a secret message to Anne Vavasour: "Curs'd be the soules that thinke to doe her wrong. / And so from Court to Cottage I depart, / My Saint is sure of mine unspotted hart." Lee's words are carefully chosen to mean one thing to the queen and the courtly lyric audience and something quite different to Anne Vavasour – which is precisely the same rhetorical strategy he used in "Sittinge alone upon my thought." If Saint Anne receives his spotless heart, does that leave Saint Elizabeth with a false heart?

Somehow, Elizabeth must have discovered Lee's betrayal, for his loss of royal favor and her subsequent forgiveness are the subject of *The Ditchley Entertainment*, a pageant performed on the occasion of the queen's visit to Lee's Oxfordshire estate two years later, in September 1592. The pageant, staged at intervals during the course of the queen's stay, is a multi-media extravaganza, complete with poetry, fairy tales, allegorical paintings, public speeches, and a courtly *débat* between Constancy and Inconstancy, all held together by the allegory of an old knight and a bevy of inconstant ladies who lie trapped in an enchanted sleep until the fairy queen arrives and sets them free.

The Ditchley Entertainment tells the story of Lee's courtship of Vavasour, and it is chock-full of allusions to their lyric exchange – to both "Sittinge alone" and "Thoughe I seeme straunge."[22] While the old knight sleeps, the knight in charge of the grove explains the situation to the fairy queen: "Heare abouts not long agoe (most vertuous ladye) did I heare a dolorous knight bewayle his hard hap in pittiful accent, there beinge growne (as it shold seeme) to some hight of expostulations with himselfe, and hearing the vere to make answer to his wordes, brack forth into the curious demandes of love & quick interrogatories, of the Nature of louers, wich passage betwixt him and the echoo, because it then lyked me, I committed to memorie" (p. 280).

The melancholy knight, the quick interrogatories, and especially "the vere" that is the "answer to his wordes" – this dense cluster of allusions to "Sittinge alone upon my thought in melancholye moode" announce that Sir Henry Lee, the melancholy knight, the pageant's author and leading man, is also the poet/lover of "Sittinge alone." Indeed, *The Ditchley Entertainment* confirms what we have already discovered: the poem's questions contain "curious" – i.e., abstruse – "demandes of love," written by Sir Henry Lee to Anne Vavasour, the woman whom (as the echo reveals) "the Vere" seduced and betrayed.

A new echo poem, complete with enigmatic questions and answers in Latin, brings the story of Lee's love for Vavasour up to date: "dic mihi crimen. E. himen." (p. 280). Tell me the crime? Hymen. The crime is not Lee's love for Anne Vavasour but Vavasour's unhappy marriage to that lynx.

The queen is then led to a hall where the old knight lies in an enchanted sleep. The page watching over him calls the queen's attention to the "charmed pictures" hanging on the walls where "secreats are con-cealed." The page, who represents the uninitiated lyric audience, cannot interpret the allegory because he is not privy to the circumstances which caused the knight to be punished: "what was his error yet I maye not knowe, / but suer it was the fayrie quenes offending." If the queen can decipher the secret meaning, the enchantment will be broken. She "looks at the pictures and divines their meaning, the Knight wakes, and it is to be supposed that the enchantment of the grove is dispelled" (p. 281).

By agreeing to venture into the enchanted room, and by successfully deciphering the allegory, Queen Elizabeth demonstrates her concern for the old knight. She also proves that she has the skill and compassion to understand his secret history. There follows "The Old Knight's Tale," which links the allegory of the knight's enchantment to the account of Lee's pursuit of Anne Vavasour. The two interwoven allegories reach a climax in the following lines:

> But loe vnhappie I was ouertaken,
> By fortune forst, a stranger ladies thrall,
> Whom when I sawe, all former care forsaken,
> To finde her out I lost my self and all,
> Through which neglect of dutie 'gan my fall: (p. 283)

As a number of scholars have pointed out, the "stranger" lady is Anne Vavasour, and the "stranger ladies thrall" is, of course, Henry Lee, the old knight who has been living in her thrall. What scholars have not realized is that Henry Lee describes Anne Vavasour as the "stranger lady" because that is how she represented herself to him in "Thoughe I seeme straunge": "Thus farwell freende I will continewe straunge." By describing her to the queen as "a stranger ladie" still, Lee fulfills his promise to protect the honor of her name.

After dinner, two maidens sing a song containing still more echoes of the woods, the sea, and the hollow caves where we first encountered Henry Lee "Sittinge alone upon my thought in melancholye mood," listening intently to "Anne Vavasour's echo." Now, thanks "To that Grace that sett us free," Lee's overwrought, seven-foot lines finally come to rest: "Eccho change thie mournefull song, / Greefes to Groues and Caues belong; / Of our new deliuerie, / Eccho, Eccho, certifie" (p. 284). The bouncy, upbeat tetrameter, hovering between a missing first syllable and a missing last syllable, looks back to all that has gone before and forward to all the rest that remains for the old knight, the stranger lady, and the fairy queen – all that the rest of us can "not heere by worde or writing."

The remainder of the pageant is sprinkled with allusions to Lee's poem, to Vavasour's poem, and to their life together at Lee's rest where "one daie aboue the rest, as he ranged abrode, hauing forgotten himself in a long sweet rauishment," the old knight finally finds a sanctuary or haven which provides "great solace" (p. 291). As Vavasour's strange past turns to something of great constancy, the pageant draws to a close. Having defended Anne Vavasour against "the soules that thinke to doe her wrong," Lee restores the queen to her position "aboue the rest, who came to giue me this blessed rest!" (p. 295)

The Ditchley Entertainment uses the courtly figure *Allegoria* to inform the queen, the court, and posterity, first, that Henry Lee wooed Anne

Vavasour with quick interrogatories, containing "curious" or concealed "demandes of love," and, second, that she is the stranger lady who accepted his proposal in veiled verse of her own. Lee writes his final answer to Vavasour's lyric in the following epitaph, written in seven-foot rhyming couplets that harken back to "Sittinge alone":

> Under this Stone intombed lies a faire & worthy Dame
>   daughter to Henry Vauasor Anne Vauasour her name
> Shee liuing wth Sr Henry Lee for loue long tyme did dwell
>   Death Could not part them but that here they rest w^{th}in one cell. (p. 237)

The verses, inscribed on a tombstone erected in Vavasour's honor while she is still alive to appreciate the tribute, conclude the lyric dialogue between Henry Lee and Anne Vavasour. By confirming his earlier promise of undying devotion, Lee proves that the echo was, if not a miracle, at least an oracle: "then faythfull will I dye." Moreover, by eternizing this "faire & worthy Dame / Daughter to Henry Vauasor Anne Vauasour her name," Lee fulfills the conditions she set for him in "Thoughe I seeme straunge": "And when thou lyste make tryall of my trouthe / So that thou save the honoure of my name . . . " "As for the rest" – Lee's answer is, "here they rest w^{th}in one cell."

TOWARDS A SET OF GENERALIZATIONS

Like Elizabeth I, Mary Sidney, and Isabella Whitney, Anne Vavasour stands "[f]ar from the reste" of the inaccessible Petrarchan sonnet ladies, the idealized Neoplatonic beauties, and the remorseful female complainants who haunt the manuscripts of Renaissance love poetry. Together "Sittinge alone" and "Thoughe I seeme straunge" celebrate the kind of clandestine love that Petrarchan ladies are honor bound to resist – and that female complainants are condemned to repent for perpetuity.

"Sittinge alone upon my thought" and "Thoughe I seeme straunge" are paradigmatic poems of courtship: their formal doubleness, ambiguous diction, and veiled figures of speech make their "secrete meaning" available to the poet's/lover's private lyric audience while keeping it "far from the reste." The conflation of revelation and mystification makes the courtship more exciting, the gossip more titillating, and the poetry more intricately multivious – its "secret meaning" dependent on an answering response that is both intrinsic to the functioning of the poem's structure and outside its boundaries.

6

A female lyric tradition

Deare Love, you write in such strains of rethorick I know not well how to answere them. Your complements terme me a godis; I know you are sensible of my frayltyes and imperfections, which will witnes that I am not devine but a poor mortall Creture, subiect to all kind of miseries . . .

Dorothy Oxinden writing to her suitor William Taylor[1]

FEMALE-AUTHORED LOVE POETRY

Elizabethan women write very little original poetry; most of the poetry they do write is religious and therefore outside the scope of this study. Yet the few secular love lyrics written and translated by Elizabethan women all strive in one way or another to construct an alternative to the male voice of Ovidean or Petrarchan poetry. The Petrarchan lyric and the Ovidean complaint are in many ways counter-genres. Together the all too earthly female complainant and the all too heavenly Petrarchan lady represent the repressive norms against which Elizabethan poetry of courtship defines itself. The sonnet lady, the symbol of spiritual beauty, is idolized and eternized by the Neoplatonic or Petrarchan poet. The female complainant, the epitome of worldly beauty and female weakness, is violated by the male gaze and judged, sometimes sympathetically and sometimes ironically, by the male poet and reader. The female complainant speaks uncontrollably, her open mouth signifying her open body; the sonnet lady is as silent as she is chaste. When she does speak, her "high holy words" are more heavenly than earthly.

This chapter examines three Elizabethan women writers who reappropriate the conventions of the Petrarchan lyric and the Ovidean complaint to wage and conceal a rebellion against those aspects of male poetic tradition which might otherwise reduce them to the object of male desire or the target of male irony and judgment.

SINGING WITH THEE

While the *Rime* is a collection of univocal lyrics which explore Petrarch's thoughts and feelings, the *Triumph of Death* is a dream vision in which Laura appears and strikes up a lyric dialogue with Petrarch. In heaven now and safely beyond fleshly temptation, it is she who first makes physical contact – "And first hir hand, sometime desyred so / Reaching to me" (2:10–11) – and she who initiates the conversation. At first, she speaks only three brief lines before pausing for Petrarch to discourse; as the dialogue continues, her speeches lengthen, becoming increasingly expansive and complex.

Speaking in the presence of God, Laura puts aside all earthly pretense: "yett now to thee more manifestlie plaine, / In face of him, who all doeth see and knowe" (2:77–8). Encouraged, Petrarch ventures to ask what he could not ask in the *Rime*: "did yow euer entretaine / Motion or thought more louinglie to me?" (2:79–80). In response, Laura admits her love more directly and unambiguously than ever before: "Neuer were / Our hearts but one, nor neuer two shall be: / Onelie thy flame I tempred with my cheere; / This onelie way could saue both thee and me" (2:88–91).[2] In the *Triumph of Death*, Laura verbalizes what she was thinking and feeling behind the veil of the *Rime*: "Thou sawe'st what was without, not what within," she says, "A thousand times wrath in my face did flame, / My heart meane-while with loue did inlie burne, / but neuer will, my reason ouercame" (2:97–102).

Using Petrarch's own imagery of burning and flaming in love, Laura explains that her flashes of anger were a guise, adopted both to control the desire burning within *him* and to conceal the desire burning within *her*. When his protestations of love became too clamorous, she checked his expectations with her disdain. When his spirits sagged to the point of collapse, she smiled encouragingly. Thousands of times she would have cast her eyes on him with sympathy and love, "Had I not fear'd in thee those coles to fyre / I thought would burne too-dangerouslie fast" (2:158–59).

The translation I have been quoting is Mary Sidney's.[3] Like so many Elizabethan texts, Mary Sidney's translation of the *Triumph* is not published during her lifetime. It does circulate in manuscript, however, where (along with her translation of Garnier's *Tragedie of Antonie*) it provides a compelling female response to the dominant male voice of the Renaissance lyric. Sidney's English reconstruction of Petrarch's dialogue with Laura is less an accolade to Laura's heavenly chastity than a corrective to the discreet, inaccessible Laura hidden behind the veil of the more famous *Rime*.[4]

Out of the three hundred years of Petrarchan poetry at her disposal Mary Sidney chooses to translate this moment when the lyric becomes a dialogue, when "a self-sufficient and closed authorial monologue, one that presumes only passive listeners beyond its own boundaries" becomes "a rejoinder in a given dialogue, whose style is determined by its interrelationship with other rejoinders in the same dialogue."[5] That strikes me as notable, especially when we think of *The Triumph* not only as Petrarch's retrospective commentary on the *Rime* but also as Mary Sidney's Elizabethan female commentary on Renaissance male love poetry.[6]

Critics praise Sidney's translation for its faithfulness both to the literal meaning of Petrarch's words and to the poetic form of his *terza rima*.[7] They note two key errors in her translation, however. The second of which deserves careful consideration:

> S'al mondo tu piacesti a gli occhi mei,
> questo mi taccio; pur quel dolce nodo
> mi piacque assai che 'ntorno al cor avei;
>   e piacemi il bel nome, se vero odo,
> che lunge e presso col tuo dir m'acquisti;
> né mai in tuo amor richiesi altro che'l modo. (2:127–32)

> If lyking in myne eyes the world did see
> I saie not, now, of this, right faine I am,
> Those cheines that tyde my heart well lyked me,
> And well me lykes (if true it be) my flame,
>   which farre and neere by thee related goes,
> Nor in thy loue could ought but measure blame.
>   (Sidney 2:127–32)

Rees's description of Sidney's mistranslation, reiterated by both Coogan and Waller, is as follows: "In this case, she has taken 'avei' to be first person singular, instead of recognizing it as second person singular, a short form of 'avevi,' and has therefore destroyed the balanced argument of the terzina, and distorted the sense."[8] It seems unlikely, however, that Sidney mistakes the verb form because she correctly translates the same shortened form only two lines later, glossing "volei," as "volevi," "thow needes wouldst shewe" (2:134).

When we compare Sidney's translation to the original, the differences look less like grammatical error than deliberate revision. Sidney translates the first part of the passage even more literally than does Wilkins, but the effect of her translation is very different from Petrarch's. Petrarch's Laura admits that she took pleasure in hearing about his love for her, but she is silent about her desires, refusing to say whether or not she took pleasure in looking at Petrarch: 'if in the world (while I was alive) you pleased my eyes, of this I am silent.' Petrarch represents Laura presenting herself as the object of Petrarch's love and the subject of his poetry.

Sidney certainly does distort Petrarch's meaning: she transforms Laura from the idolized object of Petrarch's love to a female subject who openly speaks her desire.[9] The heavy-handed repetition – "right faine I am," "well lyked me," "And well me lykes" – makes it impossible to ignore the fact that Laura is not only a beloved but also a lover. While Petrarch's Laura modestly refuses to say whether Petrarch pleased her eyes, Sidney's Laura freely acknowledges her sexual desire, refusing instead to care whether the world sees how much she enjoys gazing at Petrarch. The structure of Sidney's line – "I saie not, now, of this, right faine I am" (2:128) – makes it possible to read the middle phrase, "now, of this," both backwards and forwards. "Now" Laura no longer cares whether her love is perceived by the world because "now" she is extremely pleased with the chains which tied *her* heart with love for Petrarch.

As the passage unfolds, it becomes less and less likely that Sidney's distortion of Petrarch's meaning is merely the result of misreading the word "avei." Petrarch's Laura says, 'it pleases me, the pretty name, if I hear true, that far and near with your speaking I have acquired.' Instead, Sidney's Laura says, "And well me lykes (if true it be) my flame, / which farre and neere by thee related goes" (2:130–31). By changing "il bel nome," the beautiful name, to "my flame," Sidney's Laura claims a very different kind of pleasure: the heat of passion. The change is all the more striking because a literal translation, the beautiful name, would have rhymed perfectly with "blame." The parenthetical qualification, "(if true it be)," occupies an odd position in Sidney's sentence, signaling that something is awry, prompting us to remember that it is Petrarch's flame, not Laura's, that is described throughout the *Rime*.

Sidney's revision strengthens Laura's pleasure, both the pleasure she derives from her own burning love of Petrarch and the pleasure she derives from the role her passion plays in Petrarch's poetry. The final line of the terzina adds another surprising twist. Petrarch's Laura says, 'nothing in thy love have I sought for other than the measure.' Sidney's Laura says, "Nor in thy loue could ought but measure blame," which raises the possibility that Laura blames Petrarch for "the measure," the control, which prevented him from asking whether she too was burning in love.[10]

In a long, impassioned speech that is the climax of their encounter, Sidney's Laura tells Petrarch she was as inflamed by love as he was:

> In equale flames our louing hearts were tryde.
>> At leaste when once thy loue had notice gott,
>> But one to shewe, the other sought to hyde.
> Thow didst for mercie calle with wearie thro[at]
>> In feare and shame, I did in silence goe,
>> So much desire became of little note.
> But not the lesse becoms concealed woe,
>> Nor greater growes it uttèred, then before,
>> Through fiction, Truth will neither ebbe nor flowe.
>
> (2:139–47)

Afraid of her anger and ashamed of his passion, Petrarch asks only for mercy, not for love. Afraid of her desire and ashamed of her flaming cheeks, Laura hides her love in anger. If Petrarch had been less eager to turn his love into poetry, Laura would have been less compelled to hide her love in anger. Still, his passion is no more increased by the need to proclaim his woes to the world than her passion is diminished by the correspondent need to conceal her love from the world.

Here too, Sidney alters Petrarch's language to intensify Laura's passion:

> Fûr quasi equali in noi fiamme amorose,
> almen poi ch'i m'avidi del tuo foco;
> ma l'un le palesò, l'altro l'ascose.
>> Tu eri di mercé chiamar giá roco,
> quando tacea, perché vergogna e téma
> facean molto desir parer si poco. (2:139–44)

Most significantly, Sidney omits the qualification, "quasi equali," *almost* equally. In Petrarch's text there are no pronouns telling us who feels fear, shame, and desire, though the narrative makes it clear that the emotions are Laura's, which only makes sense since shame is a characteristic female response to ethical codes which suppress female sexuality and female agency.[11] Taking advantage of Petrarch's unattributed nouns, Sidney's syntax again encourages us to read backwards and forwards – to apply the "feare and shame" to Petrarch and Laura alike. In Sidney's version, Petrarch and Laura not only share the loving heat of their "equale flames," but they also share the painful results of a moral code that requires women to be chaste and silent, no matter how "much desire" they feel within.

The passionate intensity of Sidney's language seems even more striking in comparison to an earlier English translation by Henry Parker, Lord Morley, written for Henry VIII and published during Mary's reign. Petrarch's Laura admits her desire, so Morley cannot but acknowledge it: "And yet I loued as hoote and true as you" (line 62). Yet he seems almost embarrassed by the confession, surrounding it with continual reassurances that Laura is nonetheless honorable – "There was no dyfference in our loue at all / But that my true loue was ioyned all / In moost honest wyse." While Sidney's *Triumph* matches Petrarch's, terzina for terzina, Morley's is one and a half times the original length, in large measure because he is so anxious to reiterate and elaborate Laura's honor: "allwayes saving the chosen honest" path, she speaks "Swetely and gently," reminding Petrarch (and us), "Thys was euer my wise honest wayes / That I honestly vsed with the[e] in those dayes."[12] By contrast, Sidney's succinct translation of the same lines pointedly emphasizes Laura's shaping influence on Petrarch's poetry: "These artes I us'd with thee" (2:109).

For Morley every incident is an opportunity to defend Laura's chastity: "When that thy swete balettes I dyd synge / Dyddest thou then doubte of me in any thynge? / I thynke playnly nay."[13] For Mary Sidney, the same incidents are an opportunity to declare Laura's passion and to dramatize her influence on Petrarch's poetry:

> But clear'd I not the darkest mists of yore?
> when I thy words alone did entretaine
> Singing for thee? my loue dares speake no more. (2:148–50).

Sidney's syntax is extremely confusing, but the basic situation is clear, especially when we take Petrarch's Italian into consideration: "Ma non si ruppe almen ogni vel, quando, / soli, i tuo' detti, te presente, accolsi, / 'di piú non osa il nostro amor' cantando?" (2:148–50) Laura is recalling an incident when she entertained Petrarch by singing his lyric.[14] By repeating his words of love back to him in her own voice, Laura lets Petrarch know that she loves him, even though she dares not say so openly, in her own words. Sidney's version of the incident, although more literal than Morley's, changes "il nostro amor," our love, to "my love." In so doing, Sidney again revises the text to emphasize Laura's declaration of her feelings.

This stanza is particularly dense and ambiguous, even for Sidney.

Since in Italian, "soli" is a plural modifying "detti" (thy sayings alone), Sidney's translation captures Petrarch's meaning: I accepted your verses alone (i.e., thy words of love and no one else's), singing, "my loue dares speake no more." However, the English word, "alone," is both an adjective and an adverb, meaning: rare or unique; taking action by itself, exclusively; alone, by themselves; subjectively. Sidney's formulation – "when I thy words alone did entretaine / Singing for thee?" – asks to be read in a number of ways which do not exist in the Italian: (1) when I alone, taking action by myself, thy words did entertain, singing for thee; (2) when alone, by ourselves, I did entertain thee, singing for thee; (3) when I did entertain thee, singing thy words, giving them my own unique meaning.

At first, the verb "entertain" seems like an awkward choice for Petrarch's "accolsi," meaning I accepted your verses; however, the various senses of entertain [receive as a guest; deal with; discourse of; please or amuse; accommodate; admit to consideration; give reception to] perfectly reinforce the additional meanings Sidney gives Petrarch's verse. Not only does Laura receive Petrarch as a guest, not only does she amuse and please him by singing to him when they are alone by themselves, but she also accommodates his words to please herself. When she admits his words to her consideration, and then discourses of them "alone" [in the sense of subjectively], she gives his verse her own personal meaning.[15]

What makes Sidney's translation so remarkable is that it both dramatizes and thematizes the way control of the poem's meaning fluctuates between poet and reader. Whose meaning is uttered when Laura sings Petrarch's words back to him: his or hers? Do Petrarch's words "alone" say, "My loue dares speake no more"? Or is it Laura "alone" who in singing the words takes sole responsibility for their meaning? Clearly, she is also singing the words to him "alone," using his words as a circumlocution for her feelings, afraid to say more lest he repeat her words in his poems. By making space for all these possibilities, Sidney's language encourages us to re-experience the fluidity and befuddlement of language which "dares speake no more" as it circulates from the love poet to a private female reader and back again to subsequent lyric audiences and their reading of Petrarch's words.

Petrarch's "cantando" means "singing." Sidney's "singing for thee" gives the verse a brilliant new twist, providing yet another set of "cues for analyzing the sort of *eventfulness* that the poem contains."[16] In "singing for thee" Sidney's Laura not only clarifies the meaning of Petrarch's love poetry, but she also adds her own distinctive intonation, shedding the light of her desire on his dark words, giving her meaning "alone" – her rare and unique meaning – to his verse. In "singing for thee," she is appropriating his role, becoming the singing master of his soul, and his poetry.

When Mary Sidney sings Petrarch's words back to him from an even greater cultural distance, she reconstructs his words once again, taking over his role as poet, adjusting Petrarchan poetic conventions to suit Elizabethan social conventions. "If we grant that a genre is a construction by writer and reader, then it follows that readers interpret the genre differently at the same time or at different times."[17] A dazzling tour de force, Sidney's *terza rima* dramatizes what a poetics of courtship posits: (1) poetry of courtship succeeds when it manages to *do* something for both the poet and his reader; (2) the reader's participation is essential to understanding the functioning of the structure. By reconstructing Petrarch's Italian, Mary Sidney reinterprets the Petrarchan genre to suit her interests and needs as an Elizabethan female reader.

The particular, ambiguous meanings of Sidney's words, many of which do not exist in Petrarch's original (or, for that matter, in twentieth-century English), combined with the extraordinary fluidity of her syntax – the way the syntactical units are constantly floating backwards and forwards from one line to the next, pivoting from the first part of the line to the last – shifts the emphasis from Petrarch's former meaning to Laura's current meaning. The intricate rhyme scheme, which echoes what has gone before even as it introduces a new note, strengthens the syntactical thematics of looking back in order to move forward. Because Sidney's verse is as multiform as her syntax is multivious, Laura's ability to give Petrarch's verse her own distinctive note becomes a trope for Sidney's ability to give new meaning to lyric complexities recovered from the past and interinanimated with the present.

Mary Sidney's English reconstruction of Laura's hidden feelings offers both a powerful critique of the Renaissance moral code, where "so much desire" produces so much "shame and fear," and an intriguing analog for the ways in which an active, female lyric audience transforms the monologic male voice of the Renaissance lyric which takes the listener for a person who passively understands, into a lyric dialogue, where "every word is directed toward an answer and cannot escape the profound influence of the answering word that it anticipates."[18] Using her English art to reassert and emphasize Laura's power and passion, Sidney's translation redefines Petrarch's Italian art, publicizing the artful role of the female lyric audience: "The[se] artes I us'd with thee" (2:109).

In reiterating the "shame and fear" experienced by all those Petrarchan women whose passion and power "did in silence goe," Sidney's translation calls attention to the ethical and social constraints that render female passion invisible and unspeakable: "my loue dares speake no more" (2:150). Laura's poignant sigh, "So much desire became of little note," makes female desire seem all the more compelling precisely because it is so thoroughly silenced by the "fiction" of the *Rime*. The challenge facing Elizabethan women, Sidney seems to be suggesting, is to use their reason to assert their will, either by writing poems of their own or by responding more actively and critically to the lyric and social conventions which keep them silent in order to make them obedient. Elizabethan women can only overcome the "shame" of thinking the unspeakable if they conquer the "fear" of breaking the social and ethical codes that suppress female speech and female sexuality.

ELIZABETH I'S DIALOGUE WITH PETRARCH

In her unpublished manuscript poem, "On Monsieur's Departure," Elizabeth I constructs a female version of the Petrarchan lyric which includes her own response to the male voice of Petrarchism. As the poem opens, Elizabeth is struggling to make sense out of her thoughts and feelings:

> I grieve and dare not show my discontent,
> I love and yet am forced to seem to hate,
> I do, yet dare not say I ever meant,
> I seem stark mute but inwardly do prate.
> I am and not, I freeze and yet am burned,
> Since from myself another self I turned.[19]

Constrained by the lack of lyric conventions expressing female thoughts and feelings, Elizabeth also turns to Petrarch whose characteristic oxymorons enable her to explore the frustrations of her own personal and political situation: "e temo et spero, et ardo et son un ghiaccio / et volo sopra 'l cielo et giaccio in terra . . . et non ò lingua et grido . . ." ("I fear and hope, and burn and am of ice; and I fly above the heavens and lie on the ground . . . I have no tongue, and yet cry out," *RS* 134:2–3, 9).

"I grieve," "I love," "I do" – the repetitive syntax, the bluntness of the assertions, the allusion to the marriage vow, all make it seem clear that Elizabeth loves Monsieur and grieves at his departure but "dare[s] not say" or show she does. As the stanza unfolds and one clause after another breaks off unfinished, the language begins to look less bland and more enigmatic: discontent with what? forced by what? Exactly what did she mean to do or say? Is Elizabeth unable to say that it is Monsieur she loves, that she "meant to say" "I do" when asked, Do you Elizabeth take this man to be your lawfully wedded husband? Or does she feel constrained to say she loves him because she dares not say she is discontented with him? And just what does she mean by "I am and not"? Is she torn between saying I am in love, I am not in love? Or is she saying, I am what I claim, I am not what you think I am? As the stanza unfolds, the initial, relatively simple distinction between outer appearance and inner truth is replaced by vacillation and paradox.

The sudden shift to the past tense ("I do, yet dare not say I ever meant") suggests that everything has changed "Since from myself another self I turned." If the language is Petrarch's, the point of view is Laura's, for it is Laura who "turned" Petrarch away as we learn in Canzone 23: "She spoke, so angry to see that she made me tremble within that stone, hearing, 'I am not perhaps who you think I am'"; "Ella parlava sì turbata in vista / che tremar mi fea dentro a quella petra, / udendo: 'I' non son forse chi tu credi'" (*RS* 23:81–4). Because Petrarch's syntax pivots on the word "forse," the lines can either mean that Laura is uncertain how Petrarch sees her ('I am not who perhaps you think I am') or that she is herself not sure whether the way he sees her is an accurate representation of the way she is ('Perhaps I am not who you think I am'). Laura's words are not only tentative but also ambiguous, very like Elizabeth's "I am and not."

Canzone 23 is a watershed moment not only because it is so unusual for the *Rime* to quote Laura's words directly, but also because communication ceases at this moment of misunderstanding. Having ignored Laura's injunction, "make no word of this," "Di ciò non far parola" (*RS* 23:74), Petrarch faces the full force of her prohibition: Laura retreats behind a veil, and Petrarch seeks refuge in myths that dramatize his metamorphosis into what the world now calls a Petrarchan lover.[20] What he regrets, above all, is the loss of their conversation: "and I pardon more easily every other offense but the denial of that kind angelic greeting, which used to awaken my heart to its powers with a burning desire"; "et perdono / più lieve ogni altra offesa / che l'essermi contesa / quella benigna angelica salute" (*RS* 37:89–92). Banished from her presence, he writes poems about her, not to her. Since "[s]he does not deign to look so low as to care about our words" ("Ella non degna di mirar sì basso / che di nostre parole / curi," *RS* 70:25–7), he stops trying to use poetry to elicit her love and begins writing poetry to eternize his own love; i.e., he gives up trying to write poetry of courtship in order to explore instead the *monotonia*, the variations on a single theme, that are the essence of Petrarchan poetry.

In Canzone 23 the words Petrarch attributes to Laura remain unexplained, as enigmatic as they are ambiguous. Petrarch continues to pray that Laura will have her part of the fire that signifies passion (*RS* 65), and even imagines that one day she will be without her ice, and without her customary outer cloud (*RS* 66). Yet, it is not until Laura has died and gone to heaven that *The Triumph of Death* explains the cause of her anger: "Thou sawe'st what was without, not what within," Laura tells Petrarch, "A thousand times wrath in my face did flame, / My heart meane-while with loue did inlie burne" (*RS* 2:97–102).[21]

When Elizabeth writes, "I seem stark mute but inwardly do prate. / I am and not, I freeze and yet am burned," she sounds like Petrarch who writes because he cannot speak: "Words spoken aloud were forbidden me; so I cried out with paper and ink"; "le vive voce m'erano interditte, / ond' io gridai con carta et con incostro" (*RS* 23:98–9). By leaving one thought after another unfinished, Elizabeth hints at a secret meaning that lies both deep within the poem, at the level of the subtext, and outside the poem, in extenuating circumstances she "dare not" put into words.

Yet when Elizabeth writes "I do, yet dare not say I ever meant," she sounds less like Petrarch who has no qualms about broadcasting his love to the world, than like Laura, both the enigmatic Laura of Canzone 23 who takes Petrarch's heart saying, "make no word of this" – "Di ciò non far parola" (*RS* 23:74) and the more outspoken Laura of the *Triumph* who discloses her passion only to break off, saying "My loue dares speake no more" (*RS* 2:150). Elizabeth also sounds like Whythorne, whose songs and sonnets convey a "secret meaning" to those readers who are privy to the poet's "private affairs and secrets."[22]

Although the circumstances surrounding "On Monsieur's Departure" are unclear, the title, which appears in two of the three extant manuscripts, connects the poem with the departure of François, Duke of Alençon and later Anjou whose official title is Monsieur Frère du Roi. Monsieur, Elizabeth's last and most persistent foreign suitor, comes to England to court the queen on two separate occasions. The first time, he arrives traveling incognito, charms Elizabeth with his amorous talk, excites considerable gossip, and, after a brief but promising courtship, departs in January, 1579.

When Monsieur returns for the second time in 1581, the situation is far more complicated, and his suit elicits a bewildering array of responses from the queen. Elizabeth is distinctly less encouraging, for by then the Council has expressed serious reservations, and Stubb's *Gaping Gulf* has galvanized opposition to the marriage. Yet it is during this second visit that Elizabeth and Monsieur act out the betrothal ceremony, complete with an exchange of rings, described by the Spanish ambassador and recounted by Camden. Is Elizabeth sincere in her trothplight, moved by one last flurry of romantic yearning for a husband and child? Or is this a staged performance, calculated to placate Alençon so that he will agree to leave the country? Interpretations differ.

"On Monsieur's Departure" could conceivably be linked to either visit, depending on how one interprets both the poem and the courtship, but the long-standing acquaintance implied by "His too familiar care" (line 10) and the finality of the rupture in line 6 make the second visit more likely.[23] The problem is that by the time Monsieur is finally convinced to depart in February 1582, the courtship is essentially defunct, and Elizabeth is positively relieved to see him go. At that point, it is hard to imagine her writing, "I love and yet am forced to seem to hate, / I do, yet dare not say I ever meant."

The tumult, the vacillation and distress which give the poem its emotional intensity seem closer to what Elizabeth is feeling just after the betrothal ceremony when, having been convinced by her advisors to send Monsieur away, she "dare[s] not say" she "ever meant" to marry him. I would therefore gloss the title to mean, "in regard to Monsieur's departure," not, "at the time of Monsieur's departure."

The ambiguity of the language expresses a continuing vacillation between amorous desire and political design that plagued her in wake of the betrothal ceremony, when she knew the marriage was politically impossible, but when she also knew it was her last chance to marry and have a child. The evasive, mysterious imagery captures her conflicting feelings: "My care is like my shadow in the sun, / Follows me flying, flies when I pursue it, / Stands and lies by me, doth what I have done" (lines 7–9). The allusion to the care-cloth that is held over a couple's heads during the marriage-service implies that Elizabeth is still entertaining fantasies of a loving, caring bridegroom who "stands and lies by" her in the marriage bed [stands is slang for having an erection]. Monsieur's attentiveness makes her empathize with the suffering that her flight, her rejection, has caused him: "His too familiar care doth make me rue it" (line 10). She is still caught up in the excitement of the chase ("follows me flying"), though it has continued so long that it is losing its novelty and becoming a bit "too familiar." Bound by her "care" or public responsibility to suppress her "care" or personal desire, Elizabeth is left with the care, the mental suffering or burdened state of mind, which grows all the more oppressive the more she tries to escape.[24]

"Since from myself another self I turned" sounds definitive, implying that Elizabeth has turned away Monsieur, an other self she hoped to love. The line also implies that she has turned away "another" construction of herself, not only a self that has been "burned" by love but also a self that still at some level yearns to burn in love. Indeed, the more one examines the poem, the more conflicting the language seems.

As the poem ends, Elizabeth is still struggling to make peace with her decision to send Monsieur away: "Let me or float or sink, be high or low. / Or let me live with some more sweet content, / Or die and so forget what love ere meant" (lines 16–18). In representing herself as "soft and made of melting snow," Elizabeth resembles the aging Petrarch who is "Inwardly fire though outwardly white snow"; "Dentro pur foco et for candida neve" (*RS* 30:31–2). Yet she also distinguishes herself from him.

Petrarch continues to wonder whether "base desire" can ever be completely "extinguished by highest beauty" ("Or quando mai / fu per somma beltà vil voglia spenta?" *RS* 154:13–14), but as time passes, he is increasingly influenced by Laura's "speech full of high sweet high insights" ("col dir pien d'intelletti dolci et alti," *RS* 213:12) to "push on toward Heaven" ("sforzati al cielo," *RS* 204:12). One part of Elizabeth would also like to die and go directly to heaven where, freed from those low desires which are a momentary fantasy in *Rime* 22 and a fond memory in the *Triumph*, she could finally forget everything that love ever meant to her. Yet as the word "ere" [meaning both *earlier* and *ever*] also implies, another part of her would like to forget what love meant earlier – to Petrarch and Laura and their poetic heirs – so that she can be free to discover what love means now, to her. Part of her still yearns for "some more sweet content" – for some sweeter pleasure more like the climactic deaths of Donne's *Songs and Sonets* than like the living deaths of Petrarch's *Rime*.

On first reading, "On Monsieur's Departure" seems awfully vague, the images familiar and flat, the syntax held together by the loosest of logical connections, the dramatic situation a reworking of the conventional Petrarchan situation. Upon closer inspection, however, what emerges is not the "heavenly singing," "celeste cantar" (*RS* 220:10), the "high holy words," "l'alte parole sante" (*RS* 204:4) which make Laura the symbol of everything that is most high, exalted, and unreachable – but an Englishwoman's struggle to define herself, vaguely at first and more passionately by the end, as lyric author and speaker.

Constructed in three stanzas, each with the rhyme scheme of an English sestet, the formal structure of "On Monsieur's Departure" represents Elizabeth I's efforts to break away from the passivity and stasis imposed by the Petrarchan sonnet.[25] "[U]ntuned between two contraries" ("tra du contrari mi distempre" (*RS* 55:14)), Petrarch loves *and* hates, laughs *and* weeps, joys *and* suffers, simultaneously, eternally. Elizabeth's imagery seems virtually indistinguishable from these classic Petrarchan oxymorons – but only at first. By the end of the poem, the pounding repetition of Elizabeth's *or, or, or,* strives to sever the oxymoron so as to break away from the everlasting, undeniable, contradictory Petrarchan situation.

WHITNEY'S LETTER AND ADMONITION

Published in London in 1556–7, and forgotten by English literary history until recently, *The Copy of a letter to her Unconstant Lover, With an Admonitio^n to al yong Gentilwomen and to al other Mayds in general to beware of men'nes flattery* inserts into Elizabethan discourse the voice of a gentlewoman writing in verse, exercising an active, vocal role in her own courtship.

The Copy of a letter is not Petrarchan or Neoplatonic poetry, addressed to a literary elite; rather, it is a female-authored female complaint and a poem of courtship – and an epistolary one at that – written by an Elizabethan woman *"to her unconstant Louer."* As a genre, the male-authored female complaint traces its literary heritage back to Ovid's *Heroides*. Rather like the dramatic monologue, the complaint invites sympathy for its female speaker, even as it exposes her to the ironic judgment of the male writer and reader.

Whitney's letter combines the Ovidean tradition of the heroic epistle with popular epistolary verse and colloquial English speech. By publishing *The Copy of a letter* along *With an Admonitio^n to al yong Gentilwomen and to al other Mayds in general*, Whitney advises other Elizabethan women how to judge and use the rhetoric of courtship for themselves. By pairing the complaint with an *admonition*, Whitney extends one woman's personal experience of courtship to women in general.

The title, *The Copy of a letter, lately written in meeter* identifies the poem as the copy of an earlier amatory verse epistle that was actually sent to her unconstant lover.[26] Thus, the poem epitomizes and publicizes the

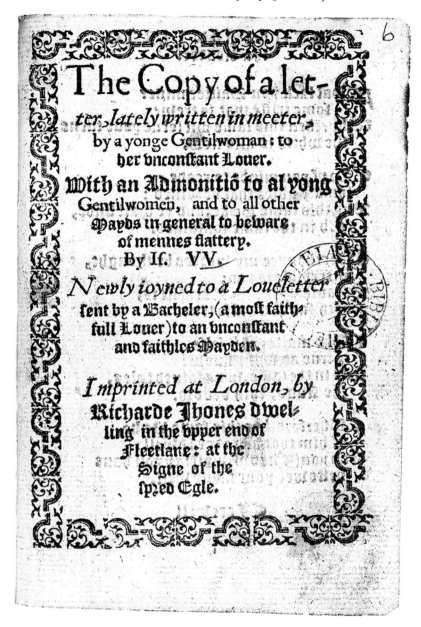

Figure 10 The title page from the only known copy of
The copie of a letter By Is[abella] W[hitney]

tendency of Elizabethan love poetry, not simply to represent a courtship, but to transact one. Perhaps Whitney's unconstant lover originally wooed her in poetry, or perhaps Whitney simply took it upon herself to construct the female side of a lyric dialogue of courtship. Whatever the actual circumstances, the letter and the admonition offer a rare opportunity to study the words of an Elizabethan woman, drawing on personal experience to teach other Elizabethan women the critical and interpretive skills they need if they are to judge and use the rhetoric of courtship for themselves.

The Copy of a letter begins by explaining that Whitney has just learned her betrothed is secretly planning to marry another woman: "As close as you your weding kept / yet now the trueth I he[ar]" (fo. A.2.r). Hoping that her skill "in meeter" will prove her worth and thus regain her betrothed's affections, *The Copy of a letter* begins positively with a combination of moral conviction that "the promises be kept / that you so firmly made" and amorous persuasion: "And yet it is not so far past / but might agayne be wonne" (fo. A.2.v, r).

Whitney has no desire to speak or act like Laura who "did in silence goe" because her "love dare[d] speak no more." Instead, she turns to mythological female figures such as Dido, Ariadne, and Medea who use their powers to win their love, only to be betrayed by male inconstancy. The bevy of classical allusions which pervade the body of the letter demonstrate Whitney's initiative and learning, giving her personal experience the force of mythic generalization. They also betray negative, angry undertones which it would be impolitic to express more openly. Instead of the conventional Petrarchan lover, blown hither and thither by the sighs and tears of unrequited, unfaltering love, Whitney tells the tale of Jason, who is condemned by the gods to wander the seas because he broke "the vowes: / That he dyd make so faithfully, / unto his louing Spowes" (fo. A.3.r). Alluding to Jason – and implicitly to her own unconstant lover – Whitney "muse[s] how he durst shew his face / to them that knew his wife" (fo. A.3.r).

Whitney cannot escape either the anger that the myths betray or the insecurity that her epistolary verses strive to contain. She frankly admits her limitations: for example, she knows she lacks Helen's beauty. Yet, the strength of her character and the force of her argument speak for themselves: "Thou knowst by prof what I deserue / I nede not to informe thee" (fo. A.4.v). By boldly admitting her love, Whitney coaches her unconstant lover, providing a text she hopes he will complete: "full boldly may you boast: / That once you had as true a Loue, / as dwelt in any

Coast" (fo. A.2.r). These lines are a particularly effective rhetorical strategy for a poem of courtship: they prepare an image for action, stressing
the role of the participant, urging her interlocutor to make it so by saying
so. The formulation reminds Whitney's unconstant lover that he can still
turn her directive speech act into the performative speech of marriage:
"then take me to your wife. / So shall the promises be kept, / that you
so firmly made: / Now chuse whether ye wyll be true, / or be of SINONS
trade" (fo. A.2.v).

Given the circumstances, Whitney knows her plea may fail. She
demonstrates her integrity and magnanimity by wishing him, "No
worser then I wish my selfe, / untill thy lyfe shal end" (fo. A.5.r). But
Whitney remains at once poignant and dignified, offering to release her
lover from his vows if she has lost his love and respect: "But if I can not
please your minde / for wants that rest in me: / Wed whom you list, I
am content, / your refuse for to be" (fo. A.4.r).

The title, *The Copy of a letter, lately written in meeter, by a yonge Gentilwoman:
to her vnconstant Louer,* exploits the reader's desire to eavesdrop on a "real"
courtship by claiming that the printed text is "the copy" of an epistolary
love poem Isabella Whitney actually sent to her erstwhile fiancé. Like so
many Elizabethan prefatory epistles, "The Printer to the Reader" encourages Whitney's readers to believe they are overhearing a lyric dialogue that
actually took place between the poet and a particular reader. It implies
that the story of her broken marriage contract is true, and suggests that
"many" of Whitney's readers "know" as much. Yet it also includes a
tantalizingly enigmatic disclaimer: "The matter of it selfe, / is true as
many know: / And in the same, some fained tales, / the Auctor doth
bestow." The "fained tales" refer both to the poetic license which enables
Whitney to tell a good story, and to the mythological tales that illustrate
the moral of her tale. Like Daniel's prefatory reference to the "priuate passions of my youth," the mention of "true" "matter," or real-life experience, makes the letter more tantalizing, while the "fained tales" make it
more widely applicable "to al other Maids being in Loue" (fo. A.5.v).

Perhaps the printer also means that the original letter has been corrected or altered to protect Whitney's reputation, but it seems unlikely
that the letter is completely fictional, for Whitney's second volume of
poetry, published six years later, contains a motley assortment of prescriptive verses and "familyar and friendly Epistles," which return again
and again to the chronic pain of her broken marriage contract, the way
one's tongue constantly returns to a sore in the mouth. The title poem,
A Sweet Nosgay, is a compendium of pious posies and practical advice

which defends free choice in marriage, while warning its readers to be wary of rejection and betrayal: "In louing, ech one hath free choyce, / or euer they begin, / But in their power it lyeth not, / to end when they are in" (fo. B. viii. r).

"A carefull complaynt by the vnfortunate Auctor" develops an image briefly mentioned in *The Copy of a letter*, comparing Whitney's own "endles griefes" to Dido's plight when Aeneas "tooke his flight, / And fowly brake his oth, / and promise made before" (fo. D.iii.r). The volume also contains an exchange of verse letters with a friend in which Whitney is still "bewaylynge her mishappes" (fo. D.v.v.), trying to come to grips with her thwarted engagement. In response, her friendly correspondent expresses sympathy and tries to cure Whitney's "heauy hart: and mind opprest" (fo. D.vi.v). Another verse epistle, addressed to her sister, implies that Whitney has become a professional writer because she no longer expects to become a housewife: "I know you huswyfery intend, / though I to writing fall / . . . / Had I a husband, or a House, / and all that longes therto / My selfe could frame about to rouse, / as other women doo" (fo. D.ii.r). The volume's last and probably best poem, "The Auctour's Wyll and Testament," begins with a barely veiled allusion to Whitney's own broken privy contract: "But many Women foolyshly, / lyke me, and other moe. / Doe such a fyxed fancy set, / on those which least desarue, / That long it is ere wit we get, / away from them to swarue. / But tyme with pittie oft wyl tel" (fo. E.ii.v).

The repeated references to Whitney's broken engagement, along with the growing confidence in her role as published poet and unmarried woman, suggest that *The Copy of a letter* represents a turning point in Whitney's life story, a watershed moment when the authority of poetry begins to transform the pain of rejection into the power of knowledge. The result is "a philosophical exercise" of the sort Foucault describes in *The History of Sexuality*: "[t]he object was to learn to what extent the effort to think one's own history can free thought from what it silently thinks, and so enable it to think differently."[27]

Whether *The Copy of a letter, lately written in meeter, by a yonge Gentilwoman*, is the copy of a letter actually sent by Isabella Whitney "to her vnconstant Louer" as the title and Whitney's other epistolary verses all suggest, or a fictionalized version of a letter which an Elizabethan woman like Isabella Whitney could send "to her vnconstant Louer," or personal testimony embroidered by poetic license as the dedicatory epistle implies and the evidence seems to suggest, the printed text nonetheless comprises, and gives us access to, an Elizabethan female discourse of courtship.

While the title asks us to read *a letter* as a poem of courtship, written to persuade Whitney's unconstant lover to honor his privy contract, the act of publication asks us to read *The Copy of a letter* as a female-author's rewriting of literary tradition. Whereas the conventional male-authored female complaint expresses the shame of an abandoned woman, Whitney's complaint lays the dishonor on her unconstant lover: "It shal your kindred stayne" (fo. A.2.v). By publishing *The Copy of a letter,* along with her initials and a title that declares the biographical truth of her charges, Whitney does, in fact, make her truth and his "falsenes manyfest in time" (fo. A.3.v). Mary Sidney's multivious syntax implies that Petrarch "didst for mercie calle with wearie thro[at] / In feare and shame" (*The Triumph of Death* 2:142–43); Isabella Whitney goes one step further, declaring that the shame and dishonor are not hers, but her unconstant lover's.

Whitney's letter addresses a specific social issue: a privy contract or private agreement to marry made in secret and broken in secret. Whitney might have retaliated by angrily denouncing all men, or she might have warned against the dangers of female passion, urging her female readers to accept marriages arranged by their parents. Or she might have threatened her unconstant lover with a lawsuit, since the ecclesiastical courts were regularly used to settle such disputes, and a prior contract took precedence over any subsequent contract.[28] But instead of casting herself as the weaker vessel and seeking protection from male authorities, from lawyers, judges, and kinfolk, Whitney takes action herself.[29]

Donning the conventional male garb of poet and suitor, she uses the strongest weapon available to her, the written word, to plead her case. By extending her moral indignation from her unconstant lover "whose falshood now is playne" (fo. A.2.v) to all those unconstant lovers through-out history and literature who "for their vnfaithfulnes, / did get per-petuall fame: / Fame: wherfore dyd I terme it so: / I should haue cald it shame" (fo. A.3.v), Whitney constructs her complaint as "a rejoinder in a given dialogue whose style is determined by its interrelationship with other rejoinders in the same dialogue."[30] But Whitney doesn't stop there. She publishes *The Copy of a letter to her Unconstant Lover, With an Admonitio^n to al yong Gentilwomen and to al other Mayds in general to beware of men'nes flattery,* thereby challenging cultural constraints on female silence and shamefastness, adding her voice to the larger social conversation about freely chosen courtships, secret marriage contracts, and clandestine marriages.

Figure 11 "Heere Learning Sits" – an emblem, written and illustrated by Isabella Whitney's brother Geffrey, which depicts learning as a woman holding a book.

Whitney's admonition, addressed "to all yong Gentilwomen: And to al other Maids being in Loue" (fo. A.5.v), begins with a peroration: "Ye virgins [that] from Cupids tentes / do beare away the foyle / Whose hartes as yet wth raginge loue / most paynfully do boyle. / To you I speake: for you be they, / that good aduice do lacke" (fo. A.5.v).[31] If this were written by a man to other men "whose hartes as yet wth raginge loue / most paynfully do boyle," it might sound like conventional Petrarchan love language. But as the poetry of "a *yonge Gentilwoman*," writing for publication to "*al yong Gentilwomen*" and "*all other Mayds in general*" (fo. A.I.r), this is completely novel and unprecedented. As female discourse, it is positively subversive. Given the code of ethics that equates female virtue with shamefastness and silence, it is hard to know what is more daring: Whitney's spirited kinship with all the other Elizabethan women who are boiling and raging with libidinous urges, or her claim to be a judge of men and a teacher of women. By appropriating male poetic

tradition and male instructional literature, Isabella Whitney joins
Margaret Tyler's challenge to those Elizabethans who say "that women
may not at al discourse in learning, for men lay in their claim to be sole
possessioners of knowledge."[32]

Whitney uses the power of print to urge other women to seize and
use the foil which they themselves are free to "beare away" from
Cupid's tent. [A "foil" is a wrestling throw which is almost a fall; a
weapon used in fencing; a mixture of tinfoil and mercury which is
placed behind a mirror to create a reflection; anything which serves to
adorn or set off another thing.] First, she urges "al other Maids being
in Loue" to pick themselves up after they are thrown down and before
they are completely fallen. Second, she punctures the ethical façade of
female silence, reminding Elizabethan women that they also have a
weapon, the power of speech, which they can and should use in the
fencing match of courtship. Third, she provides a mirror, or a contrast,
in which Elizabethan women can see themselves differently, set off or
adorned by a new and more beneficial set of ethical and social practices.

Although she begins by speaking as intrepidly as she can, Whitney
also expresses "some fear to speak and bashfulness besides." Yet, she hes-
itates to write, not because women are supposed to be silent (although,
of course, she knows they are), but because she realizes that giving "good
advice" about courtship is an enormously complex and difficult undertaking: "Oh, if I could good counsell g[iv]e, / my tongue should not be
slacke" (fo. A.5.v). Though she feels not quite equal to the task, Whitney
proceeds nonetheless: "But such as I can g[iv]e, I wyll, / here in few
wordes expresse." Much as Whythorne represents his life story as an
example for other men, "By which they may, if like chance do them
charge / That happed to me, the better know to deal / Therein,"
(Preface, lines 12–14). Whitney believes the knowledge derived from her
experiences will help other Elizabethan women who find themselves in
similar situations: "Which if you do obserue, it will / some of your care
redresse" (fo. A.5.v).[33]

Whitney thinks Elizabethan women ought to be free to choose their
own suitors, but she also thinks they need better counsel if they are to
decide for themselves "whether he be a louer true, / or do intend to
shrink" (fo. A.6.v). Citing her own experience as proof that courtship is
a risky venture, drawing analogies with sexually liberated female figures
such as Scylla "who thought her self most sure / to haue her whole
desyre" only to find herself like Whitney "cleane re[j]ect, and left

behind" (fo. A.7.r), Whitney's *Admonition* instructs her female readers how to claim the liberty and beware the dangers courtship offers.

Above all, women must learn to detect the artful performances of poet/lovers who, schooled by Ovid's "Arte of loue [which] doth teach them this same knacke," use "pleasant Songs" to woo and deceive:

> Some use the teares of Crocodiles,
>   contrary to their hart:
> And yf they cannot alwayes weep:
>   they wet their cheekes by Art. (fo. A.6.r)

At this climactic moment, Whitney turns and speaks directly to Elizabethan men: "Why haue ye such deceit in store: / haue you such craft wile: / Lesse craft the^n this god knows woll soon / us simple soules begile" (fo. A.6.r). The sudden shift in tone and audience shows that Whitney herself is not entirely free from the social codes that instruct Elizabethan women to rely on men's greater wisdom and strength. But, Whitney tells her female contemporaries, she herself has learned the hard way that Elizabethan men cannot be trusted to play their part honestly, "but still / delude us in this wise."

Elizabethan women simply cannot afford to think and act like "simple soules." Instead, they need to develop a more critical approach to male rhetoric, especially the poetry of courtship:

> Beware of fayre and painted talke,
>   beware of flattering tonges:
> The Mermaides do pretend no good,
>   for all their plesant Songs. (fo. A.6.r)

Citing the last two lines, Jones comments: "Even when her aim is to criticize the opposite sex, the ammunition that comes to hand is determined by a history of suspicious and condemnatory discourses about women."[34] That seems as telling as it is unfortunate, yet it is only the beginning of the story. By comparing deceitful male love songs to mermaids' songs, Whitney challenges sexual stereotypes, suggesting that anti-feminist stereotypes of vanity and inconstancy pertain not to Renaissance women but to Renaissance men.

Except for this momentary aside, Whitney's admonition is addressed to a female audience – "to all yong Gentilwomen: And to al other Maids being in Loue" (fo. A.5.v) and especially to "Ye virgins . . . whose hartes as yet wth raginge loue / most paynfully do boyle" (fo. A.5.v). The question she poses is this: how should virgins speak and act when they are "raging" and "boiling" with desire? Whitney does *not* tell them to be chaste, silent, and obedient. There are plenty of prescriptive texts which provide that kind of advice, but it is *not* "good advice." Instead, Whitney advises her female readers:

> Trust not a man at the fyrst sight,
>   but trye him well before:
> I wish al[l] Maids within their brests
>   to kepe this thing in store. (fo. A.6.v)

Clearly, this is a moment of great import, for Whitney interrupts the narrative to say that she wishes *all* maids to keep this particular piece of advice "in store" [meaning in their possession or in value and esteem]. Admittedly, the vagueness of "this thing" makes the last line sound somewhat anticlimactic. Yet, this is not merely a lapse in poetic authority. Rather, it is a clue (like Vavasour's and Elizabeth's evasive diction) that Whitney is referring to something so daring as to be unspeakable – and unprintable.

Whitney is not simply advising Elizabethan women to test their suitors before allowing themselves to fall in love, for the admonition addresses women whose hearts are already raging with love: "To you I speake: for you be they, / that good aduice do lacke" (fo. A.5.v). Whitney *is* urging her female readers to test their lovers "before" making a promise to marry, since, as *The Copy of a letter* asserts, she herself has been "paynfully" hurt by a broken marriage contract. This is certainly "good advice," but there is nothing particularly remarkable about it since Elizabethan sermons and marriage manuals are constantly warning men and women to beware hasty, clandestine marriage contracts. Therefore, I suspect that Whitney is offering her female readers some other "nugget of pure truth," not "to wrap up between the pages of your notebook and put on the mantelpiece forever," but "within their brests to ke[ep]."[35]

It is, Whitney declares, terribly important for women to test their suitors "before." Before what? Before making love, presumably. Premarital sex is not the sort of thing "a yonge Gentilwoman" is supposed to discuss – never mind write about and publish for all the world to see. (I don't even want to speculate about the kind of "proof" of her love which Whitney gave her own unconstant lover! "Thou knowst by prof what I deserue / I nede not to informe thee" [fo. A.4.v]) Whitney's advice to Elizabethan virgins is not only "good advice" – "Which if you do observe, it will / some of your care redress" (fo. A.5.v) – but it is also the kind of advice Elizabethan women clearly "lacke" and dearly need, for Elizabethan couples often begin sleeping together as soon as they are fast betrothed. In theory, a promise to marry followed by coitus constitutes a legally binding common law marriage; in practice, however, privy contracts are frequently broken, as the records of the ecclesiastical courts demonstrate.

Prescriptive texts are constantly warning young women to beware privy contracts: "For many men whan they can not obteyn theyr unclene desyre of the woman wyll promyse mariage, & thervpon make a contracte . . . after that done, they suppose they may lawfully vse theyr vnclene behauuor, and somtyme the acte and dede dothe folowe, vnto the great offence of god & theyr owne soules . . . for many tymes, after the vnlawful pleasure is past, discorde doth fall bytwene the partyes."[36] Unlike Whitforde and so many male moral authorities, Whitney does not denounce clandestine courtships and secret marriage contracts. Instead, she urges her female reader to "trye him well before," i.e., to postpone sexual intercourse until she has tested her suitor and determined whether he is planning to treat her the way the Earl of Oxford treated Anne Vavasour: "For triall shal declare his trueth, / and show what he doth think: / Whether he be a Louer true, / or do intend to shrink" (fo. A.6.v).

By agreeing to print an epistolary love poem and a didactic verse epistle written by an Elizabethan woman, the printer and bookseller are not only making a bold and unprecedented decision, they are making literary and social history. Yet, they seem uncomfortable about the fact that Whitney sets herself up as a critic of male rhetoric and a defendant of female sexuality, for they pair Whitney's poems with "A loue letter, or an earnest perswasion of a Louer: sent of late to a yonge Mayden, to whom he was betrothed . . . by W. G."

Unlike Whitney, W. G. does not declare his love in order to plead for his betrothed's answering love. Instead, he denounces and exposes his fiancée to the world: "thy fraude, (O faithlesse thou) / I mind to bring to light" (fos. B.2.r). When one stops to think about it, W. G.'s complaint is a rather odd substitute for the missing voice of Whitney's inconstant lover. What makes the manufactured dialogue between I. W. and W. G. seem peculiarly Elizabethan is that the composite text, constructed to expand the book's market, constitutes a far-reaching debate about courtship, women, and poetry. As Virginia Cox writes, "the use of the dialogue form may be seen as a symptom of an unease with the conventions which govern the transmission of knowledge within a society, and a desire to reform them by returning to a study of the roots of persuasion.

If a writer, or a group of writers, can no longer recognize themselves in the conventionalized 'addresser' of the prevailing monological genres, it makes sense to bring addresser and addressee together out into the open and leave them to thrash out for themselves a new and more acceptable statute of discourse."[37]

By pairing the two otherwise unconnected complaints, the composite text represents courtship and anti-feminism as alternative responses to a similar situation. To male readers angry at or hostile to women, W. G.'s conventional male complaint offers the definitive response to Whitney's novel and unprecedented female complaint. To readers who sympathize with Whitney, W. G.'s refusal to listen to his beloved's response proves that he is incapable of understanding or answering Whitney's letter. For readers prepared to consider both sides, the implied dialogue suggests a way out. Let Elizabethan women follow Whitney's advice and "trye him well before . . . For triall shal declare his trueth." Let Elizabethan men follow her lead, addressing Elizabethan women more directly, saying, "Ye, whose harte as yet wth raginge loue / most paynfully do[es] boyle. / To you I speake"(fo. A.5.v). The resulting dialogue will benefit both sexes, "Which if they do observe, it will / some of their care redress" (fo. A.6.v).

Together, Elizabeth's Petrarchan lyric and Mary Sidney's translation of the *Triumph of Death* reinterpret Petrarch's poetry, first from Laura's point of view and then from the point of view of an Elizabethan female reader and writer. Elizabeth's elusive diction embodies the ethical and verbal constraints which Elizabethan society imposes on Elizabethan women, even as her ambiguous syntax presses to the limit the ambiguities and contradictions of male poetic language. In "On Monsieur's Departure," Elizabeth I constructs an alternative female voice, enigmatic enough to raise fundamental questions about what "I am and not," and ambiguous enough both to preserve a politic silence and to express her desire for another self – a desire she cannot express as openly, either in her speeches to parliament or in marriage negotiations with the foreign ambassadors.

Much as Petrarch makes a lyric dialogue out of Laura's words, so too Mary Sidney and Elizabeth I make poetry by singing Laura's words back to Petrarch. In "singing for thee," they reconstruct his poems to suit their poetic and social purposes. By emphasizing the artful role Laura plays as participant in the lyric dialogue, they show that "true knowledge can only be attained through the battle, stressing the role of the participant, who in the course of [her] participation, it is hoped, will define situations with sufficient realistic accuracy to prepare an *image* for action."[38]

Mary Sidney and Elizabeth I are by no means typical Elizabethan women. Yet precisely because they are exceptional, they are in a position to exercise a powerful symbolic impact on Elizabethan discourse. "[O]pening up the range and richness of existing cultural traditions as potentially accessible and adaptable to the specific political and aesthetic interests of women," their initiative in wit and art is available to be taken up by other Elizabethan women such as Isabella Whitney, Anne Vavasour, or the Maydens of London.[39] Finally, the views expressed in Whitney's amatory, epistolary verse are closer to Mary Sidney's translation of the *Triumph* and Elizabeth Tudor's reconstruction of Petrarch's lyric than the differences in status and genre might suggest. By claiming the language of female desire, Whitney also takes active steps to overcome the "feare and shame" on account of which Laura "did in silence goe." By writing and publishing what had not yet been said in print by an Englishwoman, Whitney does in fact change the world by saying so.[40]

Together Mary Sidney's translation of Petrarch's *Triumph*, Elizabeth I's "On Monsieur's Departure," and Whitney's *Copy of a letter* and *Admonition* demonstrate that Elizabethan women are beginning to speak out as desiring subjects and resisting readers. When Mary Sidney translates Petrarch's fourteenth-century Italian into sixteenth-century English, infusing his words with her own intonation and interpretation, when Elizabeth I rejects the self-reflexivity of Petrarchan idolatry, "Since from myself another self I turned," and defines herself as a female agent and speaker, when Isabella Whitney dons the roles of poet and suitor, using her own experience and the idiom of daily life "to obtaine her wyll" and to urge *"al yong Gentilwomen"* and *"al other Mayds in general"* to do likewise (fo. A.7.r), their oppositional discourse declares the passion and pain of Elizabethan female subjects, even as it extends the critical faculties and rhetorical power of Elizabethan female readers and listeners.

7

Daniel's lyric dialogue of courtship

PETRARCHISM AND PSEUDO-PETRARCHISM

Renaissance poetry is a living language, adapting to a wide range of ideological, cultural, and social forces. In the preceding chapters, we examined some of the ways in which Elizabethan women use Renaissance lyric conventions: (1) as the given, or ready-made discourse of love, the generic type which can be adapted and altered, turned upside down or inside out, to woo a private, female lyric audience; (2) as the law, or norm, according to or against which lyric poets and audiences define themselves; (3) as the veil behind which more unconventional, and oftentimes explicitly sexual, aspects of courtship and seduction are both transacted and concealed; (4) as the conservative mode to which male rhetoric reverts when persuasion fails and courtship turns into its opposite, anti-feminism. This chapter analyzes one talented Elizabethan male poet, Samuel Daniel, who transforms both the lyric genre and the female complaint in corresponding ways.

Daniel's poetry of courtship, like Gascoigne's, dramatizes the transition from private manuscript to broader manuscript circulation to print. When *Astrophil and Stella* is pirated, Mary Sidney edits and publishes an authorized edition. When Daniel's sonnets are pirated in the same volume, he not only hastens to publish an expurgated, authorized edition, but he also continues to revise the text for years to come. Indeed, Gascoigne's revisions and concealments seem slight by comparison.

PIRATED POETRY

This untitled and largely forgotten sonnet sequence, identified only by the initials S. D., is at once one of the most conventionally Petrarchan and one of the most boldly innovative English Renaissance sonnet sequences. The pirated text bends and stretches conventional codes and tropes to elicit and accommodate the responses of a particular but unnamed Elizabethan female reader. For the sake of convenience, this chapter calls her Delia, although that name does not appear until 1592 when the sequence is revised and published with Samuel Daniel's signature and the title, *Delia*.[1]

The shorter, pirated version is a classic example of private love poetry, what Barthes calls "lover's discourse."[2] The "private passions" and "secrets" Daniel "neuer ment" for the public epitomize the ways in which poetry of courtship transacts a courtship. The pirated text, comprising a dedication and twenty-seven sonnets, tightly connected by repeated words, phrases, classical allusions, and images of law, finance, and religion, enacts a passionate but finally unsuccessful courtship and seduction of a particular though unidentified woman to whom the sequence is addressed. The first three poems, written after the courtship has reached an impasse, are Daniel's attempt to define the rules of the genre, and to explain how his private poetry of courtship should be read. The opening lines, filled with "wayling," "cares," and "griefe," introduce the traditional tale of a Petrarchan poet, frustrated by a cold, heartless Petrarchan lady. Yet no sooner does the unnumbered prefatory sonnet "Sigh out a storie of her cruell deedes / with interrupted accents of dispaire" than its conventional accents are "interrupted."

As the English sonnet form suggests and the last four lines of the prefatory sonnet explain, Daniel is adapting the lyric tradition to his own purposes, turning Petrarchan poetry of praise and blame into pseudo-Petrarchan poetry of courtship and seduction: "Presse to her eyes, importune me some good, / Waken her sleeping crueltie with crying, / Knock at her hard hart: say I perish for her" (lines 9–13). The clamorous verbs – say, press, importune, waken, knock, say – announce that the poems are deeds, directive speech acts addressed to a particular female reader. By collecting the poems and sending them off to make one last consummate plea, Daniel makes a concerted effort to carry on the courtship that the poems themselves enact.

Much like *The Copy of a letter* which lays the "shame" on Whitney's inconstant lover, Daniel's sonnet expresses his "feare this deed wil make the world abhor her." The shift from the present to the future tense highlights the contingent nature of the lyric act, dependent for its meaning on the female reader whom the poet/lover woos but does not control. The "deed" refers both to the poem itself, the embodiment of Daniel's act of courtship, and to her answering deed. Much as the poems in *A Hundreth Sundrie Flowres* – "Written by a Gentlewoman" and "An other

Sonet written by the same Gentlewoman" – fuse what is written *by* the poet/lover with what is said or done *by* the woman, Daniel's prefatory sonnet represents the female reader as an active participant in the lyric dialogue of courtship. Indeed, his deed is inseparable from hers because her reading recomposes his meaning. If she gives her assent, Daniel implies, the sequence will no longer need to be construed as a "monument" to Petrarchism, "that whosoeuer reedes, / May iustly praise and blame my loueles *Faire.*" But if the courtship fails, the sequence will revert to Petrarchan poetry of praise and blame, and Daniel's deed will make her both admired and abhorred.

The third sonnet, "The Onely Bird Alone that Nature Frames," is usually read as a talented, faithful translation of *Olive* 36. Daniel may well have chosen to translate this particular poem in order to develop the hint of female desire introduced by Du Bellay's phoenix, which seems, at first, to describe Olive, reborn into a new, more passionate self: "son âme est par flammes ravie / Des cendres naist un autre à luy semblable."[3] Daniel's remark, "Her ashes to hir shape new essence giues" (*PS* 3:14), uses the conventional trope of the phoenix but adjusts the meaning to suit his pseudo-Petrarchan persuasion.

Du Bellay's opening line – "L'unicq' oyseau (miracle esmerveillable)" – emphasizes the miraculous, unique quality of the phoenix. Daniel's revision emphasizes the monologic self-absorption (the "onely bird alone") which isolates the Petrarchan poet from his mistress. At first, Daniel's conceit seems to be talking about Delia in the third person; however, it soon becomes clear that Daniel is speaking directly to her, urging her to acknowledge and act on the passion that he sees that she feels – or that he says he sees that she feels.

Developing the hint of female desire implicit in Du Bellay's conceit, Daniel specifically associates the phoenix with his mistress who, "weary of the tedious life she liues, by fi[re] dies, yet finds new life in flames" (*PS* 3:2–3). Daniel urges his mistress to relinquish the lonely existence of the conventional sonnet lady who, phoenix-like, "flies haughty through our own skies" while the "silent flint of Love draws from it a subtle liquid fire that burns me in the coldest frost" (*RS* 185:5–12).[4] Rather than the cold, haughty Laura of the *Rime*, who veils her face to hide her desire, Daniel urges Delia to act more like the Laura of the *Triumph*, who makes her love "manifestlie plaine," saying, "In equale flames our louing heats were tryde" (*PS* 2:139); or like the female speaker of Elizabeth 1's "On Monsieur's Departure," who yearns both for a male lover – "another self" who "Stands and lies by me" – and for another, more passionate construction of herself, not cold and stony but "soft and made of melting snow."

Du Bellay's sestet begins with conventional Petrarchan oxymorons:

> O grand' douceur! o bonté souveraine,
> Si tu ne veux dure et inhumaine estre
> Sous ceste face angelique et seraine,
> Puis qu'ay pour toy du Phœnix le semblant,
> Fay qu'en tous points je lui sois ressemblant,
> Tu me feras de moy-mesme renaistre.

For a brief moment, it seems that Olive has more in common with the fiery, ravishing phoenix than her angelic, serene appearance suggests. Yet, in the end, the Petrarchist in Du Bellay pleads not for her answering love, but for the eternizing, narcissistic power of art.

Daniel's sestet also begins with the language of spiritual exaltation ("O Soueraigne light that with thy sacred flame") so characteristic of Petrarch's *Rime*, but ends with an erotic climax closer to *Astrophil and Stella* 71 or "The Canonization":

> thy sacred flame
> Consumes my life, reuiue me after this,
> And make me (with the happie bird) the same
> That dies to liue, by fauour of thy blisse.
> This deed of thine shall shew a Goddesse power,
> In so long death, to grant one liuing hower. (*PS* 3:9–14)

Although it is difficult to know how Daniel read Du Bellay, his sonnet redoubles the phoenix's power and passion, associating it not only with himself but also with Delia. Rather like Donne and his mistress who are joined in passion and "at [their] owne cost die," Daniel's phoenix combines the spiritual and erotic double meanings of "die" [meaning both the end of life and sexual climax] and "blisse" [meaning both spiritual ecstasy and sexual climax]. Alluding back to the seductive pun that concludes the preceding poem, "Once let her loue indeed"(*PS* 2:14) – and in deed! – Daniel urges Delia to act on her desire: "reuiue me," "make me," "this deede of thine shall shew a Goddesse power." One has only to imagine what a Greek goddess is capable of doing in one living hour to understand why Daniel removed this sonnet from the first and all subsequent authorized editions.

At times, Delia looks and acts very much like a conventional sonnet lady, but at other times she seems to be giving Daniel some distinctly unconventional encouragement, or so the next poem implies: "Teares, vowes and praiers gaines the hardest hearts" (*PS* 4:1). Just as Daniel's repetitive, gloomy rhetoric is on the verge of sinking into conventional Petrarchan idolatry – "Though frozen will may not be thawed with teares, / Though my soules Idol skorneth all my vowes, / Though all my praiers be made to deafned eares, / No fauour though, the cruel faire allowes" (*PS* 4:9–12) – the final couplet suddenly finds Delia warming to his persuasion:

> Yet will I weepe, vowe, praie to cruel shee,
> Flint, frost, disdaine, weares, melts and yeelds we see. (*PS* 4:13–14)

If one begins with the assumption that Daniel is a weak, imitative poet, one will perceive and catalogue his indebtedness, as virtually all twentieth-century scholars and critics of Daniel's poetry have done. If, on the other hand, one entertains the possibility that he, like "[e]very strong poet caricatures tradition," and is "necessarily mis-read by the tradition that he fosters," then one will be prepared to see that Daniel, like all strong poets, is "so severely mis-read that the generally accepted, broad interpretations of [his] work actually tend to be the exact opposites of what the poems truly are." Earlier twentieth-century scholars, discovering profound debts to Italian and French poetry, describe his sonnets as translations, not perceiving how radically and systematically Daniel transforms the tropes he appropriates.[5] Rees astutely observes that Daniel regularly condenses Du Bellay's sonnets into three quatrains, only to conclude that Daniel destroys the drama of the original conclusions. I would argue that, rather than being insensible to Du Bellay's artistry, Daniel is deliberately making room for his own unconventional, extremely dramatic conclusions, staging a characteristically Elizabethan undoing of Petrarchan idolatry.

Daniel's "Why doth my Mistres credit so her glasse" is a skillful translation of Desportes' *Amours d'Hippolyte* 18. Daniel may have admired the Frenchman's more erotic and persuasive language. Regardless of how Daniel read Desportes, Daniel's use of the English sonnet form signals an affinity (as so often happens in *Astrophil and Stella*) with Elizabethan challenges to Petrarchan convention.[6] Daniel begins by echoing Desportes, and asking the reasons for Delia's narcissism. He concludes by asking her directly, in his own words, whether it must persist:

> Why doth my Mistres credit so her glasse,
> Gasing hir beautie dein'd hir by the skies,
> And doth not rather looke on him (alas)
> Whose state best shewes the force of murthering eies. (*PS* 5:1–4)

What is the appropriate answer to such a question? Because Laura did? Because Petrarchan poetry offers no alternative? "With an awareness of the games played with his own poetic traditions," a poet "can seem a considerable craftsman at the very least, and a considerable innovator at the very best," Colie writes, for "reliance on the system" can "in fact subvert the system."[7] In asking why Delia sits gazing at herself – in the sense of *looking vacantly about* – Daniel raises the possibility that Delia might gaze in another sense, opening her eyes with astonishment as she looks beyond the idealized, objectified image of "Woman" to a new vision of herself – a self that burns in love.

In *Rime* 45, Petrarch chastises Laura for a narcissism that is the poetic reflection of his own self-absorption. Separated from Laura by the "miserable exile" which begins in Canzone 23, Petrarch imagines himself looking over Laura's shoulder as she gazes at herself in the mirror. As he extols her beauty and condemns her female vanity, Petrarch describes what she sees, in effect defining what she sees as the reflection of what he imagines. The very terms of the fantasy show that the narcissistic impasse has already inevitably occurred: "Ma s' io v'era con saldi chiovi fisso, / non dovea specchio farvi per mio danno / a voi stessa piacendo aspra et superba" ("But if I had been nailed there firmly, a mirror should not have / made you, because you pleased yourself, harsh and proud to my harm," *RS* 45:9–11).

It is tempting to dismiss these lines as conventional Petrarchan rhetoric and move on. Yet one cannot pause to visualize the image without squirming. Just where does the poet wish to have been nailed? To a cross, perhaps, across from Laura's dressing table, in place of her mirror, so that she will see her beauty reflected in his objectifying and controlling gaze? Or does he wish to be nailed to her eyes so that her narcissistic gaze can never drive him – "m'avete / scacciato del mio dolce albergo fora; / misero esilio" (*RS* 45:5–7) – from his sweet dwelling there? Regardless, he is nailed, which places her in an intolerable position, watching him pinned and wriggling on the wall, feeling his pain driven straight into her eyes.

This is not a Christ-like image of self-sacrifice, designed to save Laura from her narcissism. Instead, it is a performative gesture, constructed to eternize Petrarch's power over her. What can a woman say to such a poem? Nothing. She is successfully silenced by an image that obliterates any possibility of response. "By accusing his persona of an idolatrous passion Petrarch was affirming his own autonomy as a poetic creator," Freccero writes in "The Fig Tree and the Laurel: Petrarch's Poetics." "[T]he love must be idolatrous for its poetic expression to be autonomous."[8]

In his mirror poem, Desportes also represents Hippolyte's beauty as a reflection of his art – "Mirez-vous dessus moy pour les connoistre mieux."[9] Her narcissism, like that of Laura and so many Petrarchan ladies, is the reflection of the poet's idolatrous love. A reader familiar with Petrarch and Desportes may well be tempted to read Daniel's version in much the same way: "Then leaue your glasse, and gaze your selfe on mee, / That myrror showes the power of your face" (*PS* 5:9–10); i.e., admire yourself mirrored upon me if you wish to know the power of your beauty. But unlike the French "mirez-vous," the English word, "gaze," is not a reflexive verb; therefore, Daniel's translation makes better sense grammatically as an intensification of the imperative, i.e., "you yourself gaze on me."

When Hippolyte looks at Desportes, what she sees is her conventional power ("Aussi vous connoistrez le pouvoir de vos yeux," line 7) to kill the poet with her disdain: "Ma mort de vos beautez" (my death from your beauties, line 9). When Daniel transposes the "force of murthering eies" from line 9 to the first quatrain, he establishes Delia's conventionally murderous power, only to overturn it in the following lines. Just as G. G.'s riddle invites his quick-witted female interlocutor to look at him and say, "I would that eye were mine," Daniel's sestet urges Delia to look back, and to see the "power of [her] face" as a positive force. By placing the emphasis on *her* gaze, Daniel urges her to act on *her* desire.[10] Passion lends her power, he seems to be saying – the power to say, "I do," which English marriage law gives both men and women, in theory if not always in practice.

In *Rime* 45 Petrarch seeks closure in a reminder of Narcissus's fate: "certo, se vi rimembra di Narcisso, / questo et quel corso ad un termino vanno" ("Certainly, if you remember Narcissus, this and that course lead to one goal," *RS* 45:12–13). This charge, more a lugubrious acceptance of what will happen, because it has already happened over and over again, than a persuasive warning against what need not happen, dissolves into a final sigh of admiration: "ben che di sì bel fior sia indegna l'erba" ("although the grass is unworthy of so lovely a flower," *RS* 45:14). In comparing Laura to Narcissus, a creature so self-involved that she is incapable of loving another, Petrarch implicitly allies himself with Echo, the nymph who falls in love with Narcissus and eventually withers away with frustration, her body turned to flint, her voice reduced to echoing a never-to-be-answered desire. But ironically, the Petrarchan poet is less like Echo than like Narcissus, so absorbed in the reflection of his own desire that he is incapable of hearing Echo's answering love.

When Echo first falls in love with Narcissus, she still has a body and a voice.[11] Daniel's version of the Narcissus myth reminds Delia that Echo retains the crucial power of deciding which syllables to infuse with her own particular preferences. Citing this power to deconstruct logic and to re-construe meaning as a model for the female lyric audience, Daniel urges Delia to choose a more active role – the role Laura plays in the *Triumph*, where, "singing for thee," she infuses his words with her desire.

Daniel invites Delia to reclaim the voice of female desire, lest she end up even colder than Narcissus:

> To admire your forme too much may danger bee,
> *Narcissus* changd to flower in such a case:
> I feare your change not flower nor *Hiacynth*,
> *Medusas* eye may turne your heart to flint. (*PS* 5:9–14)

Petrarch complains that Laura's chilling virtue has "the power over [him] that Medusa had over the old Moorish giant" (*RS* 197:5–6). By contrast, Daniel warns Delia that she "may" be changed to a stone. He hopes to prevent her from becoming what she is not yet: a typical Petrarchan lady, cold, hard, and unyielding. Petrarch strikes the flint of his memory to turn Laura into gorgeous poetry; Daniel strikes the flint of Delia's heart in the hopes of setting her passions aflame.

Daniel's concluding reference to Narcissus is not a melancholy acceptance of Petrarchan love, "begotten by despair / Upon Impossibility" (to borrow Marvell's brilliant "Definition of Love"). Rather, it is a sharp warning that if Delia accepts the traditional female role, both she and he will lose the power to choose pleasure, to exercise knowledge, and to construct lovers' discourse.[12] But if Delia has the courage, she can redefine the role of the sonnet lady, thereby saving them both from being petrified by literary and social convention.

Encouraged by signs that his lyric courtship is melting her resistance, Daniel presses his suit more aggressively in Sonnet 6, a translation of *Olive* 10, which ends with another original and highly seductive couplet: "Yet, least long trauels be aboue my strength; / Good Ladie, lose, quench, heal me now at length!" (*PS* 6:13–14). The double puns on "travels," referring both to the endlessly frustrating Petrarchan sea voyage and to the travail of a prolonged sexual encounter, and "lose," meaning both ruin and merge with, make Daniel's persuasive purpose quite clear. Yet despite the imperatives – or perhaps because of the imperatives – the result is disappointing. Daniel has no power over Delia; his commands have no illocutionary force without her assent. He has yet to realize that the more empathetic or conciliatory his persuasion, the more likely its chance of success.

The next sonnet represents the poet/lover as a failed Pygmalion, unable to enjoy the beautiful statue he himself created and now so passionately desires:

> For haplesse Io euen with mine owne desires,
> I figured on the table of my hart
> The goodliest shape that the worlds eye admires,
> And so did perish by my proper arte.
>
> And still I toyle to change the Marble brest
> Of her, whose sweete Idea I addore,
> Yet cannot finde her breath vnto my rest,
> Hard is her heart, and woe is me therefore.
>   O blessed he that ioyes his stone and arte,
>   Vnhappie I to loue a stonie harte. (*PS* 7:5–14)

As long as Daniel sees Delia as the reflection of "mine owne desires," as a marble statue of his own making, as "my proper arte," his persuasion is bound to fall on deaf ears. Petrarch recognizes the problem and explains it brilliantly: "Misero me, che volli / quando primier sì fiso / gli tenni nel bel viso / per iscolpirlo, imaginando, in parte / onde mai né per forza né per arte / mosso sarà fin ch' i' sia dato in preda / a chi tutto diparte! / né so ben anco che di lei mi creda"; "Miserable me! What was I doing when for the first time I kept them so fixed on her lovely face, to sculpture it for imagination in a place whence it would never be moved by any art or force, until I became the prey of Death, who separates all things? Nor do I know what to think of her" (*RS* 50:63–70). Even as the years pass and her face begins to show the signs of age, Laura remains the same heavenly figure, frozen forever by Petrarch's imagination, eternized by his poetry. Having become a work of art, she can "never be moved by any art or force." But when Daniel fails to bring his Galatea to life, he is forced to admit that Delia is not his construction but his lyric audience, a female subject whose thoughts and deeds are not his but hers.

Daniel's Pygmalion sonnet seems to end gloomily, almost lapsing back into a frustrated Petrarchism Daniel ardently wishes to escape. Yet the final couplet still offers Delia a choice: "O blessed he that ioyes his stone and arte / Vnhappie I to loue a stonie harte." Either she can keep her stony heart, reducing him to the sad state of a Petrarchan lover, or, Daniel hints ever so delicately, she can quicken his desires with her art. By speaking and acting so that her "breath" enlivens his "rest," she can "joy" both his "art" and her "heart." Since, "joy," as a transitive verb means both to enjoy and to bring enjoyment to, she is free both to enjoy his art and to fill it with joy, even as she is free to fill her own heart with joy which he too enjoys. Indeed, the pun on stone as testicles evokes the image of a hardness capable of producing even more joy.

GLORYING IN HER ART

If genre is a mechanism for excluding undesirable readings, what happens to traditional codes of meaning when an Elizabethan male poet/lover invites a female reader/listener to answer that overwhelming question Petrarch's *Rime* never quite asks: what do *you* desire?[13] For a pseudo-Petrarchan poet whose goal is to court or seduce a female reader or listener, the sonnet sequence is especially appealing precisely because as a genre it is so malleable. Composed incrementally in brief, fourteen line segments, it readily adapts to the responses it both anticipates and generates.

When the more overtly erotic constructions of Sonnets 3–7 fail to warm Delia's heart, Daniel tries a very different rhetorical strategy. Rather than emphasizing the arts he uses to construct her according to his desire, he describes her role as lyric audience, delineating the arts she uses with him:

> Her voice betraies me to hir hand and eie,
> My freedomes-tyrant, glorying in hir art:
> But (ah) sweete foe, small is the victorie
> With three such powers to plague one silly hart. (*PS* 8:9–12)

Petrarch's catalogues of praise conventionally include Laura's heavenly voice, her golden hair, and her glorious eyes. Daniel mentions but does not describe Delia's voice, hand, and eye. Unmodified, the nouns stand for the power and art she claims as participant in the lyric dialogue of courtship: her voice has the power to say, yes, I do, her hand the power to give herself in marriage, her eye/I/aye the power to accept a suitor who joys her hand and eyes. "[G]lorying in hir art" rather than submitting to his poetic authority, "her voice" expresses symbolically what "hir hand and eie" enact physically: the legal and spiritual freedom to marry or not as she so desires.

Daniel is teasing her, accusing her of betraying him and destroying his freedom. Yet in calling her a tyrant, he betrays his residual belief that power is by rights his to wield: with his voice (symbolic of his rhetorical power), his hand (symbolic of his superior strength and art), and his eyes (symbolic of his male desire). Yet, the lyric dialogue of courtship has taught him that she will never be moved by any art that tries to force her into a role she does not choose. Accordingly, he sets out to seek her assent with tenderness, deference, and self-deprecating humor: "But (ah) sweete foe, small is the victorie / With three such powers to plague one silly hart." At this point, Daniel's only recourse is to submit himself to her: "Yet my soules sovereigne, since I must resigne, / Raigne in my thoughts, my loue and life are thine" (*PS* 8:12–14). Unless he wants to play the hated tyrant, he "must resigne" his position of power, surrendering his "loue and life" to her governance.

By introducing the language of female sovereignty, Daniel situates the poem firmly in Elizabethan England, where Elizabeth I's presence on the throne raises such important questions about the relationship between power and courtship.[14] How can patriarchy, which subordinates women to men, coexist with courtship which gives a mistress power over the man who woos her? Conversely, how can Elizabethan men, living in a patriarchal society which gives them power over women, submit themselves to female sovereignty? Not surprisingly, this sonnet, which comes as close as any of Daniel's sonnets to exploring the sexual politics inherent in the politics, poetry, and practice of Elizabethan courtship, also does not appear in the authorized first edition.

In the pirated sequence, the next sonnet begins where this one ends: "Raigne in my thoughts, faire hand, sweete eye, rare voice, / Possesse me whole, my harts Triumuirate: . . . What can I doo but yeeld, and yeeld I doo, / And serue them all, and yet they spoyle me too!" (*PS* 9:1–2, 13–14). This poem tries to transform Daniel's previous submission into a yet another barely veiled, pseudo-Petrarchan proposition. The boldly seductive suggestion, "Possesse me whole," the repeated promise of yielding, and the final suggestion that she "spoyl" him (meaning to strip him of clothes and armor, to plunder and ravage him) all conspire to revive the erotic pressure of the preceding sonnets. The result is disastrous, as the following poem reports: her "nayes sharp poynted set vpon my brest, / Martyres my life" (*PS* 10:10–11).

As Daniel's courtship unfolds, the political and sexual conflicts which these poems attempt to resolve overwhelm them, disrupting their happy endings. Unable to spark her desire with his art, Daniel proceeds to portray Delia, not as a Petrarchan lady, benevolently concealing her passion to assure his salvation, but as "the Slie Inchanter" – a black magician plotting his death, sticking pins into a voodoo image of him. With this angry and, from an Elizabethan woman's point of view, incendiary charge of witchcraft, the courtship is in danger of reverting to its binary opposite: anti-feminism. No wonder this complex and intriguingly unconventional sonnet is also omitted from the first and all subsequent authorized editions.

Remembering his persuasive purpose, Daniel once again tries to moderate his criticism with a more solicitous final couplet: "Naught could (saue this) my sweetest faire suffice / To trie her arte on him that loues her best" (*PS* 10:13–14). By making himself the object of her art, Daniel recognizes her power as female lyric audience, the power Sidney's Laura declares when she says, "These artes I us'd with thee" (*PS* 2:109). But the gesture is too little, too late.

After Delia's "nayes" squelch the exuberant, erotic persuasions of Sonnets 3–7, Daniel sounds more and more like a conventional Petrarchan poet, complaining bitterly of her icy disdain. In Sonnet 11, a translation of Du Bellay, *Olive* 91, instead of subverting the Petrarchan posture by adding a persuasive, seductive couplet of his own making, Daniel strengthens Du Bellay's anger and misery. Making the comparison to "lions," "*Hircan* Tygers," and "ruthlesse Beares" much harsher, Daniel preserves the bleakness of the conclusion: "Yeeld to the Marble thy hard heart againe: / So shalt thou cease to plague, and I to paine" (*PS* 11:12–14).

In Sonnet 12 Daniel admits that, despite his optimistic expectations, unbeknownst to himself, he has been lost at sea, foundering in that archetypal Petrarchan ship:

> Hard by th'inconstant sands of false reliefe,
> Where two bright starres which led my view apart,
> A Sirens voice allur'd me come so neare,
> To perish on the marble of her hart. (*PS* 12:8–11)

Was he deliberately led astray by false signals from her eyes and voice? Or was he mistaken in reading her glances as signs of encouragement? Regardless of who misunderstood whom, what makes this sonnet so moving is the simple, parenthetical comment, "A danger which my soule did neuer feare" (*PS* 12:12). Despite their differences, Daniel never thought he would reach these desperate straits.

His witty seduction having failed miserably, Daniel, still very much enamored, tries to win Delia's good graces with the idealizing language of Petrarchism. Sonnet 13 describes her as the chaste Cinthia. Sonnet 14 professes his "chast desire," his "true heart and faith vnfaigned" (*PS* 14:1–2). Alluding to but trying to put behind him the erotic subtexts that

"Bewraye[d] my Loue with broken words halfe spoken" (*PS* 14:6), Sonnet 14 exalts Delia as an angel or goddess – "her which sits in my thoughts temple sainted" *PS* 14:(7) – only to dissolve into a bitterness so uncontrollable that it disrupts the very rhythms of the poetry: "Ănd layes / tŏ víew / mў vúl / tŭre-gnáwen / héart ópen" (*PS* 14:8). Feeling as if he has been flayed open by a rapacious vulture, and sounding very much like Petrarch when he complains, "et la colpa è di tal che non à cura," "and the fault is hers who does not care" (*RS* 71:45), Daniel cannot stop himself from laying the blame entirely on her: "Let this suffice; the whole world it may see, / The fault is hers, though mine the most hurt bee" (*PS* 14:13–14). Daniel is on the verge of sinking into the kind of frustration that turns all too easily into anti-feminism.

Still hoping to find a way of resolving their differences, Sonnets 15 and 16 confront Delia's objections more openly, insisting that his "young desires" are the result, not of a base desire to deceive and dishonor her, but of an exalted desire for the spiritual and physical conversation of reciprocal love: "Oft haue I told hir that my Soule did loue hir" (*PS* 15:9, 13).[15] Yet this more elevated Petrarchan rhetoric fails just as miserably as did the earlier pseudo-Petrarchan persuasion, and the sequence plummets to its emotional nadir:

> Way but the cause, and giue me leaue to plaine me,
> For all my hurt, that my harts Queene hath wrought it,
> Shee whom I loue so deare, the more to paine me,
> Withholds my right, where I haue dearely bought it.
>
> Dearely I bought that was so highly rated,
> Euen with the price of bloud and bodies wasting,
> Shee would not yeeld that ought might be abated,
> For all shee saw my Loue was pure and lasting.
>
> And yet now scornes performance of the passion,
> And with hir presence Iustice ouerruleth,
> Shee tels me flat hir beauty beares no action,
> And so my plee and proces shee excludeth: (*PS* 16:1–2)

On one level, the sonnet elevates Delia, depicting her in language worthy of Queen Elizabeth herself: "my harts Queene." On another level, however, it implies once again that Delia is a tyrant who has taken advantage of his courtship to exercise her power in a cruel, unjust manner: "And with hir presence Iustice ouerruleth." On yet another level, it continues to transact the courtship, reminding her that his long-suffering suit – "For all shee saw my Loue was pure and lasting" – has given her ample opportunity to "trye him well before," as Isabella

Whitney advises her female readers. On still another level, it makes explicit the coded erotic persuasion that has been implicit throughout: "she scornes performance of the passion." The uneasy conjunction of sexual seduction, justice, and material considerations implies that the courtship is foundering over the differences in both sexual mores and social status.

When Daniel complains, "Shee tels me flat hir beauty beares no action," he sounds less like a Petrarchan lover than like an Elizabethan man, complaining to a male peer. Daniel clearly expects his male interlocutor to affirm his own view of the situation. Yet the poem's meaning and purpose continue to be informed by the ongoing lyric dialogue with Delia: "Shee tels me flat . . . " "Shee" is much more than a metaphor for his worldly aspirations; rather "Shee" is the locus or embodiment of his aspirations, social, spiritual, and physical.

The poem concludes by seeking wider moral support: "What wrong shee doth, the world may well perceiue it, / To accept my faith at first, and then to leaue it" (*PS* 16:13–14). Ironically, Daniel invokes a broad, public audience at the very moment when he prostitutes himself, reducing both the poetry and the courtship to a financial transaction in which she cheats him of the sexual pleasure he has paid for dearly by writing poem after poem: "Shee whom I loue so deare, the more to paine me, / Withholds my right, where I haue dearely bought it." Extremely painful from his point of view but deeply insulting from hers, this remarkable poem is yet another secret suppressed by the authorized first edition.

For a number of poems Daniel indulges in self-justification, chastising Delia for misleading him, and actually expecting her to confirm his criticism of her: "Yet let hir say that shee hath done me wrong, / To vse me thus and know I lou'd so long" (*PS* 20:13–14). Whitney's *Copy of a letter* uses an analogous but much more tactful rhetorical strategy, when she asks her inconstant lover to say how much she loves him. Daniel writes the speech he hopes she will utter which might be an effective, persuasive strategy for a poem of courtship, if it were not for the fact that Daniel asks Delia to abrogate her point of view – to "say that shee hath done me wrong." Not surprisingly, this rhetorical strategy fails just as miserably as all the previous ones.

SO HIGH ASPIRING

As time passes, Daniel's fury begins to abate. Sonnet 23 begins with the traditional Petrarchan trope of the poet, dying of frustrated desire. But unlike Petrarch who continues to write sonnets long after Laura's death, Daniel imagines himself dead and waiting to welcome his beloved to a heavenly bed. Filled with a new sense of hope that the relationship will begin over again, more positively this time, Daniel spontaneously shields her from criticism: "If anie aske, why that so soone I came? / Ile hide her fault, and say, it was my lot" (*PS* 23:9–10).

This fantasy of feigned absolution produces an expression of heart-felt forgiveness, and in the following poem, for the first time, Daniel accepts his share of the blame:

> Yet her I blame not, though she might haue blest me
> But my desi[re]s wings so high aspiring;
> Now melted with the Sunne that hath possest me,
> Downe doo I fall from of[f] my high desiring (*PS* 24:5–8).

Alluding to the spiritual transcendence, the "high holy words," Laura represents in the *Rime*, Daniel's "high desiring" and "high aspiring" strive to rise above the physical passion, social aspirations, and material considerations which caused the courtship go awry. This sonnet is a peace offering: "These Oliue braunches mercie still exorteth. / These tributarie plaints with chast desires. / I send those eyes" (*PS* 25:4–6). Not addressed directly to her, intended to assuage rather than to pressure or force, the persuasion remains indirect and attenuated.

Then, without warning, Daniel falls from the height of his "high desiring" to a new low, at once psychological, literary, and social:

> Raising my hope on hills of high desire,
> Thinking to scale the heauen of her hart,
> My slender meane presumes too high a part:
> For disdaines thunderbolt made me retire,
> And threw me downe to paine in all this fire,
> Where lo I languish in so heauie smart. (*PS* 27:1–6)

The entire poetic seduction plunges from the transcendent level of Petrarch's *Rime* to the base economic calculations of Whythorne's auto-biography, and Daniel frankly admits that a poetics of courtship only allows for human agency within structural constraints imposed by wealth and status.

The sequence comes to an end with a sobering recognition of the limits of poetic power: "th'attempt was far aboue my Art, / Her state brooks not poore soules should come so nie hir" (*PS* 27:7–8). Banished from her presence for pressing his suit too aggressively, Daniel collects the poems and sends them to her as one final, desperate attempt to win her love and forgiveness. He now realizes that the poetry with which he hoped to buy her love is worthless unless she agrees to recognize the sonnets as currency, worthy of exchange for her higher social status and greater material wealth.

A cocky young man at the beginning of the sequence, Daniel sounds older and sadder but also more compassionate and fair-minded by the end. Events beyond his control have forced him to confront what remains implicit throughout: all his artistic talent cannot command her love. She is what he cannot construct or control – the private lyric audience, a female subject whose existence outside the poem enables her either to affirm or to scorn his lyric suit. Having no authority over her, being, in fact, socially inferior to her, he cannot bring the sonnet sequence to a happy conclusion unless she decides to affirm his lyric "deeds" with her lyric response.

PRIVATE PASSIONS AND SECRETS

The pirated sonnet sequence we have been examining is printed among the "Poems and sonnets of sundry other noblemen and gentlemen," in Newman's pirated edition of Sidney's *Astrophil and Stella*. Some scholars suspect Daniel of conspiring with Newman to have the book printed, but he is no Gascoigne. Not only is Daniel traveling in Italy when the poems are published in September, 1591, but he also returns home immediately, and works feverishly, revising the sequence in ways that suggest it was never intended for publication.[16]

Only five months later, in February 1592, the authorized first edition appears in print, prefaced by a dedication to Mary Sidney: "Right honorable, although I rather desired to keep in the priuate passions of my youth, from the multitude, as things uttered to my selfe, and consecrated to silence: yet seeing I was betraide by the indiscretion of a greedie Printer, and had some of my secrets bewraide to the world, vncorrected: doubting the like of the rest, I am forced to publish that which I neuer ment."[17] Daniel's disavowal is an astute advertising gimmick, for what is more enticing to potential book-buyers than hints of private love talk and traces of secret passions? Still, the bitterness of Daniel's tone, combined with an odd syntactic obfuscation, suggests that something less transparently self-advertising and more anxiously self-protective is taking place. Manuscripts and type can be corrected or uncorrected, but how can secrets be corrected – or uncorrected? And what is Daniel so anxious to hide?

Having read the pirated text, and especially poems that are subsequently omitted from the authorized first edition, I think we know. The first edition corrects a few scribal or printer's errors, but most of the changes are deliberate attempts to conceal the erotic seduction and angry accusations the pirated sonnet sequence enacts. To avoid further scandal and to create the impression that the sonnet lady is an exemplary love object, not a real woman, Daniel chooses the persona Delia, an anagram for *ideal*. Most modern critics have been all too willing to take Daniel at his word: "we are not supposed to ask whether he actually had a lover," twentieth-century poetics teaches us, "what is at stake is a *way of talking* about a woman, rather than any particular real-life woman."[18]

Because the authorized edition bemoans the inaccuracies of the pirated text and almost doubles the number of poems, the earlier, pirated version is virtually unknown and unread today, even by the most dedicated scholars and critics. The first edition, edited by Sprague and published by Harvard in 1930, remains the authoritative text.[19] Several scholars have studied variants subsequent to the first edition, but no one has analyzed the much more revealing revisions that distinguish the first edition from the pirated sequence. As it turns out, therefore, the authorized edition does precisely what Daniel hoped it would do: it does in fact "keep in the priuate passions of my youth, from the multitude, as things uttered to my selfe, and consecrated to silence." The critics all seem to agree that "[t]here is no story, not even an implied series of events," and "consistency, or sameness is the keynote."[20]

To my mind, Daniel's real brilliance and originality appear not only in the melodious "poetical" phrases so admired by C. S. Lewis and subsequent critics, but also in the remarkable drama these two carefully constructed and distinctive, though overlapping and interdependent, sonnet sequences "keep in," both contain and conceal. When read alone, the expanded, rearranged, and expurgated 1592 sequence is just what its name signifies: a wonderfully lyrical and idealized portrait of "a lover more generous and dedicated than any other in Tudor verse, one whose sensitive regard for beauty and complete dedication to his mistress are recorded in verses promising to eternize his lady."[21] When read as a reinterpretation and correction of the original failed seduction – precisely what Daniel wants Delia and no one else to do – the authorized edition suggests a fascinating dialogue between Daniel and Delia which continues the courtship but obscures the nature of their earlier conversation.

In the authorized edition, the original introductory sonnet appears second, preceded by a new sonnet that pays tribute to "the boundles Ocean of thy beautie." In place of the highly critical, but still tentative final line ("And fear this deed will make the world abhor her"), Daniel inserts a milder, more conventional conclusion: "And tell th'vnkind, how deerely I haue lou'd her" (*PS* 2:14). Daniel still depicts Delia as the lyric audience: "Reade it sweet maide" (Sprague 1:1, 13). Yet even though he encourages the public to read the poems "as if I were a mistress," the gentle, distant tone sweetens Delia's character, making her into a thoroughly conventional sonnet lady.

To show Delia how much he has changed, and how much more he now deserves her favor, Daniel censors all the most scandalous poems: the veiled sexual propositions; the hints that Delia herself is sexually aroused; the troublesome disparity in rank and wealth; the struggle for power; the nasty *quid pro quo*; the vituperative charges of witchcraft, and, above all, the bitter anger that verges on anti-feminism. By eliminating all the " 'watershed moments,' changes of slope, when some new quality enters," Daniel conceals the functioning of the sequence as the enactment or transaction of a courtship. In sum, he makes Delia's resistance and his own resentment thoroughly unexceptionable and entirely inexplicable.[22]

Having removed the most objectionable and unconventional poems, Daniel turns his artistic talent to smoothing out the remaining poems. Moments of erotic expectation, bitter hostility, and intense self-loathing lapse into conventional Petrarchan complaint: "Loathing the light, the world, myself and all" (*PS* 23:10) becomes "Haunting vntroden pathes to waile apart" (Sprague 9:10). Warnings that keep passion alive and icy disdain at bay turn into regretful acknowledgments of Delia's cold, hard heart. What is only a possibility in the pirated sequence – "I *fear* your change! . . . Medusa's eye *may* turn your heart to flint" (*PS* 5:13–14, my emphasis) – becomes a *fait accompli*: "And you *are* chaung'd . . . I feare your eye *hath turn'd* your hart to flint" (Sprague 29:13–14; my emphasis).

When his "secrets" are exposed to the world, Daniel recasts his passionate lyric persuasion ("Presse to her eyes, importune me some good") to suit the conventional expectations of the public lyric audience. Daniel rearranges the order, giving many of the original sonnets a new context that conceals and alters their earlier meaning – precisely what Gascoigne does when he transforms *A Hundreth Sundrie Flowres* into *The Posies*. For example, the earlier erotic innuendo of "wears, melts and yields, we see" (*PS* 4:14) is muted by a new sonnet which begins: "My spotles loue hoouers with white wings, / About the temple of the proudest frame" (Sprague 12:1–2).

By reordering the entire collection and interspersing twenty-seven new poems, many of which use the poet's eternizing power to idolize and idealize Delia, Daniel masks the courtship and seduction, which, I believe, the pirated sequence once enacted and still betrays. By rearranging poems, changing a few key words, eliminating offending lines or potentially scandalous poems, interspersing new poems at crucial moments, altering the order, recasting the beginning and ending, Daniel conceals his courtship and seduction behind the eternizing rhetoric of public praise.[23]

Remarkably, Daniel continues to treat the published text with the provisionality of manuscript poetry. Even while correcting and expanding the first edition, he already foresees further changes: "my lines heereafter better labored, shall purchase grace in the world" – or so he hopes. The continued revisions from 1592 on trace and retrace the psychological effects of Daniel's life-long obsession with Delia. Still hoping to make his persuasion more appealing to her, between 1592 and 1594 Daniel continues to intersperse new sonnets and to alter key words and phrases. As Daniel's hopes of winning Delia's love fade, later revisions dampen his original passion, further weakening the poems.[24] After 1594, there are ten more editions of *Delia* and *Rosamond*, but they contain only minor verbal changes, largely applications of poetic principles developed in the "Defence of Ryme," which eliminate the mixture of feminine and masculine rhymes.

Daniel preserves the lyric sequence's fundamental capacity to promote and incorporate change even after the sonnets appear in print, for he continues to revise the sequence as his relationship with Delia evolves over the years. From a certain point of view, this seems like a naive, literal-minded devotion to fact – as if he needed to update his emotional situation, both for Delia and posterity. Yet from another point of view, it combines the fluidity of the oral tradition and manuscript circulation with a surprisingly modern conception of truth – not one eternal, universal *Truth* but truths, contingent, historically located, shifting and evolving through time, the meaning changing, quite literally, according to the response the poem receives.

Instead of going on to explore the uncouth, unseemly conflicts between poetry's idealizations and the body's material and physical needs, Daniel transforms his private lyric dialogue into public poetry of praise, designed to suit the conventional social and literary expectations of a broader public audience. Daniel and Delia both pay a heavy price. She becomes indistinguishable from all the other Lauras and Delias, and he becomes a conventional, highly imitative poet who gets what he seems to deserve: minor fame and minimal critical attention.

WHAT CANNOT WOMEN DO

In the authorized 1592 edition, the sonnet sequence, *Delia*, is followed by "The Complaint of Rosamond." Churchyard's complaint is Daniel's model. Narrated entirely in the ventriloquized voice of its female protagonist, it tells "Howe Shores wife, Edwarde the fowerthes concubine, was by king Richarde despoyld of all her goodes, and forced to open penance."[25] In Daniel's complaint, Rosamond tells how she was badly misadvised by a court matron and then deflowered by King Henry II. Henry then constructed a labyrinth to imprison and hide her from the world, all to no avail, for she was discovered and murdered by Henry's jealous queen.

According to Kerrigan, Daniel's "greatest innovation was the simple complicating one of describing events from Rosamond's point of view."[26] Equally important, I would argue, is the much greater complication of using the complaint to continue, in an encoded form, the lyric dialogue begun in the private sonnet sequence. Rosamond's ghost simply begins speaking, without any introduction or description by the male poet/narrator. She has been consigned to wandering the earth, seeking a writer to redeem her "name, / And that disgrac'd, for time hath wrong'd the same" (lines 20–1). Oddly enough, her soul has been denied passage to Elysium "Till Louers sighes on earth shall it deliuer" (line 14). This is the pretext (or pre-text) that prompts Rosamond to ask Daniel to write *our* story, for "*Delia* may happe to deygne to read our story" (line 43).

Thus, Rosamond and Daniel join in a collaborative effort, motivated by the common goal of needing to convince Delia to accept Daniel's courtship. The idea is that Rosamond will tell her story to Daniel, and he will write it down for Delia to read: "I knowe thy iust lamenting Muse, / Toylde in th' affliction of thine owne distresse, / In others cares hath little time to vse, / And therefore maist esteeme of mine the lesse: / Yet as thy hopes attend happie redresse, / Thy ioyes depending on a womans grace" (lines 36–41). Daniel's "merit" – both as a poet and a suitor – "would suffice for both our glorie, / Whereby thou might'st be grac'd, and I be blest" (lines 45–6); however, his "merit" is like his "ioyes depending on" Delia's answering response. Delia "might" save Rosamond from eternally wandering the earth, telling her tale over and over again like the Ancient Mariner, just as she "might" save Daniel from endlessly reiterating his plaint, repeatedly recasting the sonnets in the hopes of winning her love – if only she "would." Daniel's carefully qualified, conditional formulation acknowledges what the pirated sonnet sequence discovers: "*Delia* may happe to deygne to read our story" (line 43), but only if she deigns to do so – and even then, there is no guarantee that she will interpret the poem as he would like.

"The Complaint of Rosamond" speaks through Rosamond *to* Delia – but not, it is important to note, *for* her. "*Delia*, left to adorne the West" (line 525), remains outside the poem's margins and beyond the poet's/lover's control. Kerrigan notes that "line 525 is usually taken as complimenting Daniel's dedicatee, Mary Sidney."[27] It also functions as a crucial reminder *in medias res* that Daniel's primary lyric audience is Delia – a particular Elizabethan woman, who, like the innocent young Rosamond, has "liu'd at home a happy Country mayde" (line 539).

Speaking through Rosamond, Daniel urges Delia to realize she has the "power" not only to bless Rosamond but also to "joy" Daniel and herself: "Such powre she hath by whom thy youth is lead, / To ioy the liuing and to blesse the dead" (lines 48–9). Delia's power derives not only from her symbolic status as the ideal of feminine beauty and virtue, but also from her material existence as "the real reader" of Daniel's poetry and the real objective of his courtship.

The guise of the historical fiction and the female persona enables Daniel to state what the sonnet sequence can only imply. "The Complaint" explains, for example, that Rosamond's kinfolk convinced her to leave her home in the country and go to court, where they hoped to barter her beauty for wealth and status: "my frinds mine honour sought to rayse, / To higher place, which greater credite yeeldes, / Deeming such beauty was vnfit for feeldes" (lines 89–91). The end of the pirated sonnet sequence implies that Delia has been persuaded to reject Daniel – "My slender meane presumes too high a part / ... / Her state brooks not poore soules should come so nie hir" (27:3, 7–8) – so that she can be married to a husband with greater means and higher status.

"The Complaint of Rosamond" argues, even more forcefully and persistently than the sonnets do, that the innocent pleasures of young love – "The sweet-stolne sports, of ioyfull meeting Louers" (line 434) which drew Daniel and Delia together – should not be sacrificed for wealth and status: "Loue's not constrain'd, nor yet of due required, / Iudge they who are vnfortunately wed, / What tis to come vnto a loathed bed" (lines 439–41). Without mincing words, Rosamond tells Delia through Daniel – or rather, Daniel tells Delia through Rosamond – what a chaste, young woman might not be able to imagine: the unpleasantness of sex with a man she does not love: "When loe I ioyde my Louer not my Loue, / And felt the hand of lust most vndesired: / Enforc'd . . ." (lines 435–37) Rosamond's deflowering offers the predominantly male, public lyric audience the specular pleasure of seeing a woman subjugated by male force – but only for a moment. The story is told so graphically from Rosamond's point of view that the reader is immediately "Enforc'd" along with Rosamond "th' vnprooued bitter sweete to proue" (line 437).[28] The episode, as Rosamond tells it, leads to a blunt and compelling conclusion: "My nakednes had prou'd my sences liers" (line 446).

Daniel's complaint is a veiled coda to the poetic persuasion of the sonnets. It is also an allegorical exploration of how poetry of courtship works in practice. The poem contains three central tropes – the casket, the labyrinth, and the concourse – which symbolize the three conventional aspects of Renaissance love poetry. Before deflowering Rosamond, Henry sends her "a Casket richly wrought" (line 373) decorated with scenes of mortal women being raped by the gods, reminding us that, traditionally, the male-authored female complaint represents female weakness for male pleasure. As the mythic violence against women implies, the box also serves as a trope for the larger category of male art that represents women as beautiful objects to be enjoyed and violated by the male gaze: "Tis shame that men should vse poore maydens so" (line 385).

The labyrinth symbolizes the "cultural imprisonment of feminine erotic experience" which the "repetitive, often formulaic rhetoric" of the complaint traditionally depicts.[29] When the complaint is read as the continuation of Daniel's lyric dialogue with Delia, the labyrinth also represents the extraordinary lengths to which Elizabethan poets go to conceal their courtships and seductions, using deeply circuitous rhetoric, only to have their secrets betrayed to the world. Daniel finds himself "betraide by the indiscretion of a greedie Printer," his "secrets bewraide to the world." Henry's labyrinth proves as vulnerable as Daniel's poetry: "Fame doth explore what lyes most secrete hidden . . . Abroade reuealng what is most forbidden, / Of trueth and falshood both an equall teller" (lines 561–64).

Daniel transforms his private poetry of courtship into public poetry of praise, symbolized by the concourse where Elizabethan women go to parade their beauty, and Elizabethan men go to "Contemplate beauty gloriously attired" (line 527).[30] Although the idealized praise of female beauty leads women to think "heerein all our cheefest glory lyes" (line 528), "the wondrous concourse of the glittering Faire" (line 520) has its own hidden dangers, as Rosamond tries to tell Delia: "O how we ioy to see our selues admired, / Whilst niggardly our fauours we discouer, / We loue to be belou'd, yet scorne the Louer" (lines 530–32).

Henry Lee offers Anne Vavasour a choice: she can accept the role of the abandoned woman who bemoans her fate in the male-authored female complaint or she can choose the role of the female reader in the lyric dialogue of courtship. Daniel encourages Delia to consider the alternatives. If she chooses wealth and status instead of love, she, like Rosamond, will be forced to submit to male domination. Imprisoned in the labyrinth of jealously guarded male control, she will have no choice but to sacrifice her "libertie: / The onely good that women holde so deare" (lines 499–500). If, on the other hand, she chooses to seek satisfaction in being "prais'd and most desired" (line 529), she will end up embittered and cynical like the old court matron, for idolatry and narcissism also preclude reciprocal love. But if she sees herself not as a "belou'd" but as "the Louer" who freely selects her own beloved, then she need never know "What tis to come vnto a loathed bed" (line 441).

Established genres carry a conventional code of behavior shared by writer and reader, or a set of rules for practice designed, at least in theory, to prevent readers from making mistaken assumptions or undesirable inferences. Yet genre is not only "an invitation to form," it is also "an invitation to reformulate and an invitation to reform."[31] In its more conventional forms, the complaint, rather like the dramatic monologue, exposes female weakness to the combined sympathy and irony of the male poet and reader. Daniel echoes Lee's radical reformulation of the genre, for his ventriloquized female voice also lures the reader into sympathizing with an exceptional or unconventional female point of view, redirecting the poet's irony and the reader's judgment from the female persona's weakness to the social and literary codes that deny her power.

Just as our close reading of Daniel's pirated sonnet sequence shows Renaissance lyric conventions being used to subvert conventional generic expectations, so too a more probing analysis of Daniel's complaint shows the ventriloquized female voice being used to interrogate conventional generic and social codes of behavior. Rosamond, who ruined her own life by making the wrong decision, asks Daniel to "Exemplifie my frailtie" and to "teach to others, what I learnt too late" (lines 68, 67). What Rosamond "learnt too late" – and what Delia can still learn before it is too late – is that she has the strength to challenge the social and ethical codes that suppress female speech and female plea-sure. "What might I then not doe whose powre was such?" (line 127), Rosamond asks Delia and all Daniel's readers.

Daniel's attentiveness to his private female reader, learned outside the context of the court and the noble households, stands him in good stead when he redirects his "humble rhymes" to a mistress with a very different kind of power:

> Great Patroness of these my humble Rymes:
> Which thou from out thy greatnes doost inspire:
> Sith onely thou hast deign'd to rayse them higher,
> Vouchsafe now to accept them as thine owne,
> Begotten by thy hand, and my desire,
> Wherein my Zeale, and thy great might is showne. (lines 5–8)

The second edition of 1594 begins with this new prefatory sonnet addressed to "The Right Honorable, the Lady Mary, Countesse of Pembrooke." Calling upon her "greatnes" and "great might," Daniel asks the countess to "rayse" his poems and status "higher" by accepting the poems as "thine own."[32] As the translator of the *Rime* and her brother's collaborator, reader, and editor, Mary Sidney is perfectly situ-ated to appreciate Daniel's efforts both to empower his female reader and to conceal the private passions of his youth. Of course, Daniel's failure to win the wealthy Delia's hand in marriage makes his need for the countess's patronage all the more pressing.

Interrupting Rosamond's monologue for the length of a stanza, Daniel agrees to be her audience, scribe, and champion: "And I more willing tooke this charge assign'd" (line 61). We know that Mary Sidney commissioned other works by Daniel; it therefore seems likely, as line 61 implies, that she also encouraged Daniel to write and publish "The Complaint of Rosamond."[33] That would also explain why Daniel's dedication describes the volume as a collaborative venture, "Begotten by thy hand, and my desire." And it would further explain why Daniel gives Rosamond such a forceful articulation of female power: "What cannot women doe that know theyr powre?" (line 127). By addressing the sonnets and the complaint to Delia and showing that her response escapes the poet's control, by then dedi-cating the published text to Mary Sidney and showing that her patronage also exceeds his control, Daniel acknowledges the female reader's power to approve or gainsay.

Sidney's translation of Petrarch's *Triumph* circulates in manuscript between 1592 and 1594, when Daniel is preparing the first and second editions of *Delia* for the press. In adapting the complaint genre to his own persuasive purposes, Daniel deploys many of the rhetorical strategies used by Mary Sidney's translation of Petrarch's *Triumph*. Much as Sidney's syntactical ambiguities link Petrarch and Laura, Daniel relies on syntactical slippage to infuse Rosamond's complaint with his own: "To forme my case, and register my wrong" (line 35). Instead of telling her own story in her own voice, Sidney translates the *Triumph* into English, giving Petrarch's poetry and Laura's voice her own female intonation and interpretation. Instead of reiterating his misery in the male voice of the sonnet, Daniel displaces his complaint onto Rosamond, and then re-translates it into coded poetry of courtship. Sidney's version of *The Triumph* transforms Laura from the idolized object of Petrarch's love to a female subject who, returning from heaven, openly speaks her desire to Petrarch, and through Petrarch to Mary Sidney, and through Mary Sidney to other Elizabethans. Daniel writes the complaint in a ventriloquized female voice which speaks to him from beyond the grave, and through him to Delia, Mary Sidney, and other Elizabethan men and women.[34]

When poetry of courtship is *first* addressed to an amorous mistress and *later* redirected to a female patron, the second lyric dialogue with yet another powerful female interlocutor further heightens the poet/lover's attentiveness to the female point of view.[35] Some Elizabethan poems originally written to woo Elizabethan women (Whythorne's are the perfect example) are re-addressed to male patrons or male coteries. Yet, female patrons, such as Mary Sidney, Mary Wroth, and Elizabeth Tudor are also highly sought after by poets such as Daniel, Donne, and Spenser because they, as women, seem especially likely to appreciate the poet/lover's attentiveness to the female point of view.

The authorized edition ends as it began, by hinting that both the sonnets and the complaint conceal "secrets" that were "bewraide to the world, vncorrected" by the pirated sonnet sequence: "So vanisht shee, and left me to returne, / To prosecute the tenor of my woes:/ Eternall matter for my Muse to mourne" (lines 736–38). At the very moment when he is again in danger of sounding like Petrarch whose "woes" are the "Eternall matter" of so much Renaissance love poetry, Daniel lapses into enigmatic silence:

But ah the worlde hath heard too much of those,
My youth such errors must no more disclose.
  Ile hide the rest, and greeue for what hath beene,
  Who made me knowne, must make me liue vnseene.

(lines 739–42)

Like Isabella Whitney, Elizabeth I, Anne Vavasour, and Mary Sidney, Daniel "dares speake no more."

In isolation, "The Complaint of Rosamond" may seem like a ventriloquized female voice that violates the female body, invites male voyeurism, and precludes female subjectivity. But in the larger context of Daniel's ongoing lyric dialogue with Delia, and Elizabethan women's ongoing lyric dialogue with male literary tradition, Daniel's complaint protests the cultural confinement of female sexuality and advocates an alternative social code based on mutual respect, reciprocal sexual pleasure, and conjugal freedom of choice. By urging Delia to join him in defending female "libertie: / The onely good that women holde so deare" (lines 499–500), Daniel adds his ventriloquized female voice to the voices of other Elizabethan women and men who (like contemporary feminists) are "reappropriating ventriloquism to infiltrate, interrogate, and dismantle a language and a cultural lexicon that has confined women to a marginal and metaphoric status."[36]

Like Elizabeth I's redefinition of the Petrarchan lyric and the Petrarchan lady, Whitney's reappropriation of the Ovidean epistle, Mary Sidney's Elizabethan female adaptation of Petrarch's *Triumph*, Vavasour's coded poem of courtship, and Lee's transformation of the complaint into a veiled poem of courtship, *Delia* and "The Complaint of Rosamond" redefine the genres they inherit. Indeed Daniel's complaint gives the genre a rich, new life, for it sparks two decades of male-authored female complaints ranging from Shakespeare's "A Lover's Complaint" to Drayton's *Heroicall Epistles*. Thanks to Lee and Daniel, the female complaint becomes a locus of social and literary controversy. As "The Complaint of Rosamond" is imitated and adapted by other English Renaissance poets, Daniel's lyric dialogue with his female reader and his female patron continue to disturb the univocal male voice of English lyric tradition, adding a female subtext, or gender unconscious, to "processes of copying, printing, and circulation largely commanded by male interests."[37]

8

Spenser's Amoretti

Perchaunce my wordes be thought,
  uncredible to you:

Because I say this Treatise is,
  both false and also true.[1]

SEEK HER TO PLEASE ALONE

A volume containing the *Amoretti* and the *Epithalamion* appears in the
Stationer's Register on November 19, 1594.[2] The first edition, published
in 1595, announces on the title page that it was "Written not long since
by Edmunde Spenser." The joint publication invites the public lyric
audience to see the sonnets as private poems of courtship that were originally used, and that should still be read, as the transaction of the courtship which culminates in the *Epithalamion*. A series of verbal signs,
strategically placed throughout, confirm the expectation that the sonnets
are the verbal constituents – the "engins," the "playnts, prayers, vowes,
ruth, sorrow, and dismay," (14:11–12) – of the poet's own courtship: "one
long entreaty . . . that she will once vouchsafe my plaint to heare"
(18:6–7).

    Early modern English marriage contracts are customarily sealed by
the offering and accepting of lovers' tokens. Thus, the very title, *Amoretti,*
meaning "intimate little tokens of love," characterizes the sequence as a
pledge of Spenser's love and a token of his engagement. Unlike Daniel's
and Sidney's sequences, Spenser's breaks off in anticipation of a felicitous conclusion: "Happy ye leaues when as those lilly hands, / which
hold my life in their dead doing might / shall handle you and hold in
loues soft bands / lyke captiues trembling at the victors sight"(1:1–3). The
future tense, combined with the references to her "lilly hands" and
"loues soft bands," implies that Spenser's female reader has promised,

but not yet actually given, her hand in marriage. Sounding eager to woo and win her but still slightly afraid of offending her, Spenser celebrates the power "those lamping eyes" direct on him and his poems. The neologism, "lamping," suggests that conventional poetic language cannot capture the enlightening viewpoint which her reading brings to the poems – even as it indicates that her role as prototypical lyric audience continues to clarify all subsequent readings of the poems. Like Gascoigne's riddling final line, "I would those eyes were mine," her lamping eyes illuminate the poet/lover's rhetorical persuasion, even as they escape his control.

The conclusion announces that she is the only reader, and the only woman, about whom he cares. Looking forward to the consummation of their relationship ("when ye behold that Angels blessed looke, / my soules long lacked foode, my heauens blis" l:11–12), he collects the poems for her reading pleasure.[3] The confident expectation of a felicitous reception ("Happy ye leaues," "And happy lines," "And happy rhymes"), along with numerous, specific verbal allusions to the battles that take place in the following poems, suggests that Spenser and his fiancée have discussed and even fought over her responses to the poems. Yet, it seems, there are also a few poems, composed during moments of estrangement – "written with teares in harts close bleeding book" (1:8) – that have not yet been seen by her.

The punning final couplet reinforces what the previous lines so boldly and unequivocally assert, that even poems not directly addressed to her (and Sonnet 1 is a case in point) aim only to please her, and to please her only:

> Leaues, lines, and rymes, seeke her to please alone,
>   whom if ye please, I care for other none. (1:13–14)

This does not literally mean that Spenser's mistress is the only reader of the *Amoretti*; subsequent sonnets mention other readers, ranging from a friend named Lowick, to Spenser's mother, Elizabeth 1, and posterity. It does give his mistress an important symbolic significance: it makes her "alone" the primary and prototypical lyric audience.

A Petrarchan poet can praise or curse to his heart's content or misery, all by his lonesome, but an Elizabethan poet/lover must perforce recognize his mistress's power to accept or refuse his suit. When Petrarch writes about "loving her to whom I said: 'you alone please me'" ("col dolce onor che d'amar quella ài preso / a cui io dissi: 'Tu sola mi piaci'" *RS* 205:7–8), the lines emphasize his words and his love. When Spenser's

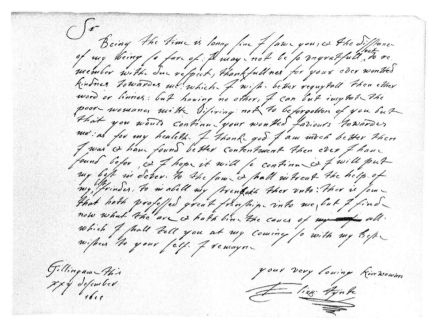

Figure 12 A letter written by Elizabeth Tynt [Boyle] who married Edmund Spenser around the time the *Amoretti* and the *Epithalamion* were published.

"Leaues, lines, and rymes, seeke her to please alone" (1:13) the emphasis shifts to her response to his love and his poems.

The *Amoretti* is a charged, complicated lyric sequence which has been frequently praised for its imagery, its numerological patterns, and its Neoplatonic allegorizing, but repeatedly criticized for its narrative inconsistencies and verbal contradictions. Yet, the sequence, with its shifting, contradictory tropes and attitudes, makes better sense both aesthetically and emotionally, when read as a lyric dialogue of courtship. Edmund Spenser marries Elizabeth Boyle around the time the *Amoretti* and the *Epithalamion* are published. The standard biography, Judson's *The Life of Edmund Spenser*, reconstructs Spenser's courtship of Elizabeth Boyle almost entirely on the basis of the poems themselves.[4] Subsequent critics debate whether the *Amoretti* is autobiography or fiction or a collection of discrete poems written upon different occasions about any number of different women. Since the evidence is inconclusive, there is little to be gained from rehashing the arguments pro and con.

Even if the *Amoretti* was never used by Spenser to court Elizabeth Boyle, which seems theoretically possible but unlikely given what we have learned about the use of poetry in courtship, he certainly went to a lot of trouble to make his readers think the poems were the means by which he conducted his own courtship. Regardless, the *Amoretti* is a brilliant dramatization of an Elizabethan courtship, as well as one of the period's most insightful analyses of what it means for Elizabethan poetry to transact a courtship.

Written in the mid-1590s at the apex of the Elizabethan love poetry and the height of the socio-political controversy over poetry, courtship, and women, the *Amoretti* explores the fundamental questions that both poetry and courting pose for Elizabethan men and women. By interpolating what early modern women from Elizabeth I to Isabella Whitney are writing and saying about poetry and courtship, we can begin to understand what Spenser and his Elizabethan readers are themselves trying to understand: how would an Elizabethan woman, being wooed in poetry, respond to the poet's/lover's various attempts to convince her that he is the man for her to marry?

Clearly, Spenser's poems would have been interpreted in any number of different ways by different types of Elizabethan readers, just as they are interpreted differently by different readers today. The following pages are one late twentieth-century female reader's attempt to reconstruct some of the many ways in which one late sixteenth-century female reader might have responded to the courtship which the *Amoretti* seeks (or at least purports) to transact.

PREPARE YOUR SELF NEW LOUE TO ENTERTAIN

The opening poems run the gamut from apostrophes to the poem, public encomiums, and private musings, to intimate conversations with a sympathetic male friend, to direct pleas to his mistress. Yet no matter what the poet/lover says, or whom he addresses, the female reader's unwritten response is always present, the subtext and measure of his persuasion.

The courtship per se begins with the second sonnet, an apostrophe to the poem. The witty allusion to Astrophil's famous outburst – "Desire still cries, give me some food" (*AS* 71:14) – hints at the physical gratification he hopes to attain: "Breake forth at length out of the inner part / . . . / and seeke some succour both to ease my smart / and also to sustayne thy selfe with food" (2:5–8). Fearing that he may have expressed his hunger too boldly, he immediately begs her pardon: "fall lowly at her feet: / and with meeke humblesse and afflicted mood, / pardon for thee, and grace for me intreat" (2:10–12). The combination of erotic persuasion and apology comprises a classic instance of the rhetorical figure "*Parisia*, or the Licentious": "The fine and subtill per-swader when his intent is . . . to declare his mind in broad and liberal speeches, which might breede offence or scandall, he will seeme to bespeake pardon before hand, whereby his licentiousnes may be the better borne withall."[5]

Does *Amoretti* 2 reach the beloved through a servant or a mutual acquaintance? Does she respond, and if so, is her tone encouraging or disapproving? At this point, it is difficult to say. Like the letters of first entreaty in the letter writing manuals, this amatory epistle seeks permis-sion to woo her: "But if in presence of that fayrest proud / thou chance to come . . ." (2:9–10).

The following poem is an encomium, appropriate to be recited at a social gathering or circulated in manuscript among mutual acquain-tances: "The souerayne beauty which I doo admyre, / witnesse the world how worthy to be prayzed" (3:1–2). The imagery – "the light wherof hath kindled heauenly fyre" (3:3) – hints at the fiery passion Sonnet 2 introduces, while the elevated, heavenly diction – "by her from basenesse raysed" (3:4) – allays any doubts which may have been caused by that overly precipitate first entreaty:

> So when my toung would speak her praise dew,
>   it stopped is with thoughts astonishment:
>   and when my pen would write her titles true,
>   it rauist is with fancies wonderment:
> Yet in my hart I then both speake and write
>   the wonder that my wit cannot endite. (3:9–14)

The uncontrolled pouring forth of clause after clause uses all the resources of art to imply what (it says) cannot be said: the astonishment of a pen "rauist" with uncontrollable desires.

The most effective compliments tend to be those that are overheard. How might the woman feel upon overhearing this wondrous paean of praise? Perhaps she is overcome by passion she cannot acknowledge, like Mary Sidney's Laura who later confesses, "In equale flames our louing heats were tryde" (2:139). Or perhaps she is wary "of fayre and painted talke / beware of flattering tonges," like Isabella Whitney, or Jane Anger who complains that men "are rauished w´ y delight of those dainties, which allure and draw the sences of them to serue vs, wherby they become rauenous haukes, who doe not only seize vpon vs, but deuour vs."[6]

Still knowing almost nothing about her thoughts and feelings, the poet/lover presses for greater intimacy, again using poetic apostrophe to intimate what cannot be said directly. The new year, the subject of the sentence, "bids all old thoughts to die in dumpish spright" and "promise[s] hope of new delight," while that lusty trickster Cupid "wils [fresh loue] awake, and soon about him dight / his wanton wings and darts of deadly power" (4:4–8). But who does our poet/lover think he is kidding? This rhetorical strategy is also easily recognizable: "hee putteth the fault in his pen, when it was his passion that deserued reproofe," Jane Anger warns Elizabethan women.[7]

Like the follow-up letters that regularly appear in letter writing manuals, the couplet graciously requests the favor of a private meeting: "Then you faire flowre, in whom fresh youth doth raine, / prepare your selfe new loue to entertaine" (4:13–14). "Entertain" means receive as a guest; to keep in mind with favor; to keep oneself in the frame of mind for; the primary meaning is to hold mutually, to hold intertwined. Spenser asks her to accept the poem, sent by him to her as a sign of the mutual love which he hopes will bind them together like the flowers earth in "her faire mantel weaue[s]." Is she charmed by the carefully woven wreath of words, or put off by the presumption of the imperative? He seems to think that she is in his debt and at his command ("entertain" also means to be at his charge in return for services rendered) because he has been singing her praises to the world, not wanting to admit that the invitation is not necessarily his for the asking.

Apparently she responds coolly, or so the next poem suggests: "Rudely thou wrongest my deare harts desire / In finding fault with her too portly pride" (5:1–2). The poem is addressed to an unidentified male interlocutor, but sounds as if it is also intended for her to overhear. Her resistance is a sign, not of moral weakness, he tells his critical friend, but of strong character and firm principles: "For in those lofty lookes is close implide, / scorn of base things, and sdeigne of foul dishonor . . ." (5:5–6). In case his earlier sexual innuendos have given her pause, he insists that he is not one of those base suitors – "Their glozing tongues, the preface to the execution of their vilde mindes, and their pennes the bloody executioners of their barbarous maners" – who use poetic rhetoric to seduce and deceive. Hoping to make amends, he compares their love to an oak tree that catches fire slowly but which, once ignited, produces "great heat, and makes his flames to heauen aspire" (5:8). The strength of mind which enables her to challenge and resist his rhetoric will also give her the feisty independence necessary "to obtaine her wyll" and "to haue her whole desyre" – or so he hopes.[8] Musing to himself but choosing words appropriate for a coterie of mutual friends, he assures her that he is willing to wait "to knit the knot, that euer shall remaine" because he knows, and wants her to know, that it is "hard" to "kindle new desire, in gentle brest, that shall endure for euer" (6:9–10).

In these initial epistolary verses, Spenser's poet/lover is overcome with wonder at the beauty of her "Fayre eyes," but also, at the same time, "mazed" (caught in a maze, or confused) by the contradictory signals he is receiving from her – and from Elizabethan culture at large. He continues to see her "Fayre eyes, the myrrour of my mazed hart" (7:1), as the object or reflection of his desire, even though he realizes that by wooing her he is making himself "into the object of your mighty view" (7:4).[9] Speaking directly to her, he places her in the magisterial, and conventionally male, position of judge and critic.

He urges her to take responsibility for kindling the fire of his desire – "For when ye mildly looke with louely hew, / then is my soule with life and loue inspired" (7:4–6) – but he also intimates that his passions are aroused by her fiery resistance: "when ye lowre, or looke on me askew, / then doe I die, as one with lightning fyred." When she looks at him "askew" (meaning literally, out of the corner of her eye, but also awry), it is difficult to know whether she is looking at him askance, signaling her disapproval, or looking at him sidelong, expressing a veiled desire which might look awry if expressed more openly. Depending on how the lines are read, he could either be dying from her icy disdain, or hoping to die like "one with lightning fyred" at the moment of sexual climax.

The third quatrain maintains the ambiguity:

> But since that lyfe is more then death desyred,
>   looke euer louely, as becomes you best,
>   that your bright beams of my weak eies admyred,
>   may kindle liuing fire within my brest.

In urging her to stop frowning and "looke euer louely," he might be saying that he will find her always lovely, or lovable, if she remains "louely," or worthy of love, i.e., chaste, silent, and obedient. But he might be suggesting that she will seem all the more *lovable* if she is "louely" in the broadest sense of the word, i.e., loving, kind, affectionate, and, that's right, amorous. This could either be a Petrarchan poem of unrequited, idealized love, or an encoded, pseudo-Petrarchan poem of courtship and seduction. Rather than simply mirroring his desire, Spenser's female interlocutor is the locus of his cultural confusion.

The couplet sums up the interpretive conundrum: "Such life should be the honor of your light, / such death the sad ensample of your might" (7:13–14). She could be dishonored in his eyes either by lowering and rejecting him, or by returning and enflaming his passionate desire. In the first case, "such death should be the honor" which makes him the "sad example" of the Petrarchan lady's conventional power to kill. In the second case, "the sad ensample of your might" ("sad" also means satisfied, sated, having had one's fill; strong, valiant; steadfast, firm; serious, trustworthy) would instead give her the courage to act on her desire, leaving them both sated with love.

Caught in an ideological and poetic impasse, unable to acknowledge that idolatry precludes seduction, even as seduction makes a mockery of idolatry, these initial sonnets fluctuate disconcertingly between idealized praise and lusty desire. For this reason, Lever and a number of subsequent critics conclude that the *Amoretti* is a collection of disparate lyrics, written upon discrete occasions about very different sorts of women. The problem with this explanation is that the opposing, irreconcilable conceptions of love and lust generally occur simultaneously – in a single sonnet or amphibolous phrase.

When read as the enactment, or dramatization, of a lyric courtship, the conflicting viewpoints make much better sense both dramatically and ideologically. The challenge of reading the text epitomizes the difficulty of conducting a lyric courtship: the male poet's struggle to interpret her confusing eye signals matches the female reader's effort to interpret his ambivalent verbal signals. Unclear whether she would be more or less lovely to his eyes if she chose to act on the erotic subtext lurking beneath his idealized rhetoric, Spenser's enigmatic, amphibolous language allows his female reader to interpret his courtship as she chooses, either as a conventional tribute to her chastity or as a radical redefinition of the very notion of honor.

Finally, instead of praising and criticizing her as a conventional sonnet lady, the poet/lover tries to capture her rare appeal: "But that which fairest is, but few behold, / her mind adornd with vertues manifold" (15:13–14). All his concerted attempts to describe her have left out precisely what is most distinctive and impressive about her:

> many wondrous things there are beside.
> The sweet eye-glaunces, that like arrowes glide,
> the charming smiles, that rob sence from the hart:

the louely pleasance and the lofty pride,
cannot expressed be by any art.
A greater craftesmans hand thereto doth neede,
that can expresse the life of things indeed. (17:8–14)

This fresh and "wondrous" sense of her "louely pleasance" combines the action of pleasing with the freedom to be pleased, to satisfy her own pleasure. To be truly "lovely," both lovable and amorous, her "sweet eye-glaunces" must be free, like arrows, to glide where they will. In sum, she must be seen not as "my deare harts desire" (5:1), not as the object of his desire or his construction of his poem, but as the lyric audience, a subject who exists outside the poem, part of "the life of things indeed," both truly and in deed.[10]

I KNOW THE ART

In Sonnet 18 Spenser pauses to review the situation, hoping to figure out why the courtship is going nowhere:

But when I pleade, she bids me play my part,
and when I weep, she says teares are but water:
and when I sigh, she sayes I know the art,
and when I waile, she turnes hir selfe to laughter. (18:9–12)

"[S]uch extravagant exaggeration of the conventional poses," Martz writes, "strike[s] me as close to mock-heroic. These are the conventions of love, the poet seems to say; these are the usual rituals of courtship; he will gladly pay these tributes, and even overpay them, since this is what his delightful damsel seems to expect." Martz's wonderful essay teaches us to appreciate both the poet/lover's good-humored self-irony and the lady's wit and intelligence, but it fails to recognize that there is a serious critique embedded in the female reader's laughter. She says, "I know the art," or "Go on, play the part of the Petrarchan lover," not because she wants him to be a Petrarchan lover, but because she, like Isabella Whitney, wants him to know that she knows "Some [men] use the teares of Crocodiles, / contrary to their hart: / And yf they cannot alwayes weep: / they wet their Cheekes by Art."[11] When he banters back, admitting that his wailing deserves her mirth, his witty self-irony offers her some hope that he is beginning to understand her objections. Then the teasing stops. The final couplet reproduces the problem her laughter exposes: "so doe I weepe, and wayle, and pleade in vaine, / whiles she as steele and flint doth still remayne" (18:13–14).

Throughout the first part of the sequence, Spenser's poet/lover complains that his mistress vacillates between cold, chaste pride and vibrant, smiling encouragement, but the problem is as much his as hers. By attributing her resistance to moral and spiritual rectitude, he implicitly associates the active encouragement for which he yearns and sues with the moral and spiritual degradation which he deplores. He exalts her to the sun, the moon, the stars in Sonnet 9, only to complain four sonnets later that she "thinke[s] how she to heauen may clime: / treading downe earth as lothsome and forlorne" (13:10–11).[12] What Spenser's poet/lover and female reader need, but do not yet have, is an ethics and a poetics that will enable them to escape the ideological stasis of Petrarchism.

The solution comes not from male literary tradition, but from the female reader: "Thus doth she traine and teach me with her lookes, / such art of eyes I neuer read in bookes" (21:13–14). At this moment of symbolic inversion – of discourse or behavior which inverts, contradicts, abrogates the prevalent belief that the man is supposed to be the judge and teacher, Spenser makes a point of telling us that he has learned the art of courtship, not from earlier poets, but from the experience of communicating to and with a particular Elizabethan woman.[13] Significantly, this important turning point in the sequence reenacts the moment where Laura tells Petrarch, as Mary Sidney tells Elizabethan readers of Petrarch's *Triumph*, "these artes I used with thee." Shortly thereafter, the poet/lover again steps back from the turmoil of events to analyze his poetic rhetoric and her response. The result, *Amoretti* 23, is about as probing an enunciation of an Elizabethan poetics of courtship as we are likely to find.

PENELOPE'S WEB

Rather than turning to conventional male poetry, with its eternizing tropes and universal verities, Spenser chooses as his models two mythic, female performance artists whose impermanent, unstable arts and crafts provide an alternative way to "conceive" poetry and courtship. The first stanza retells the story of Penelope who "for her *Vlisses* sake, / Deuiz'd a Web her wooers to deceaue: / in which the worke that she all day did make / the same at night she did againe vnreaue." Penelope is regularly depicted as the ideal Elizabethan woman. In *Penelopes Web*, for example, she preaches what she represents: "those three speciall poynts that are requisite in euery woman, Obedience, Chastitie, and Silence." But Greene's Penelope offers "forceful examples of the simultaneous construction and subversion of this ideology," and so too does Spenser's.[14] By placing himself in the traditional female role, passively waiting for the wandering Odysseus to return, Spenser gives his mistress the role of the adventurous hero who may or may not return to her faithful, constant lover. Just as Penelope's weaving can do nothing to hasten Ulysses' return, Spenser's artistry continually fails to bring his errant beloved to the marital bed.

At first glance, Spenser's trope may seem to give his female reader less initiative than Penelope because he, not she, weaves the tapestry. Yet Spenser has even less power, as it turns out, than Penelope. She laboriously weaves and unweaves her own cloth, whereas the lyric tapestry Spenser weaves is continually undone by his resisting female reader:

> Such subtile craft my Damzell doth conceaue,
> th'importune suit of my desire to shonne:
> for all that I in many dayes doo weaue,
> in one short houre I find by her vndonne (23:5–8).

When the female reader's oppositional response unravels the poet/lover's persuasion, the conceit of Penelope's web collapses, and Spenser begins again, turning to the myth of Arachne, another mortal but mythic female weaver who challenges Athena to a weaving contest. Arachne's tapestry depicts the Gods raping their mortal, female victims which makes Athena so furious that she destroys Arachne's work. Devastated, Arachne kills herself. In pity, Athena transforms Arachne into a spider who continues to weave and catch insects in her web, but who never attains the immortality of art because her web is constantly "broken with least wynd."

Spenser is clearly frustrated by his inability to complete the tapestry that is the sonnet sequence, but he does not sound bitter or angry. By comparing himself to Arachne, Spenser expresses sympathy with Elizabethan women who are prevented by the ethics of silence and obedience from using their artistic and intellectual talents – the "subtile craft" that his resisting reader has in such abundance – to produce immortal works of art. In this crucial moment of reassessment, Spenser's poet/lover seems to finally understand that his female reader, like the wind that tears Arachne's web apart, is not to be confined by his tropes or defined by his art.[15]

"To put on femininity with a vengeance suggests the power of taking it off." By donning and doffing the classic female roles of Penelope and Arachne, Spenser acknowledges that his female reader also has the power to doff the constraints imposed by the Elizabethan code of ethics and to don a garb of her own fashioning. He has been trying to catch her in the web of his words, but she, more like Penelope or Athena than a trapped fly, continues to elude his "fruitlesse" efforts, rejecting one trope after another, forcing him to start over and over again.[16] Both Penelope and Arachne continue to weave, Penelope for her Ulysses sake, and Arachne, to sustain herself through art. So too, Spenser continues to write sonnets, expressing "th'importune suit of my desire," still hoping to convince his mistress that he, like the returning Ulysses, deserves to be welcomed into the marital bed.[17]

Blurring the roles of poet and reader, artist and critic, her response to his web not only becomes an intrinsic part of the web in question, but it also offers a critique of the ways in which he has been constructing her and her sex: "for with one looke she spils that long I sponne, / and with one word my whole years work doth rend" (11–12). With a single word or look, she undoes his poetic constructions and prevents his courtship from reaching closure. Though rarely analyzed or anthologized, *Amoretti* 23 is a probing exploration of how a poetics of courtship works in practice – one of those " 'watershed moments,' changes of slope, when some new quality enters."[18]

THE STUBBORN DAMSEL DOTH DEPRAVE MY SIMPLE MEANING

Still the days pass without providing any respite from uncertainty. Caught "twixt feare and hope depending doubtfully" (25:4), Spenser's poet/lover again complains that she "torment[s] mee thus with cruelty" (25:7). He accuses her of torturing him "to proue your powre" (25:8), not quite wanting to admit that he is also tormenting her by repeatedly testing her "power, / which I too wel haue tride" (25:8). At stake is a larger ideological dispute over male mastery and female subordination. As Whately writes in *A Care-cloth*, "diuers houses are none other, but euen very Fencing-Schooles, wherein the two sexes seeme to haue met together for nothing, but to play their prizes, and to trie masteries." The submerged struggle for power breaks into a full-scale battle in Sonnet 28, one of the most enigmatic and devious poems in the sequence.[19]

Spenser pays his mistress a visit, and is pleased to find her wearing a laurel leaf, the symbol of poetic immortality, and "the badg" (28:3) he himself wears as poet. Having urged her in the previous poem to accept his suit in exchange for immortality – "Faire be no longer proud of that shall perish, / but that which shal you make immortall, cherish" (27:13–14)

– he interprets her wearing the laurel as a sign "of your relenting mynd" (28:2). Finally, it seems as if she is as ready as he to collaborate on a conclusion to the courtship: "ye bearing it doe seeme to me inclind: / The powre thereof, which ofte in me I find, / let it lykewise your gentle brest inspire" (28:2, 4–6). This offer of shared "powre" sounds like a happy solution to their previous power struggle, at least until we think more carefully about Spenser's version of Apollo and Daphne.

Laura/laurel, the symbol of eternally verdant poetry, is the central symbol of Petrarch's *Rime*. In Canzone 22, Petrarch imagines himself falling down in the "amorous wood," alone with Laura "just one night and let the dawn never come! and let her not be transformed into a green wood to escape from my arms as the day when Apollo pursued her down here on earth." This, perhaps the most erotic of Petrarch's fantasies, is followed by Canzone 23 which recounts his fight with Laura. Furious that he has broken his promise to "Make no word of this," Laura makes that enigmatic comment, "I am not perhaps who you think I am!" The misunderstanding puts an end to their conversation, making poetry of courtship impossible, and Petrarch undergoes a number of metamorphoses, including Daphne's: "ei duo mi trasformaro in quel ch' i' sono, / facendomi d'uom vivo un lauro verde / che per fredda stagion foglia non perde" ("those two transformed me into what I am, making me of a living man a green laurel that loses no leaf for all the cold season," *RS* 23:35–7). The image of the laurel merges poet and lady. It not only transforms Petrarch from a living man into a green laurel, but it also turns Laura from a living, breathing woman into a heavenly icon, the reflection of his unfulfilled desire and the construction of his poetry.

Ovid's version of the story is rather different. His Daphne is one of those independent women – rather like Spenser's mistress or, indeed, his queen – who has already rejected many a suitor, much to her father's dismay. Struck by Cupid's arrow, Apollo falls desperately in love with Daphne. He tries to woo her with words, but she flees in terror, leaving him "With many words unsaid." "Too young a god to waste his time in coaxing," he chases her as a hound starts a rabbit. But just as "[h]e has her, or thinks he has, and she is doubtful / Whether she's caught or not," she sees "the river of her father," and crying out for help, is transformed by the gods into a laurel tree.

In both Ovid's version of the myth and in Petrarch's Canzone 23, the pursuit of Daphne ends the conversation between the poet/lover and his mistress. By contrast, Spenser's use of the myth produces one of those watershed moments when it is absolutely essential to posit a private lyric dialogue, occurring in the inter-lyric space.[20] When read together, *Amoretti* 28 and 29 dramatize a struggle between Spenser's poet/lover and his female reader over how to interpret Petrarch and Ovid – or how to conduct a lyric courtship. Spenser would like to use the myth, not only as Petrarch uses it in Canzone 22, to indulge his erotic fantasies but also as it is used by Elizabethan letter writers: as a coded means of sexual seduction. His female reader would like to use the myth as Whitney, Anger, and Sidney's Laura do – to assert her interpretive power over his poetry and courtship.

Like those multivious lines in Mary Sidney's *Rime* which refer simultaneously to both Petrarch and Laura, Spenser's retelling of the Ovidean tale makes one wonder who is being blamed "for which" act: "Proud Daphne scorning Phæbus louely fyre . . . from him did flee: / for which the gods in theyr reuengefull yre / did her transforme into a laurell tree" (28:9–12). Knowing the myth, one would naturally assume that the Gods are angry at Phæbus Apollo; however, Spenser's diction implies that the Gods are angry instead with "Proud Daphne" who is somehow to blame for "scorning Phæbus louely fyre." Just think what Apollo would have done to Daphne, had the Gods sided with him rather than her!

Amoretti 28 ends by making Spenser's identification with Apollo's chase all too clear:

> Then fly no more fayre loue from Phebus chace,
> but in your brest his leafe and loue embrace. (28:13–14)

The diction sounds tender and loving, but the imperative is disturbing. What the myth implies but Spenser's poet/lover is not prepared to acknowledge is the interpretive violence. Making her into the object of his desire is a kind of symbolic rape: it subjugates her body to his will, her "brest" to his verbal "embrace."

To my knowledge, not one of Spenser's modern critics has realized that *Amoretti* 28 contains a sexual proposition, allegorically veiled and loving but surprisingly aggressive nonetheless. I suspect Elizabethan readers would have been more canny. "Will the Gods permit it, the Goddesses stay their punishing iudgments, and we ourselues not pvrsue their vndoinges for such d[ev]ilish practises?," Jane Anger asks her female readers to consider. Similarly Whitney's *Admonitio*[n] *to al yong Gentilwomen and to al other Mayds in general* warns her readers that Elizabethan men deceive them with "pleasant Songs" of love: "Ouid, within his Arte of loue, / doth teach [men] this same knacke, / To wet their ha[n]d, & touch their eies: / so oft as teares they lacke."[21]

Whythorne, that wooing master *par excellence*, explains how a coded poetic seduction works in practice: "I made this song somewhat dark and doubtful of sense, because I knew not certainly how she would take it, nor to whose hands it might come after that she had read it. If she would take it to be written to herself, she might best do it" – do what?! – "But if she would not take it to herself or in good part, but would scoff thereat and show it to such whom she thought would take her part, yet it is so made as neither she nor none other could make any great matter therof . . ."[22] Whythorne explains how the game works. If the woman is pleased by the poet's/lover's proposal, she can respond with secret encourage- ment, and he can then proceed with more overt poetic and/or physical advances. If, on the other hand, she is offended by his proposition or deterred by social and material impediments, he can invoke the defense amphibology provides, saying, 'but that is not what I meant at all.'

Spenser's poet/lover proceeds to do exactly what Puttenham, Whythorne, Gascoigne, and the letter writing manuals all advise: he tries to save face by denying the erotic subtext: "See how the stubborne damzell doth depraue / my simple meaning with disdaynfull scorne" (29:1–2). Although twentieth-century critics have failed to notice any- thing awry, Spenser's female reader knows exactly what he is doing, and she is furious.

Unlike Apollo and Petrarch, Spenser's poet/lover pauses to consider her objections, giving her the opportunity to explain her "meaning" more fully than ever before. She says she is wearing the laurel leaf not as a sign of her subjection to his poetic authority, lines 4–8 explain, but as a sign of her power to vanquish her opponents. The spoils of victory are hers to award to those who have earned her favor, and he is not among them. Though a direct quotation, the lines are not, of course, what the private female reader actually says. Not even the cleverest Elizabethan woman talks in iambic pentameter, epic diction, and alter- nating rhymes.

Having constructed this lyric dialogue as a symbolic act of atonement, he blazons her glorious victory:

> But sith she will the conquest challeng needs,
>   let her accept me as her faithfull thrall,
>   that her great triumph which my skill exceeds,
>   I may in trump of fame blaze ouer all. (29:5–12)

Martz treats this bright young lady with the gentle but ultimately con- descending forbearance of an older professor, humoring a clever but willful pupil who must in the end submit to the poet's authority. "The poet's tone here," Martz writes, is "intimate, smiling, affectionate, respectful, reproachful, and courtly, all at once: it strikes exactly the tone that an older man, of experience and wisdom (someone a bit like Emma's Mr. Knightly) might adopt toward a bright and beautiful and willful young lady for whom he feels, not awe, but deep admiration and affection." In the context of the earlier, allegorical seduction, however, Spenser's poet/lover sounds less like a principled Mr. Knightly, than like a sheepish Whythorne caught trying to seduce his female pupils with enigmatic, amorous verses, or an equivocating Gascoigne complaining that Master F. J.'s poetic persuasion has "bene offensive for sundrie wanton speeches and lascivious phrases" which "have beene doubtfully contrued, and (therefore) scandalous."[23]

The upshot is a new round of Petrarchan complaints, but this time the tone is considerably less playful and more fraught. Quite a number of critics from Lever to Gibbs conclude that the sequence falls apart at this point because the sonnet lady seems to be "not only proud and disdainful – familiar attributes of the Petrarchan heroine – but also . . . sly, licentious, savage, and guileful." Yet, given the provocation of Sonnets 28 and 29, the ensuing cycle of anger, distrust, and mutual misunderstanding makes perfect sense. Having humbled himself by proclaiming his subjection, "sith she will the conquest challeng needs," the poet/lover cannot understand why she does not accept his apologies and save them both untold anguish. Irked by his presumption and infuriated by his suggestion that she perverted his "simple meaning," she thinks, understandably, that he is like all those other Elizabethan men who "run so into Rethorick, as often times they ouerrun the boundes of their own wits . . . If they may once encroch so far into our presence, as they may but see the lyning of our outermost garment, they straight think that Apollo honours them." No matter how often he protests his love, she is afraid to trust him: "Though loue be sure and firme: yet Lust fraught with deceit, / And mens fair wordes do worke great wo, vnlesse they be suspected." Only time will tell whether he is still as heedless of her wishes as Apollo is of Daphne, or whether he will prove as "constant, true and iust" as Penelope.[24]

NOT FINISHING HER QUEEN OF FAERY

Soon after the Apollo/Daphne catastrophe creates irreconcilable differences between the poet/lover and his female reader, a sonnet appears which seems to come out of nowhere:

> Great wrong I doe, I can it not deny,
>   to that most sacred Empresse my dear dred
>   not finishing her Queene of faery,
>   that mote enlarge her liuing prayses dead (33:1–4).

The opening quatrain identifies the writer and speaker as Edmund Spenser, the well-known author of three books of the *Faerie Queene*. The second quatrain addresses "lodwick," thus identifying the poem as one side of a private dialogue with a male peer, presumably Spenser's friend, Lodwick Brisket. The third quatrain identifies the poet/lover as the author of both the *Amoretti* and the *Faerie Queene*, thereby connecting the lyric courtship with Spenser's own life-story.

In response to Lodwick's criticism, Spenser explains that he has carefully considered the consequences of his courtship and decided to take a calculated risk, "that greater meede at last may turne to mee" (25:14). With patience, he still hopes to win his beloved's hand, along with the material possessions and social contacts she will presumably bring to the marriage. Moreover – as Sonnet 33 implicitly reminds his mistress should she overhear the poem – Spenser is not simply a ridiculous creature undone by love; he is also a public figure who cannot afford to neglect his professional obligations to the queen indefinitely. His female reader had better make up her mind soon, the sonnet implies, lest her resistance cause irreparable damage to his professional prospects and their future financial security. At the same time, Spenser informs the queen, should she read the sequence at some later date as he clearly hopes she will, that he has not forgotten his duty to her.

Sonnet 33 reasserts and clarifies what the introductory sonnet announces: the *Amoretti* is constructed – and should be read – as poetry of courtship, written by the real historical figure, Edmund Spenser. He has been neglecting the *Faerie Queene* because he is under a powerful psychological compulsion he can neither control nor escape – "tost with troublous fit, / of a proud loue, that doth my spirite spoyle" (33:9–12). He is greatly concerned about both the queen's and Lodwick's opinions, but he is *even more* concerned, inordinately concerned, with her, "whom if ye please, I care for other none" (1:14). Spenser's mistress is not simply a disembodied reflection of his thoughts and desires, or a metaphor for his worldly aspirations. Instead, she is his primary lyric audience – the locus of his most intense worldly, emotional, and spiritual aspirations. He is going to all that trouble, avidly writing sonnet after sonnet, because she completely eludes his control.

ERE SHE COULD THY CAUSE WELL UNDERSTAND

The misunderstanding between Spenser and his mistress reaches a point of crisis in Sonnet 48 when he reports, in a tone of absolute outrage, that she has destroyed one of his poems, throwing the "Innocent paper" into the fire to "avenge her yre" (48:1–3). Critics who assume that "the woman is static," or that "the central drama is within the lover himself," do not stop to ask why she resorts to such drastic measures.[25] Yet we have only to accept the premise that the sequence is a lyric dialogue between a poet/lover and a private female reader to discover the reason. The preceding sonnet is an exceptionally nasty attack on her character and behavior:

> So she with flattring smyles weake harts doth guyde
>   vnto her loue, and tempte to theyr decay,
>   whome being caught she kills with cruell pryde,
>   and feeds at pleasure on the wretched pray:
> Yet euen whylst her bloody hands them slay,
>   her eyes looke louely and vpon them smyle:
>   that they take pleasure in her cruell play,
> and dying doe them selues of payne beguyle. (47:5–12)

Many a Petrarchan lady has been charged with the poet's death, but not many are represented as sadists, playing with their prey and then devouring the poet live for supper.[26]

Kellogg finds this talk of "torture, bloodshed, humiliation, captivity, and death," "repulsive" and "improbable." Assuming that "[w]e would not like to believe that the author of the *Faerie Queene* was ever so abjectly enamored that his mistress could despise and disdain him with haughty cruelty for months on end,"[27] Kellogg concludes that poems like this one could not possibly have been written to Spenser's future wife. Yet if we pause to ask why Spenser's female reader responds as she does, the lyric situation makes perfect sense, both psychologically and dramatically. By throwing the offending poem into the fire, she expresses her objections to, and does her best to eradicate, the poet/lover's violent attack on her character and behavior. Taking the lyric dialogue into her own hands, her destructive action dramatizes in concrete terms what Penelope's web represents in symbolic form: "for all that I in many dayes doo weaue, / in one short houre I find by her vndonne" (23:7–8).

The confrontation dramatized by Sonnets 47 and 48 prompts Spenser to face the difference between praising and cursing. He did not mean that she was really tearing him apart with her bare hands and devouring him raw for supper. "[C]onstrayned / to vtter forth the anguish of his hart," he was simply trying to make her understand how badly her behavior had been making him feel; but "she all carelesse of his griefe . . . would not heare, when he to her complayend / the piteous passion of his dying smart" (48:9–12). Daniel's authorized first edition omits his lustiest persuasions and nastiest attacks, thereby concealing the courtship which the private sequence enacts. Spenser does not eliminate the poem his private female reader tried to obliterate because he does not want to destroy the courtship the sonnets transact. Instead, Spenser apologizes for his transgression, and explains that his aggressive rhetoric was not caused by any flaw in her character – for he "neuer thought you ill" (49:7).[28] If she acted precipitously, "ere she could thy cause wel vnderstand," he was at least partially to blame, he now admits, for not realizing how offensive his language must have seemed to her.

Instead of making her response fit his desires as he did in the Apollo/Daphne fiasco, Spenser's poet/lover alters his poetry to accommodate her words and actions. At the end of Sonnet 48 he "speake[s] her good" in a decidedly more conciliatory tone of voice, and in Sonnet 49, "at your footstoole humbled lies" (49:11), the very image of contrition. In Sonnet 51 he explains that his lack of experience in love prevented him from grasping her meaning: "Why then doe I, vntrainde in louers trade, / her hardnes blame which I should more commend?" (51:5–6) Banished in punishment but still yearning for "her presense," he sounds saddened but chastened in Sonnet 52. He repudiates all "pleasure vaine" (52:14, 9), all hint of erotic satisfaction, and professes his subjection more unconditionally than ever before: "So doe I now my selfe a prisoner yeeld" (52:5).

Lacking an alternative lover's discourse, he still cannot do without the language of battle, but now he pleads openly for an end to the hostilities: "Sweet warriour when shall I haue peace with you? / High time it is, this warre now ended were" (57:1–2). He renounces angry recriminations and cogently asks, "what glory can be got, / in slaying him that would liue gladly yours?" (57:11–12). His plea, "graunt me timely grace" (57:11), spoken more directly and simply than ever before, has an emotional resonance and persuasive power far surpassing either his idealized praise or his aggressive imperatives.

BY HER THAT IS MOST ASSURED TO HER SELF

Among the eighty-nine sonnets of the *Amoretti*, only Sonnet 58 is singled out by a title: "By her that is most assured to her selfe."[29] If "by" means not only *concerning*, as Martz suggests, but also *nearby*, as in Gascoigne's headnotes, it sets the scene: standing next to her, the poet/lover recites the poem to her, carefully observing her response. Since "assured" could, but need not, carry the negative connotation of presumptuous, the title recalls the poems' repeated attempts to curtail her "power, / which I too wel haue tride" (25:8) and to master her will: "the whiles she lordeth in licentious blisse / of her freewill" (10:3–4). Since "assured" also means betrothed, the title also acknowledges more clearly than ever before that she has repeatedly rejected his offer of marriage in order to assure "her owne powre" (58:2).

Spenser summons his considerable authority to show her – not to bully her or to deceive her, but to persuade her – that it would be better for her to relinquish her independence and become his wife: "Weake is th'assurance that weake flesh reposeth / In her owne powre, and scorneth others ayde" (58:1–2). From a certain point of view, these lines challenge her power more directly than ever before.[30] Yet the tone sounds muted, generalized, wary of giving offense. Moreover, as soon as line 8 mentions "her glories pride," the sonnet turns into a Christian sermon on the vanity of all earthly possessions: "Ne none so rich, or wise, so strong or fayre, / but fayleth trusting on his owne assurance" (58:9). As if already anticipating her objections to his budding anti-feminist attack on female vanity and inconstancy, Spenser includes himself in the moral: no one, neither man nor woman, poet nor sonnet lady, can ever be entirely self-reliant.

Recalling her proud self-assurance, the poet/lover seems about to reassert his male authority when he suddenly stops lecturing and asks: "Why then doe ye proud fayre, misdeeme so farre, / that to your selfe ye most assured arre?" (58:13–14). As Isabella Whitney advises her readers in *A Sweet Nosegay*: "Ech louer knoweth what he lykes / and what he doth desire, / But seld, or neuer doth he know, / what thing he should require."[31] By concluding with a question rather than an imperative, Spenser shows that he has finally begun to consider the woman's point of view.

The language of Sonnets 58 and 59 is so stylized and artful that a modern reader might well assume the "meaning" or "message" is altogether conventional.[32] Yet here, as so often in Elizabethan poetry of courtship, the most strikingly unconventional observations are expressed through ever so delicate modulations of familiar symbols. One must know the codes – not only the familiar Petrarchan conceit of the ship but also the popular Elizabethan trope of Woman as the weaker vessel – to understand what happens in the marginal inter-lyric space between *Amoretti* 58 where the poet/lover tries to convince his female reader to submit herself to his authority and Sonnet 59 where he praises her for being "so well assured / Vnto her selfe and setled so in hart: / that nether will for better be allured, / ne feard with worse to any chaunce to start" (59:1–4).

To get a handle on the larger symbolic frame of reference, consider for a moment Henrie Smith's *Preparatiue to Mariage*: "the Wife is as much despised for taking rule ouer her Husband, as he for yeelding it unto her." Even if such wives are "despised," they are not, it seems, always prevented. The very choice of the verb "is" suggests a state of being in which "the wife is . . . taking rule" over the husband who is "yeelding it unto her." Smith disapproves, but he is less rigidly patriarchal than such a remark might lead one to assume, for just when his tone seems most uncompromising, the diction and imagery become surprisingly egalitarian: "It becomes not the Mistris to be Master, no more than it beseemeth the Master to be Mistris, but both to saile with their owne winde."[33] Returning in his characteristic way to correct or qualify assertions that might, in other cultural circumstances, have issued from an uncompromising voice of male authority, Smith's text produces a feeling of a parity between the spouses, syntactically, by balancing master and mistress, and metaphorically, by allowing the woman an equivalent right to sail freely, following a course set by her own will and desire.

Spenser's poet/lover uses the same image to represent his new-found respect for "her that is most assured to her selfe":

> But like a steddy ship doth strongly part
>   the raging waues and keeps her course aright:
>   ne ought for tempest doth from it depart,
>   ne ought for fayrer weathers false delight. (59:5–8)

Amoretti 34 represents the poet/lover as a conventional Petrarchan ship, blown endlessly hither and thither by the sighs and tears of unrequited love.[34] Sonnet 59 depicts the female reader/listener as a strong, firm, unwavering ship, following her own straight course, unswayed by friends or enemies alike:

> Such selfe assurance need not feare the spight
>   of grudging foes, ne fauour seek of friends:
>   but in the stay of her owne stedfast might,
>   nether to one her selfe nor other bends. (59:9–12)

A number of critics have complained that the diametrically opposed viewpoints of Sonnets 58 and 59 prove that the *Amoretti* has no psychological or narrative coherence.[35] Yet when we apply a dialogic poetics, Sonnets

58 and 59 constitute neither the irresolvable contradiction Lever sees, nor the "slight" qualification to the poet's happiness Martz perceives, but one of those heightened symbolic moments that are the lyric equivalent of cross-dressing. Far from being the "weaker vessel," this strong, self-reliant female vessel keeps "her course aright." Knowing where she is headed, swerving neither for tempests nor for the false pleasure of fairer weather, she is entirely capable of getting there on her own volition.[36]

By contrast to the Daphne/Apollo incident where the poet/lover turns the female reader's words to his own persuasive purposes, Sonnet 59 retracts Sonnet 58's attempt to define her viewpoint and determine her response. Spenser is "most happy" now, both because he loves such a one best, and also because he is the one whom such a one loves best: "Most happy she that most assured doth rest, / but he most happy who such one loues best" (59:13–14). The syntactical ambiguity of the final couplet does not manipulate or deceive; rather, it captures the respectful exchange of views which transforms idolatry and narcissism into lyric dialogue. The poet/lover's newly discovered capacity to love the female reader *for* her strength and self-assurance – as the Elizabethans were expected to love their queen – is precisely what wins her strong, freely chosen love. By allowing himself to become the object of her active, freely bestowed love, he gains the double pleasure of satisfying her desires and having her satisfy his desires.

Although it is tempting to end our examination of the *Amoretti* at this point, the sequence does not end here because the poet/lover and his female reader/listener need time to absorb and integrate the gender redefinitions that these paired poems dramatize. The following poems reveal the painful intransigence of sexual stereotypes, but they also strive to fashion a new-made idiom which re-negotiates relationships between the sexes and redefines conventional gender roles.

NEW BEGINNINGS

The fresh, new vision of their relationship is symbolized by Lady Day, the onset of spring and the beginning of the liturgical calendar when the "new begins his compast course anew" (62:2). The insistent emphasis on newness announces the spiritual renovation and poetic innovation that emerge from their recent conflict. The mild mornings are a sign, "betokening peace and plenty to ensew" (62:4), while the "compast course" recalls the steady self-assurance of Sonnet 59 which "keeps her course aright."

In language that is thoroughly egalitarian and scrupulously free from recriminations, this sonnet acknowledges that he offended her as much as she offended him: "the old yeares sinnes forepast let vs eschew, / and fly the faults with which we did offend" (62:7–8). Recalling earlier poems in which classic Petrarchan conceits – the hunt (20), the storm (34), the tree (6), and the shipwreck (56) – criticize her for treating him so cruelly, this sonnet rewrites the Petrarchan conceit of the ship yet again. She did not actively set out to wreck, ruin, or destroy him, he now realizes. Her ship was simply proceeding on its own self-assured, straight course, while his "silly" (meaning foolish, feeble, ignorant) "barke" blundered into storms and tempests, led astray by his own foolish, misguided sense of direction: "After long stormes and tempests sad assay, / . . . with which my silly barke was tossed sore" (63:1, 4).

As he finally glimpses the happy shore, these remembered tempests intensify "the ioyous safety of so sweet a rest" (63:10), promising "eternall blisse" (63:14) – at once heavenly and erotic. Now that she has said he may, he gathers these roses with no delay: "Coming to kisse her lyps, (such grace I found) / Me seemd I smelt a gardin of sweet flowres" (64:1–2). Moving from her lips which "smell lyke vnto Gillyflowres" down her neck like "Cullambynes," to her brest "lyke lillyes, ere theyr leaues be shed," and on to "her nipples lyke yung blossomd Iessemynes," and "her goodly bosome lyke a Strawberry bed" (64:4–13) ready to be plucked and eaten, his unrestrained sexual exuberance is heading towards an unmistakeable climax when, quite suddenly, his self-assured female reader announces that she still has some doubts.

In response, he tries to reassure her that marriage to him, far from imposing subjection upon her, will redouble her liberty:

> The doubt which ye misdeeme, fayre loue, is vaine,
>   That fondly feare to loose your liberty,
>   when loosing one, two liberties ye gayne,
>   and make him bond that bondage earst dyd fly. (65:1–4)

The earlier sonnets repeatedly complain that she uses her power to torment and entrap him. Sonnet 10 asked the "Vnrighteous Lord of loue what law is this, / That me thou makest thus tormented be? / the whiles she lordeth in licentious blisse / of her freewill, scorning both thee and me" (10:1–4). Sonnet 12 complained that her eyes, "me captiuing streight with rigorous wrong, / haue euer since me kept in cruell bands" (11–12). Sonnet 37, the gorgeous, "What guyle is this, that those her golden tresses," described his enormous attraction to her, only to recoil in fear of "that guilefull net" (37:10). Now, he freely yields up his liberty without complaint, arguing that marriage imposes no constraints when both members of the couple freely choose each other: "Sweet be the bands, the which true loue doth tye, / without constraynt or dread of any ill" (65:5–6).[37]

Then, quite suddenly, a problem arises: "the gentle birde feeles no captiuity / within her cage, but singes and feeds her fill" (65:7–8). To the bird's owner, it may look as if the bird "feeles no captiuity"; however, to the caged bird, even if she is well nourished and free to sing her heart out, a cage still "feeles" like a cage. The preceding poems clearly show that Spenser's female interlocutor, like Æmelia Lanyer, is fully capable of objecting, "Then let vs haue our Libertie againe, / And challendge to your selues no Sou'raigntie." When the poet/lover criticized her behavior too harshly, she threw his sonnet into the fire. When he attacked her self-assurance, she bluntly refused to submit, sounding like Elizabeth 1 telling the members of parliament, "My Lords, do whatever you wish. As for me, I shall do no otherwise than pleases me."[38] Having fought so hard to exercise her lawful liberty during courtship, this self-assured, early modern woman may not like the prospect of being locked up in her husband's house, as Spenser's poet/lover immediately suspects. Even before she has time to object, he tries to make amends: "simple truth and mutuall good will, / seekes with sweet peace to salue each others wound" (65:9–12).

From the magisterial imposition of male authority to the acceptance of gender equality is not an instantaneous Ovidean metamorphosis, but a slow, painstaking process of social change. Perhaps Spenser is still hoping to reassert his sovereignty once he is safely married, as the metaphor of the caged bird implies, whether deliberately or inadvertently. Yet, his female reader, like her queen and "[m]any such wiues," who "from the least difference in iudgement and opinion, euen in the smallest matters, take occasion to refuse subiection, and thinke they haue warrant enough so to do,"[39] is still free to exercise the liberty that courtship grants early modern women, the freedom to say no, unless or until a suitor provides sufficient assurances that she will be allowed to maintain her self-assurance even after she is married.

In the twenty-four sonnets that follow, Spenser makes numerous attempts, some more overt than others, to acknowledge her power and assure her liberty. The beautiful and justly famous, "Lyke as a huntsman after weary chace," rewrites another favorite Petrarchan conceit, the poet hunting his dear/deer:

> So after long pursuit and vaine assay,
>> when I all weary had the chace forsooke,
>> the gentle deare returnd the selfe-same way,
>> thinking to quench her thirst at the next brooke.
> There she beholding me with mylder looke,
>> sought not to fly, but fearless she still did bide.

When Laura appears to Petrarch as a white doe, he falls into the water and she disappears into the distance, metamorphosed forever into an object of unattainable desire: " 'Nessun mi tocchi,' al bel collo d'intorno / scritto avea di diamanti et di topazi. / 'Libera farmi al mio Cesare parve' " (" 'Let no one touch me,' she bore written with diamonds and topazes around her lovely neck. 'It has pleased my Caesar to make me free'," *RS* 190:9–11). Petrarch leaves every other task to follow his dear, although, as his symbolic immersion in the waters of the mind reveals, she has already become an intangible, idealized vision.

Instead of disappearing, Spenser's Elizabethan dear/deer returns, searching for a brook to satisfy her "thirst," and then gazes straight at him, not with the fierce look of a wild beast ready to bloody and devour her prey, nor with maddeningly ambiguous eye glances, but "with mylder looke" of one who likes what she sees. She stands her ground, "fearless," prepared to take a deep thirst-quenching drink. At moments like this, the *Amoretti* sounds less like Petrarchan or Neoplatonic poetry, extolling the virtues of heavenly chastity, than like an Elizabethan sermon, extolling the reciprocal joys of marriage: "And therefore, *Pro.* 5.19. wee see that the wife should bee to him, as the louing Hinde: namely, delightful, and one in whom hee may delight, that as the Harte delighteth in the Hinde, so the wife, should bee a delight vnto her husband: and so in like manner, shee ought to take delight in him."[40]

A liberated modern woman might still object to the outcome – "till I in hand her yet halfe trembling tooke / and with her owne goodwil hir firmely tyde" (67:11–12) – although, to be fair, we should acknowledge that this Elizabethan woman is no longer caged by duplicitous poetic conceits. Instead, "halfe trembling" from the excitement of his touch, she is tied her "with her owne goodwill." Her "goodwill," meaning her cheerful acquiescence or freewill but also her determination to act; her desire, and specifically her erotic desire, liberates both the male poet/lover and the female reader from the painful frustrations of the Petrarchan deer hunt.[41]

In the original springtime sonnet which initiates the courtship, the impertinence of the imperative – "prepare your selfe new loue to entertaine" (4:14) – initiates the cycle of idealization and aggression that disturbs the poetry and stymies the courtship for so long. Now Spenser sends her an exquisite new *carpe diem* poem, "Fresh spring the herald of loues mighty king" (70:1). Pausing to imagine his sleepyhead "where she is carelesse layd, / yet in her winters bowre not well awake" (70:5–6), his poetic apostrophe dresses spring "in goodly colours gloriously arrayd" (70:4) for her pleasure. This fresh, new spring shows his loving concern for her feelings, and explicitly recognizes her freedom of choice and action: "tell her the ioyous time wil not be staid / vnlesse she doe him by the forelock take" (70:7–8).

Conventional *carpe diem* poems such as Herrick's "To the Virgins, to Make Much of Time" conclude by subjecting frail female bodies to male verbal power: "Then be not coy, but use your time, / And, while ye may, go marry; / For, having lost but once your prime, / You may forever tarry" (13–16). Dropping the apostrophe and speaking directly to her, Spenser avoids the expected conclusion that she had better marry quickly before *she* loses *her* fragile beauty: "Make hast therefore sweet loue, whilest it is prime, / for none can call againe the passed time" (70:13–14). At once tenderly solicitous and passionately impatient, this gender-free language includes male poet/lover and female reader equally.

Sonnet 71, recalling and inverting the trope of Penelope's web, describes his response to her artwork:

> I Ioy to see how in your drawen work,
>   Your selfe vnto the Bee ye doe compare;
>   and me vnto the Spyder that doth lurke,
>   in close awayt to catch her vnaware. (71:1–4)

As the poem unfolds, Spenser's poet/lover becomes so caught up in his own rhetoric that he begins to reproduce the poetry of entrapment which caused her to rend his "whole years work" and forced him to "begin and neuer bring to end" (23:12, 10):

> Right so your selfe were caught in cunning snare
>   of a deare foe, and thralled to his loue:
>   in whose streight bands ye now captiued are
>   so firmely, that ye neuer may remoue. (71:5–8)

In attempting to impose meaning on her art, this image of captivity comes dangerously close to repeating the affronts of Apollo's chase or the bird cage, although the exaggerated self-irony suggests that the poet/lover realizes he is in danger of being "caught in the cunning snare" of his own rhetoric.

Once again, the turn to the sestet anticipates her objections: "so sweet your prison you in time shall proue, / with many deare delights bedecked fine" (11–12). The promise of luxury and pleasure resembles Martha Moulsworth's description of her loving third marriage: "wth him I led an easie darlings life. / I had my will in house, in purse in Store / what would a women old or yong haue more?"[42] In yet another attempt to release his mistress from the prisonhouse of his language, Spenser represents her "drawen work" as an alternative to the competitive, military discourse of the earlier sonnets. Thanks to her artful representation of their relationship, entrapment and duplicity are no longer necessary: "all thensforth eternall peace shall see, / betweene the Spyder and the gentle Bee" (71:13–14).

In Sonnet 72 his "spirit doth spred her bolder winges" (72:1), and male poetic tradition again threatens to draw him ever upwards toward the high, heavenly realms of Petrarchan idolatry. But then he looks down and glimpses her, standing firmly on the earth:

> There my fraile fancy fed with full delight,
>> doth bath in blisse and mantleth most at ease:
>> ne thinks of other heauen, but how it might
>> her harts desire with most contentment please. (72:9–12)

Unlike Sidney's famous outburst – "Desire still cries, 'give me some food'" (71:14) – or his own first entreaty – "seeke some succour both to ease my smart / and also to sustayne thy selfe with food" (2:7–8) – this blissful moment is "fed with full delight." Instead of seeing her as "*my* deare harts desire" (5:1, my emphasis), he happily recognizes her heart's desires: "Hart need not wish none other happinesse, / but here on earth to haue such heauens blisse" (72:13–14). The closing couplet transcends gender stereotypes, merging spiritual and physical bliss, satisfying both male and female desire.

In the following poem, the climax of the courtship, Spenser sends her an epistolary love poem, bearing his heart in the likeness of a captive bird:

> Being my selfe captyued here in care,
>> My hart, whom none with seruile bands can tye,
>> but the fayre tresses of your golden hayre,
>> breaking his prison forth to you doth fly.
> Lyke as a byrd that in ones hand doth spy
>> desired food, to it doth make his flight:
>> euen so my hart, that wont on your fayre eye
>> to feed his fill, flyes backe vnto your sight. (73:1–8)

The language is packed with allusions to its poetic ancestors, to Petrarch's descriptions of Laura's golden hair, to Astrophil and Stella 71 and 81, "Leave that sir Phip, least off your necke be wroong," and above all, to the preceding *Amoretti*. For example, "whom none with seruile bands can tye" allays his earlier fear of being "entrapped" by her golden hair (37). "My hart" in search of "desired food" not only echoes *Astrophil and Stella* 71 and *Amoretti* 2, but it also recalls the pivotal moment in Sonnet 67 when she, in the guise of a hart or deer, returned to quench her thirst and yield up her love.

Striving to release her from his masterful conceits, offering to make amends for imprisoning her in Sonnet 65, Spenser offers himself as her thrall: "Doe you him take, and in your bosome bright, gently encage, that he may be your thrall" (73:9–10). The syntax is so tentative and the diction so gentle that the lines sound more like a question than an imperative. Now he asks her whether she will teach him how she wishes to be identified and known: "perhaps he there may learne with rare delight, / to sing your name and prayses ouer all" (73:11–12). Perhaps! It is at precisely this moment of gender reversal, when he willingly subordinates his authority to her teaching, that Spenser addresses her by name for the first time in the sequence.

Earlier in the sequence Spenser complained to his friend Lodwick that he could not finish the *Faerie Queene* "till she vouchsafe to grawnt me rest" (33:9, 13). Now that she has promised him her hand – for that is apparently what happens in the space between Sonnets 73 and 74 – he writes a celebratory sonnet addressed to "ye three Elizabeths," thanking them for giving him the invaluable "guifts of body, fortune and of mind." First, he thanks his mother, Elizabeth Spenser, for "my being"; then his "souereign Queene," Elizabeth 1, for providing "honour and large richesse"; and finally, in the pride of place, his "loue," Elizabeth – presumably Elizabeth Boyle Spenser, the woman whom Edmund Spenser did, in fact, marry "not long" before the *Amoretti* was published with the *Epithalamion*.

Though certainly not the sole readers of the *Amoretti*, these three bona fide Elizabethan women are Spenser's most cherished readers. They are not only responsible for making him what he is, but they are also in some sense responsible for his creating the sonnets.

Sonnet 73 blazons what the introductory sonnet and the sonnet to Lodwick have already announced: the *Amoretti* is constructed – and should be read – as poetry of courtship, written by the real historical figure Edmund Spenser to a particular Elizabethan woman, named

Elizabeth. Whether Spenser's claim that the *Amoretti* is the enactment of his own courtship "be altogether fayned," as the prefatory letter to Willobie's *Avisa* observes, "or in some part true, or altogether true, and yet in most part Poetically shadowed, you must giue me leaue to speake by coniecutre, and not by knowledge. My coniecture is doubtfull, and therfore I make you the Iudges."[43] What is important about these flagrant avowals of biographical truth is not what they tell us about Spenser's life, but what they tell us about his conception of the lyric dialogue and the lyric audience. Even if Spenser didn't actually use the *Amoretti* to woo Elizabeth Boyle – which seems increasingly unlikely – he goes to great lengths to instruct us to read the sequence as if he did.

SO LONG A RACE

To order or command requires the speaker to be in a position of authority over the hearer; however, a poet/lover has no more authority over his female reader/listener than a poet has over his patron, which is why the *Amoretti* can be addressed *both* to Spenser's beloved Elizabeth *and* his queen, Elizabeth I. Once his beloved Elizabeth accepts his proposal of marriage, Spenser starts to worry once again about his professional obligations to the queen. By re-identifying the poet/lover of the *Amoretti* with the epic poet, Edmund Spenser, by revealing that his witty, self-assured female reader is named Elizabeth, and by wooing her in words calculated to please both her and her namesake, a queen famous for "outwittinge the wittiest ones; for few knew how to aim their shaft against hir cunninge," Spenser connects his poetics of courtship with Elizabeth I's politics of courtship.[44]

Citing the great effort he has already made – "After so long a race as I haue run / Through Faery land, which those six books compile" (80:1–2) – he asks her leave to recover his strength so that he can re-dedicate himself "as a steed refreshed after toyle" to her praise:

> Till then giue leaue to me in pleasant mew,
>   to sport my muse and sing my loues sweet praise:
>   the contemplation of whose heauenly hew,
>   my spirit to an higher pitch wil rayse.
> But let her prayses yet be low and meane,
>   fit for the handmayd of the Faery Queene. (80:9–14)

For the first time in the sequence, Spenser seems as eager to please Queen Elizabeth as his beloved Elizabeth. Having gained the latter's promise of marriage, he is all the more eager for the *Amoretti* to advance his professional prospects, making him "one of that great number of Learned men who through [Queen Elizabeth's] Favour and Bounty did abound both with Wealth and Leisure."[45]

In the following sonnet, "One day I wrote her name vpon the strand," Spenser pays tribute to his mistress's wit. Eternizing poems like Shakespeare's proclaim the poet's power to conquer time: "Gainst death and all oblivious enmity / Shall you pace forth; your praise shall still find room / Even in the eyes of all posterity."[46] *Carpe diem* poems like Herrick's "Gather ye rosebuds" summon poetic authority to urge young ladies to marry. In Spenser's witty rewriting of lyric convention, the female interlocutor seizes the occasion to point out the vanity and limits of male poetic authority: "Vayne man, sayd she, that doest in vaine assay, / a mortall thing so to immortalize, / for I my selue shall lyke to this decay, and eek my name bee wyped out lykewize" (75:5–8).

Here, as in that first, retrospective sonnet where he expressed the wish to "please her alone," verbal ambiguity is not a duplicitous rhetorical strategy, designed to seduce and master her, but a tribute to the disruptive, revitalizing power of conversation: "Where whenas death shall all the world subdew, / our loue shall liue, and later life renew" (75:13–14). Their lyric dialogue will not only rejuvenate their later years, keeping their relationship flexible and alive, but it will continue in times to come, reread, recreated by later readers such as we, to whom their "rare delight" (73:11) continues to speak anew.

These later sonnets are such a remarkable exchange of respectful, empathetic love, disturbed and complicated but not in the end prevented by Spenser's culturally conditioned impulse to assert his masculine authority, that I have indulged the temptation to linger over them, to illustrate what Spenser applies his extraordinary poetic power to demonstrating in sonnet after sonnet: that he has learned to love Elizabeth *for* the "frewil," the "power," the "self-assurance," the "virtues rare" that undo all his efforts at mastery, causing him to rethink his own most deeply held assumptions and to refashion some of the most treasured lyric tropes: "So when I thinke to end that I begonne, / I must begin and neuer bring to end" (23:9–10).

Close to the end of the sequence Elizabeth sends him away to await their wedding, lest his exuberant "blisse" get out of control. During this period of separation, someone tries to defame his character and motives, and Spenser briefly fears that the slander will jinx the courtship, as it does Whythorne's. At this moment of worry and separation, the *Amoretti* sounds more like a Petrarchan complaint than like a lyric dialogue of

Elizabethan courtship. However, the temporary note of uncertainty only confirms Elizabeth's continuing power to unweave the web of his words, to rend his most artful constructions, to undo any falsely complacent gestures towards stability and closure.

The sequence ends by dramatizing, yet again, the contingency of courtship, the difficulty of maintaining love even as one is on the verge of attaining it. While the persistent undertone of joy suggests that now Spenser trusts Elizabeth to follow her own self-assured course, undeterred by enemies or friends, these later poems also recognize the difficulty of maintaining self-assurance after courtship succeeds and intimacy begins. "It becomes still more difficult to find / Words at once true and fair, / Or not untrue and not unfair," as Larkin observes in "Talking in Bed."

SUCH IS THE POWER OF LOVE

This study concludes with Spenser, although it began as a book on Donne, because Spenser is much readier than Donne to explain the powerful role the Elizabethan female lyric audience plays in deconstructing and recomposing the English Renaissance lyric genre. Spenser's more theoretical poems provide a poetics of the genre, dramatizing his mistress's role as resisting reader and cultural critic, exploring conflicts between the sexes that less magisterial poets such as Daniel or Donne enact but do not explain.

At the outset of the *Amoretti*, the poet/lover addresses his private female reader indirectly, through poetic apostrophes. The early poems, spoken to her from afar, reveal almost nothing about her responses because the poet/lover hardly knows her. As the courtship progresses, the sonnets, addressed directly to her, dramatize the poet/lover's side of an increasingly heated conversation. Her responses, though still remaining on the poem's margins, become somewhat easier to detect or infer from the gaps and contradictions – by weighing what one sonnet anticipates or desires and what a subsequent sonnet amends or revises.

As the conflicts between them intensify, Elizabeth voices her objections more boldly, and he begins to understand the ideological and gender differences which separate them. The more bluntly she disputes his assumptions, the more clearly her oppositional voice peeks through. Yet whenever her responses leave the margins and enter the text, it is difficult to know whether the poet/lover is unwittingly distorting her words or deliberately misconstruing her views in the hopes of advancing his own persuasive purpose. After the Apollo/Daphne fiasco produces a physical and psychological separation, Spenser again writes to himself, or to a friend, or to no one in particular, hoping she will overhear his complaint. Eventually, the lyric dialogue resumes. Earlier images recur, transformed by changes in his attitude and their relationship. Elizabeth withholds her acceptance of Spenser's suit until he retracts his criticism of her "pride" and "licentious free-wil," hears and heeds what she is saying, and agrees to honor her self-assurance even after marriage – in short, until he leaves behind all the male -isms, Petrarchism, Neoplatonism, anti-feminism, which subject early modern women to male authority.

The sequence represents "her that is most assured to her selfe" as "a determinate and signifying absence in the text."[47] Even if the courtship dramatized in the *Amoretti* is fictional, it represents the poet's mistress not as the object of the poet's desire, silent, iconic, powerless, but as the lyric audience – as she "that is most assured to her selfe."[48]

The *Amoretti* asks to be read not only as the dramatization of Spenser's own courtship but also as a symbolic move in an ideological confrontation between the sexes, for the emotional conflicts and verbal incongruities of the sonnets parallel the larger sexual conflicts and social contradictions of the culture. As the poet/lover comes to appreciate the female reader's wit and intelligence, she begins to resemble the bold, young woman in Tilney's *Flower of Friendshippe* who says, "I know not . . . what we are bounde to do, but as meete is it, that the husbande obey the wife, as the wife the husband, or at the least that there bee no superioritye betweene them . . . For women haue soules as wel as men, they haue wit as wel as men, and more apte for procreation of children than men. What reason is it then, that they should be bound, whome nature hath made free?" As Spenser begins to admire Elizabeth's power and to recognize her lawful liberty, she sounds more and more like the Maydens of London who write, "Yet when he hath sayd what he can: he can shewe no good cause why our liberties should be restrained, as he so earnestly desired." [49]

By the end of the *Amoretti*, Spenser's female reader seems less like a conventional sonnet lady than like Elizabeth I, declaring her right to remain single unless or until she finds a suitor who not only arouses her desire but who also acknowledges her liberty: "nothing would suffice to make her think of marrying, or even treating of marriage; but the person she was to marry pleasing her so much as to cause her to desire what at present she ha[d] no wish for."[50]

In *English Literature in the Sixteenth Century* Lewis praises the *Amoretti*'s "devout, quiet, harmonious pattern," but concludes that "Spenser was not one of the great sonneteers."[51] I think the *Amoretti* is an extraordinary literary achievement, as well as a remarkable cultural document, precisely because its devout, quiet, harmonious pattern is continually controverted by the presumption of a "self-assured" female reader who undoes Spenser's rhetoric, refutes his conceptions of women, love, sex, and marriage, and prompts him to undertake a far more probing exploration of what it means for the lyric to be in the business of transacting a courtship: "Such is the power of loue in gentle mind, / that it can alter all the course of kynd" (30:13–14).

The published volume, printed along with the *Epithalamion* about the time of Edmund Spenser's marriage to Elizabeth Boyle, is enormously popular, adding its private lyric courtship to the larger cultural debate about poetry and courtship and providing new ways for Elizabethan women and men to represent themselves and woo each other. By identifying his mistress as "th'author of my blisse" (22:9), Spenser eternizes the female reader's power over his poetry, giving "her words so wise" an important critical voice in English literary tradition, even today.

EPILOGUE

To end that I begun

> So when I thinke to end that I begonne,
>   I must begin and neuer bring to end:
>   for with one looke she spils that long I sponne,
>   and with one word my whole years work doth rend.
>   Spenser's *Amoretti* 23:9–12

In the dedicatory epistle to her translation of a Spanish romance, Margaret Tyler writes, "Thou hast heere gentle Reader, the historie of Trebatio, an Emperour in Greece: whether a true storie of him in deede, or a fained fable, I wot not, neither d[i]d I greatlye seeke after it in [the] translation."[1] Like Daniel's pirated, private sonnet sequence, some Elizabethan lyric sequences are the embodiment of the poet's own courtship. Like Whythorne's *Autobiography*, Gascoigne's *Hundreth Sundrie Flowres,* and the authorized edition of Daniel's *Delia*, some combine original poems, written to woo a particular woman, with later revisions and additions, made either to explain the original lyric courtship or to conceal anything too scandalous. Still others are "a fained fable," which, like Shakespeare's *As You Like It* or *Much Ado about Nothing*, dramatize the role lyric poetry plays in Elizabethan courtship.

Whether the *Amoretti* is "a fained fable" or "a true storie of him in deede" like Tyler's translation, or "both false and also true" like Isabella Whitney's letter to her unconstant lover, I wot not, neither did I greatly seek after it, for "the poet, he nothing affirms, and therefore never lieth."[2] A suitor cannot conduct a courtship without artfulness, for what is acted "in deed" can only be dramatized in story – in fable that is "fained" because it is both desired and constructed. Yet, what is written in verse can also be enacted – and not only on the stage. Reading Elizabethan love poetry *as if* it is a courtship – whether real or imaginary – does not diminish its aesthetic and formal characteristics. Rather it means that the lyric dialogue between the male poet/lover and the female interlocutor is as artfully constructed as any other aspect of Elizabethan poetry.

In "Cartographies of Silence," Adrienne Rich writes:

> Silence can be a plan
> rigorously executed
>
> the blueprint to a life
>
> It is a presence
> It has a history of form
>
> Do not confuse it
> with any kind of absence[3]

By making our literary history and cultural conversation more responsive to early modern women's voices – both by reconstructing the dialogue between the male poet/lover and the female lyric audience which takes place in the marginal, inter-lyric spaces, and by heeding the voices and the views of Elizabethan women writers – we can produce alternative histories of form which contain blueprints to the lives of Elizabethan women.

By attending to the female lyric tradition and the female lyric audience, we can begin to break the silence that has been "rigorously executed" on Elizabethan women from Elizabeth I, Mary Sidney and Isabella Whitney to Delia, Penelope Rich, Elizabeth Boyle, and Ann More, and all those unknown Elizabethan women, from Jane Anger to the Maydens of London. As their "self-assured" voices provide a critique of or a counterpoint to the male lyric tradition, poetry becomes "the gate"

> throgh which her words so wise do make their way
> to beare the message of her gentle spright.
> The rest be works of natures wonderment,
> but this the worke of harts astonishment. (*Am* 81:12–14).

In the early seventeenth century, Mary Wroth claims the right which Elizabethan women from Elizabeth I and Mary Sidney to Isabella Whitney and the Maydens of London struggle so hard to assert: the right to remain both "true vnto your selues" (34:3) and free to express female desire: "Catch you alwatching eyes ere they be past, / Or take yours fixt, where your best Loue hath sought / The pride of your desires" (34:5–7). Instead of demurely lowering her eyes, Wroth boldly returns the gaze of all those who search her face for a clue to her desires. Moving from a Petrarchan octave, where Pamphilia, like Laura, hides her "heart's most secret thought" (34:2), to an English sestet where she, like Isabella Whitney, seizes the opportunity to "enioy ful sight of Loue" (34:13), Wroth's sonnet constructs a voice, a strategy, and a form for female desire.

The coded autobiographical allusions in Wroth's *Pamphilia to Amphilanthus*, the first complete and still extant sonnet sequence written by an Englishwoman, are both explained and concealed by the thinly veiled topical allusions in *The Countess of Montgomery's Urania*. Like Wroth herself, Wroth's heroine writes autobiographical love poetry – her veiled erotic persuasion betrayed by the heat of her flushed skin. In fact, the *Urania* describes a number of women poets who "pretend to desire an aesthetic response to their poetry while their real hope is for an amorous one."[4] As *Pamphilia to Amphilanthus* and *Urania* demonstrate, Wroth is as cognizant as Whythorne, Gascoigne, Sidney, Daniel, and Spenser of the ways in which English Renaissance men and women use poetry for courtship and seduction.

In the mid-seventeenth century, Dorothy Oxinden writes to her lover, telling him to drop his idolatrous rhetoric – "you write in such strains of rethorick I know not well how to answere them. Your complements terme me a godis; I know you are sensible of my frayltyes and imperfections." Like the female letter-writer in Angel Day's *English Secretory*, who complains that her suitor's eloquent rhetoric is "fitter for a Poeticall Goddess" than for "any such earthlie" woman, Dorothy Oxinden seeks a more forthright and serious conversation: "If you could get some frend that weare acquainted in the ships for to get thee som place there, for I think 'tis safer being there then in the wares . . ."[5]

Dorothy Oxinden's female predecessors and contemporaries challenge poetic and social convention, resisting or reinterpreting conventional love language, *both* upon those rare occasions when they translate Petrarch or write poetry of their own *and* upon those much more frequent occasions when, "poor mortal creatures," they are the recipients of "such strains of rethorick" that they "know not well how to answere." Yet answer they do, and their responses provide a compelling critique of "complements" which "term [them] a godis."

In telling their male suitors, "I know you are sensible of my frayltyes and imperfections," these women also make their suitors and readers sensible of the frailties and imperfections which male poetic "rhetorick" strives to conceal.[6] As female authors, auditors, and readers begin to formulate alternatives to the monologic male voice of Renaissance lyric tradition, male poets/lovers, eager to win their female reader's/listener's

approval and acceptance, begin to anticipate and incorporate their
female readers' and listeners' admonitions.

It is during the first half of the seventeenth century that Lucy
Hutchinson rejects numerous suitors favored by her mother and friends
until, finally, Colonel Hutchinson wins her consent, "after about 14
months various exercise of his mind, in the persuite of his love" (1:98),
not with the idealizing rhetoric of Petrarchan idolatry but with the intel-
lectually engaged and impassioned conversation represented by
Elizabethan poetry of courtship: "never was there a passion more ardent
and lesse idolatrous; he lov'd her better than his life, with inexpressable
tendernesse and kindnesse, [and] had a most high obliging esteeme of
her."[7]

According to her own account, as a young woman Lucy eagerly
"learne[s] or heare[s] wittie songs and amorous sonnetts or poems, and
twenty things of that kind." Moreover, as Hutchinson's diary goes on to
explain, the women in her mother's household – like the women represented in the letter writing manuals, Gascoigne's *Hundreth Sundrie Flowres*,
Whythorne's *Autobiography*, and Puttenham's *Arte of English Poesie* – avidly
learn "twenty things of that kind" so that they can answer their suitors
or perhaps even initiate a courtship or seduction of their own: "wherein
I was so apt that I became the confident in all the loves that were
managed among my mother's young weomen, and there was none of
them but had many lovers, and some particular friends belov'd above the
rest."[8]

There is no evidence that Lucy Hutchinson recites or writes "wittie
songs and amorous sonnetts" to her own numerous suitors, for the diary
suddenly breaks off in mid-sentence: "among these I have . . ." As the
editor explains, "[a]t this place is a great chasm, many leaves being torn
out apparently by the writer herself." Knowing Lucy's private passion
for "wittie songs and amorous sonnetts," and also knowing her prolific
literary productivity (in addition to the diary, she wrote a multi-volume
biography of her deceased husband), it is tempting to imagine that this
"great chasm" of history contains Lucy Hutchinson's love lyrics, silently
entombed along with the love letters and love songs of many another
early modern Englishwoman.[9]

In reconstructing a dialogic poetics of courtship, we have been trying
to read Elizabethan love poetry as the Elizabethans themselves read it:
first and foremost, as "if I were a mistresse"; second, as voyeurs, avidly,
pruriently wondering what "really" happened between the poet/lover
and his mistress; third, as scavengers and consumers, reconstruing the

poem, perhaps even revising the poem, to suit their own immediate purposes; finally, as critics of *both* poetry *and* courtship, seeking, debating, defending "the right use of the material point" of both poetry and courtship.

The intrigue and interpretive uncertainty that make courtship all-consuming also make the process of reading Elizabethan poetry of courtship vastly different from the demands and pleasures of reading Petrarchan love poetry. The recurrent tropes and eternizing purpose, the *monotonia* and oxymoronic stasis, nourish infinite changes on a single theme. Elizabethan poetry of courtship is constantly adapting to the lyric situation and the lyric audience: it is a "forme of Poesie variable, inconstant, affected, curious, and most witty of any others."[10]

"[D]esire must always be transgressive, must always have a repressive law or norm through which to burst and against which to define itself."[11] The idolatrous, narcissistic mirroring of Petrarchan poet and Petrarchan lady represents the repressive norm through which the Elizabethan lyric dialogue of courtship breaks and against which it defines itself. Elizabethan poetry arises from, rebels against, and sometimes, but not always, lapses back into and continues to rebel against Petrarchan idolatry, either overcoming, or overcome by, the sexual conflicts and social differences it strives to ameliorate.

Ultimately, the veering of conversation, empowered by passion, disturbed by sexual conflict, and grounded by material constraint, is the characteristic Elizabethan lyric note. As this revolution in poetic language merges with the ongoing cultural revolution, female voices find their way into early modern English culture and English Renaissance literary tradition, having "added to their own an oversound, / Her tone of meaning but without the words" – or without the words' traditional tone and meaning. "Never again would birds' song be the same."[12]

Notes

I AN INTRODUCTION TO ELIZABETHAN COURTSHIP

1 John Donne, "Loves growth" lines 11–14, *The Complete Poetry of John Donne*, John T. Shawcross (ed.) (Garden City, NY: Anchor Books, 1967).

2 William Shakespeare, *The Sonnets; and, A Lover's Complaint*, John Kerrigan (ed.) (New York: Viking, 1986; Harmondsworth: Penguin, 1986), 29:1–2. Sonnet sequences are cited parenthetically, the poem number followed by line numbers. All quotations from Shakespeare's sonnets and *A Lover's Complaint* refer to Kerrigan's edition. Quotations from Shakespeare's plays, also cited parenthetically, are from *The Riverside Shakespeare*, G. Blakemore Evans, *et al.* (eds.) (Boston: Houghton Mifflin, 1974).

3 *The Poems of Sir Philip Sidney*, William A. Ringler, Jr. (ed.) (Oxford: Clarendon Press, 1962). All future quotations of Sidney's poetry are from this edition.

4 George Herbert, "The Forerunners," quoted from *The Works of George Herbert*, F. E. Hutchinson (ed.) (Oxford: Clarendon Press, 1970).

5 Unless otherwise noted, all definitions, based on Elizabethan usage, are taken from the *Compact Edition of the Oxford English Dictionary* (Oxford University Press, 1971). See Bates, *The Rhetoric of Courtship in Elizabethan Language and Literature* (Cambridge University Press, 1992), p. 8: "An identical semantic shift" in the word for courtship, "took place in the major European languages, and did so – fascinatingly enough – at more or less the same time: around the turn of the sixteenth century."

6 These thoughts were prompted by Kenneth Burke's observation in *The Philosophy of Literary Form*, 1941 (Rev. edn., Berkeley: University of California Press, 1973), p. 301, that American slang "developed out of the fact that new typical situations had arisen and people needed names for them."

7 On the literature of courtesy and the arts and practice of courtiership, see Bates, *The Rhetoric of Courtship;* Stephen Jay Greenblatt, *Sir Walter Raleigh: The Renaissance Man and His Roles* (New Haven: Yale University Press, 1973); Richard Helgerson, *The Elizabethan Prodigal* (Berkeley: University of California Press, 1976), and *Self-Crowned Laureates: Spenser, Jonson, Milton and the Literary System* (Berkeley: University of California Press, 1983); Clark Hulse, "Stella's Wit: Penelope Rich as Reader of Sidney's Sonnets," *Rewriting the Renaissance: The Discourses of Sexual Difference in Early Modern*

Europe, Margaret W. Ferguson, Maureen Quilligan, and Nancy Vickers (eds)
(University of Chicago Press, 1986), pp. 272–86; Jonathan Goldberg, *James I
and the Politics of Literature: Jonson, Shakespeare, Donne and their Contemporaries*
(Baltimore: Johns Hopkins University Press, 1983); Daniel Javitch, *Poetry and
Courtliness in Renaissance England* (Princeton University Press, 1978); Ann
Rosalind Jones and Peter Stallybrass, "The Politics of *Astrophil and Stella*,"
Studies in English Literature 24 (1984): 53–68; Guy Fitch Lytle and Stephen
Orgel, *Patronage in the Renaissance* (Princeton University Press, 1981); Eleanor
Rosenberg, *Leicester, Patron of Letters* (New York: Columbia University Press,
1955); Arthur F. Marotti, *John Donne, Coterie Poet* (Madison: University of
Wisconsin Press, 1986); Richard C. McCoy, *The Rites of Knighthood: The
Literature and Politics of Elizabethan Chivalry* (Berkeley: University of California
Press, 1989), and *Sir Philip Sidney: Rebellion in Arcadia* (New Brunswick, New
Jersey: Rutgers University Press, 1979); Louis Adrian Montrose, "Eliza,
Queene of Shepheardes, and the Pastoral of Power," *English Literary
Renaissance* 10 (1980): 153–82; Wayne A. Rebhorn, *Courtly Performances:
Masking and Festivity in Castiglione's Book of the Courtier* (Detroit: Wayne State
University Press, 1978); Michael Schoenfeldt, *Prayer and Power: George Herbert
and Renaissance Courtship* (University of Chicago Press, 1981); Frank
Whigham, *Ambition and Privilege: The Social Tropes of Elizabethan Courtesy Theory*
(Berkeley: University of California Press, 1984).

8 Ringler, *Poems of Sidney*, p. 490, writes, "The 'great cause' more probably
refers to public service in general, which requires 'use' (experience) and 'art'
(knowledge of the principles of government and statesmanship)." McCoy,
Sir Philip Sidney, p. 109, cites Ringler's note to the poem and concludes that
"Sidney begins to return to the world of public and political concerns after
deliberately banishing them from his protracted meditation on love."
McCoy recognizes that Sidney "attempts one of the more explicit formula-
tions of sexual politics, defining precisely the issues of power and autonomy." Yet he makes sexual politics seem like an auxiliary issue rather than
a central facet of the public world. Jones and Stallybrass, "Politics of
Astrophil" p. 61, offer an intriguing analysis of Stella's "double role: the
barrier to but also the potential aider of public service." Yet for them too, it
is "the public world" of the court that is "the place of a great cause which
it would be blameworthy to ignore."

9 In *The Elizabethan Courtier Poets: The Poems and their Contexts*, (Columbia:
University of Missouri Press, 1991), Steven W. May demonstrates that very
few of the great Elizabethan lyrics are written to be read at court. *Astrophil and
Stella* looks like the one example of canonical courtly poetry, but it was actually written when Sidney withdrew from court, having offended the queen by
objecting to her marriage with the Duke of Alençon (McCoy, *Rites* p. 63,
Arthur F. Marotti, " 'Love Is Not Love': Elizabethan Sonnet Sequences and
the Social Order," *English Literary History* 49 (1982): 396–428.) As May explains,
p. 84, in Sonnet 23, "Astrophil notes that others interpret his preoccupation
with Stella as concern over politics 'because the Prince my service tries.' "

10 This book could not have been written without the scholarship on English Renaissance women that has appeared in the last two decades. Among the studies that helped me with my own investigations are: Elaine V. Beilin, *Redeeming Eve: Women Writers of the English Renaissance* (Princeton University Press, 1987); Pamela Joseph Benson, *The Invention of The Renaissance Woman* (University Park: Pennsylvania State University Press, 1992); Philippa Berry, *Of Chastity and Power: Elizabethan Literature and the Unmarried Queen* (London: Routledge, 1989); Jean R. Brink, Allison P. Coudert, and Maryanne C. Horowitz (eds.), *The Politics of Gender in Early Modern Europe, Sixteenth-Century Essays & Studies* 12 (1989); Carroll Camden, *The Elizabethan Woman*, 1952 (Mamaroneck, New York: Appel, 1975); Ann Jennalie Cook, *Making a Match: Courtship in Shakespeare and his Society* (Princeton University Press, 1991); Stevie Davies, *The Feminine Reclaimed: The Idea of Woman in Spenser, Shakespeare, and Milton* (Lexington: University of Kentucky Press, 1986); Natalie Zemon Davis, *Society and Culture in Early Modern France: Eight Essays by Natalie Zemon Davis* (Stanford University Press, 1975); Heather A. Dubrow, *A Happier Eden: The Politics of Marriage in Stuart Epithalamium* (Ithaca: Cornell University Press, 1990); Juliet Dusinberre, *Shakespeare and the Nature of Women* (London: Macmillan, 1975); Margaret J. M. Ezell, *The Patriarch's Wife: Literary Evidence and the History of the Family* (Chapel Hill: University North Carolina Press, 1987); Kirby Farrell, Elizabeth H. Hageman, and Arthur F. Kinney (eds.), *Women in the Renaissance: Selections from English Literary Renaissance* (Amherst, University of Massachusetts Press, 1988); Margaret W. Ferguson, Maureen Quilligan, and Nancy Vickers (eds.), *Rewriting the Renaissance: The Discourses of Sexual Difference in Early Modern Europe* (University of Chicago Press, 1986); Moira Ferguson (ed.), *First Feminists: British Women Writers: 1578–1799* (Bloomington: Indiana University Press; Old Westbury, New York: Feminist Press, 1985); Marjorie B. Garber, *Cannibals, Witches, and Divorce: Estranging the Renaissance* (Baltimore: Johns Hopkins University Press, 1987); Margaret George, *Women in the First Capitalist Society: Experiences in Seventeenth-Century England* (Urbana: University of Illinois Press, 1988); Elspeth Graham, Hilary Hinds, Elaine Hobby, and Helen Wilcox (eds.), *Her Own Life: Autobiographical Writings by Seventeenth-Century Englishwomen* (London: Routledge, 1989); Margaret Patterson Hannay, *Silent but for the Word: Tudor Women as Patrons, Translators, and Writers of Religious Works* (Ohio: Kent State University Press, 1985); Elizabeth D. Harvey and Katharine Eisaman Maus (eds.), *Soliciting Interpretation: Literary Theory and Seventeenth-Century English Poetry* (University of Chicago Press, 1990); Anne M. Haselkorn and Betty S. Travitsky (eds.), *The Renaissance Englishwoman in Print: Counterbalancing the Canon* (Amherst: University of Massachusetts Press, 1990); Katherine Usher Henderson and Barbara F. McManus, *Half Humankind: Contexts and Texts of the Controversy about Women in England 1540–1640* (Urbana: University of Illinois Press, 1985); Jean E. Howard, "Crossdressing, The Theatre, and Gender Struggle in Early Modern England," *Shakespeare Quarterly* 39 (1988): 418–40; Suzanne Hull, *Chaste, Silent & Obedient: English Books for Women 1475–1640* (San Marino,

California: Huntingdon Library, 1982); Lisa Jardine, *Still Harping on Daughters: Women and Drama in the Age of Shakespeare* (Totowa, New Jersey: Barnes, 1983); Ann Rosalind Jones, *The Currency of Eros: Women's Love Lyric in Europe 1540–1620* (Bloomington: Indiana University Press, 1990); Constance Jordan, *Renaissance Feminism: Literary Texts and Political Models* (Ithaca: Cornell University Press, 1990); Joan Kelly, *Women, History, & Theory: The Essays of Joan Kelly* (University of Chicago Press, 1984); Margaret L. King, *Women of the Renaissance* (University of Chicago Press, 1991); Joan Larsen Klein (ed.), *Daughters, Wives, and Widows: Writings by Men about Women and Marriage in England, 1500–1640* (Urbana: University of Illinois Press, 1991); Mary Ellen Lamb, *Gender and Authorship in the Sidney Circle* (Madison: University of Wisconsin Press, 1990); Carolyn Ruth Swift Lenz, Gayle Greene, and Carol Thomas Neely (eds.), *The Woman's Part: Feminist Criticism of Shakespeare* (Urbana: University of Illinois, 1980); Carole Levin, *The Heart and Stomach of a King: Elizabeth I and the Politics of Sex and Power* (Philadelphia: University of Pennsylvania Press, 1994); Barbara Kiefer Lewalski, *Writing Women in Jacobean England* (Cambridge: Harvard University Press, 1993); Leah S. Marcus, *Puzzling Shakespeare: Local Reading and Its Discontents,* the New Historicism Studies in Cultural Poetics 6 (Berkeley: University of California Press, 1988); Sara Heller Mendelson, *The Mental World of Stuart Women: Three Studies* (Amherst: University of Massachusetts Press, 1987); Karen Newman, *Fashioning Femininity and the English Renaissance Drama* (University of Chicago Press, 1991); Mary Nyquist and Margaret W. Ferguson (eds.), *Re-membering Milton: Essays on the Texts and Traditions* (New York: Methuen, 1988); Mary Prior (ed.), *Women in English Society 1500–1800* (London: Methuen, 1985); Mary Beth Rose, *The Expense of Spirit: Love and Sexuality in English Renaissance Drama* (Ithaca: Cornell University Press, 1988); Mary Beth Rose (ed.), *Women in the Middle Ages and the Renaissance: Literary and Historical Perspectives* (Syracuse University Press, 1986); Hilda Smith, *Reason's Disciples: Seventeenth-Century English Feminists* (Urbana: University of Illinois Press, 1982); Julia M. Walker (ed.), *Milton and the Idea of Woman* (Urbana: University of Illinois Press, 1988); Retha M. Warnicke, *Women of the English Renaissance and Reformation* (Westport, Conn.: Greenwood Press, 1983); Merry Wiesner, *Women and Gender in Early Modern Europe* (Cambridge University Press, 1993) and Linda Woodbridge, *Women and the English Renaissance: Literature and the Nature of Womankind, 1540 to 1620* (Urbana: University of Illinois Press, 1984).

11   For a comparative study of English women writers and European female challenges to Petrarchism, see Jones, *The Currency of Eros.* On the similarities among English, French, and Italian conceptions of courtship, see Bates, *Rhetoric of Courtship* chapter 2. For a study of medieval women poets who were "claiming the power to speak – to represent themselves," see Laurie A. Finke, *Feminist Theory, Women's Writing* (Ithaca: Cornell University Press, 1992), p. 33. In the case of male poets, Finke argues, p. 48, that "it is in the withholding of her favors, in her silence, that [the woman] exercises her power." On the continuities between medieval and Renaissance, see

Mariann Sanders Regan, *Love Words: The Self and the Text in Medieval and Renaissance Poetry* (Ithaca: Cornell University Press, 1982).

12 In *The Renaissance Dialogue: Literary Dialogue in its Social and Political Contexts, Castiglione to Galileo* (Cambridge University Press, 1992), p. 5, Virginia Cox argues that "by duplicating its primary communication with a fictional double, the dialogue has the effect of calling attention to the act of communication itself . . . the act of persuasion is played out before us, and we cannot simply absorb the message without reflecting on the way in which it is being sent and received." The lyric dialogue has a similar, dynamic impact: it calls attention both to the act of communication and the act of courtship, making it difficult for us to absorb the message of the poem without reflecting on the ways in which the courtship is transacted and the message sent and received.

13 For a survey of Petrarchism as one of the three major systems of international love see Irving Singer, *The Nature of Love*, 3 vols., 1966 (University of Chicago Press, 1984–1987), vol. II, pp. 129–64; Dennis de Rougement, *Love in the Western World*, Montgomery Belgion (trans.), 1940 (Rev. and aug. edn. New York: Harper Colophon, 1974), pp. 180–87. For an astute study of Petrarchism and its impact on subsequent literature, including Sidney's *Astrophil and Stella*, see Greene, *Post-Petrarchism*. For studies of Petrarchism and continental humanism and their relation to English Renaissance poetry, see Mary Thomas Crane, *Framing Authority: Sayings, Self, and Society in Sixteenth-Century England* (Princeton University Press, 1993); Heather A. Dubrow, *Echoes of Desire: English Petrarchism and Its Counterdiscourses* (Ithaca: Cornell University Press, 1995); Lewis Einstein, *The Italian Renaissance in England* (New York: Columbia University Press, 1902); Barbara L. Estrin, *Laura: Uncovering Gender and Genre in Wyatt, Donne, and Marvell* (Durham: Duke University Press, 1994); Roland Greene, *Post-Petrarchism: Origins and Innovations of the Western Lyric Sequence* (Princeton University Press, 1991); David Kalstone, *Sidney's Poetry: Contexts and Interpretations* (New York: Norton, 1965); William Kerrigan and Gordon Braden, *The Idea of the Renaissance* (Baltimore: Johns Hopkins University Press, 1988); J. W. Lever, *The Elizabethan Love Sonnet*, 1966 (London: Methuen, 1978); Jerome Mazzaro, *Transformations in the Renaissance English Lyric* (Ithaca: Cornell University Press, 1970); Lu Emily Pearson, *Elizabethan Love Conventions* (New York: Barnes & Noble, 1967); Anne Lake Prescott, *French Poets and the English Renaissance: Studies in Fame and Transformation* (New Haven: Yale University Press, 1978); Hugh M. Richmond, *The School of Love: The Evolution of the Stuart Love Lyric* (Princeton University Press, 1964); Thomas P. Roche, *Petrarch and the English Sonnet Sequences* (New York: AMS Press, 1989); Neil L. Rudenstine, *Sidney's Poetic Development* (Cambridge: Harvard University Press, 1967); A. Lytton Sells, *The Italian Influence in English Poetry, from Chaucer to Southwell* (Bloomington: Indiana University Press, 1955); A. J. Smith, *The Metaphysics of Love: Studies in Renaissance Love Poetry from Dante to Milton* (Cambridge University Press, 1985); Michael R. G. Spiller, *The Development of the Sonnet:*

An Introduction, (London: Routledge, 1992); Sara Sturm-Maddox, *Petrarch's Laurels* (University Park: Pennsylvania State University Press, 1992), and *Petrarch's Metamorphoses: Text and Subtext in the Rime Sparse* (Columbia: University of Missouri Press, 1985).

14 Burke, *Philosophy of Literary Form*, p. 109. M. M. Bakhtin, *The Dialogic Imagination: Four Essays*, Michael Holquist (ed.), Caryl Emerson and Michael Holquist (trans.) (Austin: University of Texas Press, 1981), p. 276, makes a similar point: "The living utterance, having taken meaning and shape at a particular historical moment in a socially specific environment, cannot fail to brush up against thousands of living dialogic threads, woven by socio-ideological consciousness around the given object of an utterance; it cannot fail to become an active participant in social dialogue."

15 Thomas Whythorne, *The Autobiography of Thomas Whythorne*, James M. Osborn (ed.), Modern spelling edn. (London: Oxford University Press, 1962), p. 23.

16 For a review of the scholarship, see Farrell, Hageman, Kinney, *Women in the Renaissance*, pp. 228–309.

17 For a study of the complex bonds linking male poet and male reader, see Eve Kosofsky Sedgwick's classic study, *Between Men: English Literature and Male Homosocial Desire* (New York: Columbia University Press, 1985).

18 For further information about women's literacy, see Julia Boffey, "Women Authors and Women's Literacy in Fourteenth- and Fifteenth-Century England," *Women and Literature in Britain 1150–1500*, Carol M. Meale (ed.) (Cambridge University Press, 1993); R. A. Houston, *Literacy in Early Modern Europe: Culture and Education, 1500–1800* (London: Longman, 1988); Josephine Kamm, *Hope Deferred: Girls' Education in English History* (London: Methuen, 1965); Ruth Kelso, *Doctrine for the Lady of the Renaissance* (Urbana: University of Illinois Press, 1956); Norma McCullen, "The Education of English Gentlewomen 1540–1640," *History of Education* 6 (1977): 87–101; Diane Willen, "A Comment on Women's Education in Elizabethan England," *Topic* 36 (1982): 66–73; David Cressy, "Literacy in pre-industrial England," *Societas* 4 (1974): 229–40; David Cressy (ed.), *Education in Tudor and Stuart England* (New York: St. Martin's, 1975); Keith Thomas, "The Meaning of Literacy in Early Modern England," *The Written Word: Literacy in Transition*, Gerd Baumann (ed.) (Oxford, 1986), pp. 116–17; Hull, *Chaste, Silent & Obedient*; Margaret Spufford, "First Steps in Literacy: the Reading and Writing Experiences of the Humblest Seventeenth-Century Spiritual Autobiographers," *Social History* 4 (1979): 407–35; Louise Schleiner, *Tudor and Stuart Women Writers* (Bloomington: Indiana University Press, 1994), chapter 1, "Women's Household Circles as a Gendered Reading Formation."

19 Roy Strong, *The English Icon: Elizabethan & Jacobean Portraiture* (The Paul Mellon Foundation for British Art. London: Routledge, 1969), includes two portraits of Dorothy Petre Wadham, both with a book. The one on p. 209 is inscribed "*Dorothy Wadham Wife of / Nicholas Wadham Esq; and / Foundress of Wadham College / in Oxford.*"

20 In "From 'Listen, Lordings' to 'Dear Reader'," *University of Toronto Quarterly* 46 (1976/77): 113, William Nelson notes that "books of every conceivable kind, whether in prose or in verse, were commonly read aloud, sometimes by the author himself, sometimes by members of a household taking turns, sometimes by a professional reader." Robert Darnton, "History of Reading," in *New Perspectives on Historical Writing*, Peter Burke (ed.) (University Park: Pennsylvania State University Press, 1992), p. 150, writes, "for most people throughout most of history, books had audiences rather than readers. They were better heard than seen." See also Walter J., Ong, S.J., *Rhetoric, Romance, and Technology: Studies in the Interaction of Expression and Culture* (Ithaca: Cornell University Press, 1971), pp. 23–47. On the singing of lyrics, see John E. Stevens, *Music & Poetry in the Early Tudor Court* (Lincoln: University of Nebraska Press, 1961). Alberto Manguel's *A History of Reading* (New York: Viking, 1996), offers an intriguing review of the history of silent reading. *The Practice and Representation of Reading in England*, James Raven, Helen Small, and Naomi Tadmore (eds.) (Cambridge University Press, 1996), reexamines the activity of reading from a number of different angles. What still needs to be studied more fully, I think, is the degree to which silent reading was practiced, and the role it played in Elizabethan culture.

21 Evelyn Fox, "The Diary of an Elizabethan Gentlewoman," *Transactions of the Royal Historical Society*, 3rd series (London, 1908), vol. II, p. 161.

22 Quoted from L. M. Ruth Kuschmierz, "'The Instruction of a Christian Woman': A Critical Edition of the Tudor Translation," PhD thesis, University of Pittsburgh (1961), p. 28. For further information on Vives' influence, see Beilin, *Redeeming Eve*, pp. 4–8; Gloria Kaufman, "Juan Luis Vives on the Education of Women," *Signs* 3 (1978): 891–96; Valerie Wayne, "Some Sad Sentence: Vives' *Instruction of a Christian Woman*," Hannay, *Silent but for the Word*, pp. 15–29.

23 M[argaret] T[yler] (trans.), *The Mirrour of Princely deedes and Knighthood* (London, 1578), fos. A.4.r, A.4.v., A.2.r.

24 Gayle Greene and Coppélia Kahn, "Feminist Scholarship and the Social Construction of Woman," *Making a Difference: Feminist Literary Criticism*, Greene and Kahn (eds.) (London: Methuen, 1985), p. 5.

25 For a theory of human agency within structural constraints, see Anthony Giddens, *Central Problems in Social Theory: Action, Structure and Contradiction in Social Analysis* (Berkeley: University of California Press, 1979). There is little reason to rehearse the argument here since a number of excellent studies have argued that such a theory is crucial to feminism: Linda Alcoff, "Cultural Feminism Versus Post-structuralism: The Identity Crisis in Feminist Theory," *Signs* 13 (1988): 405–36; Rita Felski, *Beyond Feminist Aesthetics: Feminist Literature and Social Change* (Cambridge: Harvard University Press, 1989), chapter 2, "Subjectivity and Feminism"; Teresa de Lauretis, "Feminist Studies/Critical Studies: Issues, Terms, and Contexts," *Feminist Studies/Critical Studies*, de Lauretis (ed.) (Bloomington: Indiana University Press, 1986), 1–19; Nancy K. Miller, "Changing the Subject: Authorship,

Writing and the Reader," de Lauretis, 102–20; Carol Thomas Neely, "Constructing the Subject: Feminist Practice and the New Renaissance Discourses," *English Literary Renaissance* 18 (1988): 5–18; Judith Newton, "History as Usual?: Feminism and the 'New Historicism,'" *Cultural Critique* 9 (1988): 87–121; Camille Roman, Suzanne Juhasz, and Cristanne Miller (eds.), *The Women and Language Debate: A Sourcebook* (New Brunswick, New Jersey: Rutgers University Press, 1994); Chris Weedon, *Feminist Practice and Poststructuralist Theory* (Oxford: Basil Blackwell, 1987), chapter 4, "Language and Subjectivity."

26 As Montrose writes, "The Elizabethan Subject and the Spenserian Text," in *Literary Theory / Renaissance Texts*, ed. Patricia Parker and David Quint (Baltimore: Johns Hopkins University Press, 1986), p. 306: "To speak, then, of the social production of 'literature' or of any particular text is to signify not only that it is socially produced but also that it is socially productive – that it is the product of work and that it performs work in the process of being written, enacted, or read."

27 I am indebted to Judith Newton and Deborah Rosenfelt's definition of ideology in the Introduction to *Feminist Criticism and Social Change: Sex, Class and Race in Literature and Culture* (New York: Methuen, 1985), p. xix, as "a complex and contradictory set of representations through which we explore ourselves." As Newton and Rosenfelt remind us, ideology has a power and life of its own that can, at certain moments in history, contradict the interests of the ruling class or the dominant sex/gender system. In "Ideology and Scholarship," Jerome J. McGann (ed.), *Historical Studies and Literary Criticism*, 4th edn. Caltech-Waingart Conference in the Humanities, 1984 (Madison: University of Wisconsin Press, 1985), p. 116, Terry Eagleton also provides a useful working definition of ideology "as a set of discourses which wrestle over interests which are in some way relevant to the maintenance or interrogation of power structures central to a whole form of social and historical life."

28 For a more thorough account of the reasons why it is important to "explore the gap between prescriptive and public representations of gender and the way that gender relations were constructed by individuals in their private lives," see Newton, "History as Usual?: Feminism and the 'New Historicism'," p. 119, and Carroll Smith-Rosenberg, "The New Woman and the New History," *Feminist Studies* 3 (1975): 185–98.

29 Klein, *Daughters, Wives, and Widows*, p. xii, notes that "the further our texts move from theological assumptions about woman's place and the nearer they come to describing the actual conditions of women's lives, the less emphasis we find on notions of women's subordination, inferiority, and frailty."

30 Bates, *Rhetoric of Courtship*, pp. 37–40, cites a number of instances where the word "courtship" is associated with lust, seduction, and deceit.

31 In *Writing Women's Literary History* (Baltimore: Johns Hopkins University Press, 1993), p. 4, Margaret J. M. Ezell questions "the theoretical model of

women's literary history and the construction of women's literary studies as a field" which "rest upon the assumption that women before 1700 either were effectively silenced or . . . contained and co-opted in patriarchal discourse." In "Surprising Fame: Renaissance Gender Ideologies and Women's Lyric," *The Poetics of Gender*, Nancy K. Miller (ed.) (New York: Columbia University Press, 1986), p. 79, Ann Rosalind Jones also argues that "the poetic collections of Renaissance women show that they did not simply accede to the silencing logic of their culture." Thomas Wyatt, "Madam, withouten many words," quoted from *Sir Thomas Wyatt: The Complete Poems*, Ronald A. Rebholz (ed.) (New Haven: Yale University Press, 1981).

32 Based on the limited number of works dedicated to Queen Elizabeth, some scholars inferred that her patronage was limited. In *Leicester: Patron of Letters*, Rosenberg demonstrates that Elizabeth relies on the nobility and especially favorites such as Leicester to dispense patronage on her behalf.

33 Judith Fetterley, *The Resisting Reader: a Feminist Approach to American Fiction* (Bloomington: Indiana University Press, 1978); Elaine Showalter, "Towards a Feminist Poetics," *Women Writing and Writing about Women*, Mary Jacobus (ed.) (London: Croom Helm, 1979), p. 25; Caroline Lucas, *Writing for Women: the Example of Woman as Reader in Elizabethan Romance* (Stony Stratford: Open University Press, 1989), p. 4.

34 Elaine Showalter, "Feminist Criticism in the Wilderness," *The New Feminist Criticism: Essays on Women, Literature, and Theory*, Showalter (ed.) (New York: Pantheon Books, 1985), p. 266.

35 Burke, *Philosophy of Literary Form*, p. 89; Bakhtin, *Dialogic Imagination*, p. 280.

36 [George Puttenham], *The Arte of English Poesie*, 1589 (Ohio: Kent State University Press, 1970), p. 170.

37 Clifford Geertz, *The Interpretation of Cultures* (New York: Basic Books, 1973), p. 218.

38 C. L. Barber, *Shakespeare's Festive Comedy; a Study of Dramatic Form and its Relation to Social Custom* (Princeton University Press, 1959), p. 36.

39 In "The Stigma of Print: A Note on the Social Bases of Tudor Poetry," *Essays in Criticism* 1 (1951), p. 151, J. W. Saunders observes that poetry, "the agent of flattery, of ego-titillation, of love-making, and of condolence," is "used to grace and comment on virtually every happening in life." The function of love-making, though sometimes mentioned in passing, has received little sustained critical attention.

40 Bakhtin, *Dialogic Imagination*, p. 281.

41 Newton and Rosenfelt, *Feminist Criticism*, p. xxx.

2 AN ELIZABETHAN POETICS OF COURTSHIP

1 Robert Frost, *Selected Poems of Robert Frost* (New York: Holt, Rinehart and Winston, 1963), p. 224.

2 Philip Sidney, *Defence of Poesy*, from *The Covntesse Pembrokes Arcadia* (London, 1598), p. 516. All further references are cited parenthetically.

3 *The Norton Anthology of English Literature*, M. H. Abrams, *et al.* (eds.), 5th edn. (New York: Norton, 1986).

4 T. S. Eliot, *On Poetry and Poets* (New York: Farrar, Straus, 1943, rpt. 1979), pp. 105, 107, 107. In *Intentionality and the New Traditionalism: Some Liminal Means to Literary Revisionism* (University Park: Pennsylvania State University Press, 1991), p. 86, John T. Shawcross responds, "The voice does not turn his or her back on the audience." Whereas Shawcross's critique of Eliot emphasizes "the author's intention" in "the creation of the literary artifact," mine stresses the transformative impact of the lyric audience.

5 Ibid., pp. 97, 106, 97–8. In some ways, this is a surprising comment, since Eliot himself acknowledges that "it is poetry rather than prose that is concerned with the expression of emotion and feeling" (p. 9). Yet it certainly does explain why "The Love Song of J. Alfred Prufrock" first raises and then explodes the reader's expectation that the speaker is communicating with a beloved.

6 "Persuasion," as Neil L. Rudenstine writes in *Sidney's Poetic Development* (Cambridge: Harvard University Press, 1967), p. 152, "lies at the heart of Sidney's entire theory of poetry."

7 John Donne, "Loves growth," line 12, quoted from *The Complete Poetry of John Donne*, John T. Shawcross (ed.) (Garden City, NY: Anchor Books, 1967). In *Trials of Desire: Renaissance Defenses of Poetry* (New Haven: Yale University Press, 1983), p. 138, Margaret W. Ferguson observes that Sidney "dissimulated so well that many of his later readers have failed to notice the political and autobiographical issues at stake in his *Defence of Poesie*." Ferguson also notes, p. 146, that Sidney "sees the threat that poetry poses as an erotic one," but she does not pursue the connections between Sidney's poetics and *Astrophil and Stella*. Ferguson, p. 158, argues that Sidney's "hypothetical clause" creates "a space of 'as if,' a space in which the play of same and different replaces the work of ascertaining truth and falsehood."

8 Clark Hulse, "Stella's Wit: Penelope Rich as Reader of Sidney's Sonnets," in *Rewriting the Renaissance: The Discourses of Sexual Difference in Early Modern Europe*, Margaret W. Ferguson, Maureen Quilligan, and Nancy Vickers (eds.) (University of Chicago Press, 1986), p. 273, cites this passage and comments: "Here Sidney contemplates the male reader entering into the poem only by imagining himself as a woman, and this strategy works most easily if that woman is a critic." Sidney was accustomed to considering the female reader. He not only wrote *Astrophil and Stella* for Penelope Rich, and the *Arcadia* for his sister Mary Sidney, but he also collaborated with Mary on a metrical translation of the psalms which she completed after his death and dedicated "To the Thrice Sacred Queen Elizabeth." For a more thorough study of Mary Sidney's role as editor, translator, and patron, see Mary Ellen Lamb, *Gender and Authorship in the Sidney Circle* (Madison: University of Wisconsin Press, 1990), pp. 28–71.

9 Jonathan D. Culler, *On Deconstruction: Theory and Criticism after Structuralism* (Ithaca: Cornell University Press, 1982), p. 57. For a range of views, see

Elizabeth A. Flynn and Patrocinio P. Schweickart (eds.), *Gender and Reading: Essays on Readers, Texts, and Contexts* (Baltimore: Johns Hopkins University Press, 1986).

10 Fredric Jameson, *The Political Unconscious: Narrative as a Socially Symbolic Act* (Ithaca: Cornell University Press, 1981), p. 219. On the revolutionary impact of print, see Henry Stanley Bennett, *English Books & Readers: 1558–1603* (Cambridge University Press, 1952); Natalie Zemon Davis, *Society and Culture in Early Modern France: Eight Essays* (Stanford University Press, 1975), chapter 7, "Printing and the People"; Elizabeth Eisenstein, *The Printing Press as an Agent of Change*, 2 vols. (Cambridge University Press, 1979); Neil Fraistat, "Introduction: The Place of the Book and the Book as Place," *Poems in their Place: The Intertextuality and Order of Poetic Collections*, Neil Fraistat (ed.) (Chapel Hill: University of North Carolina Press, 1986), pp. 3–17.

11 Eliot, *On Poetry and Poets*, p. 98; Jameson, *The Political Unconscious*, pp. 81–2.

12 For studies of these related genres, see Virginia Cox, *The Renaissance Dialogue: Literary Dialogue in its Social and Political Contexts, Castiglione to Galileo* (Cambridge University Press, 1992); John Kerrigan (ed.), *Motives of Woe: Shakespeare and 'Female Complaint': a Critical Anthology* (Oxford: Clarendon Press, 1991); K. J. Wilson, *Incomplete Fictions: The Formation of English Renaissance Dialogue* (Washington, DC: Catholic University of America Press, 1985).

13 As William Nelson writes in *Fact or Fiction: the Dilemma of the Renaissance Storyteller* (Cambridge: Harvard University Press, 1973), pp. 8–9, "Before the conventionalizing of the novel the signs by which we readily distinguish fiction from nonfiction – place on library shelves, format, style – were not available, so that only the quite incredible tale could be free from confusion with historical report." Judith Anderson develops the point in *Biographical Truth: The Representation of Historical Persons in Tudor-Stuart Writing* (New Haven: Yale University Press, 1984).

14 As William A. Ringler, Jr. (ed.), remarks in *Philip Sidney's Poems* (Oxford: Clarendon Press, 1962), p. xliv, "Sidney went out of his way to identify himself as Astrophil and Stella as Lady Rich, and even wrote three sonnets to reveal her married name." Richard A. Lanham, "Astrophil and Stella: Pure and Impure Persuasion," *English Literary Renaissance* 2 (1972): p. 107, presses the point even further: "There is no Astrophil in the poem except as a name. It is Sidney who speaks. . . Sidney did not title the work." For a review of biographical facts, see Steven W. May, *The Elizabethan Courtier Poets: The Poems and their Contexts* (Columbia: University of Missouri Press, 1991), p. 87.

15 Kenneth Burke, *The Philosophy of Literary Form* (1941, rev. edn. Berkeley: University of California Press, 1973), p. 109; Richard Helgerson offers a particularly apt description of the biographical dilemma in *The Elizabethan Prodigals* (Berkeley: University of California Press, 1976), p. 141: "One does not so easily pick truth from fiction in *Astrophil and Stella* as to put a biographer at his ease, but this much is clear: the poems invite us to see Sidney in Astrophil and they suggest that his purpose in writing was the simple, if ignoble, desire to seduce Lady Rich."

16 [George Puttenham], *The Arte of English Poesie.* 1589 (Ohio: Kent State University Press, 1970), p. 60.

17 Abraham Fraunce, *The Arcadian Rhetorike*, Ethel Seaton (ed.) (Oxford: for the Lutrell Society by Blackwell, 1950), pp. 3, 106; Baldassare Castiglione, *The Book of the Courtier From the Italian of Count Baldassare Castiglione: Done into English by Sir Thomas Hoby. Anno 1561* (London: David Nutt, 1900), p. 64; Burke, *Philosophy of Literary Form*, p. 159.

18 Thomas Whythorne, *The Autobiography of Thomas Whythorne*, James M. Osborn (ed.), Modern spelling edn. (London: Oxford University Press, 1962), p. 40.

19 Ibid., p. 72.

20 Ibid., pp. 196–8, 267, 196, 196.

21 Ibid., p. 518.

22 As J.W. Saunders, "The Stigma of Print: A Note on the Social Bases of Tudor Poetry," *Essays in Criticism* 1 (1951): 139–64, explains, p. 153, "The transcription of transcriptions . . . was a process with which [the poet] had nothing to do. The poet himself could never tell how many copies were abroad . . . He had very little control therefore over the ultimate destinations of his poems, and there was next to nothing he could do to prevent an occasional manuscript from falling into the hands of a compiler who might print it."

23 In *Cultural Aesthetics: Renaissance Literature and the Practice of Social Ornament* (University of Chicago Press, 1991), p. 87, Patricia Fumerton suggests a fascinating connection between "the 'publication' of the private miniature at court" and "the way the love poem was increasingly published in print. The poet published his private love – carrying it not only to the court but to the 'commonality' of the public beyond – by enclosing his poems in what amounted to a literary locket: the 'case' of prefatory letters."

24 See Ted-Larry Pebworth, "Manuscript Poems and Print Assumptions: Donne and his Modern Editors," *John Donne Journal* 3 (1984): 1–21, and Arthur F. Marotti, *Manuscript, Print, and the English Renaissance Lyric* (Ithaca: Cornell University Press, 1995), p. 135. Marotti concludes that "it was normal for lyrics to elicit revisions, corrections, supplements, and answers, for they were part of an ongoing social discourse. In this environment texts were inherently malleable, escaping authorial control to enter a social world in which recipients both consciously and unconsciously altered what they received." Puttenham, *Arte of English Poesie*, p. 60.

25 Terry Eagleton, *Literary Theory*, pp. 7–8. This may sound like an odd stance for a Marxist like Eagleton; at this point, however, Eagleton is not developing his own literary theory but summarizing the prevailing tenets of modern literary criticism. Robert C. Elliott, *The Literary Persona* (University of Chicago Press, 1981), p. 43, makes the point absolutely clear: "Despite its personal form, erotic poetry cannot be taken to reflect the true feelings or conduct of the writer. There are conventions for love poetry as for other forms of artistic expression, and the poets themselves insist on the distinction between art and life." But if Elizabethan poets rely on lyric conventions

to provide the poetic license they need, they also toy with the conventions to call the distinctions between art and life into question.

26 Eagleton, *Literary Theory*, p. 7. The self-compounds continue to proliferate. In *The Reinvention of Love: Poetry, Politics and Culture from Sidney to Milton* (Cambridge University Press, 1993), p. 23, Anthony Low writes, "Men court patrons and mistresses because they want some material return, financial or sexual, or both. They want to satisfy their lusts, to seek position, power, and social aggrandizement. Less noticed is another aspect of desire, which is less interested in a crude immediate return than in a kind of self-validation." By representing the poet's self-validation as a higher ideal, Low, like so many earlier critics, reduces the female lyric audience to the object of male lust.

27 Eliot, *On Poetry and Poets*, pp. 106, 105, 107. On the private subtext of Shakespeare's sonnets, see Kerrigan, Introduction to *The Sonnets; and, A Lover's Complaint*. On the dialogue with the young man, see Joel Fineman, *Shakespeare's Perjured Eye: The Invention of Poetic Subjectivity in the Sonnets* (Berkeley: University of California Press, 1986).

28 Ann Rosalind Jones and Peter Stallybrass, "The Politics of *Astrophil and Stella*," *Studies in English Literature* 24 (1984): 67.

29 Puttenham, *Arte of English Poesie*, p. 170; Eliot, *On Poetry and Poets*, p. 107; Sidney, *Defence*, p. 518.

30 For a review of the ways in which structuralism and deconstruction have redefined the lyric, see Antony Easthope, *Poetry as Discourse* (London: Routledge, 1983) and Jonathan D. Culler, "Changes in the Study of the Lyric," in *Lyric Poetry Beyond New Criticism*, Chaviva Hosek and Patricia Parker (eds.) (Ithaca: Cornell University Press, 1985). Culler cites a number of prominent feminist critics, though feminism per se plays little role in the five major changes Culler enumerates: "attention to babble and doodle, exploration of intertextuality, interest in voice as figure, a new understanding of self-reflexivity, and the deconstruction of the hierarchical opposition of symbol and allegory" (p. 54).

31 John Carey, *John Donne: Life, Mind and Art* (New York: Oxford University Press, 1981), p. 118; R. L. Kesler, "The Idealization of Women: Morphology and Change in Three Renaissance Texts," *Mosaic* 23 (1990): 116; Howard Felperin, "Canonical Texts and Non-Canonical Interpretations. The Neohistoricist Rereading of Donne," *Southern Review* 18 (1985): 245.

32 Quoted from Marotti, *Manuscript, Print*, p. 11; Culler, "Changes in the Study of the Lyric"; Alexander Dunlop, "The Unity of Spenser's *Amoretti*"; Kesler, "Idealization of Women", pp. 117–18; Alastair Fowler, *Kinds of Literature: An Introduction to the Theory of Genres and Modes* (Cambridge: Harvard University Press, 1982), p. 163; Don M. Ricks, "Persona and Process in Spenser's 'Amoretti,'" *Ariel* 3 (1972): 7; J. E. V. Crofts, "John Donne: A Reconsideration"; Gardner, *Collection*, p. 82; Theodore Spencer, "The Poetry of Sir Philip Sidney," *English Literary History* 12 (1945): 270; Ricks, "Persona and Process," pp. 7–8; Wendy Wall, *The Imprint of Gender: Authorship and Publication in the English Renaissance* (Ithaca: Cornell University Press,

1993), p. 69. For a more extensive deconstruction of the lyric genre, see Antony Easthope, *Poetry as Discourse* (London: Routledge, 1983).

33 Eagleton, *Literary Theory*, p. 7; Eliot, *On Poetry and Poets*, p. 107; James Winny, *The Master-Mistress: a Study of Shakespeare's Sonnets* (New York: Barnes & Noble, 1968), p. 23; Low, *Reinvention of Love*, p. 45; Walter J. Ong, S.J.,"The Writer's Audience is Always a Fiction," *PMLA* 90 (1975): 12. In *John Donne, Coterie Poet*, pp. 150–51, Marotti also looks beyond "the lover's concern for and sensitivity to his beloved's emotional state . . . to a coterie readership that could appreciate [the poems'] skill, inventiveness, and force."

34 The notion of both/ands comes from Newton and Rosenfelt's Introduction to *Feminist Criticism and Social Change: Sex, Class and Race in Literature and Culture* (New York: Methuen, 1985), p. xxix, which "actively encourages us to hold in our minds the both-ands of experience: that women at different moments in history have been both oppressed and oppressive, submissive and subversive, victim and agent, allies and enemies both of men and one another."

35 Hallett Darius Smith, *Elizabethan Poetry; A Study in Conventions, Meaning, and Expression* (Cambridge: Harvard University Press, 1952), p. 166; Louis L. Martz, "The *Amoretti*: 'Most Goodly Temperature'," in *The Prince of Poets: Essays on Edmund Spenser*, John R. Elliott Jr. (ed.) (New York University Press, 1968), p. 125; Peter M. Cummings, "Spenser's *Amoretti* as an Allegory of Love," *Texas Studies in Language and Literature* 12 (1970): 170; Martz, *Prince of Poets*, p. 134; Jacqueline T. Miller, " 'Love Doth Hold My Hand': Writing and Wooing in the Sonnets of Sidney and Spenser," *English Literary History* 46 (1979): 556.

36 Patrick Cruttwell, "The Love Poetry of John Donne: Pedantique weedes or Fresh Invention?" *Metaphysical Poetry*, Malcolm Bradbury and David Palmer (eds.) (Bloomington: Indiana University Press, 1971), p. 22. Ilona Bell, "The Role of the Lady in Donne's *Songs and Sonets*," *Studies in English Literature* 23 (1983): 127; Jones and Stallybrass, "Politics of *Astrophil and Stella*" p. 61; Gary F. Waller, "Struggling into Discourse: The Emergence of Renaissance Women's Writing," *Silent but for the Word: Tudor Women as Patrons, Translators, and Writers of Religious Works*, Margaret Patterson Hannay (ed.) (Ohio: Kent State University Press, 1985), p. 243; Fienberg, "The Emergence of Stella," *Studies in English Literature* 25 (1985): 5; Hulse, *Rewriting the Renaissance*, p. 279.

37 In the introduction to *Seeking the Woman in Late Medieval and Renaissance Writings* (Knoxville: University of Tennessee Press, 1990), p. 6, Sheila Fisher and Janet E. Halley complain that studies of male-authored texts "altogether ignore the historical existence of real women and their experience of selfhood." They urge critics to consider "the materiality of women's lives – the conditions in which they grew up, worked, worshipped, married, gave birth, and learned."

38 Martz, *Prince of Poets*, p. 125; Bell, "Role of the Lady" p. 128; Jones and Stallybrass, "Politics of *Astrophil and Stella*" p. 67.

39 Waller, *Silent but for the Word*, p. 245; Hulse, *Rewriting the Renaissance*, p. 286; Janet E. Halley, "Textual Intercourse: Anne Donne, John Donne, and the

Sexual Poetics of Textual Exchange," in *Seeking the Woman in Late Medieval and Renaissance Writings: Essays in Feminist Contextual Criticism*, Sheila Fisher and Janet Halley (eds.) (Knoxville: University of Tennessee Press, 1989), p. 188.

40 Ibid., pp. 50, 38, 42, 50. 50.

41 Northrop Frye, *The Anatomy of Criticism: Four Essays* (Princeton University Press, 1957; New York: Atheneum, 1966), p. 249; M. Thomas Hester (ed.), *John Donne's 'desire of more': The Subject of Anne More Donne in his Poetry* (Newark: University of Delaware Press, 1996) begins to redress the lack of interest in Donne's female lyric audience.

3 THE PRACTICE OF ELIZABETHAN COURTSHIP

1 Maydens of London, *A Letter Sent by the Maydens of London, to the vertuous Matrones & Mistresses of the same, in the defense of their lawfull Libertie*, 1567, R. J. Fehrenbach (ed.), *English Literary Renaissance* 14 (1984): 300. For a more detailed study, see my essay, "The Maydens of London: In Defense of their Lawful Liberty," *Women, Writing, and the Reproduction of Culture in Tudor and Stuart Britain*, Mary Elizabeth Burke, Jane Donawerth, Linda Dove, and Karen Nelson (eds.) (Syracuse University Press, 1998).

2 Lawrence Stone's *The Family, Sex, and Marriage In England 1500–1800*, Abridged (New York: Harper & Row, 1979), first published in 1977 and still probably the most influential history of early modern English marriage, focuses on marriages arranged among the aristocracy and upper gentry for the express purpose of producing social and economic bonds. Stone's views have been challenged by feminists, literary critics, and historians, including Alan Macfarlane, "Review Essay: *The Family, Sex, and Marriage in England*," *History and Theory* 18 (1979): 103–26, and Keith Thomas, "The Changing Family," *Times Literary Supplement*, 21 October 1977: 1226–27. Later social and legal histories defend the role of romantic love, sexual attraction, and personal choice in marriage. For example, in *Church Courts, Sex, and Marriage in England, 1570–1640*, Past and Present Publications (Cambridge University Press, 1987), p. 141, Martin Ingram writes: "personal attraction played a much more significant role in matchmaking than contemporary moralists recommended or modern historians like Stone have supposed." My own understanding of early modern marriage is also indebted to Susan Dwyer Amussen, *An Ordered Society: Gender and Class in Early Modern England* (Oxford: Blackwell, 1988); Margaret J. M. Ezell, *The Patriarch's Wife: Literary Evidence and the History of the Family* (Chapel Hill: University of North Carolina Press, 1987); John R. Gillis, *For Better, For Worse: British Marriages 1600 to the Present* (Oxford University Press, 1985); Ralph A. Houlbrooke, *The English Family 1450–1700* (London: Longman, 1984); Michael MacDonald, *Mystical Bedlam: Madness, Anxiety, and Healing in Seventeenth-Century England* (Cambridge University Press, 1981); Alan Macfarlane, *The Family Life of Ralph Josselin, a Seventeenth-Century Clergyman: an Essay in Historical Anthropology* (New York: Norton, 1977); *Marriage and Love in England: Modes of Reproduction*

1300–1840 (Oxford: B. Blackwell, 1986); Steven E. Ozment, *When Fathers Ruled: Family Life in Reformation Europe* (Cambridge: Harvard University Press, 1983).

3 James Clifford, Introduction to *Writing Culture: The Poetics and Politics of Ethnography*, J. Clifford and George E. Marcus (eds.) (Berkeley: University of California Press, 1986), p. 10.

4 Henrie Smith, *A Preparatiue to Mariage* (London, 1591), p. 38.

5 As Catharine R. Stimpson writes in the introduction to *Feminist Issues in Literary Scholarship*, Shari Benstock (ed.) (Bloomington: Indiana University Press, 1987), p. 2, "For women, if choked, have still spoken. For women, if on the borders of culture, have still smuggled messages past border sentries. Their sentences begin in resistance." In *Literary Fat Ladies: Rhetoric, Gender, Property* (London: Methuen, 1987), pp. 26–31, Patricia Parker explores the issues involved in "the supposed copiousness of the female tongue."

6 Ozment, *When Fathers Ruled*, p. 38.

7 The Canons of 1604 forbade marriage without parental consent for children under 21 and required parental consent for anyone (except widows and widowers) seeking a marriage license, thereby bringing England into closer conformity with the rest of Europe. Yet freedom of choice was so firmly entrenched in the popular culture that even the Jacobean Parliament, eager as it was to establish the political and ideological power of patriarchy, "did not declare marriages made in contravention of these regulations to be invalid." R.B. Outhwaite (ed.), *Marriage and Society: Studies in the Social History of Marriage* (London: Europa, 1981), p. 47.

8 Jack Goody, "Inheritance, Property, and Women," in *Family and Inheritance: Rural Society in Western Europe, 1200–1800*, Jack Goody, Joan Thirsk, and E. P. Thompson (eds.) (Cambridge University Press, 1976), p. 20. Gillis, *For Better*, p. 35. Also see Amussen, *Ordered Society*, p. 68.

9 Gillis, *For Better*, p. 35. Alan Macfarlane, *The Family Life of Ralph Josselin, A Seventeenth-Century Clergyman: an Essay in Historical Anthropology* (New York: Norton, 1977), p. 92.

10 See Ian W. Archer, *The Pursuit of Stability: Social Relations in Elizabethan London* (Cambridge University Press, 1991); Vivien Brodsky Elliott, "Single Women in the London Marriage Market: Age, Status and Mobility, 1598–1619," *Marriage and Society: Studies in the Social History of Marriage*, R. B. Outhwaite (ed.) (London: Europa, 1981), pp. 81–100; Steven Rappaport, *Worlds within Worlds: Structures of Life in Sixteenth-Century London* (Cambridge University Press, 1989). *The copie of a letter, lately written in meeter, by a yonge gentilwoman to her vnconstant Louer. With an Admonition to al yong Gentilwomen and to al other Mayds in general. By Is. W[hitney]* (London, 1567), fo. A.i.r. *A sweet nosgay; or pleasant posye: contayning a hundred and ten phylosophicall flowers* (London, 1573), fo. C.vii.v.

11 Muriel St. Clare Byrne (ed.), *The Lisle Letters*, 6 vols. (University of Chicago Press, 1981), vol. III, pp. 1–35. For more information on women's work, see Barbara A. Hanawalt (ed.), *Women and Work in Preindustrial Europe* (Bloomington: Indiana University Press, 1986).

12 John Stubbs, *John Stubbs's Gaping Gulf with Letters and Other Relevant Documents*, Lloyd E. Berry (ed.) (Charlottesville: University Press of Virginia, 1968), p. 174. William Whately, *A Care-Cloth: Or A Treatise of the Troubles of Marriage* (London, 1624). line 3; Elizabeth Grymeston, *Miscelanea, Meditations, Memoratives*. 1604, The English Experience 933 (Norwood, NJ: Johnson, 1979), fo. A.3.v.

13 See Amussen, *Ordered Society*; Anthony Fletcher and John Stevenson (eds.), *Order and Disorder in Early Modern England* (Cambridge University Press, 1985), Introduction; Keith Wrightson, *English Society 1580–1680* (New Brunswick: Rutgers University Press, 1982), chapter 1, "Degrees of People." Thomas Whythorne, *The Autobiography of Thomas Whythorne*, James M. Osborn (ed.), Modern Spelling edn. (London: Oxford University Press, 1962), p. 61.

14 Amussen, *Ordered Society*, p. 70, Macfarlane, *Marriage and Love in England*, p. 270. Thomas Powell, *Tom of all Trades, or The plaine Path-way to Preferment*, Frederick J. Furnivall (ed.), (1631, London, 1876), p. 172.

15 Ibid., p. 15. Anne Halkett, *The Memoirs of Anne, Lady Halkett and Ann, Lady Fanshawe*, John Loftis (ed.) (Oxford: Clarendon Press, 1979), p. 14.

16 William Whately, *A Care-cloth*, fo. A.6.r. Social histories of English marriage generally span at least a century, often several centuries. Whenever possible, I have selected data from the Elizabethan period, especially in court cases and prescriptive texts where there is considerable evidence. Statistics and autobiographical sources relating specifically to the Elizabethan period are harder to come by. For a review of histories of Renaissance marriage, see Barbara B. Diefendorf, "Family Culture, Renaissance Culture," *Renaissance Quarterly* 40 (1987): 661–81. For a survey of Shakespeareans who apply family history from this period to literary criticism, see Linda Boose, "The Family in Shakespeare Studies; or – Studies in the Family of Shakespeare; or – The Politics of Politics," *Renaissance Quarterly* 40 (1987): 706–42.

17 On this point, Amussen and Underdown correct Alice Clark's *Working Life of Women in the Seventeenth Century*, 1919 (London: Routledge, 1982).

18 Macfarlane, *Marriage and Love*, p. 276. James Gairdner (ed.), *The Paston Letters, AD 1422–1509*, 5 vols. (London: Chatto & Windus, 1904), vol. v, p. 15.

19 Gillis, *For Better*, p. 15. For a review of the literature, see Katherine Gaskin, "Age at First Marriage in Europe Before 1850: a Summary of Family Reconstitution Data," *Journal of Family History* 31 (1978): 23–36. Most of the statistics come from the Cambridge Group for the History of Population and Social Structure.

20 Lawrence Stone, *The Crisis of the Aristocracy, 1558–1641* (Oxford: Clarendon Press, 1965), p. 661; Natalie Zemon Davis, *The Return of Martin Guerre* (Cambridge: Harvard University Press, 1983).

21 "Unlike a single or married woman, a widow could legitimately maintain her own household and conduct a business," Charles Carlton writes in "The Widow's Tale: Male Myths and Female Reality in 16th and 17th Century England," *Albion* 10 (1978): 126. "Recent widows often moved to London, perhaps to enjoy its freer society . . . to drive hard bargains with second

husbands, or to protect their inheritances by suing in chancery." Both Margaret L. King, *Women of the Renaissance* (University of Chicago Press, 1991), pp. 52–62, and Barbara J. Todd, "The Remarrying Widow: A Stereotype Reconsidered," Mary Prior (ed.), *Women in English Society 1500–1800* (London: Methuen, 1985), pp. 54–92, argue that the widow, whether remarried or single, poses a challenge to the patriarchal social order.

22 Samuel Rawson Gardiner (ed.), *The Fortescue Papers* (Westminster, England, 1871), p. xi.

23 Ibid., p. xi. Barbara J. Harris, "Power, Profit, and Passion: Mary Tudor, Charles Brandon, and the Arranged Marriage in Early Tudor England," *Feminist Studies* 15 (1989): 59–60; Carlton, "The Widow's Tale" p. 123; Martha Moulsworth, *"My Name Was Martha": A Renaissance Woman's Autobiographical Poem*, Robert C. Evans and Barbara Wiedemann (eds.) (West Cornwall, Conn.: Locust Hill Press, 1993), line 54. All further references will be cited parenthetically. On "The Poem as Autobiography," see Evans and Wiedemann, pp. 71–91.

24 Jane Meautys Cornwallis Bacon, *The Private Correspondence of Jane Lady Cornwallis*, 1613–1644 (London, 1842). Cornwallis, p. 3.

25 Maydens of London, *A Letter Sent*, p. 301. See Maurice Ashley, "Love and Marriage in Seventeenth-Century England," *History Today* 8 (1958): 667–75; Kathleen M. Davies, "Continuity and Change in Literary Advice on Marriage," R. B. Outhwaite (ed.), *Marriage and Society: Studies in the Social History of Marriage* (London: Europa, 1981), pp. 58–79; William Haller and Malleville Haller, "The Puritan Art of Love," *Huntingdon Library Quarterly* 5 (1942): 235–72; Roland Mushat Frye, "The Teachings of Classical Puritanism on Conjugal Love," *Studies in the Renaissance* 2 (1955): 148–59; Irving Singer, *The Nature of Love*, 3 vols., 1966 (University of Chicago Press, 1984–1987).

26 Desiderus Erasmus, *A Ryght Frutefull Epystle in laude and prayse of matrymony*, Richard Tauernour (trans.) (London, 1536), fos. D.9.v-D.10.r. William Gouge, *The Workes of William Govge. In Two Volumes: The First, Domesticall Dvties. The Second, The Whole Armovr of God* (London, 1627), vol. I, pp. 131–32; Desiderus Erasmus, *A Ryght Frutefull Epystle in laude and prayse of matrymony*, Richard Tauernour (trans.) (London, 1536); Bucer, quoted in Ozment, *When Fathers Ruled*, p. 63.

27 MacDonald, *Mystical Bedlam*, p. 90.

28 Maydens of London, *A Letter Sent*, p. 300. For a classic example of marriage negotiations between wealthy parents, see Byrne, *The Lisle Letters*, vol. III, pp. 10–11. John Strype, *Annals of the Reformation and Establishment of Religion, and other Various Occurrences in the Church of England, during Queen Elizabeth's Happy Reign*, 4 vols. (Oxford, 1824), vol. IV, p. 477, vol. III, pp. 85–6.

29 Smith, *Preparature to Marriage*, p. 2. *The copie of a letter*, fo. A.6.v. For two extremely useful studies of marriage manuals and English Renaissance literature, see Heather A. Dubrow, *Happier Eden: The Politics of Marriage in Stuart Epithalamium* (Ithaca: Cornell University Press, 1990), pp. 1–41, and James

Grantham Turner, *One Flesh: Paradisal Marriage and Sexual Relations in the Age of Milton* (Oxford: Clarendon Press, 1987).

30 Simonds D'Ewes, *The Diary of Sir Simonds D'Ewes, 1622–1624*, Elisabeth Bourcier (ed.), Publications de la Sorbonne, Littératures 5 (Paris: Didier, 1974), p. 171. Macfarlane, *The Family Life of Ralph Josselin*, p. 96. Lucy Apsley Hutchinson, *Memoirs of the Life of Colonel Hutchinson . . . with original anecdotes of many of the most distinguished of his contemporaries . . . to which is prefixed the life of Mrs. Hutchinson, written by herself*, 2 vols. (London, 1822) vol. ii, p. 93.

31 John Chamberlain, *The Chamberlain Letters: A Selection of the Letters of John Chamberlain Concerning Life in England from 1597–1626*, Elizabeth McClure Thomson (ed.) (New York: Putnam, 1965), p. 239.

32 Gillis, *For Better*, p. 21. Joel Hurstfield, *The Queen's Wards; Wardship and Marriage under Elizabeth I* (Cambridge, Harvard University Press, 1958). For additional examples of women's role in negotiating process, see Barbara J. Harris, "Women and Politics in Early Tudor England," *The Historical Journal* 33 (1990): 259–81. Cornwallis, *Private Correspondence*, p. 11.

33 Ibid., pp. 57–8.

34 Baldassarre Castiglione, *The Book of the Courtier From the Italian of Count Baldassare Castiglione: Done into English by Sir Thomas Hoby. Anno 1561* (London: David Nutt, 1900), p. 284; Lady Anne Newdigate-Newdegate (ed.), *Gossip from a Muniment Room, Being Passages in The Lives of Anne and Mary Fitton, 1574–1618* (London, 1897); Halkett, *Memoirs of Anne* p. 12.

35 John Donne Papers. *Original Letters of John Donne Relating to his Secret Marriage* (Folger Library, Washington, DC), p. 120.

36 MacDonald reports, *Mystical Bedlam*, pp. 88, 89, 94: "Their tales make nonsense of historians' confident assertions that romantic love was rare in seventeenth-century England or that it was unimportant in choosing marital partners . . . These young people suffered the unmistakable pangs of romantic love . . . [I]n most cases the children appear to have assumed the initiative in courting." Amussen, *Ordered Society*, p. 76.

37 Henry Percy, *Advice to His Son by Henry Percy Ninth Earl of Northumberland*, 1609, G. B. Harrison (ed.) (London: Ernest Benn, 1930), p. 94; Strype, *Annals of Reformation*, vol. iv, p. 476.

38 Charlotte F. Otten (ed.), *English Women's Voices 1540–1700* (Miami: Florida International University Press, 1992), p. 169.

39 Ibid., p. 2.

40 Ibid., fo. a.4.r. Mary Wroth, *The Countesse of Mountgomeries URANIA* (London 1621; Women Writer's Project, Providence, Rhode Island: Brown University), p. 141.

41 Macfarlane, *Family Life*, p. 95. Roger Lowe, *The Diary of Roger Lowe of Ashton-in-Makerfield, Lancashire 1663–1674*, William L. Sachse (ed.) (New Haven: Yale University Press, 1938), p. 24.

42 Halkett, *Memoirs of Anne*, pp. 12, 15.

43 Gardiner, *Fortescue Papers*, pp. xiii, xv.

44 Lowe, *Diary of Roger Lowe*, p. 27; Halkett, *Memoirs of Anne*, p. 18.

45 Halkett, *Memoirs of Anne*, pp. 15, 27. John Loftis, Introduction to *The Memoirs of Anne, Lady Halkett and Ann, Lady Fanshawe*, p. xii.

46 According to P. E. Hair, "Bridal Pregnancy in Rural England in Earlier Centuries," *Population Studies* 20 (1966): 233–66 and "Bridal Pregnancy in Rural England Further Examined," *Population Studies* 24 (1970): 59–70, roughly one-fifth of all brides between 1540 and 1700 were pregnant. Macfarlane and Gillis claim about 10 percent. David Levine and Keith Wrightson, "The Social Context of Illegitimacy in Early Modern England," in *Bastardy and its Comparative History: Studies in the History of Illegitimacy and Marital Nonconformism in Britain, France, Germany, Sweden, North America, Jamaica and Japan*, Peter Laslett, Karla Oosterveen, and Richard M. Smith (eds.) (Cambridge: Harvard University Press, 1980), pp. 174–75, describe the "explosion of bastardy at the turn of the sixteenth and seventeenth centuries" as "a point of crisis in a growing disequilibrium between customary attitudes, expectations and sexual behavior and deteriorating social and economic circumstances."

47 MacDonald, *Mystical Bedlam*, p. 91.

48 Ibid., p. 42. For additional information on birth control and illegitimacy, see Audrey Eccles, *Obstetrics and Gynaecology in Tudor and Stuart England* (Ohio: Kent State University Press, 1982); Peter Laslett, Karla Oosterveen and Richard M. Smith (eds.), *Bastardy and its Comparative History*; Angus McLaren, *Reproductive Rituals: the Perception of Fertility in England from the Sixteenth Century to the Nineteenth Century* (New York: Methuen, 1984); Beryl Rowland (ed. and trans.), *Medieval Woman's Guide to Health: the First English Gynecological Handbook* (Ohio: Kent State University Press, 1981); Edward Shorter, *A History of Women's Bodies* (New York: Basic Books, 1982); Schnucker, "Elizabethan Birth Control and Puritan Attitudes." Amussen, *Ordered Society*, pp. 114–15, cites instances of women who try to abort an illegitimate child, sometimes successfully, sometimes unsuccessfully.

49 Gardiner, *Fortescue Papers*, p. xi.

50 Ibid., p. xvii.

51 Evelyn Fox, "The Diary of an Elizabethan Gentlewoman," *Transactions of the Royal Historical Society*, 3rd series (London, 1908), vol. II, p. 158. Margaret Dakins Hoby, *Diary of Lady Margaret Hoby*, Dorothy M. Meads (ed.) (Boston: Houghton, 1930), p. 23.

52 Gardiner, *Fortescue Papers*, pp. xv–xvi. Margaret Hoby's voice is not entirely lost to history, for her diary provides a detailed account of her daily life and spiritual devotion. The absence of passionate affection for Hoby might possibly provide an illuminating footnote to the story we have been reconstructing.

53 Gardiner, *Fortescue Papers*, p. v.

54 The episode from which all the following quotations are taken can be found on pp. 61–8 of Whythorne's autobiography.

55 Maydens of London, *A Letter Sent*, p. 300.

56 Ibid., pp. xii–xiii.

4 THE LYRIC DIALOGUE OF ELIZABETHAN COURTSHIP

1 Thomas Whythorne, *The Autobiography of Thomas Whythorne*, James M. Osborn (ed.), Modern spelling edn. (London: Oxford University Press, 1962), p. 1. On the conception of music as "an inspiration to both heavenly rapture and carnal lust," see Linda Phyllis Austern, "'Sing Againe Syren': Female Musicians and Sexual Enchantment in Elizabethan Life and Literature," *Renaissance Quarterly* 42 (1989): 420.

2 George Gascoigne, *George Gascoigne's A Hundreth Sundrie Flowres*, C. T. Prouty (ed.), *University of Missouri Studies* 17 (Columbia: University of Missouri, 1942), pp. 111, 125, 133, 119, 136. Jane Hedley, "Allegoria, Gascoigne's Master Trope," *English Literary Renaissance* 11 (1981): 149, also believes that these "lyrics were not aesthetically autonomous: they were social gestures."

3 For further publication information, see the introduction to George Puttenham, *The Arte of English Poesie*, Gladys Doidge Willcock and Alice Walker (eds.) (Cambridge University Press, 1936), pp. xliv–liii. On links between political rhetoric and literary secrets, see John Kerrigan, Introduction to *The Sonnets; and, A Lover's Complaint* (New York: Viking, 1986; Harmondsworth: Penguin, 1986), pp. 7–63; Annabel M. Patterson, *Censorship and Interpretation: The Conditions of Writing and Reading in Early Modern England* (Madison: University of Wisconsin Press, 1984); Christopher Pye, *The Regal Phantasm: Shakespeare and the Politics of Spectacle* (London: Routledge, 1990), pp. 142 ff.; Leonard Tennenhouse, *Power on Display: The Politics of Shakespeare's Genres* (New York: Methuen, 1986) and "Sir Walter Ralegh and the Literature of Clientage," Guy Fitch Lytle, and Stephen Orgel, *Patronage in the Renaissance* (Princeton University Press, 1981), pp. 235–58.

4 For a fuller discussion of Elizabethan posies, see chapter 2. Whythorne, *Autobiography of Thomas*, pp. 21, 22.

5 Ibid., pp. 23, 21, 23, 21.

6 Ibid., p. 23.

7 Ibid., p. 34.

8 Ibid., p. 34; Kenneth Burke, *The Philosophy of Literary Form*, 1941 (rev. edn. Berkeley: University of California Press, 1973), p. 150.

9 Whythorne, *Autobiography of Thomas*, pp. 34, 36, 41.

10 Ibid., p. 41.

11 Gascoigne, *Hundreth Sundrie Flowres*, p. 116, Puttenham, *Arte of English Poesie*.

12 Ibid., p. 117.

13 Ibid., p. 118.

14 Ibid., pp. 117–18.

15 Gascoigne, *Hundreth Sundrie Flowres*, p. 118.

16 Gascoigne, pp. 114–15.

17 M. M. Bakhtin, *The Dialogic Imagination: Four Essays*, Michael Holquist (ed.), Caryl Emerson and Michael Holquist (trans.) (Austin: University of Texas Press, 1981), p. 282.

18 Whythorne, *Autobiography of Thomas*, p. 1.

19 Ibid., p. 1.

20 Philip Sidney, *Defence of Poesy*, from *The Covntesse of Pembrokes Arcadia* (London, 1598), p. 495; Whythorne, *Autobiography of Thomas*, p. 21.

21 Whythorne, *Autobiography of Thomas*, pp. 24, 23, 24, 27.

22 Ibid., p. 33.

23 Wendy Wall, *The Imprint of Gender: Authorship and Publication in the English Renaissance* (Ithaca: Cornell University Press, 1993), p. 69.

24 Whythorne, *Autobiography of Thomas*, p. 33, (my emphasis).

25 Ibid., p. 24.

26 Ibid., p. 1. Wall sees the female reader as a supernumerary third term, "the 'turn' or trope for the conversation of the Renaissance [male] coterie." Wall, *Imprint of Gender*, p. 50. Yet Whythorne's own account suggests that the supernumerary third term is not the female reader but the male reader.

27 Gascoigne, *Hundreth Sundrie Flowres*, pp. 47, 49, 50, 49.

28 Helgerson, *The Elizabethan Prodigal* (Berkeley: University of California Press, 1976), p. 45, remarks, "poems like these do inevitably have occasions; they are an integral part of the courtly conversation that goes on between lover and mistress, friend and friend, hopeful job seeker and potential patron." Gascoigne, *Hundreth Sundrie Flowres*, pp. 112, 142.

29 George Gascoigne, *The Complete Works of George Gascoigne*, John W. Cunliffe (ed.), 2 vols. (Cambridge University Press, 1907), vol. 1, pp. 6–7.

30 Ibid., vol. 1, p. 3. In "Certayne Notes of Instruction Concerning the Making of Verse" (1575), one of the earliest pieces of English literary criticism, Gascoigne assumes that his readers will write love lyrics "in prayse of a gentlewoman" or to "disclose my pretence in love." Gascoigne, *Complete Works*, vol. 1, pp. 465–66. Like the pun on "layes of lust," the word "pretence," meaning aim or purpose as well as deception, indicates that Elizabethan poetry of courtship relies on "the depths and secrets of some conceytes" (vol. 1, p. 3).

31 Gascoigne, *Hundreth Sundrie Flowres*, p. 142. As he explains in the introduction, Prouty reaches this conclusion after making a detailed comparison of the two editions.

32 Gascoigne, *Complete Works*, vol. 1, pp. 5, 7.

33 Ibid., vol. 1, pp. 9, 12.

34 Ibid., vol. 1, pp. 3, 12, 12, 12, 9.

35 Ibid., vol. 1, pp. 15, 16, 16.

36 Ibid., vol. 1, p. 17. Billingsgate is one of the gates of the city where the fish market was. Seventeenth-century references to foul, abusive language there were so common that the word came to mean foul language.

37 Gascoigne, *Complete Works*, vol. 1, p. 16; Wall, *Imprint of Gender*, p. 50.

38 Puttenham, *Arte of English Poesie*, p. 170. Citing this passage, Elaine V. Beilin, *Redeeming Eve: Women Writers of the English Renaissance* (Princeton University Press, 1987), p. 8, concludes: "If, surmounting all these barriers, a woman should still seriously wish to write poetry, she is confronted by hostility and

by poetic traditions and conventions that had been adapted to masculine experience." Puttenham's remark may sound condescending to our ears, but it couldn't have been intended that way, since only a fool would single out the most likely users of his book for ridicule.

39 Puttenham, *Arte of English Poesie*, pp. 196, 197.
40 Ibid., p. 197; Whythorne, *Autobiography of Thomas*, p. 1.
41 Puttenham, *Arte of English Poesie*, pp. 197–8.
42 Ibid., p. 68.
43 Angel Day, *The English Secretary, or Methode of Writing of Epistles*, 2 pts. (London, 1599), p. 11.
44 Claudio Guillén in "Notes toward the Study of the Renaissance Letter," Barbara Kiefer Lewalski, *Renaissance Genres: Essays on Theory, History, and Interpretation*, Harvard English Studies 14 (Cambridge: Harvard University Press, 1986): 81, argues that the "notorious growth of both the social practice of correspondence and the printing of books incorporating that practice" epitomizes "the interplay between literature and social life during the Renaissance."
45 W[illiam] F[ulwood], *The Enimie of Idlenesse: Teaching a Perfect Platforme How to Endite, Epistles and Letters of All Sortes* (London, 1582), pp. 294, 296, 287, 291.
46 Ibid., pp. 146–47.
47 Baldassarre Castiglione, *The Book of the Courtier From the Italian of Count Baldassare Castiglione: Done into English by Sir Thomas Hoby. Anno 1561* (London: David Nutt, 1900), p. 261.
48 Day, *English Secretary*, p. 148.
49 Angel Day, *The English Secretorie. Wherein is Contayned, A Perfect Method, for the Inditing of all Manner of Epistles and Familiar Letters* (London, 1586), p. 238. The different spelling of "Secretorie" to that in 1599 edition is intentional and original.
50 Fulwood, *The Enimie of Idlenesse*, p. 290.
51 Ibid., pp. 285–86.
52 Philomusus, *The Academy of Complements: Wherein Ladyes, . . . May Accommodate Their Courtly Practiices* (London, 1640), pp. 71, 77, 79, 90, 112, 114, 159, 160.
53 Ibid., A.8.
54 Don M. Ricks, "Persona and Process in Spenser's 'Amoretti,'" *Ariel* 3 (1972): 7.
55 Arthur F. Marotti, *John Donne, Coterie Poet* (Madison: University of Wisconsin Press, 1986), p. 11.
56 Wall, *Imprint of Gender*, p. 69.
57 Whythorne, *Autobiography of Thomas*, p. 31.

5 ANNE VAVASOUR AND SIR HENRY LEE

1 Kenneth Burke, *The Philosophy of Literary Form*, 1941 (rev. edn. Berkeley: University of California Press, 1973), pp. 73–4.

2   Both poems are printed by E. K. Chambers in *Sir Henry Lee: an Elizabethan Portrait* (Oxford: Clarendon Press, 1936), pp. 152–54. The first poem is quoted from "The Poems of Edward De Vere, Seventeenth Earl of Oxford and of Robert Devereux, Second Earl of Essex, An Edition and Commentary by Steven W. May," *Studies in Philology* 77 (1980): 38, in a group of "Poems Possibly by Oxford." The second poem, having been printed by A. B. Grosart, *Miscellanies of the Fuller Worthies' Library* (Blackburn, 1876), is reprinted but not edited by Marotti in *Manuscript, Print, and the English Renaissance Lyric* (Ithaca: Cornell University Press, 1995), p. 58. I want to thank the reader for Cambridge University Press for calling the poems to my attention.

3   Some manuscripts, including the one published by Chambers, *Sir Henry Lee* have the variant "her secret feare to wayle, / Cladd all in colour of a Nun." The word "nun" seems more literal and less evocative than "vow," although "secret feare" still hints that the narrator is privy to her secret.

4   For further information on the tradition of the male-authored female complaint, see John Kerrigan, *Motives of Woe: Shakespeare and 'Female Complaint': a Critical Anthology* (Oxford: Clarendon Press, 1991).

5   I have removed the quotation marks, added by May, which is how the poem would have been read by the Elizabethans.

6   For a more comprehensive account of Oxford's position in the Elizabethan aristocracy, see Bernard Mordaunt Ward, *The Seventeenth Earl of Oxford, 1550–1604* (London: J. Murray, 1928).

7   Chambers, *Sir Henry Lee*, pp. 155–56.

8   Ruth Hughey (ed.), *The Arundel Harington Manuscript of English Poetry*, 2 vols. (Columbus: Ohio State University Press, 1960), vol. ii, p. 257.

9   The poem is quoted by Hughey, *Arundel Harington*, vol. i, pp. 215–16, and annotated, vol. ii, pp. 258–59. May, *Studies in Philology*, pp. 79–81, thinks it doubtful that either Oxford or Vavasour wrote the poem, but he nonetheless prints the text among "Poems Possibly by Oxford" on the grounds that Harington makes "a certain attribution to Oxford": "his testimony must carry some weight for he was a courtier who was both interested in verse and in a position to know who wrote it."

10 For the complete collection and an introduction, see *The Paradise of Dainty Devices*, Hyder Edward Rollins (ed.) (Cambridge: Harvard University Press, 1927). The poems are quoted here from May, *Studies in Philology*, p. 272.

11 Quoted by Chambers, *Sir Henry Lee*, p. 156. Hughey, *Arundel Harington*, vol. ii, pp. 258–59, writes: "the comment at the head of the poem suggests that Sir John knew Oxford's poetry well" which "was not so easy to do."

12 Hughey, *Arundel Harington*, vol. ii, p. 257.

13 Puttenham, *Arte of English Prose*, pp. 196–8.

14 May writes, *Studies in Philology*, p. 81, the poem "flatters [Oxford] with references to his beauty and birth, while suggesting that Anne *might* be worthy of his favors. If she wrote the poem, she went far out of her way to debase herself and glorify her lover." Rather than saying that the poem debases Vavasour, I would say the poem emphasizes Oxford's greater rank and status.

15 In order to support her attribution of the poem to Oxford, Hughey suggests that Harington is among a "lesser number" of readers capable of enjoying "the ironic mockery of the poem, which reverses the role of the suffering Petrarchan lover and skillfully presents the author as scorning himself for his pride and unfaithfulness in love." To me, the tone sounds less like gentle self-irony than like a scathing critique of Vere's vanity and self-absorption.

16 Chambers, *Sir Henry Lee*, p. 132. The armor is also described by Roy Strong, *The Cult of Elizabeth: Elizabethan Portraiture and Pageantry* (London: Thames and Hudson, 1977), p. 163.

17 There is as yet no modern edition listing all the textual variants. Based on Cummings' reproduction of the Finet ms. with a few emendations from the Cornwallis ms., Marotti prints the poem in a single block. I prefer Lee's version, based on Bodleian Rawlinson Poet Manuscript 85, fo. 17, because the division into quatrains enhances the meaning, and is more consistent with Elizabethan practice. Lee's version of the final phrase, "I leave it to thy thoughte," makes more sense than "I leave It to hy thoughte." Marotti's version of line 2, "Do not anoye thy self," is more accessible to today's readers, but the variant, "accoy," meaning quiet, soothe, silence, more aptly expresses the speaker's concern for the reader's "sullen will."

18 Chambers, *Sir Henry Lee*, p. 156; Marotti, *Manuscript and Print*, p. 57

19 Chambers, *Sir Henry Lee*, pp. 58–9. Marotti, *Manuscript and Print*, p. 58, cites Laurence Cummings' unpublished dissertation which mentions "elements in the poems that conflict with the circumstances of Ann Vavasour's life" but makes no attempt to assess the reasons for or validity of Cummings' conclusion.

20 Chambers, *Sir Henry Lee*, p. 55.

21 Ibid., p. 135.

22 For a detailed summary of the plot, see Chambers, *Sir Henry Lee*, 145–49. The full text is reprinted in Appendix E, to which the parenthetical references refer.

6 A FEMALE LYRIC TRADITION

1 Dorothy Gardiner (ed.), *The Oxinden and Peyton Letters 1642–1670* (London: Sheldon Press, 1937), p. xxvi.

2 Citing these lines in the original, Robert Coogan, "Petrarch's *Trionfi* and the English Renaissance," *Studies in Philology* 67 (1970): 324, observes: "This triumph reviews the love between Petrarch and Laura, offers an *apologia* for Laura's coldness to Petrarch, and contains Laura's most unequivocal protestation of love for Petrarch – 'mai diviso da te non fu 'l mio cor, né già mai fia'."

3 The text is from *The Triumph of Death, and Other Unpublished and Uncollected Poems*, by Mary Sidney, Countess of Pembroke (1561–1621) G. F. Waller (ed.), Elizabethan & Renaissance Studies 65 (Institut für Englische Sprache und Literatur, University of Saltzburg, 1977). For further information on Mary

Sidney, see Margaret Patterson Hannay, *Philip's Phoenix: Mary Sidney, Countess of Pembroke* (New York: Oxford University Press, 1990); Coburn Freer, "Mary Sidney," *Women Writers of the Renaissance and Reformation*, Katharina M. Wilson (ed.) (Athens: University of Georgia Press, 1987), pp. 481–90; Pearl Hogrefe, *Women of Action in Tudor England: Nine Biographical Sketches*, chapter 5, "Mary Sidney Herbert, Countess of Pembroke 1561–1621" (Ames: Iowa State University Press, 1977); G. F. Waller, *Mary Sidney, Countess of Pembroke: a Critical Study of her Writings and Literary Milieu* (Institut für Anglistik und Amerikanistik, Universitat Salzburg, 1979). For an annotated bibliography, see Josephine A. Roberts, Mary Sidney, Countess of Pembroke," *Women in the Renaissance: Selections from English Literary Renaissance*, Kirby Farrell, Elizabeth H. Hageman, and Arthur F. Kinney (eds.) (Amherst, University of Massachusetts Press, 1988), pp. 245–58.

4 For a thoughtful analysis of Sidney's *Triumph* from a quite different perspective, see Mary Ellen Lamb, *Gender and Authorship in the Sidney Circle* (Madison: University of Wisconsin Press, 1990), pp. 138–41. After describing the beauty and "the passivity of Laura's death," which "shows how any woman can fulfill the function of spiritual guide, molding her words and actions to benefit her man on his pilgrimage to heaven," Lamb astutely remarks that the countess's translations embody a female literary strategy through which "women could be perceived as heroic" without challenging the patriarchal culture of Elizabethan England.

5 M. M. Bakhtin, *The Dialogic Imagination: Four Essays*, Michael Holquist (ed.), Caryl Emerson and Michael Holquist (trans.) (Austin: University of Texas Press, 1981), p. 274.

6 In his introduction to *The Triumph*, p. 17, Waller writes, "As Petrarch encounters Laura in his dream, the poem becomes a dialogue between lovers, the tone more dramatic and less expository. Laura becomes a complex composite figure – the religious ideal, certainly, but as well what by the late sixteenth century had developed into the familiar Petrarchan mistress of love-poetry."

7 Sidney's translation receives high praise "verbally as well as metrically" by D. G. Rees, "Petrarch's 'Trionfo Della Morte' in English," *Italian Studies* 7 (1952): 83, and Coogan, *"Petrarch's Trionfi"* p. 324, who calls it "the finest translation of this triumph in the English language." Waller's judgment, *The Triumph*, pp. 11, 18, is first, that "Petrarch's *Trionfi* was probably the most influential poem of the Renaissance," and second, that Sidney's translation "is by the highest poetical standards, a remarkable piece of work."

8 Petrarch's *Rime Sparse* is quoted from the bilingual edition of *Petrarch's Lyric Poems: The Rime Sparse and Other Lyrics*, Robert M. Durling (ed. and trans.) (Cambridge: Harvard University Press, 1976). Rees, *Italian Studies* 7, p. 85.

9 Elaine V. Beilin, *Redeeming Eve: Women Writers of the English Renaissance* (Princeton University Press, 1987), is surely right to point out, p. 137, that "Laura radiates the spiritual sense of chastity as an expression of God's will and the path to blessedness, and redeems her lover rather than destroys

him." My point is that by intensifying her passion while applauding her chastity, Mary Sidney's language makes Laura one of those "seemingly paradoxical cases" described in Beilin's introduction, pp. xvii–xviii, where the "concept of women" not only circumscribes "what women wrote and how they wrote it" but also provokes them "to subvert cultural expectations of women's writing."

10 Ernest Hatch Wilkin's modern translation, *The Triumphs of Petrarch* (University of Chicago Press, 1962), p. 65, helps to clarify what is distinctive about Sidney's version: "Whether thou didst bring pleasure to my eyes / I will not say; but pleasure that sweet knot / Did give me that thou hadst around thy heart, / And pleasure the fair name thy poetry / Hath won for me, I ween, both near and far. / All that I sought was measure in thy love."

11 For a more thorough philosophical exploration of the issue, see "Shame and Gender," Sandra Lee Bartky, *Femininity and Domination: Studies in the Phenomenology of Oppression* (New York: Routledge, 1990), pp. 83–98.

12 *The Triumphes of Petrarch*, Henry Parker Lord Morley (trans.), 1554 (rpt. London, 1887), pp. 64, 63. The 1887 reprint has no line numbers.

13 Ibid., p. 64.

14 For a thoughtful analysis of Laura's singing in the *Rime*, see Sara Sturm-Maddox, *Petrarch's Laurels* (University Park: Pennsylvania State University Press, 1992), pp. 53–61. Sturm-Maddox also notes that in the *Trionfi*, "the burden of the song is love and its concealment . . . Its function is to reveal what words cannot say, and its concern is precisely the word of love that may not be spoken."

15 Lynn Enterline, "Embodied Voices: Petrarch Reading (Himself Reading) Ovid," *Desire in the Renaissance: Psychoanalysis and Literature*, Valeria Finucci and Regina Schwartz (eds.) (Princeton University Press, 1994), p. 138, argues that the "seemingly fetishized female figures . . . become signs of what the culturally fashioned male subject of poetic language must renounce if 'he' is to acceede to symbolic form." I would argue that Sidney's translation, by representing herself reading Laura reading Petrarch, transforms the beloved from fetishized object to speaking subject.

16 Kenneth Burke, *The Philosophy of Literary Form*, 1941 (rev. edn. Berkeley: University of California Press, 1973), p. 73.

17 Ralph Cohen, "Genre Theory, Literary History, and Historical Change," in *Theoretical Issues in Literary History*, David Perkins (ed.) (Cambridge: Harvard University Press, 1991), p. 104.

18 Bakhtin, *Dialogic Imagination*, p. 280.

19 Elizabeth I, "On Monsieur's Departure," lines 1–6. Quoted from *The Poems of Elizabeth I*, Leicester Bradner (ed.) (Providence: Brown University Press, 1964), p. 5.

20 This reading of Canzone 23 is indebted to a paper, presented by Nora Fienberg at the Modern Language Association Convention (1994), and to Barbara Estrin, *Laura: Uncovering Gender and Genre in Wyatt, Donne, and Marvell* (Durham: Duke University Press, 1994), p. 113. Estrin also identifies this

sonnet as a pivotal moment, in which Laura "takes on the poet's role, denies his power to circumscribe her, and asserts her elusiveness in terms of her exclusive control over the field that seemed, until then, the realm where only Petrarch functioned."

21 Estrin, *Laura*, p. 12, makes a similar point: "Complicating the sexual failure in Petrarchism is the presence in some poems of a desiring, albeit short-lived Laura-Eve." For a summary of the "elusive and enticing" history of Petrarch's love for Laura, see Peter Hainsworth, *Petrarch the Poet: An introduction to the Rerum vulgarium fragmenta* (London: Routledge, 1988), pp. 108 ff.

22 Thomas Whythorne, *The Autobiography of Thomas Whythorne*, James M. Osborn (ed.), Modern Spelling Edition (London: Oxford University Press, 1962), p. 1.

23 Bradner writes, *Poems of Elizabeth I*, p. 73: "Both Ashmore and Stowe say that Elizabeth wrote the poem on Monsieur's departure, which would connect it with the ending of the negotiations with Anjou in 1582."

24 One of the manuscripts reads "this care" rather than "his care" which shifts the emphasis from the pressures of Alençon's courtship to the cares of life as monarch.

25 In "Diana Described: Scattered Woman and Scattered Rhyme," *Critical Inquiry* 8 (1981): 278–79, Nancy J. Vickers writes: "by the time we arrive at the end that 'crowns' his song, her speech has been written out and his has been written in. . . Silencing Diana is an emblematic gesture; it suppresses a voice, and it casts generations of would-be Lauras in a role predicated upon the muteness of its player. . . His speech requires her silence." It is this muteness which, I believe, Mary Sidney and Elizabeth I call into question.

26 "One strategy in 'The Copy of a letter' is that it purports to be a private communication," Ann Rosalind Jones writes in *The Currency of Eros: Women's Love Lyric in Europe 1540–1620* (Bloomington: Indiana University Press, 1990), p. 43. "But the fact that the letter is 'written in meeter' proves that it was a literary performance from the start, not a text meant only for the lover's eyes." I would add that the Elizabethans are accustomed to addressing poems of courtship to a particular reader, knowing full well that they will also be read by other private and public audiences. Such poems are none the less artful than poems written for a wider public audience.

27 Michel Foucault, *The Use of Pleasure*, Robert Hurley (trans.), *The History of Sexuality* (New York: Vintage-Random House, 1980–1990), vol. II p. 9.

28 The courts are full of disputes over marriage contracts. For a fuller account, see Martin Ingram, *Church Courts, Sex, and Marriage in England, 1570–1640*, Past and Present Publications (Cambridge University Press, 1987).

29 "Whitney maneuvers for a positive position as a woman speaker," Jones writes, *Currency of Eros*, p. 43. "This is not easy, given that she adopts the newly fashionable mode of Ovid's *Heroides*." Unlike the male-authored female complaints, Whitney "writes to her 'unconstant lover' not as his victim but as his superior. She then turns to an audience of women as a

social and literary critic, to expose men's deceptions of women. Her protest against her own mistreatment in 'The Copy of a letter' becomes in 'An Admonition' a generalized protest against gender arrangements in the society at large."

30 Bakhtin, *Dialogic Imagination*, p. 274.

31 Beilen, *Redeeming Eve*, p. 100, reads "The Copy of a Letter" and "The Admonition" as "conventional warnings to young women to protect their virtue against lust." To me, Whitney's poems sound more like those "seemingly paradoxical cases" Beilin describes in her introduction, p. xviii, which "subvert cultural expectations of women's writing."

32 M[argaret] T[yler] (trans.), *The Mirrour of Princely deedes and Knighthood* (London, 1578), fo. A.4.r.

33 Ibid., preface.

34 Ann Rosalind Jones, "Nets and Bridles: Early Modern Conduct Books and Sixteenth-Century Women's Lyrics," in *The Ideology of Conduct: Essays on Literature and the History of Sexuality*, Nancy Armstrong and Leonard Tennenhouse (eds.) (New York: Methuen, 1987), p. 66.

35 Virginia Woolf, *A Room of One's Own* (New York: Harcourt, Brace and Company, 1929), p. 3.

36 Richard Whitford, *A Werke for Housholders* (London, 1530), fos. E.iii.r–v.

37 Virginia Cox, *The Renaissance Dialogue: Literary Dialogue in its Social and Political Contexts, Castiglione to Galileo* (Cambridge University Press, 1992), p. 7,

38 Burke, *Philosophy of Literary Form*, pp. 149–50.

39 Rita Felski, *Beyond Feminist Aesthetics: Feminist Literature and Social Change* (Cambridge: Harvard University Press, 1989), p. 43.

40 John R. Searle and Daniel Vanderveken, *Foundations of Illocutionary Logic* (Cambridge University Press, 1985), p. 93.

7 DANIEL'S LYRIC DIALOGUE OF COURTSHIP

1 Clark Hulse, *Metamorphic Verse: the Elizabethan Minor Epic* (Princeton University Press, 1981), p. 68, quotes the dedication of *Musophilus* as proof that "Daniel rejects the successively borrowed manners of sonnet and epic in favor of a personal style which holds him apart." Hulse, p. 59, accepts the traditional view of Delia – "as much a chapbook of polite social postures as the record of a passion. Its vocabulary is Petrarchan." I am suggesting that *Delia* has already begun to reject the borrowed manners of the sonnet tradition in favor of the "idiosyncratic plain style" (p. 56) which Hulse finds in Daniel's later writing.

2 Roland Barthes, *A Lover's Discourse: Fragments*, Richard Howard (trans.) (New York: Hill and Wang–Farrar, Strauss, and Giroux, 1978).

3 Joachim Du Bellay, *L'olive*, E. Caldarini (ed.) (Genève: Droz, 1974).

4 On Petrarch's use of the phoenix myth, and other versions of the myth, see Marjorie O'Rourke Boyle, *Petrarch's Genius: Pentimento and Prophecy* (Berkeley: University of California Press, 1991), p. 134.

5 Harold Bloom, *Kabbalah and Criticism* (New York: Continuum, 1984), p. 103. See George Keyports Brady, *Samuel Daniel; A Critical Study* (Urbana: University of Illinois Press, 1923); Janet Girran (Scott) Espiner, *Les Sonnets élisabéthains* (Paris: Champion, 1929); Sidney Lee, *Elizabethan Sonnets*, (Westminster: Archibald Constable, 1904), vol. 1, pp. liii–lxiii; L. E. Kastner, "The Italian Sources of Daniel's 'Delia,'" *Modern Language Review* 7 (1912): 153–56; C. Ruutz-Rees, "Some Debts of Samuel Daniel to Du Bellay," *Modern Language Notes* 24 (1909): 134–37; Pierre Spriet, *Samuel Daniel (1563–1619) Sa Vie – Son Oeuvre, Études Anglaises* 29 (Paris: Didier, 1968). Lars-Hakan Svensson, *Silent Art: Rhetorical and Thematic Patterns in Samuel Daniel's Delia* (Lund: Gleerup, 1980), p. 20, gives Daniel considerably more credit: "Obviously, such a term as 'translation' does not account for the subtle play on responses and expectations that is the main effect of this sonnet."

6 Daniel may well have known Petrarch's original Italian; there are no earlier English translations of Sonnet 45 cited in: *Petrarch in England: An Anthology of Parallel Texts from Wyatt to Milton*, Jack D'Amico (ed.) (Ravenna: Longo, 1979); Stephen Minta, *Petrarch and Petrarchism: the English and French Traditions* (New York: Barnes & Noble, 1980); *Petrarch's Canzoniere in the English Renaissance*, Anthony Mortimer (ed.) (Florence: Minerva Italica, 1975); or George Watson, *The English Petrarchans: A Critical Bibliography of the Canzoniere* (Warburg Institute–University of London, 1967).

7 Rosalie L. Colie, *The Resources of Kind: Genre-Theory in the Renaissance*, Barbara Kiefer Lewalski (ed.) (Berkeley: University of California Press, 1973), p. 26.

8 John Freccero, "The Fig Tree and the Laurel: Petrarch's Poetics," *Diacritics* 5 (1975): 40.

9 Philippe Desportes, *Les Amours D'Hippolyte*, Victor E. Graham (ed.) (Genève: Droz; Paris: Minard, 1960), p. 3.

10 *George Gascoigne's A Hundreth Sundrie Flowres*, C. T. Prouty (ed.), *University of Missouri Studies* 17 (Columbia: University of Missouri, 1942), p. 118. The poem is discussed more fully in chapter 4.

11 On the symbolic significance of Echo, see Caren Greenberg, "Reading Reading: Echo's Abduction of Language," *Women and Language in Literature and Society*, Sally McConnell-Ginet, Ruth Borker, and Nelly Furman, (eds.) (New York: Praeger, 1980), pp. 300–9; John Hollander, *The Figure of Echo: a Mode of Allusion in Milton and After* (Berkeley: University of California Press, 1981); Joseph Loewenstein, *Responsive Readings: Versions of Echo in Pastoral, Epic, and the Jonsonian Masque*, Yale Studies in English 192 (New Haven: Yale University Press, 1984).

12 Quoted from *Andrew Marvell: Complete Poetry*, George de F. Lord (ed.) (New York: Modern Library, 1968). As Michel Foucault's oft-cited remark in *Power/Knowledge: Selected Interviews and Other Writings, 1972–1977*, Colin Gordon (ed.), Colin Gordon, Leo Marshall, John Mepham, Kate Soper (trans.) (New York: Pantheon, 1980), p. 119, asserts, "What makes power hold good, what makes it accepted, is simply the fact that it doesn't only

weigh on us as a force that says no, but that it traverses and produces things, it induces pleasure, forms knowledge, produces discourse."

13 Peter Hainsworth, *Petrarch the Poet: An introduction to the Rerum vulgarium fragmenta* (London: Routledge, 1988), pp. 119–20, describes the erotic impulse and persuasive purpose as omnipresent but "inevitably tainted. Poem after poem is nothing more than a testimonial to a sinfulness which is made worse through being concealed or prettified."

14 In *The "Inward" Language: Sonnets of Wyatt, Sidney, Shakespeare, Donne* (University of Chicago Press, 1983), p. 206, Anne Ferry writes: "One of the commonest metaphors for representing the lover's state in sixteenth-century verse is the comparison of him to a subject ruled by a sovereign mistress. While it had the support of long-established literary tradition, and the encouragement of current fashion in continental poetry, the metaphor also corresponded to the actual situation of the Elizabethan courtier, who paid daily tribute to such a ruler not only in his verses." For a study of Elizabeth's politics of courtship, see my essay, "Elizabeth I – Always her Own Free Woman," *Political Rhetoric, Power, and Renaissance Women*, Carole Levin and Patricia Ann Sullivan (eds.) (Albany: State University of New York Press, 1995), pp. 57–82.

15 See Patricia Thomson, "Sonnet 15 of Samuel Daniel's *Delia*: A Petrarchan Imitation," *Comparative Literature* 17 (1965): 151–57.

16 Christopher R. Wilson, "*Astrophil and Stella*: A Tangled Editorial Web," *The Library* 6 (1979): 337. For information about Daniel's travels, see Mark Eccles, "Samuel Daniel in France and Italy," *Studies in Philology* 34 (1937): 148–67, and Joan Rees, *Samuel Daniel: A Critical and Biographical Study* (Liverpool: Liverpool University Press, 1964), pp. 13–14. In "*Astrophil and Stella*: A Tangled Editorial Web," Wilson says he "can't help feeling that Daniel was involved with Nash," though he admits, p. 339, there is "contrary evidence." Wilson argues, p. 337, that Lownes' decision to publish "the extra poems of Newman's first quarto" connects Daniel with Newman, though his reasoning seems obscure. Daniel clearly didn't want the pirated text reprinted, whereas Lownes clearly thought it would sell.

17 Samuel Daniel, *Poems and A Defence of Ryme*, Arthur Colby Sprague (ed.) (Cambridge, Harvard University Press, 1930), p. 9. Quotations from the authorized first edition are cited from this edition.

18 Terry Eagleton, *Literary Theory: An Introduction* (Minneapolis: University of Minnesota Press, 1983), pp. 7, 8.

19 The 1591 pirated edition is reprinted in Lee, *Elizabethan Sonnets* 1:88–102. Spriet, one of the few critics to comment on the pirated edition, offers a bleak assessment: "Les sonnets publiés en 1591 – et qui furent donc écrits avant le voyage en Italie, en 1590 – se caractérisaient par la relative banalité des sentiments et des images: dans la tradition pétrarquiste" (p. 87).

20 C. F. Williamson, "The Design of Daniel's *Delia*," *Review of English Studies* 19 (1968): 260, defends "Daniel's variations on a well-known theme and his 'formal ordering' of the sonnets" as "probably the high-water mark of deliberate artistry in the whole range of the Elizabethan sonnet sequences."

21 Probably the single most definitive and influential modern statement about Daniel's sonnet sequence is C. S. Lewis's in *English Literature in the Sixteenth Century, Excluding Drama,* The Oxford History of English Literature, vol. III. (Oxford: Clarendon, 1954), p. 491: "those who like their poetry 'not too darn poetical' should avoid *Delia.* It offers no ideas, no psychology, and of course no story: it is simply a masterpiece of phrasing and melody." Lewis assumes that *Delia* "of course" has "no story," not only because he himself believes, p. 328, that "the sonnet sequence does not exist to tell a real, or even a feigned, story," but also because he is judging by the expurgated first edition. Joseph Kau, "*Delia's* Gentle Lover and the Eternizing Conceit in Elizabethan Sonnets," *Anglia* 92 (1974): 334–35.

22 K. Burke, *The Philosophy of Literary Form,* 1941 (rev. edn. Berkeley: University of California Press, 1973), p. 78.

23 Svenssen provides detailed analyses of Daniel and his continental precursors, but does not analyze the pirated text.

24 In "Samuel Daniel's Revisions in *Delia,*" *Journal of English and Germanic Philology* 53 (1954): 61, Miller writes that Daniel "permitted the caution of middle age to throttle the injudiciousness of youthful passion."

25 "The Complaint of Rosamond," quoted from John Kerrigan, *The Motives of Woe: Shakespeare and 'Female Complaint': a Critical Anthology* (Oxford: Clarendon Press, 1991). The discursive title, cited by Kerrigan, p. 304, appears in Baldwin's 1563 edition of *A Myrrour for Magistrates.*

26 Kerrigan, *Myrrour for Magistrates,* p. 164.

27 Ibid., p. 164.

28 As Kerrigan observes, p. 17, Gascoigne also challenges the convention: to "disrupt the assumption (implicit in much feminine love plaint) that male readers should enjoy the victim's woe in ways not only continuous with the 'pleyinge' of an errant narrative . . . but with that of the treacherous lover," the male "writer who (like Gascoigne) wanted to question this arrangement did not write free-standing plaint but was forced to restructure the containment of the form."

29 Elizabeth D. Harvey, *Ventriloquized Voices: Feminist Theory and English Renaissance Texts* (London: Routledge, 1992), p. 141.

30 Although new authorized editions continue to appear, Daniel's original pirated text is reprinted in the second pirated edition of Sidney's sonnets, published by Matthew Lownes later in the decade. Clearly, a considerable number of Elizabethans were still eager to discover "the priuate passions" and "secrets" which the authorized editions conceal.

31 Heather A. Dubrow, *Genre* (London: Methuen, 1982), p. 23.

32 There may even be a veiled autobiographical link between Rosamond and Mary Sidney who acquired status, power, and wealth by marrying the Earl of Pembroke when she was only fourteen and he was already in his forties. The dedication of Shakespeare's sonnets, "TO. THE. ONLY. BEGETTER. OF. THESE. INSVING. SONNETS," makes a similar but even stronger claim, transferring authority entirely from poet to private lyric audience.

33 For additional information, see Mary Ellen Lamb, *Gender and Authorship in the Sidney Circle* (Madison: University of Wisconsin Press, 1990), and G. F. Waller's (ed.) introduction to *The Triumph of Death, and Other Unpublished and Uncollected Poems*, Elizabethan & Renaissance Studies 65 (Salzburg, Austria: Institut für Englische Sprache und Literatur, Univ. Saltzburg, 1977.), p. 11.

34 As Kerrigan's introduction explains, p. 16, complaints from Chaucer's to Gascoigne's use "the courtly intimacy between poet and audience" to allude to "experiences which, though deeply recessed in the poem, are part of the world he shares with his auditors." Kerrigan also warns, p. 18, that the elusive, veiled language of the complaint has produced some "forced readings *à clef*."

35 For studies of female patrons, see Margaret Patterson Hannay, *Silent but for the Word: Tudor Women as Patrons, Translators, and Writers of Religious Works* (Ohio: Kent State University Press, 1985); Lamb, *Gender and Authorship*; Guy Fitch Lytle and Stephen Orgel, *Patronage in the Renaissance* (Princeton University Press, 1981); Arthur F. Marotti, *John Donne Coterie Poet* (Madison: University of Wisconsin Press, 1986), pp. 202–44; Margaret Maurer, "The Real Presence of Lucy Russell, Countess of Bedford, and the Terms of John Donne's 'Honour is So Sublime Perfection'," *English Literary History* 47 (1980), pp. 205–34; Patricia Thomson, "The Literature of Patronage, 1580–1630," *Essays In Criticism* 2 (1952): 267–84.

36 Harvey, *Ventriloquized Voices*, p. 142.

37 Kerrigan, *Motives of Woe*, p. 17.

8 SPENCER'S AMORETTI

1 *The copie of a letter, lately written in meeter, by a yonge gentilwoman to her vnconstant Louer. With an Admonitio^{n} to al yong Gentilwomen and to al other Mayds in general. By Is. W[hitney]* (London, 1567), fo. A.I.V.

2 A. Kent Hieatt, "A Numerical Key for Spenser's 'Amoretti' and Guyon in the House of Mammon," *The Yearbook of English Studies* 3 (1973): 15, writes that "Spenser would have thought of them as one work."

3 Donna Gibbs, *Spenser's Amoretti: A Critical Study* (Aldershot, Hants, England: Scolar Press; Brookfield, Vermont: Gower, 1990), p. 41, recognizes, as previous critics do not, that the Mistress "is, after all, the reader of these 'leaves, lines and rymes', which were composed for her perusal." Yet, Gibbs sees the poet's mistress, not as a lyric audience who plays an active role throughout the sequence, but as an inconsistent and baffling figure who is often little more than a conventional lyric type.

4 Alexander C. Judson, *The Life of Edmund Spenser, The Works of Edmund Spenser, A Variorum Edition*, Edwin Greenlaw, Charles Grosvenor Osgood and Frederick Morgan Padelford *et al.* (eds.), vol. IX (Baltimore: Johns Hopkins Press, 1945), p. 171, concludes that "the sequence as it stands was intended by the poet to celebrate his courtship of Elizabeth Boyle and to suggest, at least in a broad general way, the course of this affair." Although the

biographical basis of the sequence has been challenged repeatedly, a number of critics agree with Judson. G. K. Hunter, "Spenser's *Amoretti* and the English Sonnet Tradition," in *A Theatre for Spenserians*, Judith M. Kennedy and James A. Reither (ed.), Papers of the International Spenser Colloquium, 1969 (University of Toronto Press, 1973), p. 124, writes: "the *Amoretti* themselves give *some* indication that they are arranged as the history of a courtship leading up to marriage, or the expectation of marriage – and this again is not the natural or inevitable end to a sonnet sequence." Waldo F. McNeir, "An Apology for Spenser's *Amoretti*," in *Essential Articles for the study of Edmund Spenser*, A. C. Hamilton (ed.) (Hamden, Conn: Archon Books, 1972), p. 526, argues that Spenser "intended" the *Amoretti* "as a record of his courtship of Elizabeth Boyle." For an analysis of the biographical data, see Douglas Hamer, "Spenser's Marriage," *Review of English Studies* 7 (1931): 271–90.

5 [George Puttenham], *The Arte of English Poesie*, 1589 (Ohio: Kent State University Press, 1970), p. 234. Elizabeth Bieman, " 'Sometimes I . . . mask in myrth lyke to a Comedy': Spenser's *Amoretti*," *Spenser Studies* 4 (1983), writes, p. 132, that "much of the verbal energy in the early sonnets is directed to the decorously veiled end of provoking desire in the lady."

6 Whitney, *Copy of a Letter*, fo. A.5.v–A.6.r; Jane Anger, *Iane Anger her Protection for Women. To defend them against* THE SCANDALOVS REPORTES OF *a late Surfeiting Louer, and all other like Venerians that complaine so to bee ouercloyed with womens kindnesse* (London, 1589), fo. B.3.r.

7 Ibid., fo. C .3.v.

8 Whitney, *Copy of a Letter*, fos. C.3.v., A.7.r.

9 Some scholars have suggested that this Shakespearean sonnet must predate the Spenserian sonnets which comprise the *Amoretti*. It seems equally possible, however, that Spenser chose the form to signify his kinship with all the other Elizabethan rewritings of the classic Petrarchan conceit of the mirror, including Daniel's "Why doth my Mistres credit so her glasse" and Gascoigne's quick-witted female interlocutor, *Hundreth Sundrie Flowres*, C. T. Prouty (ed.), *University of Missouri Studies* 17 (Columbia: University of Missouri, 1942) p. 117, who responds, "Looke as long as you list, but surely if I take you / looking, I will looke with you."

10 According to Hallett Smith, *Elizabethan Poetry; A Study in Conventions, Meaning, and Expression* (Cambridge: Harvard University Press, 1952), p. 166, "Her greatest glory is her mind, 'adornd with vertues manifold.' Her awareness of heaven and of earth and her power to attract the eyes of others but chasten the desires produced by these looks derive from these qualities of 'pride and meekenesse mixt by equall part.' " Smith describes her as "the real protagonist of the series," but subsequent critics disagree. "Although she is described in many of the sonnets," Alexander Dunlop writes, "The Unity of Spenser's *Amoretti*," in Fowler, A. (ed.), *Silent Poetry: essays in numerological analysis* (London: Routledge & Kegan Paul, 1970), pp. 153–69, p. 163, "it is the lover who is characterized by his own descriptions." The "assertion that

the lady is the primary object of interpretation," writes Peter M. Cummings, "Spenser's *Amoretti* as an Allegory of Love," *Texas Studies in Language and Literature* 12 (1970): 164, "ignore[s] the unrelenting, immediate presence of the lover-poet's psychological monologues, which make him the crucial personality of the sequence."

11 Louis L. Martz, "The *Amoretti*: 'Most Goodly Temperature,'" in *The Prince of Poets: Essays on Edmund Spenser*, John R. Elliott, Jr. (ed.) (New York University Press, 1968), p. 128. Ibid., fo. A.6.r.

12 William Nelson, *Fact or Fiction: the Dilemma of the Renaissance Storyteller* (Cambridge: Harvard University Press, 1973), p. 91, summarizes a prevailing critical position when he writes, "As the lady's beauty arouses sexual passion so her pride of spirit keeps it under control." I find this conflict both less controlled and less easily resolved.

13 Beginning with Martz and continuing right up to Joan Larsen Klein's 1992 essay, "Women and Marriage in Renaissance England: Male Perspectives," *Topic* 36 (1982): 20–37, Spenser has been seen as the authoritative male figure, fulfilling his social and moral responsibility to educate this witty, but proud and fickle woman. These readings fail to acknowledge what Spenser himself is loathe to admit: that he has been both fickle and duplicitous, spouting Petrarchan idealism in public while practicing pseudo-Petrarchan seduction in private.

14 Robert Greene, *Penelopes Web* (London, 1587), fo. B.4.v. Patricia Parker, *Literary Fat Ladies: Rhetoric, Gender, Property* (London: Methuen, 1987), pp. 27–8, cites Greene's text as an illustration of endless female prattle as opposed to "the wifely virtue of 'Silence'." Georgianna Ziegler, "Penelope and the Politics of Woman's Place in the Renaissance," *Gloriana's Face: Women, Public and Private, in the English Renaissance*, S. P. Cerasano and Marion Wynne-Davies (eds.) (Detroit: Wayne State University Press, 1992), p. 31.

15 On weaving and poetry, see Patricia Klindienst Joplin, "The Voice of the Shuttle Is Not Ours," *Stanford Literary Review* 1 (1984): 25–53; J. Hillis Miller, "Ariachne's Broken Woof," *Georgia Review* 31 (1977): 44–60; Nancy K. Miller, "Arachnologies: The Woman, the Text, and the Critic," *The Poetics of Gender*, Nancy K. Miller (ed.) (New York: Columbia University Press, 1986), 270–95; Nancy J. Vickers, "Diana Described: Scattered Woman and Scattered Rhyme," *Critical Inquiry* 8 (1981): 265–79.

16 Mary Russo, "Female Grotesques: Carnival and Theory," *Feminist Studies, Critical Studies*, Teresa de Lauretis (ed.) (Bloomington: Indiana University Press, 1986), p. 224. Jacqueline T. Miller, "'Love Doth Hold My Hand': Writing and Wooing in the Sonnets of Sidney and Spenser," *English Literary History* 46 (1979): 552, also explores Spenser's "method for admitting his lady's control and skill." Whereas I emphasize their conflicts, Miller merges poet and lady, "granting her resistance and distance while ensnaring her (in his poem) into a position which integrates their actions."

17 Gibbs, *Spenser's Amoretti* argues, pp. 68, 80–2, that trope of the spider places the Lover/Persona in the "bewildered victim role," making him look ridiculous, and that the metaphor of the spider cinches the humor. For all the humor, I think that the sonnet offers a more probing and serious analysis of the relation between poet/lover and lyric audience, and that the final allusion to Arachne emphasizes the poignancy of his failure to find a convincing rhetorical strategy.

18 Kenneth Burke, *The Philosophy of Literary Form*, 1941 (Rev. edn. Berkeley: University of California Press, 1973), p. 78.

19 William Whately, *A Care-cloth: Or A Treatise of the Troubles of Marriage* (London, 1624), fo. a.2.v. According to McNeir, *An Apology*, p. 532, it is "her tough sense of her own power and individual worth which prevents her from yielding to his suit." According to Miller, "Love Doth Hold My Hand," p. 556, Spenser "demonstrates the power of his poetry while exhibiting the lady's capacity to manipulate, transform, and modify his art."

20 Annabel M. Patterson's fascinating analysis of Jonson's lyrics as a "medium of covert self-expression," "Lyric and Society in Jonson's *Under-wood*," *Lyric Poetry Beyond New Criticism*, Chaviva Hosek and Patricia Parker (eds.), (Ithaca: Cornell University Press, 1985), pp. 159, 153, remarks that "Jonson's self is also, as it were, present in the ordering, in the meditative spaces between the poems, where things can be implied that could not be expressed openly." I think Spenser uses an analogous technique at climactic moments in the *Amoretti*, with the crucial difference that it is not only the poet's self, but also the female listener/reader who is, as it were, present in the spaces between the poems where things are implied that cannot be openly asserted.

21 Anger, *Iane Anger* fo. a.4.v; Whitney, *Copie of a letter* fo. a.6.r. On the erotic subtext of Ovidean verse, see Clark Hulse, *Metamorphic Verse: the Elizabethan Minor Epic* (Princeton University Press, 1981), and William Keach, *Elizabethan Erotic Narratives: Irony and Pathos in the Ovidian Poetry of Shakespeare, Marlowe, and Their Contemporaries* (New Brunswick, New Jersey: Rutgers University Press, 1976).

22 Thomas Whythorne, *The Autobiography of Thomas Whythorne*, James M. Osborn (ed.), Modern Spelling edn. (London: Oxford University Press, 1962), pp. 31–2.

23 Gascoigne, *Hundreth Sundrie Flowres*, p. 126. Whythorne, *Autobiography of Thomas*, p. 20.

24 J. W. Lever, *The Elizabethan Love Sonnet*, 1966 (2nd edn. London: Methuen, 1978), p. 102. Anger, *Iane Anger* fos. b.1.r, b.1.v., a.7.v.

25 Pamela Joseph Benson, *The Invention of The Renaissance Woman* (University Park: Pennsylvania State University Press, 1992), p. 185; Alexander Dunlop, "The Drama of the *Amoretti*," *Spenser Studies* 1 (1980): p. 119.

26 V. Kostic, "Spenser's *Amoretti* and Tasso's Lyrical Poetry," *Renaissance and Modern Studies* 3 (1959): 68–9, notes that Spenser's version is much harsher than either Petrarch's or Tasso's.

27 Robert Kellogg, "Thought's Astonishment and the Dark Conceits of Spenser's *Amoretti,*" *The Prince of Poets: Essays on Edmund Spenser,* John R. Elliott Jr. (ed.), 1965 (New York University Press, 1968), pp. 142, 141.

28 Cf. Gibbs, *Spenser's Amoretti* p. 42.

29 If, as I have been suggesting, the *Amoretti* constitutes the poet/lover's side of an ongoing conversation, it is tempting to conclude, as Dunlop, "Drama of Amoretti", does, that Sonnet 58 is spoken "by her" to the poet. However, the rhetoric is clearly that of a male poet/lover speaking to a female reader.

30 For a very different reading, see Arlene N. Okerlund, "The Rhetoric of Love: Voice in the *Amoretti* and the *Songs and Sonets,*" *Quarterly Journal of Speech* 68 (1982): 42, Spenser "addresses his lady from a distance and celebrates her perfections with abstractions . . . he seldom speaks *to* her; instead he speaks *about* her in the third person."

31 Isabella Whitney, *A sweet nosgay; or pleasant posye: contayning a hundred and ten phylosophicall flowers* (London, 1573), fo. B.8.r.

32 Carol V. Kaske, "Spenser's *Amoretti* and *Epithalamion* of 1595: Structure, Genre, and Numerology," *English Literary Renaissance* 8 (1978): 280, notes "sexual frustration . . . in the bride's mind too." Though "less certain" about this part of the argument, Kaske, *Spenser's Amoretti,* pp. 280–81, suggests that "Christian humility and wifely submission are not the final answer."

33 Henrie Smith, *A Preparatiue to Mariage* (London, 1591), p. 78.

34 W. B. C. Watkins, *Shakespeare and Spenser* (Princeton University Press, 1950), p. 214, argues that "unlike Sidney and Shakespeare and Drayton, Spenser does not rebel against the Petrarchan conventions. He is the last great poet to accept them and work inside their limitations with ease and mastery." Other critics, however, including Gibbs, *Spenser's Amoretti.* Reed Way Dasenbrock, "The Petrarchan Context of Spenser's *Amoretti,*" *PMLA* 100 (1985): 38–50, and Anne Lake Prescott, *French Poets and the English Renaissance: Studies in Fame and Transformation* (New Haven: Yale University Press, 1978), see Spenser moving away from Petrarchism in one way or another.

35 Martz, *The Amoretti,* p. 134, does not take the disagreement seriously: "The only qualifications to his happiness here are slight, and very easily overcome: her fear of losing her liberty (Sonnet 65) . . ." The essay later justifies this "courtly" attitude, on the grounds of "the lover's age: he is forty, . . . explains a great deal that may have puzzled us about the lover's manner and tone; it confirms our impression that the foregoing sonnets are written from the broad, experienced view of maturity."

36 For an examination of the image, and its broad cultural significance, see Antonia Fraser, *The Weaker Vessel: Woman's Lot in Seventeenth Century England* (New York: Knopf, 1984).

37 Joan Larsen Klein argues, *Daughters, Wives, and Widows: Writings by Men about Women and Marriage in England, 1500–1640* (Urbana: University of Illinois Press, 1991), p. 111, that the lady "is encouraged to overcome her pride and her desire for mastery and submit to love and to her husband, while her

poet–lover abandons both abject submission and forceful desiring and prepares to assume the role of benevolent ruler and teacher or husband."

38 Klein, *Daughters, Wives* examines prescriptive literature but not the practice of courtship or the controversy over courtship, and thus fails to see that the later sonnets upset these traditional gender roles. Æmelia Lanyer, *Salve Deus Rex Judæorvm*, (London: 1611), fo. B.2.r. J. E. Neale, *Elizabeth I and Her Parliaments*, 2 vols. (London: Jonathan Cape, 1953–57), vol. I, p. 142.

39 William Gouge, *The Workes of William Govge. Two Volumes: The First, Domesticall Dvties. The Second, The Whole Armovr of God* (London, 1627), vol. I, p. 197.

40 Robert Cleaver, *A Godly Form of Hovseholde Gouernement* (London, 1598), p. 176.

41 Gibbs, *Spenser's Amoretti*, comments, p. 26, "It is an equal kind of union, for although he is master and ties her 'fyrmely' he does so with her goodwill." Joseph Loewenstein, "A Note on the Structure of Spenser's Amoretti: Viper Thought," *Spenser Studies* 8 (1987): 314–15, writes, "Lady and lover cannot meet on equal terms, yet the poem makes as great an advance toward mutuality as can perhaps be achieved given the sexual politics that prevailed on Spenser . . . So that the good will of the lady is not only a condition, but an instrument of what cannot honestly be described except as a kind of bondage." What Loewenstein does not mention is that this is only one step in the dance of bondage and liberty, not the final number. Prescott's reading of sonnets, pp. 67–70, brings to bear not only Petrarch, Tasso, the psalms, and the Prayer Book, but also Marguerite de Navarre's *Chansons*.

42 Martha Moulsworth, *"My Name Was Martha": A Renaissance Woman's Autobiographical Poem*, (ed. with commentary) Robert C. Evans and Barbara Wiedemann (West Cornwall, Conn: Locust Hill Press, 1993), p. 7, lines 66–8.

43 Henry Willobie, *Willobie, his Avisa, or, The True picture of a modest maid and of a chast and constant wife* (London, 1594), p. 3.

44 John Harington, *Nugae Antiquae: Being a Miscellaneous Collection of Original Papers in Prose and Verse . . . By Sir John Harington, Knt. And by others who lived in those Times*, Thomas Park (ed.), 1804, 2 vols. (New York: AMS, 1966), vol. I, p. 360.

45 Camden, W., *The Historie of the . . . princesse Elizabeth.* (trans.) R. N[orton]. London, 1630, p. 4.

46 William Shakespeare, *The Sonnets; and, A Lover's Complaint*, John Kerrigan (ed.) (New York: Viking, 1986; Harmondsworth: Penguin, 1986), Sonnet 55, lines 9–11.

47 Fredric Jameson, *The Political Unconscious: Narrative as a Socially Symbolic Act* (Ithaca: Cornell University Press, 1981), p. 137.

48 Mary A. Villeponteaux, " 'With her own will beguyld': The Captive Lady in Spenser's *Amoretti*," *Explorations in Renaissance Culture* 14 (1988): 30, argues that the lady of the sonnets is "flawed by a desire for maisterie" which she must learn to overcome. I would say that it is the poet who is "flawed by a desire for maisterie" which he must learn to overcome. While Villeponteaux, p. 33, sees "the first assurance sonnet" as a measure for and

critique of the second, I see the second sonnet as a correction of and answer
to the first.

49 Edmund Tilney, *A Brief and Pleasant Discourse of Duties in Mariage, Called the
   Flower of Friendshippe* (London, 1568), fo. D.viii.r; R. J. Fehrenbach, "A Letter
   Sent by the Maydens of London (1567)," *English Literary Renaissance* 14 (1984):
   296.

50 Great Britain, *Calendar of Letters and State Papers Relating to English Affairs,
   Preserved Principally in the Archives of Simancas,* vol. 1, Elizabeth: 1558–1567,
   Martin A. S. Hume (ed.) 1892 (Nendeln/Liechtenstein: Kraus, 1971), vol.
   1:123.

51 C. S. Lewis, *English Literature in the Sixteenth Century, Excluding Drama.* The
   Oxford History of English Literature, vol. III (Oxford: Clarendon, 1954), p.
   372.

9 EPILOGUE

1 M[argaret] T[yler] (trans.), *The Mirrour of Princely deedes and Knighthood.*
  (London, 1578), fo. A.3.r.

2 Philip Sidney, *Defence of Poesy,* from *The Covntesse Pembrokes Arcadia* (London,
  1598), pp. 516, 518.

3 Adrienne Rich, "Cartographies of Silence," *The Dream of a Common
  Language: Poems, 1974–1977* (New York: Norton, 1978), 3:7–13.

4 Citing her blush as proof that Pamphilia "did not merely 'counterfeit' love
  in her verse," Mary Ellen Lamb, *Gender and Authorship in the Sidney Circle*
  (Madison: University of Wisconsin Press, 1990), p. 179, concludes: "The
  women poets in Wroth's romance write poems in the thrill of the chase as
  well as in abandonment. In using their poetry as a means of seduction,
  women poets are following a path well worn by the metrical feet of male
  poets."

5 Angel Day, *The English Secretorie. Wherein is Contayned, A Perfect Method, for the
  Inditing of all Manner of Epistles and Familiar Letters* (London, 1586), p. 147.
  Dorothy Gardiner (ed.), *The Oxinden and Peyton Letters 1642–1670* (London:
  Sheldon Press, 1937), p. xxvi.

6 Gardiner, *Oxinden and Peyton,* p. xxvi.

7 Lucy Hutchinson, *Memoirs of the Life of Colonel Hutchinson . . . with original anecdotes of many of the most distinguished of his contemporaries . . . to which is prefixed the
  life of Mrs. Hutchinson, written by herself,* 2 vols. (London, 1822), vol. 1, p. 95. For
  a more detailed study of Lucy Hutchinson's life and writings see Margaret
  George, *Women in the First Capitalist Society: Experiences in Seventeenth-Century
  England* (Urbana: University of Illinois Press, 1988), chapter 1, "Lucy
  Hutchinson: Keynote Speaker."

8 Hutchinson, *Memoirs of the Life,* 1:27.

9 Ibid., 1:27–8. For an illuminating introduction to and collection of
  seventeenth-century women's autobiographies, see *Her Own Life: Autobiographical Writings by Seventeenth-Century Englishwomen,* Elspeth Graham,

Hilary Hinds, Elaine Hobby, and Helen Wilcox (eds.) (London: Routledge, 1989). For some fascinating accounts of seventeenth-century women's writings, courtships, and marriages see Antonia Fraser, *The Weaker Vessel* (New York: Knopf, 1984); George, *Women in the First Capitalist Society;* Elaine Hobby, *Virtue of Necessity: English Women's Writing 1649–1688* (Ann Arbor: University of Michigan Press, 1988), Sara Heller Mendelson, *The Mental World of Stuart Women: Three Studies* (Amherst: University of Massachusetts Press, 1987).

10 [George Puttenham], *The Arte of English Poesie*, 1589 (Ohio: Kent State University Press, 1970), pp. 59–60.

11 Fredric Jameson, *The Political Unconscious: Narrative as a Socially Symbolic Act* (Ithaca: Cornell University Press, 1981), p. 68.

12 Robert Frost, *Selected Poems of Robert Frost* (New York: Holt, Rinehart and Winston, 1963), p. 225.

Works cited

Abrams, M. H. *et al.* (eds.). *The Norton Anthology of English Literature*, 5th edn. New York: Norton, 1986.

Alcoff, Linda. "Cultural Feminism Versus Post-Structuralism: The Identity Crisis in Feminist Theory." *Signs* 13 (1988): 405–36.

D'Amico, Jack, (ed.) *Petrarch in England: An Anthology of Parallel Texts from Wyatt to Milton.* Ravenna: Longo, 1979.

Amussen, Susan Dwyer. *An Ordered Society: Gender and Class in Early Modern England.* Oxford: Blackwell, 1988.

Anderson, Judith H. *Biographical Truth: The Representation of Historical Persons in Tudor-Stuart Writing.* New Haven: Yale University Press, 1984.

Anger, Jane. *Iane Anger her Protection for Women. To defend them against THE SCANDALOVS REPORTES OF a late Surfeiting Louer, and all other like Venerians that complaine so to bee ouercloyed with womens kindnesse.* London, 1589.

Archer, Ian W. *The Pursuit of Stability: Social Relations in Elizabethan London.* Cambridge University Press, 1991.

Armstrong, Nancy and Leonard Tennenhouse. "The Literature of Conduct, the Conduct of Literature, and the Politics of Desire: an Introduction." Armstrong and Tennenhouse, 1–24.

  (eds) *The Ideology of Conduct: Essays on Literature and the History of Sexuality.* New York: Methuen, 1987.

Ashley, Maurice. "Love and Marriage in Seventeenth-Century England." *History Today* 8 (1958): 667–75.

Attridge, Derek. *Peculiar Language: Literature as Difference from the Renaissance to James Joyce.* Ithaca: Cornell University Press, 1988.

Austern, Linda Phyllis. "'Sing Againe Syren': Female Musicians and Sexual Enchantment in Elizabethan Life and Literature." *Renaissance Quarterly* 42 (1989): 420–48.

Austin, J. L. *How To Do Things With Words.* Cambridge: Harvard University Press, 1962.

Babcock, Barbara, (ed.) *The Reversible World: Symbolic Inversion in Art and Society.* Forms of Symbolic Inversion Symposium (1972: Toronto). Ithaca: Cornell University Press, 1978.

Bacon, Jane Meautys Cornwallis. *The Private Correspondence of Jane Lady Cornwallis, 1613–1644.* London, 1842.

Bakhtin, M. M. *The Dialogic Imagination: Four Essays.* Michael Holquist. (ed.) Caryl Emerson and Michael Holquist (trans.). Austin: University of Texas Press, 1981.

Barber, C. L. *Shakespeare's Festive Comedy; a Study of Dramatic Form and its Relation to Social Custom.* Princeton University Press, 1959.

Barthel, Carol. "*Amorett!*: A Comic Monodrama?" Richardson, 288–93.

Barthes, Roland. *A Lover's Discourse: Fragments.* Richard Howard (trans.). New York: Hill and Wang-Farrar, Strauss, and Giroux, 1978.

Bartky, Sandra Lee. *Femininity and Domination: Studies in the Phenomenology of Oppression.* New York: Routledge, 1990.

Bassnett, Susan. *Elizabeth I: A Feminist Perspective.* New York: St. Martin's Press, 1988.

Bates, Catherine. *The Rhetoric of Courtship in Elizabethan Language and Literature.* Cambridge University Press, 1992.

Beilin, Elaine V. *Redeeming Eve: Women Writers of the English Renaissance.* Princeton University Press, 1987.

Bell, Ilona. "Elizabeth I – Always her Own Free Woman." Levin and Sullivan, 57–82.

"The Maydens of London: In Defense of their Lawful Liberty." Burke, Donawerth, Dove, and Nelson, 1998.

"Milton's Dialogue with Petrarch." *Milton Studies* 28 (1992): 91–120. *Riven Unities: Authority and Experience, Self and Other in Milton's Poetry,* Wendy Furman, Christopher Grose, and William Shullenberger (Guest eds.)

"The Role of the Lady in Donne's *Songs and Sonets.*" *Studies in English Literature* 23 (1983): 113–29.

"Under Y^e Rage of a Hott Sonn & Y^r Eyes: John Donne's Love Letters to Ann More." Summers and Pebworth, 25–52.

"What if it be a she? The Riddle of Donne's 'Curse'." John Donne's "desire of more". The Subject of Anne More Donne in His Poetry. M. Thomas Hester (ed.). (Newark: University of Delaware Press, 1996), pp. 106–39.

Du Bellay, Joachim. *L'olive,* E. Caldarini (ed.). Genève: Droz, 1974.

Belsey, Catherine. *The Subject of Tragedy: Identity and Difference in Renaissance Drama.* London: Methuen, 1985.

Bennett, Henry Stanley. *English Books & Readers: 1558–1603.* Cambridge University Press, 1952.

Benson, Pamela Joseph. *The Invention of The Renaissance Woman.* University Park: Pennsylvania State University Press, 1992.

Benson, Robert G. "Elizabeth as Beatrice: A Reading of Spenser's 'Amoretti'." *South Central Bulletin* 32 (1972): 184–88.

Benstock, Shari. *Textualizing the Feminine: on the Limits of Genre.* Norman: University of Oklahoma Press, 1991.

(ed.) *Feminist Issues in Literary Scholarship.* Bloomington: Indiana University Press, 1987.

Bernardo, Aldo S. *Petrarch, Laura, and the Triumphs.* Albany: State University of New York Press, 1974.

Berry, Philippa. *Of Chastity and Power: Elizabethan Literature and the Unmarried Queen.* London: Routledge, 1989.

Bieman, Elizabeth. "'Sometimes I . . . mask in myrth lyke to a Comedy': Spenser's *Amoretti.*" *Spenser Studies* 4 (1983): 131–41.

Black, L. G. "A Lost Poem by Queen Elizabeth I." *Times Literary Supplement.* 23 May, 1968: 535.

Bloom, Harold. *Kabbalah and Criticism.* New York: Seabury Press, 1975.

Blount, Thomas. *The Academie of Eloquence.* 2nd edn. London, 1656.

Boffey, Julia. "Women Authors and Women's Literacy in Fourteenth- and Fifteenth-Century England," *Women and Literature in Britain 1150–1500,* Carol M. Meale (ed.) Cambridge University Press, 1993.

Boose, Linda. "The Family in Shakespeare Studies; or – Studies in the Family of Shakespeans; or – The Politics of Politics." *Renaissance Quarterly* 40 (1987): 706–42.

Boyle, Marjorie O'Rourke. *Petrarch's Genius: Pentimento and Prophecy.* Berkeley: University of California Press, 1991.

Bradbrook, Muriel Clara. *The Queen's Garland; Verses Made by her Subjects for Elizabeth I, Queen of England, Now Collected in Honour of her Majesty Queen Elizabeth II.* Oxford: Published for the Royal Society of Literature by Geoffrey Cumberlege, Oxford University Press, 1953.

Brady, George Keyports. *Samuel Daniel; A Critical Study.* Urbana: University of Illinois Press, 1923.

Breton, N. *A Poste With a Madde Packet of Letters.* London: 1602.

Brink, Jean R., Allison P. Coudert and Maryanne C. Horowitz, (eds.) *The Politics of Gender in Early Modern Europe.* Sixteenth Century Essays & Studies 12 (1989).

Burke, Kenneth. *The Philosophy of Literary Form.* 1941. Rev. edn. Berkeley: University of California Press, 1973.

Burke, Mary, Jane Donawerth, Linda Dove, and Karen Nelson, (eds.) *Women, Writing, and the Reproduction of Culture in Tudor and Stuart Britain.* Syracuse University Press, 1998.

Burke, Peter (ed.). *New Perspectives on Historical Writing.* University Park: Pennsylvania State University Press, 1992.

Butler, Judith P. *Gender Trouble: Feminism and the Subversion of Identity.* New York: Routledge, 1989.

Buxton, John. "On the date of *Syr P.S. His Astrophel and Stella* . . . Printed for Matthew Lownes." Bodleian Library Record 5 (1960): 614–16.

Byrne, Muriel St. Clare, (ed.) *The Lisle Letters.* 6 vols. Chicago: University of Chicago Press, 1981.

Camden, Carroll. (1952) *The Elizabethan Woman.* Rev. edn. Mamaroneck, New York: Appel, 1975.

Camden, William. *The Historie of the . . . princesse Elizabeth.* R. N[orton] (trans.). London, 1630.

    Remains concerning Britain. R. D. Dunn (ed.). Toronto: University of Toronto Press, 1984.

Carey, John. *John Donne: Life, Mind and Art.* New York: Oxford University Press, 1981.

Carlton, Charles. "The Widow's Tale: Male Myths and Female Reality in 16th and 17th Century England." *Albion* 10 (1978): 118–29.

Carroll, Berenice A. (ed.) *Liberating Women's History: Theoretical and Critical Essays.* Urbana: University of Illinois Press, 1976.

Castiglione, Baldassarre. *The Book of the Courtier From the Italian of Count Baldassare Castiglione: Done into English by Sir Thomas Hoby. Anno 1561.* London: David Nutt, 1900.

Cerasano, S. P. and Marion Wynne-Davies (eds.) *Gloriana's Face: Women, Public and Private, in the English Renaissance.* Detroit: Wayne State University Press, 1992.

Chamberlain, John. *The Chamberlain Lettters: A Selection of the Letters of John Chamberlain Concerning Life in England from 1597–1626.* Elizabeth McClure Thomson (ed.). New York: Putnam, 1965.
   The Letters of John Chamberlain. Norman Egbert McClure (ed.). Philadelphia: American Philosophic Society, 1939.

Chambers, E. K. *Sir Henry Lee: an Elizabethan Portrait.* Oxford: The Clarendon Press, 1936.

Clark, Alice. (1919). *Working Life of Women in the Seventeenth Century.* London: Routledge, 1982.

Clark, Sandra. *The Elizabethan Pamphleteers: Popular Moralistic Pamphlets 1580–1640.* Rutherford: Fairleigh Dickinson University Press, 1983.

Cleaver, Robert. *A Godly Form of Householde Gouernement: for the Ordering of Priuate Families.* London, 1598.

Clifford, James. Introduction. Clifford and Marcus, 1–26.
   and George E. Marcus, (eds.) *Writing Culture: The Poetics and Politics of Ethnography.* Berkeley: University of California Press, 1986.

Cohen, Ralph. "Genre Theory, Literary History, and Historical Change." Perkins, 85–113.

Colie, Rosalie L. *The Resources of Kind; Genre-Theory in the Renaissance.* Barbara Kiefer Lewalski (ed.). Berkeley: University of California Press, 1973.

Colse, Peter. *Penelopes Complaint: or, A Mirrour for wanton Minions.* London, 1596.

Compact Edition of the Oxford English Dictionary. Oxford University Press, 1971.

Coogan, Robert. "Petrarch's *Trionfi* and the English Renaissance." *Studies in Philology* 67 (1970): 306–27.

Cook, Ann Jennalie. *Making a Match: Courtship in Shakespeare and his Society.* Princeton University Press, 1991.

Cox, Virginia. *The Renaissance Dialogue: Literary Dialogue in its Social and Political Contexts, Castiglione to Galileo.* Cambridge University Press, 1992.

Craig, D. H. *Sir John Harington.* Boston: Twayne, 1985.

Craig, Joanne. "The Queen, Her Handmaid, and Spenser's Career." *English Studies in Canada* 12 (1987): 255–68.

Crane, Mary Thomas. *Framing Authority: Sayings, Self, and Society in Sixteenth-Century England.* Princeton University Press, 1993.

"'Video et Taceo': Elizabeth I and the Rhetoric of Counsel." *Studies in English Literature* 28 (1988): 1–15.

Crawford, Patricia. "Women's Published Writings 1600–1700." Prior, 211–82.

Cressy, David. "Literacy in pre-industrial England." *Societas* 4 (1974): 229–40.

   (ed.) *Education in Tudor and Stuart England*. New York: St. Martin's Press, 1975.

Crewe, Jonathan V. *Trials of Authorship: Anterior Forms and Poetic* from Wyatt reconstruction to Shakespeare. Berkeley: University of California Press, 1990.

Crofts, J. E. V. "John Donne: A Reconsideration." Gardner, *Collection* 77–89.

Culler, Jonathan D. *On Deconstruction: Theory and Criticism After Structuralism*. Ithaca: Cornell University Press, 1982.

   "Changes in the Study of the Lyric." Hosek and Parker, 38–54.

Cummings, Peter M. "Spenser's *Amoretti* as an Allegory of Love." *Texas Studies in Language and Literature* 12 (1970): 163–79.

Cummings, Robert M., (ed.) *Spenser: The Critical Heritage*. New York: Barnes & Noble, 1971.

Cupids Messenger: or, A Trusty Friend Stored with Sundry Sorts of Serious, Witty, Pleasant, Amorous, and Delightfull Letters. London, 1629.

Daniel, Samuel. "Poems and Sonets of Sundrie Other Noble men and Gentlemen." Sidney, Sir Philip. *Syr P. S. his Astrophel and Stella. To the end of wh. are added sundry other rare sonnets of diuers gentlemen.* J3v-L2v.

   Poems and a Defence of Ryme. Arthur Colby Sprague (ed.). Cambridge: Harvard University Press, 1930.

Darnton, Robert. "History of Reading." Burke, 140–67.

Dasenbrock, Reed Way. "The Petrarchan Context of Spenser's *Amoretti*." *PMLA* 100 (1985): 38–50.

Davies, Kathleen M. "Continuity and Change in Literary Advice on Marriage." Outhwaite, 58–79.

Davies, Stevie. *The Feminine Reclaimed: The Idea of Woman in Spenser, Shakespeare, and Milton*. Lexington: University of Kentucky Press, 1986.

Davis, Natalie Zemon. *The Return of Martin Guerre*. Cambridge: Harvard University Press, 1983.

   Society and Culture in Early Modern France. Eight Essays by Natalie Zemon Davis. Stanford University Press, 1975.

   "'Women's History' in Transition: The European Case." *Feminist Studies* 3 (1976): 83–103.

Day, Angel. *The English Secretary, or Methode of Writing of Epistles*. 2 pts. London, 1599.

   The English Secretorie. Wherein is Contayned, A Perfect Method, for the Inditing of all Manner of Epistles and Familiar Letters. London, 1586.

Derrida, Jacques. *Of Grammatology*. Gayatri Chakravorty Spivak (trans.). Baltimore: Johns Hopkins University Press, 1976.

Desportes, Philippe. *Les Amour D'Hippolyte*. Victor E. Graham (ed.). Genève: Droz; Paris: Minard, 1960.

Diefendorf, Barbara B. "Family Culture, Renaissance Culture." *Renaissance Quarterly* 40 (1987): 661–81.

Dollimore, Jonathan. *Radical Tragedy: Religion, Ideology and Power in the Drama of Shakespeare and his Contemporaries*. Chicago: University of Chicago Press, 1984.

and Alan Sinfield, (eds.) *Political Shakespeare: New Essays in Cultural Materialism*. Ithaca: Cornell University Press, 1985.

Donne, John. *The Complete Poetry of John Donne*. John T. Shawcross (ed.). Garden City, New York: Anchor Books, 1967.

Original Letters of John Donne Relating to his Secret Marriage. John Donne Papers. Folger Library, Washington, DC.

Douglas, Mary. *Natural Symbols: Explorations in Cosmology*. New York: Pantheon, 1970.

Drayton, Michael. *The Works of Michael Drayton*. J. William Hebel (ed.). 5 vols. Oxford: Blackwell, 1931–1941.

Dubrow, Heather A. *Echoes of Desire: English Petrarchism and Its Counterdiscourses*. Ithaca: Cornell University Press, 1995.

Genre. London: Methuen, 1982.

A Happier Eden: The Politics of Marriage in Stuart Epithalamium. Ithaca: Cornell University Press, 1990.

Dunlop, Alexander. "The Unity of Spenser's *Amoretti*." Fowler, 153–69.

"The Drama of the *Amoretti*." *Spenser Studies* 1 (1980): 107–20.

Durling, Robert, (ed.) *Petrarch's Lyric Poems: The Rime Sparse and Other Lyrics*. Cambridge: Harvard University Press, 1976.

Dusinberre, Juliet. *Shakespeare and the Nature of Women*. London: Macmillan, 1975.

Eagleton, Terry. "Ideology and Scholarship." McGann, 114–25.

Literary Theory: An Introduction. Minneapolis: University of Minnesota Press, 1983.

Easthope, Antony. *Poetry as Discourse*. London: Routledge, 1983.

Eccles, Audrey. *Obstetrics and Gynaecology in Tudor and Stuart England*. Ohio Kent State University Press, 1982.

Eccles, Mark. "Samuel Daniel in France and Italy." *Studies in Philology* 34 (1937): 148–67.

Einstein, Lewis. *The Italian Renaissance in England*. New York: Columbia University Press, 1902.

Eisenstein, Elizabeth. *The Printing Press as an Agent of Change: Communications and Cultural Transformations in Early Modern Europe*. 2 vols. Cambridge University Press, 1979.

Eliot, T. S. *On Poetry and Poets*. New York: Farrar, Straus, and Cudahy, 1943, rpt. 1979.

Selected Essays. London: Faber and Faber, 1932.

Elizabeth I. *The Poems of Queen Elizabeth I*. Leicester Bradner (ed.). Providence: Brown University Press, 1964.

Elliott, John R. Jr. (ed.) *The Prince of Poets: Essays on Edmund Spenser*. New York University Press, 1968.

Elliott, Robert C. *The Literary Persona*. University of Chicago Press, 1981.

Elliott, Vivien Brodsky. "Single Women in the London Marriage Market: Age, Status and Mobility, 1598–1619." Outhewaite, 81–100.

Elton, G. R. "Parliament." Haigh, 79–100.

Enterline, Lynn. "Embodied Voices: Petrarch Reading (Himself Reading) Ovid." Finucci and Schwartz, 120–45.

Erasmus, Desiderius. *A Ryght Frutefull Epystle in laude and prayse of matrymony*. Richard Tauernour (trans.). London, 1536.

Espiner, Janet Girran (Scott). *Les Sonnets élisabéthains*. Paris: Champion, 1929.

Estrin, Barbara L. *Laura: Uncovering Gender and Genre in Wyatt, Donne, and Marvell*. Durham: Duke University Press, 1994.

D'Ewes, Simonds, Sir. *The Diary of Sir Simonds D'Ewes, 1622–1624*. Elisabeth Bourcier (ed.). Publications de la Sorbonne, Littératures 5. Paris: Didier, 1974.

(ed.) *The Journals of All the Parliaments During the Reign of Queen Elizabeth, Both of the House of Lords and House of Commons*. London, 1682.

Ezell, Margaret J. M. *The Patriarch's Wife: Literary Evidence and the History of the Family*. Chapel Hill: University North Carolina Press, 1987.

Writing Women's Literary History. Baltimore: Johns Hopkins University Press, 1993.

Farrell, Kirby, Elizabeth H. Hageman, and Arthur F. Kinney, (eds.) *Women in the Renaissance: Selections from English Literary Renaissance*. Amherst: University of Massachusetts Press, 1990.

Fehrenbach, R. J. "A Letter Sent by the Maydens of London (1567)." *English Literary Renaissance* 14 (1984): 285–304.

Felperin, Howard. "Canonical Texts and Non-Canonical Interpretations. The Neohistoricist Rereading of Donne." *Southern Review* 18 (1985): 235–50.

Felski, Rita. *Beyond Feminist Aesthetics: Feminist Literature and Social Change*. Cambridge: Harvard University Press, 1989.

Ferguson, Margaret W. *Trials of Desire: Renaissance Defenses of Poetry*. New Haven: Yale University Press, 1983.

Ferguson, Margaret W., Maureen Quilligan, and Nancy Vickers, (eds.) *Rewriting the Renaissance: The Discourses of Sexual Difference in Early Modern Europe*. University of Chicago Press, 1986.

Ferguson, Moira (ed.) *First Feminists: British Women Writers: 1578–1799*. Bloomington: Indiana University Press; Old Westbury, New York: Feminist Press, 1985.

Ferry, Anne. *The "Inward" Language: Sonnets of Wyatt, Sidney, Shakespeare, Donne*. University of Chicago Press, 1983.

Fetterley, Judith. *The Resisting Reader: a Feminist Approach to American Fiction*. Bloomington: Indiana University Press, 1978.

Fienberg, Nona. *Elizabeth, Her Poets, and the Creation of the Courtly Manner: A Study of Sir John Harington, Sir Philip Sidney, and John Lyly*. New York: Garland, 1988.

"The Emergence of Stella in *Astrophil and Stella.*" *Studies in English Literature* 25 (1985): 5–19.

" 'I'non son forse chi tu credi': 'I am not perhaps who you think I am." MLA annual meeting, 1994.

Fineman Joel. *Shakespeare's Perjured Eye: The Invention of Poetic Subjectivity in the Sonnets.* Berkeley: University of California Press, 1986.

Finke, Laurie A. *Feminist Theory, Women's Writing.* Cornell University Press, 1992.

Finucci, Valeria and Regina Schwartz, (eds) *Desire in the Renaissance: Psychoanalysis and Literature.* Princeton University Press, 1994.

Fisher, Sheila and Janet E. Halley, (eds.) *Seeking the Woman in Late Medieval and Renaissance Writings: essays in feminist contextual criticism.* Knoxville: University of Tennessee Press, 1989.

Fletcher, Anthony and John Stevenson, (eds.) *Order and Disorder in Early Modern England.* Cambridge University Press, 1985.

Flynn, Dennis. "Donne and a *Female* Coterie." *LIT* 1 (1989): 127–36.

Flynn, Elizabeth A. and Patrocinio P. Schweickart, (eds). *Gender and Reading: Essays on Readers, Texts, and Contexts.* Baltimore: Johns Hopkins University Press, 1986.

Forster, Leonard Wilson. *The Icy Fire: Five Studies in European Petrarchism.* London: Cambridge University Press, 1969.

Foucault, Michel. *The History of Sexuality.* Robert Hurley (trans.). 3 vols. New York: Vintage-Random House, 1980–1990.

    Language, Counter-Memory, Practice: Selected Essays and Interviews. Donald F. Bouchard (ed.). Donald F. Bouchard and Sherry Simon (trans.). Ithaca: Cornell University Press, 1977.

    Power / Knowledge: Selected Interviews and Other Writings, 1972–1977. Colin Gordon (ed. and trans.). New York: Pantheon, 1980.

Fowler, Alastair (ed.). "The Unity of Spenser's Amoretti." *Silent Poetry: essays in numerological analysis* (London: Routledge & Kegan Paul, 1970), pp. 153–69.

Fowler, Alastair. *Kinds of Literature: An Introduction to the Theory of Genres and Modes.* Cambridge: Harvard University Press, 1982.

Fox, Evelyn. "The Diary of an Elizabethan Gentlewoman." Transactions of the Royal Historical Society. 3rd series. London, 1908. vol. II: 153–74.

Fraistat, Neil. "Introduction: The Place of the Book and the Book as Place." Fraistat, 3–17.

    (ed.) *Poems in their Place: The Intertextuality and Order of Poetic Collections.* Chapel Hill: University of North Carolina Press, 1986.

Fraser, Antonia. *The Weaker Vessel: Woman's Lot in Seventeenth Century England.* New York: Knopf, 1984.

Fraunce, Abraham. *The Arcadian Rhetorike.* Ethel Seaton (ed.). Oxford: For the Lutrell Society by R. Blackwell, 1950.

Freccero, John. "The Fig Tree and the Laurel: Petrarch's Poetics." *Diacritics* 5 (1975): 34–40.

Frost, Robert. *Selected Poems of Robert Frost.* New York: Holt, Rinehart and Winston, 1963.

Frye, Northrop. *Anatomy of Criticism: Four Essays.* Princeton University Press, 1957. New York: Atheneum, 1966.

Frye, Roland Mushat. "The Teachings of Classical Puritanism on Conjugal Love." *Studies in the Renaissance* 2 (1955): 148–59.

Frye, Susan. *Elizabeth I: the Competition for Representation.* New York: Oxford University Press, 1993.

F[ulwood], W[illiam]. *The Enimie of Idlenesse: Teaching a Perfect Platforme How to Endite, Epistles and Letters of All Sortes.* London, 1582.

Fumerton, Patricia. *Cultural Aesthetics: Renaissance Literature and the Practice of Social Ornament.* University of Chicago Press, 1991.

Furnivall, Frederick J. *Child-Marriages, Divorces, and Ratifications, in the Diocese of Chester.* London: Kegan Paul, 1897.

  (ed.) *Thomas Powell's Tom of all trades. or The Plaine Path-Way to Preferment.* London, 1876.

  (ed.) *Tell-Trothes New-Yeares Gift and The Passionate Morrice.* 1593. London, 1876.

  and W. R. Morfill, (eds.) *Ballads from Manuscripts.* Vol. II. Hertford, 1873.

Gairdner, James (ed.) *The Paston Letters, AD 1422–1509.* 5 vols. London: Chatto & Windus, 1904.

Garber, Marjorie, B. *Cannibals, Witches, and Divorce. Estranging the Renaissance.* Baltimore: Johns Hopkins University Press, 1987.

Gardiner, Samuel Rawson, (ed.) *The Fortescue Papers.* Westminster, England, 1871.

Gascoigne, George. *The Complete Works of George Gascoigne.* John W. Cunliffe (ed.). 2 vols. Cambridge University Press, 1907–1910.

  George Gascoigne's A Hundreth Sundrie Flowres. C. T. Prouty (ed.). *University of Missouri Studies* 17 (2). Columbia: University of Missouri, 1942.

Gaskin, Katherine. "Age at First Marriage in Europe Before 1850: a Summary of Family Reconstitution Data." *Journal of Family History* 31 (1978): 23–36.

Geertz, Clifford. *The Interpretation of Cultures: Selected Essays.* New York: Basic Books, 1973.

George, Margaret. *Women in the First Capitalist Society: Experiences in Seventeenth-Century England.* Urbana: University of Illinois Press, 1988.

Gibbs, Donna. *Spenser's Amoretti: A Critical Study.* Aldershot, Hants, England: Scolar Press; Brookfield, Vermont: Gower, 1990.

Giddens, Anthony. *Central Problems in Social Theory: Action, Structure and Contradiction in Social Analysis.* Berkeley, University of California Press, 1979.

Gillis, John R. *For Better, For Worse: British Marriages 1600 to the Present.* Oxford University Press, 1985.

Goldberg, Jonathan. *James I and the Politics of Literature: Jonson, Shakespeare, Donne and their Contemporaries.* Baltimore: Johns Hopkins University Press, 1983.

Goody, Jack. "Inheritance, Property, and Women." Goody, Thirsk, and Thompson, 10–30.

  Joan Thirsk, and E. P. Thompson, (eds.) *Family and Inheritance: Rural Society in Western Europe, 1200–1800.* Cambridge University Press, 1976.

Gosson, Stephen. *The School of Abuse.* London, 1841.

Gosynhill, Edward. *Here Begynneth the Scole House of Women.* London, 1560.

Gottfried, Rudolf. "Autobiography and Art: An Elizabethan Borderland." Damon, 109–34.

"'The G. W. Senior' and 'G. W. I.' of Spenser's *Amoretti.*" *Modern Language Quarterly* 3 (1942): 543–46.

Gouge, William. *The Workes of William Gouge. Two Volumes: The First, Domesticall Dvties. The Second, The Whole Armovr of God.* London, 1627.

Graff, Harvey J. (ed.) *Literacy and Social Development in the West: a Reader.* Cambridge University Press, 1981.

Graham, Elspeth, Hilary Hinds, Elaine Hobby, and Helen Wilcox, (eds) *Her Own Life: Autobiographical Writings by Seventeenth-Century Englishwomen.* London: Routledge, 1989.

Grange, John. *The Golden Aphrodits.* London, 1577. Delmar, New York: Scholars' Facsimiles, 1978.

Great Britain. *Calendar of Letters and State Papers Relating to English Affairs, Preserved Principally in the Archives of Simancas.* vol. 1. Elizabeth. 1558–1567. Martin A. S. Hume (ed.). London, 1892. Nendeln/Liechtenstein: Kraus, 1971.

Greenberg, Caren. "Reading Reading: Echo's Abduction of Language." McConnell-Ginet, Borker, and Furman, 300–9.

Greenblatt, Stephen Jay. *Learning to Curse: Essays in Early Modern Culture.* New York: Routledge, 1990.

Sir Walter Ralegh: The Renaissance Man and His Roles. New Haven: Yale University Press, 1973.

Greene, Gayle and Coppélia Kahn. "Feminist Scholarship and the Social Construction of Woman." Greene and Kahn, 1–36.

(eds.) *Making a Difference: Feminist Literary Criticism.* London: Methuen, 1985.

Greene, Robert. *Neuer Too Late.* Vol. 8 of *The Life and Complete Works in Prose and Verse of Robert Greene.* Alexander Balloch Grosart (ed.). 15 vols. New York: Russell & Russell, 1964.

Penelopes Web: Wherein a Christall Myrror of Faeminine Perfection Represents Vertues and Graces. London, 1587.

Greene, Roland. *Post-Petrarchism: Origins and Innovations of the Western Lyric Sequence.* Princeton University Press, 1991.

Grosart, Alexander B. *The Complete Works in Verse and Prose of Samuel Daniel.* London, 1885–96.

(ed.) *The Lismore Papers*, second series, volume I, London, 1887.

Grymeston, Elizabeth. *Miscelanea, Meditations, Memoratives.* London, 1604. The English Experience, 933. Norwood, New Jersey: Johnson, 1979.

Guibbory, Achsah. *The Map of Time: Seventeenth-Century English Literature and Ideas of Pattern in History.* Urbana: University of Illinois Press, 1986.

Guillén, Claudio. *Literature as System: Essays toward the Theory of Literary History.* Princeton University Press, 1971.

"Notes toward the Study of the Renaissance Letter." Lewalski, 70–101.

Hageman, Elizabeth H. "Recent Studies in Women Writers of the English Seventeenth Century (1604–1674)." Farrell, Hageman, and Kinney, 269–309.

"Recent Studies in Women Writers of Tudor England. Part 1: Women Writers, 1485–1603, Excluding Mary Sidney, Countess of Pembroke." Farrell, Hageman, and Kinney 228–44; 258–64.

(ed.) *Women in the Renaissance II.* Special issue of *English Literary Renaissance* 18, (1988).

Haigh, Christopher, (ed.) *The Reign of Elizabeth I.* Athens: University of Georgia Press, 1985.

Hainsworth, Peter. *Petrarch the Poet: An introduction to the Rerum vulgarium fragmenta.* London: Routledge, 1988.

Hair, P. E. "Bridal Pregnancy in Rural England Further Examined." *Population Studies* 24 (1970): 59–70.

"Bridal Pregnancy in Rural England in Earlier Centuries." *Population Studies* 20 (1966): 233–66.

Halkett, Anne. *The Memoirs of Anne, Lady Halkett and Ann, Lady Fanshawe.* John Loftis (ed.). Oxford: Clarendon Press, 1979.

Haller, William, and Malleville Haller. "The Puritan Art of Love." *Huntingdon Library Quarterly* 5 (1942): 235–72.

Halley, Janet E. "Textual Intercourse: Anne Donne, John Donne, and the Sexual Poetics of Textual Exchange." Fisher and Halley, 187–206.

Hamer, Douglas. "Spenser's Marriage." *Review of English Studies* 7 (1931): 271–90.

Hamilton, A. C. *Essential Articles for the study of Edmund Spenser.* Hamden, Conn.: Archon Books, 1972.

Hanawalt, Barbara A. (ed.) *Women and Work in Preindustrial Europe.* Bloomington: Indiana University Press, 1986.

Hannay, Margaret Patterson. *Philip's Phoenix: Mary Sidney, Countess of Pembroke.* New York: Oxford University Press, 1990.

(ed.) *Silent but for the Word: Tudor Women as Patrons, Translators, and Writers of Religious Works.* Ohio: Kent State University Press, 1985.

Harington, John. *Nugae Antiquae: Being a Miscellaneous Collection of Original Papers in Prose and Verse . . . By Sir John Harington, Knt. And by others who lived in those Times.* Thomas Park (ed.). 1804. 2 vols. New York: AMS, 1966.

The Letters and Epigrams of Sir John Harington, Together with The Prayse of Private Life. Norman Egbert McClure (ed.). Philadelphia: University of Pennsylvania Press, 1930.

Harley Manuscript. 787/81; 853/16. London: British Library.

Harris, Barbara J. "Marriage Sixteenth-Century Style: Elizabeth Stafford and the Third Duke of Norfolk." *Journal of Social History* 15 (1981): 371–81.

"Power, Profit, and Passion: Mary Tudor, Charles Brandon, and the Arranged Marriage in Early Tudor England." *Feminist Studies* 15 (1989): 59–88.

"Women and Politics in Early Tudor England." *The Historical Journal* 33 (1990): 259–81.

Harrison, G. B., (ed. and trans.) *De Maisse; A Journal of All That Was Accomplished by Monsieur de Maisse, Ambassador in England from King Henri IV to Queen Elizabeth Anno Domini 1597.* London: Nonesuch, 1931.

Harvey, Elizabeth D. *Ventriloquized Voices: Feminist Theory and English Renaissance Texts*. London: Routledge, 1992.

    and Katharine Eisaman Maus, (eds.) *Soliciting Interpretation: Literary Theory and Seventeenth-Century English Poetry*. University of Chicago Press, 1990.

Haselkorn, Anne M., and Betty S. Travitsky, (eds.) *The Renaissance Englishwoman in Print: Counterbalancing the Canon*. Amherst: University of Massachusetts Press, 1990.

Heath, Stephen. "Différence." *Screen* 19 (1978): 51–112.

Hedley, Jane. "Allegoria, Gascogne's Master Trope." *English Literary Renaissance* 11 (1981): 148–64.

Heilbrun, Carolyn G. *Writing a Woman's Life*. New York: Norton, 1988.

Heisch, Allison. "Queen Elizabeth I and the Persistence of Patriarchy." *Feminist Review* 4 (1980): 45–56.

    "Queen Elizabeth I: Parliamentary Rhetoric and the Exercise of Power." *Signs* 1 (1975): 31–55.

Helgerson, Richard. *The Elizabethan Prodigal*. Berkeley: University of California Press, 1976.

    Self-Crowned Laureates: Spenser, Jonson, Milton and the Literary System. Berkeley: University of California Press, 1983.

Henderson, Katherine Usher, and Barbara F. McManus. *Half Humankind: Contexts and Texts of the Controversy about Women in England 1540–1640*. Urbana: University of Illinois Press, 1985.

Herbert, George. *The Works of George Herbert*. F. E. Hutchinson (ed.). Oxford: Clarendon Press, 1970.

Hester, M. Thomas (ed.) *John Donne's 'desire of more': The Subject of Anne More Donne in his Poetry*. Newark: University of Delaware Press, 1996.

Heywood, Thomas. *England's Elizabeth by Thomas Heywood*. Philip R. Rider (ed.). *Garland English Texts* 8. New York: Garland, 1982.

Hic Mulier: or, The Man-Woman. London, 1620. (author unknown).

Hieatt, A. Kent. "A Numerical Key for Spenser's 'Amoretti' and Guyon in the House of Mammon." *The Yearbook of English Studies* 3 (1973): 14–27.

Hobby, Elaine. *Virtue of Necessity: English Women's Writing 1649–1688*. Ann Arbor: University of Michigan Press, 1988.

Hoby, Margaret Dakins. *Diary of Lady Margaret Hoby*. Dorothy M. Meads (ed.). Boston: Houghton, 1930.

Hogrefe, Pearl. *Women of Action in Tudor England: Nine Biographical Sketches*. Ames: Iowa State University Press, 1977.

Hollander, John. *The Figure of Echo: a Mode of Allusion in Milton and After*. Berkeley: University of California Press, 1981.

Hosek, Chaviva and Patricia Parker, (eds.) *Lyric Poetry Beyond New Criticism*. Ithaca: Cornell University Press, 1985.

Houlbrooke, Ralph A. *Church Courts and the People During the English Reformation, 1520–1570*. Oxford University Press, 1979.

    The English Family 1450–1700. London: Longman, 1984.

Houston, R. A. *Literacy in Early Modern Europe: Culture and, 1500–1800.* London: Longman, 1988.

Howard, George Elliott. *A History of Matrimonial Institutions, Chiefly in England and the United States.* 3 vols. Chicago: University of Chicago Press, Callaghan, 1904.

Howard, Jean E. "Crossdressing, The Theatre, and Gender Struggle in Early Modern England." *Shakespeare Quarterly* 39 (1988): 418–40.

Hughey, Ruth, (ed.) *The Arundel Harington Manucript of English Poetry.* 2 vols. Columbus: Ohio State University Press, 1960.

Hull, Suzanne. *Chaste, Silent & Obedient: English Books for Women 1475–1640.* San Marino, California: Huntingdon Library, 1982.

Hulse, Clark. *Metamorphic Verse: the Elizabethan Minor Epic.* Princeton University Press, 1981.

    "Stella's Wit: Penelope Rich as Reader of Sidney's Sonnets." *Rewriting the Renaissance: The Discourses of Sexual Difference in Early Modern Europe.* Ferguson, Quilligan, and Vickers (eds.). (University of Chicago Press, 1986) 272–86.

    "Samuel Daniel: The Poet as Literary Historian." *Studies in English Literature* (1979) 19: 55–69.

Hunter, G. K. "Drab and Golden Lyrics of the Renaissance." Brower, 1–18.

    "Spenser's *Amoretti* and the English Sonnet Tradition." Kennedy and Reither, 124–44.

Hurstfield, Joel. *The Queen's Wards; Wardship and Marriage under Elizabeth I.* Cambridge, Harvard University Press, 1958.

Hutchinson, Lucy Apsley. *Memoirs of the Life of Colonel Hutchinson . . . with original anecdotes of many of the most distinguished of his contemporaries . . . to which is prefixed the life of Mrs. Hutchinson, written by herself.* 2 vols. 4th edn. London, 1822.

Ingram, Martin. *Church Courts, Sex, and Marriage in England, 1570–1640.* Past and Present Publications. Cambridge University Press, 1987.

Jacobus, Mary, (ed.) *Women Writing and Writing about Women.* London: Croom Helm, 1979.

Jameson, Fredric. *The Political Unconscious: Narrative as a Socially Symbolic Act.* Ithaca: Cornell University Press, 1981.

Jardine, Lisa. *Still Harping on Daughters: Women and Drama in the Age of Shakespeare.* Totowa, New Jersey: Barnes, 1983.

Javitch, Daniel. "The Impure Motives of Elizabethan Poetry." *Genre* 15 (1982): 225–38.

    Poetry and Courtliness in Renaissance England. Princeton University Press, 1978.

Jones, Ann Rosalind. *The Currency of Eros: Women's Love Lyric in Europe 1540–1620.* Bloomington: Indiana University Press, 1990.

    "Inscribing Femininity: French Theories of the Feminine." Greene and Kahn, 80–112.

    "Nets and Bridles: Early Modern Conduct Books and Sixteenth-Century Women's Lyrics." Armstrong and Tennenhouse, 39–72.

    "Surprising Fame: Renaissance Gender Ideologies and Women's Lyric." Miller, 74–95.

Jones, Ann Rosalind and Peter Stallybrass. "The Politics of *Astrophil and Stella.*" *Studies in English Literature* 24 (1984): 53–68.

Jones, Norman L. "Elizabeth's First Year: the Conception and Birth of the Elizabethan Political World." Haigh, 27–53.

Joplin, Patricia Klindienst. "The Voice of the Shuttle is Ours." *Stanford Literary Review* 1 (1984): 25–53.

Jordan, Constance. *Renaissance Feminism: Literary Texts and Political Models.* Ithaca: Cornell University Press, 1990.

Judson, Alexander C. *The Life of Edmund Spenser. The Works of Edmund Spenser, A Variorum Edition.* 1945. Greenlaw, *et al.* (eds.). Vol. IX. Baltimore: Johns Hopkins University Press, 1966.

Kalstone, David. *Sidney's Poetry: Contexts and Interpretations.* New York: Norton, 1965.

Kamm, Josephine. *Hope Deferred: Girls' Education in English History.* London: Methuen, 1965.

Kaske, Carol V. "Rethinking Loewenstein's 'Viper Thoughts'." *Spenser Studies* 8 (1987): 325–28.

  "Spenser's *Amoretti* and *Epithalamion* of 1595: Structure, Genre, and Numerology." *English Literary Renaissance* 8 (1978): 271–95.

Kastner, L. E. "The Italian Sources of Daniel's 'Delia'." *Modern Language Review* 7 (1912): 153–56.

Kau, Joseph. "*Delia's* Gentle Lover and the Eternizing Conceit in Elizabethan Sonnets." *Anglia* 92 (1974): 334–48.

Kaufman, Gloria. "Juan Luis Vives on the Education of Women." *Signs* 3 (1978): 891–96.

Keach, William. *Elizabethan Erotic Narratives: Irony and Pathos in the Ovidian Poetry of Shakespeare, Marlowe, and Their Contemporaries.* New Brunswick, New Jersey: Rutgers University Press, 1976.

Kellogg, Robert. "Thought's Astonishment and the Dark Conceits of Spenser's *Amoretti.*" 1965. Elliott, 139–51.

Kelly, Joan. *Women, History, & Theory: The Essays of Joan Kelly.* University of Chicago Press, 1984.

Kelso, Ruth. *Doctrine for the Lady of the Renaissance.* Urbana: University of Illinois Press, 1956.

Kempe, Alfred John (ed.) *The Loseley Manuscripts, and Other Rare Documents, Illustrative of Some of the More Minute Particulars of English History, Biography, and Manners, from the Reign of Henry VIII to that of James I (Loseley House in Surrey).* London, 1836.

Kennedy, Judith M. and James A. Reither, (eds.) *A Theatre for Spenserians.* Papers of the International Spenser Colloquium, 1969. University of Toronto Press, 1973.

Kennedy, William J. *Rhetorical Norms in Renaissance Literature.* New Haven: Yale University Press, 1978.

Kerrigan, John. Introduction. *The Sonnets; and, A Lover's Complaint.* Shakespeare, 7–63.

(ed.) *Motives of Woe: Shakespeare and 'Female Complaint': a Critical Anthology.* Oxford: Clarendon Press, 1991.

Kerrigan, William and Gordon Braden. *The Idea of the Renaissance.* Baltimore: Johns Hopkins University Press, 1989.

Kesler, R. L. "The Idealization of Women: Morphology and Change in Three Renaissance Texts." *Mosaic* 23 (1990): 107–16.

King, John N. "Queen Elizabeth 1: Representations of the Virgin Queen." *Renaissance Quarterly* 43 (1990): 30–74.

King, Margaret L. *Women of the Renaissance.* University of Chicago Press, 1991.

Kinney, Arthur F. (ed.) *Elizabethan Backgrounds: Historical Documents of the Age of Elizabeth 1.* Hamden, Conn.: Archon Books, 1975.

Klarwill, Victor Von. (ed.) *Queen Elizabeth and Some Foreigners.* New York: Brentano, 1928.

Klein, Joan Larsen. "Women and Marriage in Renaissance England: Male Perspectives." *Topic* 36 (1982): 20–37.

(ed.) *Daughters, Wives, and Widows: Writings by Men about Women and Marriage in England, 1500–1640.* Urbana: University of Illinois Press, 1991.

Klein, Lisa M. " 'Let us love, deare love, lyke as we ought': Protestant Marriage and the Revision of Petrarchan Loving in Spenser's *Amoretti.*" *Spenser Studies* 10 (1992): 109–37.

Knox, John. *The First Blast of the Trumpet Against the Monstruous Regiment of Women.* London, 1558.

Korda, Natasha. "Mistaken Identities: Castiglio(ne)'s Practical Joke." Finucci and Schwartz, 39–60.

Kostic, V. "Spenser's *Amoretti* and Tasso's Lyrical Poetry." *Renaissance and Modern Studies* 3 (1959): 51–77.

Krier, Theresa M. *Gazing on Secret Sights: Spenser, Classical Imitation, and the Decorums of Vision.* Ithaca: Cornell University Press, 1990.

Kuschmierz, Ruth L. M. " 'The Instruction of a Christian Woman': A Critical Edition of the Tudor Translation." Dissertation at University of Pittsburgh, 1961.

Lacan, Jacques. *Feminine Sexuality: Jacques Lacan and the école freudienne.* Juliet Mitchell and Jacqueline Rose, (eds). Jacqueline Rose (trans.). New York: Norton, 1982.

Lamb, Mary Ellen. *Gender and Authorship in the Sidney Circle.* Madison: University of Wisconsin Press, 1990.

"The Cooke Sisters: Attitudes toward Learned Women in the Renaissance." Hannay, 107–25.

Lanham, Richard A. "Astrophil and Stella: *Pure and Impure Persuasion.*" *English Literary Renaissance* 2 (1972): 100–15.

The Motives of Eloquence: Literary Rhetoric in the Renaissance. New Haven: Yale University Press, 1976.

Lanyer, Æmelia. *Salve Deus Rex Judæorvm.* London: 1611.

Laslett, Peter, Karla Oosterveen, and Richard M. Smith, (eds.) *Bastardy and its Comparative History: Studies in the History of Illegitimacy and Marital*

Nonconformism in Britain, France, Germany, Sweden, North America, Jamaica and Japan. Cambridge: Harvard University Press, 1980.

Lauretis, Teresa de. "Feminist Studies/Critical Studies: Issues, Terms, and Contexts." de Lauretis, 1–19.

(ed.) *Feminist Studies, Critical Studies*. Bloomington: Indiana University Press, 1986.

Lee, Sidney. *Elizabethan Sonnets*. vol. 1. Westminster: Archibald Constable, 1904.

Leigh, Dorothy. *The Mother's Blessing. Or the godly Counsaile of a Gentlewoman*. 7th edn. London 1621.

Lentricchia, Frank. *Criticism and Social Change*. University of Chicago Press, 1983.

Lenz, Carolyn Ruth Swift, Gayle Greene, and Carol Thomas Neely, (eds.) *The Woman's Part: Feminist Criticism of Shakespeare*. Urbana: University of Illinois, 1980.

Lerner, Gerda. *The Majority Finds Its Past. Placing Women in History*. Oxford University Press, 1979.

Lever, J. W. *The Elizabethan Love Sonnet*. 1966. 2nd edn. London: Methuen, 1978.

Levin, Carole. *The Heart and Stomach of a King: Elizabeth I and the Politics of Sex and Power*. Philadelphia: University of Pennsylvania Press, 1994.

and Patricia Ann Sullivan, (eds.) *Political Rhetoric, Power, and Renaissance Women*. Albany: State University of New York Press, 1995.

Levine, David and Keith Wrightson. "The Social Context of Illegitimacy in Early Modern England." Laslett, Oosterveen and Smith, 158–75.

Levine, Mortimer. "The Place of Women in Tudor Government." Guth and McKenna, 109–23.

Lewalski, Barbara Kiefer. *Writing Women in Jacobean England*. Cambridge: Harvard University Press, 1993.

(ed.) *Renaissance Genres: Essays on Theory, History, and Interpretation. Harvard English Studies* 14. Cambridge: Harvard University Press, 1986.

Lewis, C. S. *English Literature in the Sixteenth Century, Excluding Drama*. The Oxford History of English Literature. vol. III. Oxford: Clarendon, 1954.

A Preface to Paradise Lost. 1942. New York: Galaxy-Oxford University Press, 1961.

Lodge, Thomas. *Rosalynde, Or, Euphues' Golden Legacy*. Edward Chauncey Baldwin (ed.). Boston: Ginn, 1910.

Loewenstein, Joseph. "A Note on the Structure of Spenser's Amoretti: Viper Thought." *Spenser Studies* 8 (1987): 311–23.

Responsive Readings: Versions of Echo in Pastoral, Epic, and the Jonsonian Masque. Yale Studies in English 192. New Haven: Yale University Press, 1984.

Loftis, John. Introduction. Loftis, ix–xviii.

(ed.) *The Memoirs of Anne, Lady Halkett and Ann, Lady Fanshawe*. Oxford: Clarendon Press, 1979.

Low, Anthony. *The Reinvention of Love: Poetry, Politics and Culture from Sidney to Milton*. Cambridge University Press, 1993.

Lowe, Roger. *The Diary of Roger Lowe of Ashton-in-Makerfield, Lancashire 1663–74*. William L. Sachse (ed.). New Haven: Yale University Press, 1938.

Lucas, Caroline. *Writing for Women: the Example of Woman as Reader in Elizabethan Romance*. Stony Stratford: Open University Press, 1989.

Lytle, Guy Fitch and Stephen Orgel. *Patronage in the Renaissance*. Princeton University Press, 1981.

MacCaffrey, Wallace T. *Queen Elizabeth and the Making of Policy, 1572–1588*. Princeton University Press, 1981.

The Shaping of the Elizabethan Regime. 1968. London: Jonathan Cape, 1969.

MacDonald, Michael. *Mystical Bedlam: Madness, Anxiety, and Healing in Seventeenth-Century England*. Cambridge University Press, 1981.

Macfarlane, Alan. *The Family Life of Ralph Josselin, a Seventeenth-Century Clergyman: an Essay in Historical Anthropology*. New York: Norton, 1977.

Marriage and Love in England: Modes of Reproduction 1300–1840. Oxford: Blackwell, 1986.

"Review Essay: *The Family, Sex, and Marriage in England*." *History and Theory* 18 (1979): 103–26.

Maclean, Ian. *The Renaissance Notion of Woman: a Study in the Fortunes of Scholasticism and Medical Science In European Intellectual Life*. Cambridge University Press, 1980.

Maisse, André Hurault de. *A Journal of All That Was Accomplished by Monsieur de Maisse, Ambassador in England from King Henri IV to Queen Elizabeth Anno Domini 1597*. G. B. Harrison and R. A. Jones (trans. and ed.). Bloomsbury: Nonesuch, 1931.

Manguel, Alberto. *A History of Reading*. New York: Viking, 1996.

Manley, Lawrence. *Convention, 1500–1750*. Cambridge: Harvard University Press, 1980.

Marcus, Leah S. *Puzzling Shakespeare: Local Reading and Its Discontents*. The New Historicism Studies in Cultural Poetics 6. Berkeley: University of California Press, 1988.

Marotti, Arthur F. *John Donne, Coterie Poet*. Madison: University of Wisconsin Press, 1986.

"'Love Is Not Love': Elizabethan Sonnet Sequences and the Social Order." *English Literary History* 49 (1982): 396–428.

Manuscript, Print, and the English Renaissance Lyric. Ithaca: Cornell University Press, 1995.

Martines, Lauro. *Society and History in English Renaissance Verse*. Oxford: Blackwell, 1985.

Martz, Louis L. "The *Amoretti*: 'Most Goodly Temperature'." Elliott, 120–38.

Marvell, Andrew. *Andrew Marvell: Complete Poetry*. George de F. Lord (ed.). New York: Modern Library, 1968.

Maurer, Margaret. "The Real Presence of Lucy Russell, Countess of Bedford, and the Terms of John Donne's 'Honour is So Sublime Perfection'." *English Literary History* 47 (1980): 205–34.

"Samuel Daniel's Poetical Epistles, Especially Those to Sir Thomas Egerton and Lucy, Countess of Bedford." *Studies in Philology* 74 (1977): 418–34.

May, Steven W. *The Elizabethan Courtier Poets: The Poems and their Contexts.* Columbia: University of Missouri Press, 1991.

"The Poems of Edward De Vere, Seventeenth Earl of Oxford and of Robert Devereux, Second Earl of Essex, An Edition and Commentary by Steven W. May." *Studies in Philology* 77 (1980): 5–118.

Maydens of London. *A Letter Sent by the Maydens of London, to the vertuous Matrones & Mistresses of the same, in the defense of their lawfull Libertie.* 1567. R. J. Fehrenbach (ed.). *English Literary Renaissance* 14 (1984): 285–304. Rpt. 1567 Farrell, Hageman, and Kinney, 28–47.

Mazzaro, Jerome. *Transformations in the Renaissance English Lyric.* Ithaca: Cornell University Press, 1970.

McConnell-Ginet, Sally, Ruth Borker, and Nelly Furman, (eds.) *Women and Language in Literature and Society.* New York: Praeger, 1980.

McCoy, Richard C. *The Rites of Knighthood: The Literature and Politics of Elizabethan Chivalry.* Berkeley: University of California Press, 1989.

Sir Philip Sidney: Rebellion in Arcadia. New Brunswick, New Jersey: Rutgers University Press, 1979.

McCullen, Norma. "The Education of English Gentlewomen 1540–1640." *History of Education* 6 (1977): 87–101.

McGann, Jerome J, (ed.) *Historical Studies and Literary Criticism.* 4th edn. Caltech-Waingart Conference in the Humanities, 1984. Madison: University of Wisconsin Press, 1985.

McLaren, Angus. *Reproductive Rituals: the Perception of Fertility in England from the Sixteenth Century to the Nineteenth Century.* New York: Methuen, 1984.

McManus, Barbara F. "Eve's Dowry: Genesis and the Pamphlet Controversy about Women." Burke, Donawerth, Dove, and Nelson, 1998.

McNeir, Waldo F. "An Apology for Spenser's *Amoretti.*" Hamilton, 524–33.

Mendelson, Sara Heller. *The Mental World of Stuart Women: Three Studies.* Amherst: University of Massachusetts Press, 1987.

Miller, Edward Haviland. "Samuel Daniel's Revisions in Delia." *Journal of English and Germanic Philology* 53 (1954): 58–68.

Miller, J. Hillis. "Ariachne's Broken Woof." *Georgia Review* 31 (1977): 44–60.

Miller, Jacqueline T. "'Love Doth Hold My Hand': Writing and Wooing in the Sonnets of Sidney and Spenser." *English Literary History* 46 (1979): 541–58.

Miller, Nancy K. "Arachnologies: The Woman, the Text, and the Critic." Miller, *Poetics,* 270–95.

"Changing the Subject: Authorship, Writing and the Reader." de Lauretis, 102–20.

(ed.) *The Poetics of Gender.* New York: Columbia University Press, 1986.

Miller, Naomi J. and Gary Waller. *Reading Mary Wroth: Representing Alternatives in Early Modern England.* Knoxville: University of Tennessee Press, 1991.

Minta, Stephen. *Petrarch and Petrarchism: the English and French Traditions.* New York: Barnes & Noble, 1980.

Montrose, Louis Adrian. "Celebration and Insinuation: Sir Philip Sidney and the Motives of Elizabethan Courtship." *Renaissance Drama* new series 8 (1977): 3–35.

"The Elizabethan Subject and the Spenserian Text." Parker and Quint, 303–40.

"Eliza, Queene of Shepheardes, and the Pastoral of Power." *English Literary Renaissance* 10 (1980): 153–82.

"Professing the Renaissance: The Poetics and Politics of Culture." Veeser, 15–36.

"The Purpose of Playing: Reflections on a Shakespearean Anthropology." *Helios* 7 (1979–80): 51–74.

"Renaissance Literary Studies and the Subject of History." *English Literary Renaissance* 16 (1986): 5–12.

"'Shaping Fantasies': Figurations of Gender and Power in Elizabethan Culture." *Representations* 1 (1983): 61–94.

Mortimer, Anthony, (ed.) *Petrarch's Canzoniere in the English Renaissance*. Florence: Minerva Italica, 1975.

Moulsworth, Martha. *"My Name Was Martha": A Renaissance Woman's Autobiographical Poem*. (ed.) with commentary by Robert C. Evans and Barbara Wiedemann. West Cornwall, Conn.: Locust Hill Press, 1993.

Mountfield, David. *Everyday Life in Elizabethan England*. Geneve: Liber, 1978.

Mueller, Janel. "Women Among the Metaphysicals: A Case, Mostly, of Being Donne For." *Modern Philology* 87 (1989): 142–58.

Muir, Kenneth, (ed.) *Collected Poems of Sir Thomas Wyatt*. Cambridge: Harvard University Press, 1950.

Mullaney, Stephen. *The Place of the Stage: License, Play and Power in Renaissance England*. University of Chicago Press, 1988.

Mumford, Ivy L. "Petrarchism in Early Tudor England." *Italian Studies* 19 (1964): 56–63.

Nashe, Thomas. *The Works of Thomas Nashe*. Ronald B. McKerrow (ed.). 5 vols. London: A. H. Bullen, 1904–1910.

Neale, John Earnest, Sir. *Elizabeth I and Her Parliaments*. 2 vols. London: Jonathan Cape, 1953–1957.

Introduction. Osborn, 7–15.

Queen Elizabeth. 1934. Garden City, New Jersey: Doubleday-Anchor, 1957.

Neely, Carol Thomas. "Constructing the Subject: Feminist Practice and the New Renaissance Discourses." *English Literary Renaissance* 18 (1988): 5–18.

"The Structure of English Renaissance Sonnet Sequences." *English Literary History* 45 (1978): 359–89.

Nelson, William. *Fact or Fiction: the Dilemma of the Renaissance Storyteller*. Cambridge: Harvard University Press, 1973.

"From 'Listen, Lordings' to 'Dear Reader'." *University of Toronto Quarterly* 46 (1976/77): 110–24.

Newdigate-Newdegate, Lady Anne, (ed.) *Gossip from a Muniment Room, Being Passages in The Lives of Anne and Mary Fitton, 1574–1618*. London, 1897.

Newman, Karen. *Fashioning Femininity and the English Renaissance Drama.* University of Chicago Press, 1991.

Newton, Judith. "History as Usual?: Feminism and the 'New Historicism'." *Cultural Critique* 9 (1988): 87–121.

and Deborah Rosenfelt. "Introduction: Toward a Materialist-Feminist Criticism." Newton and Rosenfelt, xv–xxxix.

and Deborah Rosenfelt, (eds.) *Feminist Criticism and Social Change: Sex, Class and Race in Literature and Culture.* New York: Methuen, 1985.

Norbrook, David. *Poetry and Politics in the English Renaissance.* London: Routledge, 1984.

Nyquist, Mary and Margaret W. Ferguson, (eds.) *Re-membering Milton: Essays on the Texts and Traditions.* New York: Methuen, 1988.

Oakeshott, Walter Fraser. *The Queen and the Poet.* London: Faber and Faber, 1960.

Okerlund, K., Arlene, N. "The Rhetoric of Love: Voice in the *Amoretti* and the *Songs and Sonets.*" *Quarterly Journal of Speech* 68 (1982): 37–46.

Oldys, William, and Thomas Park. *The Harleian Miscellany: A Collection of Scarce, Curious, and Entertaining Pamphlets and Tracts.* London, 1808–1813.

Ong, Walter J. *Rhetoric, Romance, and Technology: Studies in the Interaction of Expression and Culture.* Ithaca: Cornell University Press, 1971.

"The Writer's Audience is Always a Fiction." *PMLA* 90 (1975): 9–21.

Orgel, Stephen. *The Illusion of Power: Political Theater in the English Renaissance.* Berkeley: University of California Press, 1975.

Osborn, James M. (ed.) *The Quenes Maiesties Passage through the Citie of London to Westminster the Day before her Coronacion.* New Haven: Yale University Press, 1960.

Osborne, Dorothy. *Letters to Sir William Temple.* Kenneth Parker (ed.). London: Penguin, 1987.

Otten, Charlotte F. (ed.) *English Women's Voices 1540–1700.* Miami: Florida International University Press, 1992.

Outhwaite, R. B. (ed.) *Marriage and Society: Studies in the Social History of Marriage.* London: Europa, 1981.

Ovid. *Metamorphoses.* Rolfe Humphries (trans.). Bloomington: Indiana University Press, 1955.

Oxinden, Henry. *The Oxinden and Peyton Letters 1642–1670.* Dorothy Gardiner (ed.). London: Sheldon Press, 1937.

Ozment, Steven E. *When Fathers Ruled: Family Life in Reformation Europe.* Cambridge: Harvard University Press, 1983.

P[hillips], E[dward]. *The Mysteries of Love & Eloquence, Or, the Arts of Wooing and Complementing; As They are Managed in the Spring Garden, Hide Park, the New Exchange, and Other Eminent Places.* 3rd edn. London, 1685.

Parker, Patricia. *Literary Fat Ladies: Rhetoric, Gender, Property.* London: Methuen, 1987.

and David Quint, (eds.) *Literary Theory / Renaissance Texts.* Baltimore: Johns Hopkins University Press, 1986.

Patterson, Annabel M. *Censorship and Interpretation: The Conditions of Writing and*

Reading in Early Modern England. Madison: University of Wisconsin Press, 1984.

"Lyric and Society in Jonson's *Under-wood*." Hosek and Parker, 148–63.

Peacham, Henry. *The Garden of Eloquence*. 1593. Gainesville, Florida: Scholars Facsimiles, 1954.

Pearson, Lu Emily. *Elizabethan Love Conventions*. New York: Barnes & Noble, 1967.

Pebworth, Ted-Larry. "The Editor, the Critic, and the Multiple Texts of Donne's 'A Hymne to God the Father'." *South Central Review* 4 (1987): 15–34.

"Manuscript Poems and Print Assumptions: Donne and his Modern Editors." *John Donne Journal* 3 (1984): 1–21.

and Claude J. Summers. " 'Thus Friends Absent Speake': The Exchange of Verse Letters between John Donne and Henry Wotton." *Modern Philology* 81 (1984): 361–77.

Pembroke, Anne Clifford Herbert. *The Diary of Lady Anne Clifford*. V. Sackville-West (ed.). London: Heinemann, 1923.

Percy, Henry. *Advice to His Son by Henry Percy Ninth Earl of Northumberland*. 1609. G. B. Harrison (ed.). London: Ernest Benn, 1930.

Perkins, David (ed.) *Theoretical Issues in Literary History*. Cambridge: Harvard University Press, 1991.

Petrarch, Francesco. *Petrarch's Lyric Poems: The* Rime Sparse *and Other Lyrics*. Robert Durling (trans. and ed.). Cambridge: Harvard University Press, 1976.

The Triumphs of Petrarch. Ernest Hatch Wilkins (trans.). Chicago: University of Chicago Press, 1962.

The Triumphes of Petrarch. Henry Parker Lord Morley (trans.), 1554. Rpt. London, 1887.

Philomusus. *The Academy of Complements: Wherein Ladyes,...May Accommodate Their Courtly Practice*. London, 1640.

Prescott, Anne Lake. *French Poets and the English Renaissance: Studies in Fame and Transformation*. New Haven: Yale University Press, 1978.

"The Thirsty Deer and the Lord of Life: Some Contexts for *Amoretti* 67–70." *Spenser Studies* 6 (1985): 33–76.

Prior, Mary (ed.) *Women in English Society 1500–1800*. London: Methuen, 1985.

The Prompters Packet of Private and Familiar Letters. London, 1612.

[Puttenham, George.] *The Arte of English Poesie*. 1589. Ohio: Kent State University Press, 1970.

Pye, Christopher. *The Regal Phantasm: Shakespeare and the Politics of Spectacle*. London: Routledge, 1990.

Quilligan, Maureen. "The Comedy of Female Authority in *The Faerie Queene*." *English Literary Renaissance* 17 (1987): 156–71.

Milton's Spenser: The Politics of Reading. Ithaca: Cornell University Press, 1983.

R., M. *President for Yong Pen-men. Or, the Letter Writer*. London, 1638.

Rappaport, Steven. *Worlds within Worlds: Structures of Life in Sixteenth-century London*. Cambridge University Press, 1989.

Raven, James, Helen Small, and Naomi Tadmore, (eds.) *The Practice and Representation of Reading in England*. Cambridge University Press, 1996.

Rebhorn, Wayne A. *Courtly Performances: Masking and Festivity in Castiglione's Book of the Courtier*. Detroit: Wayne State University Press, 1978.

Rees, D. G. "Petrarch's 'Trionfo Della Morte' in English." *Italian Studies* 7 (1952): 82–96.

Rees, Joan. *Samuel Daniel: A Critical and Biographical Study*. Liverpool University Press, 1964.

Regan, Mariann Sanders. *Love Words: The Self and the Text in Medieval and Renaissance Poetry*. Ithaca: Cornell University Press, 1982.

Reynolds, Myra. *The Learned Lady in England 1650–1760*. Boston: Houghton Mifflin, 1920.

Rice Jr., George P. *The Public Speaking of Queen Elizabeth: Selections from her Official Addresses*. 1951. New York: AMS Press, 1966.

Rich, Adrienne. *The Dream of a Common Language: Poems, 1974–1977*. New York: Norton, 1978.

Richardson, David A. (ed.) Spenser at Kalamazou. Cleveland State University Press, 1978.

Richmond, Hugh M. *The School of Love: The Evolution of the Stuart Love Lyric*. Princeton University Press, 1964.

Ricks, Don M. "Persona and Process in Spenser's '*Amoretti*'." *Ariel* 3 (1972): 5–15.

Ridley, Jasper Godwin. *Elizabeth I: The Shrewdness of Virtue*. 1987. New York: Fromm, 1989.

Riffaterre, Michael. *Semiotics of Poetry*. Bloomington: Indiana University Press, 1978.

Rimanelli, Giose and Kenneth John Atchity, (eds.) *Italian Literature, Roots and Branches: Essays in Honor of Thomas Goddard Bergin*. New Haven: Yale University Press, 1976.

Roberts, Josephine A. "Recent Studies in Women Writers of Tudor England. Part II: Mary Sidney, Countess of Pembroke." Farrell, Hageman and Kinney, 245–58; 265–69.

Roche, Thomas P. *Petrarch and the English Sonnet Sequences*. New York: AMS Press, 1989.

Roman, Camille, Suzanne Juhasz, and Cristanne Miller, (eds.) *The Women and Language Debate: A Sourcebook*. New Brunswick, New Jersey: Rutgers University Press, 1994.

Rollins, Hyder Edward (ed.) *The Paradise of Dainty Devices* Cambridge: Harvard University Press, 1927.

Rose, Mary Beth. *The Expense of Spirit: Love and Sexuality in English Renaissance Drama*. Ithaca: Cornell University Press, 1988.

(ed.) *Women in the Middle Ages and the Renaissance: Literary and Historical Perspectives*. Syracuse University Press, 1986.

Rosenberg, Eleanor. *Leicester, Patron of Letters*. New York: Columbia University Press, 1955.

Rougemont, Denis de. *Love in the Western World*. Montgomery Belgion (trans.). 1940. Rev. and aug. edn. New York: Harper Colophon, 1974.

Rowland, Beryl, (ed. and trans.) *Medieval Woman's Guide to Health: the first English gynecological handbook*. Ohio: Kent State University Press, 1981.

Rudenstine, Neil L. *Sidney's Poetic Development*. Cambridge: Harvard University Press, 1967.

Russo, Mary. "Female Grotesques: Carnival and Theory." de Lauretis, 213–29.

Ruutz-Rees, C. "Some Debts of Samuel Daniel to Du Bellay." *Modern Language Notes* 24 (1909): 134–37.

Saunders, J. W. "The Stigma of Print: A Note on the Social Bases of Tudor Poetry." *Essays in Criticism* 1 (1951): 139–64.

"From Manuscript to Print: A Note on the Circulation of Poetic MSS in the Sixteenth Century." *Proceedings of the Leeds Philosophical and Literary Society* 6–8 (1951), 507–28.

Schleiner, Louise. *Tudor and Stuart Women Writers*. Bloomington: Indiana University Press, 1994.

Schoenfeldt, Michael C. *Prayer and Power: George Herbert and Renaissance Courtship*. University of Chicago Press, 1991.

Scott, Joan Wallach. "Gender: A Useful Category of Historical Analysis." *American Historical Review* 91 (1986): 1053–75.

Gender and the Politics of History. New York: Columbia, 1988.

Searle, John R. and Daniel Vanderveken. *Foundations of Illocutionary Logic*. Cambridge University Press, 1985.

Sedgwick, Eve Kosofsky. *Between Men: English Literature and Male Homosocial Desire*. New York: Columbia University Press, 1985.

Sells, A. Lytton. *The Italian Influence in English Poetry, from Chaucer to Southwell*. Bloomington: Indiana University Press, 1955.

Seronsy, Cecil. *Samuel Daniel*. New York: Twayne, 1967.

Shakespeare, William. *The Riverside Shakespeare*. G. Blakemore Evans, *et al.* (eds.). Boston: Houghton Mifflin, 1974.

The Sonnets; and, A Lover's Complaint. John Kerrigan (ed.). New York: Viking, 1986; Harmondsworth: Penguin, 1986.

Shawcross, John T. *Intentionality and the New Traditionalism: Some Liminal Means to Literary Revisionism*. University Park, Pennsylvania State University Press, 1991.

(ed.) *The Complete Poetry of John Donne*. Garden City, New York: Anchor, 1967.

Shepherd, Simon, (ed.) *The Women's Sharp Revenge: Five Women's Pamphlets from the Renaissance*. New York: St. Martin's Press, 1985.

Shorter, Edward. *A History of Women's Bodies*. New York: Basic Books, 1982.

Showalter, Elaine. "Feminist Criticism in the Wilderness." Showalter, 243–70.

"Towards a Feminist Poetics." Jacobus, 22–41.

(ed.) *The New Feminist Criticism: Essays on Women, Literature, and Theory*. New York: Pantheon Books, 1985.

Sidney, Mary. *The Triumph of Death, and Other Unpublished and Uncollected Poems*. G. F. Waller (ed.). *Elizabethan & Renaissance Studies 65*. Salzburg, Austria: Institut für Englische Sprache und Literatur, Univ. Saltzburg, 1977.

Urania. Providence, RI: Brown Writers Project.

Sidney, Philip. *The Covntesse of Pembrokes Arcadia*. Ohio: Kent State University Press, 1970.

Poems. William A. Ringler, Jr. (ed.). Oxford: Clarendon Press, 1962.

Sir Philip Sidney's Defence of Poesy. Dorothy M. Macardie (ed.). London: Macmillan; New York: St. Martin's Press, 1964.

Syr P. S. his Astrophel and Stella. To the end of which are added sundry other rare sonnets of diuers gentlemen. London, 1591.

Singer, Irving. *The Nature of Love.* 1966. Three vols. University of Chicago Press, 1984–1987.

Smith, A. J. *The Metaphysics of Love: Studies in Renaissance Love Poetry from Dante to Milton.* Cambridge University Press, 1985.

Smith, G. Gregory (ed.) *Elizabethan Critical Essays.* 2 vols. Oxford: Clarendon Press, 1904.

Smith, Hallett Darius. *Elizabethan Poetry: A Study in Conventions, Meaning, and Expression.* Cambridge: Harvard University Press, 1952.

Smith, Henrie. *A Preparatiue to Mariage.* London, 1591.

Smith, Hilda. *Reason's Disciples: Seventeenth-Century English Feminists.* Urbana: University of Illinois Press, 1982.

Smith-Rosenberg, Carroll. "The New Woman and the New History." *Feminist Studies* 3 (1975): 185–98.

"Writing History: Language, Class, and Gender." de Lauretis, 31–54.

Sowernam, Ester. *Ester Hath Hang'd Haman: or An Answere to a Lewd Pamphlet.* London, 1617.

Speght, Rachel. *A Mouzzell for Melastomus.* London, 1617.

Spencer, Theodore. "The Poetry of Sir Philip Sidney." *English Literary History* 12 (1945): 251–78.

Spenser, Edmund. *The Amoretti.* Edwin Greenlaw, *et al.* (eds.). vol. VIII:193–232 of *The Works of Edmund Spenser: A Variorum Edition.* 10 vols. Baltimore: Johns Hopkins University Press, 1932–1949.

The Faerie Queene. 1977. A. C. Hamilton (ed.). London: Longman, 1980.

Spiller, Michael R. G. *The Development of the Sonnet: An Introduction.* London: Routledge, 1992.

Spriet, Pierre. *Samuel Daniel (1563–1619) Sa Vie – Son Oeuvre. Études Anglaises* 29. Paris: Didier, 1968.

Spufford, Margaret. "First Steps in Literacy: the Reading and Writing Experiences of the Humblest Seventeenth-Century Spiritual Autobiographers." *Social History* 4 (1979): 407–35.

Stallybrass, Peter and Allon White. *The Politics and Poetics of Transgression.* Ithaca: Cornell University Press, 1986.

Stevens, John E. *Music & Poetry in the Early Tudor Court.* Lincoln: University of Nebraska Press, 1961.

Stimpson, Catharine R. Introduction. Benstock, 1–6.

Stockwood, John. *A Bartholmew Fairing for Parentes, Shewing That Children Are Not to Marie, Without the Consent of Their Parents.* London, 1589.

Stone, Lawrence. *The Crisis of the Aristocracy, 1558–1641.* Oxford: Clarendon Press, 1965.

The Family, Sex, and Marriage In England 1500–1800. Abridged. New York: Harper & Row, 1979.

Strong, Roy. *The English Icon: Elizabethan & Jacobean Portraiture*. Paul Mellon Foundation for British Art. London: Routledge, 1969.

The Cult of Elizabeth: Elizabethan Portraiture and Pageantry. London: Thames and Hudson, 1977.

Strype, John (ed.) *Annals of the Reformation and Establishment of Religion, and other Various Occurrences in the Church of England, during Queen Elizabeth's Happy Reign*. 4 vols. Oxford, 1824.

Stubbes, Philip. *The Anatomie of Abuses*. London, 1595.

Stubbs, John. *John Stubbs's Gaping Gulf with Letters and Other Relevant Documents*. Lloyd E. Berry (ed.). Charlottesville: University Press of Virginia, 1968.

Sturm-Maddox, Sara. *Petrarch's Laurels*. University Park, Pennsylvania Press, 1992.

Petrarch's Metamorphoses: Text and Subtext in the Rime sparse. Columbia: University of Missouri Press, 1985.

Summers, Claude J. and Ted-Larry Pebworth. "Donne's Correspondence with Wotton." *John Donne Journal* 10 (1991): 136.

(eds.) *The Eagle and the Dove: Reassessing John Donne*. Columbia: University of Missouri Press, 1986.

(eds.) *Representing Women in Renaissance England*. Columbia: University of Missouri Press, 1997.

Svensson, Lars-Hakan. *Silent Art: Rhetorical and Thematic Patterns in Samuel Daniel's Delia*. Lund: Gleerup, 1980.

Swetnam, Joseph. *The Araignment of Lewde, idle, froward and unconstant women*. London, 1615.

Tanner, J. R., (ed.) *Tudor Constitutional Documents AD 1485–1603*. Cambridge University Press, 1922.

Teague, Frances. "Queen Elizabeth in her Speeches." Cerasano and Wynne-Davies, 63–78.

Tennenhouse, Leonard. *Power on Display: The Politics of Shakespeare's Genres*. New York: Methuen, 1986.

"Sir Walter Ralegh and the Literature of Clientage." Lytle and Orgel, 235–58.

Thickstun, Margaret Olofson. *Fictions of the Feminine: Puritan Doctrine and the Representation of Women*. Ithaca: Cornell University Press, 1988.

Thomas, Keith. "The Changing Family." *Times Literary Supplement* 21 October 1977: 1226–27.

"The Meaning of Literacy in Early Modern England," *The Written Word: Literacy in Transition*, Gerd Baumann (ed.) Oxford, 1986, 116–17.

Thompson, Ann. "The Warrant of Womanhood." Holderness, 74–88.

Thompson, Edward Maunde (ed.) *Correspondence of the Family of Hatton*. 2 vols. London, 1878.

Thomson, P. "Petrarch and the Elizabethans." *English* 10 (1955): 177–80.

Thomson, Patricia. "The Literature of Patronage, 1580–1630," *Essays In Criticism* 2 (1952): 267–84.

"Sonnet 15 of Samuel Daniel's *Delia*: A Petrarchan Imitation." *Comparative Literature* 17 (1965): 151–57.

Tilney, Edmund. *A Brief and Pleasant Discourse of Duties in Mariage, Called the Flower of Friendshippe*. London, 1568.

Todd, Barbara J. "The Remarrying Widow: A Stereotype Reconsidered." Prior, 54–92.

Toliver, Harold E. *Lyric Provinces in the English Renaissance*. Columbus: Ohio State University Press, 1985.

Travitsky, Betty. Introduction. "Placing Women in the Renaissance." Haselkorn and Travitsky, 3–41.

"The Lady Doth Protest: Protest in the Popular Writings of Renaissance Englishwomen." *English Literary Renaissance* 14 (1984): 255–83.

"The 'Wyll and Testament' of Isabella Whitney." *English Literary Renaissance* 10 (1980): 76–94.

(ed.) *The Paradise of Women. Writings by Englishwomen of the Renaissance*. Contributions in Women's Studies 22. Westport, Conn.: Greenwood Press, 1981.

Turner, James Grantham. *One Flesh: Paradisal Marriage and Sexual Relations in the Age of Milton*. Oxford: Clarendon Press, 1987.

(ed.) *Sexuality and Gender in Early Modern Europe: Institutions, Texts, Images*. Cambridge University Press, 1993.

T[yler], M[argaret]. Introductory Epistles. Tyler A2r–A4v.

(trans.) *The Mirrour of Princely deedes*. London, 1578.

Underdown, D. E. "The Taming of the Scold: the Enforcement of Patriarchal Authority in Early Modern England." Fletcher and Stevenson, 116–36.

Veen, Otto van. *Amorvm Emblemata*. Tr. Verstegan, pseudonym for Richard Rowlands. Antwerp, 1608.

Veeser, H. Aram (ed.) *The New Historicism*. New York: Routledge, 1988.

Vickers, Nancy J. "Diana Described: Scattered Woman and Scattered Rhyme." *Critical Inquiry* 8 (1981): 265–79.

Villeponteaux, Mary A. "'With her own will beguyld': The Captive Lady in Spenser's *Amoretti*." *Explorations in Renaissance Culture* 14 (1988): 29–39.

Vives, J. L. *A Very Frutefull and Pleasant Boke Called the Instruction of a Christen Woman*. R. Hyrd (trans.). London, 1529.

Walker, Julia M. (ed.) *Milton and the Idea of Woman*. Urbana: University of Illinois Press, 1988.

Wall, Wendy. *The Imprint of Gender: Authorship and Publication in the English Renaissance*. Ithaca: Cornell University Press, 1993.

Waller, Gary F. "Acts of Reading: the Production of Meaning in *Astrophil and Stella*." *Studies in the Literary Imagination* 14 (1981): 23–35.

Introduction. Mary Sidney, 1–64.

"Struggling into Discourse: The Emergence of Renaissance Women's Writing." Hannay, 238–56.

Mary Sidney, Countess of Pembroke: a Critical Study of her Writings and Literary Milieu. Institut für Anglistik und Amerikanistik, Universität Salzburg, 1979.

Waller, Marguerite R. *Petrarch's Poetics and Literary History*. Amherst: University of Massachuetts Press, 1980.

Walton, Isaac. *The Lives of Dr John Donne, Sir Henry Wotton, Mr Richard Hooker, Mr George Herbert.* London, 1670.

Ward, Bernard Mordaunt. *The Seventeenth Earl of Oxford, 1550–1604.* London: J. Murray, 1928.

Warnicke, Retha M. *Women of the English Renaissance and Reformation.* Westport, Conn.: Greenwood Press, 1983.

Watkins, W. B. C. *Shakespeare and Spenser.* Princeton University Press, 1950.

Watson, Foster (ed.) *English Writers on Education, 1480–1603.* Gainesville: Scholars' Facsimiles and Reprints, 1967.

(ed.) *Vives and the Renascence Education of Women.* New York: Longmans, 1912.

Watson, George. *The English Petrarchans: A Critical Bibliography of the Canzoniere.* London: Warburg Institute, University of London, 1967.

Wayne, Valerie (ed.) Introduction. *The Flower of Friendship: A Renaissance Dialogue Contesting Marriage.* Ithaca: Cornell University Press, 1992, 1–93.

"Some Sad Sentence: Vives' *Instruction of a Christian Woman.*" Hannay, 15–29.

Weedon, Chris. *Feminist Practice and Poststructuralist Theory.* Oxford: Blackwell, 1987.

Whately, William. *A Care-cloth: Or A Treatise of the Troubles of Marriage.* London, 1624.

Whigham, Frank. *Ambition and Privilege: The Social Tropes of Elizabethan Courtesy Theory.* Berkeley: University of California Press, 1984.

Whitford, Richard. *A Werke for Housholders.* London, 1530.

Whitney, Geffrey. *A Choice of Emblemes, and other Devises.* London, 1586.

Whitney, Isabella. *The copie of a letter, lately written in meeter, by a yonge gentilwoman to her vnconstant Louer. With an Admonitio*[n] *to al yong Gentilwomen and to al other Mayds in general. By Is. W[hitney].* London, 1567.

A sweet nosgay; or pleasant posye: contayning a hundred and ten phylosophicall flowers. London, 1573.

Whythorne, Thomas. *The Autobiography of Thomas Whythorne.* James M. Osborn (ed.). Modern Spelling edn. London: Oxford University Press, 1962.

Wiesner, Merry. *Women and Gender in Early Modern Europe.* Cambridge University Press, 1993.

Willen, Diane. "A Comment on Women's Education in Elizabethan England." *Topic* 36 (1982): 66–73.

Williamson, C. F. "The Design of Daniel's *Delia.*" *Review of English Studies* 19 (1968): 251–60.

Williamson, Marilyn L. *The Patriarchy of Shakespeare's Comedies.* Detroit: Wayne State University Press, 1986.

Raising their Voices: British Women Writers, 1650–1750. Detroit: Wayne State University Press, 1990.

"Toward a Feminist Literary History." *Signs* 10 (1984): 136–47.

Willoby, Henry. *Willobie, his Avisa. Or, the True picture of a modest maid and of a chast and constant wife.* London, 1594.

Wilson, Christopher R. "*Astrophil and Stella*: A Tangled Editorial Web." The Library 6 (1979): 336–46.

Wilson, K. J. *Incomplete Fictions: The Formation of English Renaissance Dialogue.* Washington, DC: Catholic University of America Press, 1985.

Wilson, Katharina M. *Women Writers of the Renaissance and Reformation.* Athens: University of Georgia Press, 1987.

Wiltenburg, Joy. *Disorderly Women and Female Power in the Street Literature of Early Modern England and Germany.* Charlottesville: University Press of Virginia, 1992.

Winny, James. *The Master-Mistress: a Study of Shakespeare's Sonnets.* New York: Barnes & Noble, 1968.

Woodbridge, Linda. *Women and the English Renaissance: Literature and the Nature of Womankind, 1540 to 1620.* Urbana: University of Illinois Press, 1984.

Woods, Suzanne. "Spenser and the Problem of Women's Rule." *Huntingdon Library Quarterly* 48 (1985): 141–58.

Woods, Suzanne (ed.) *The Poems of Aemilia Lanyer. Salve Deus Rex Judæorum.* Women Writers in English 1350–1850. New York: Oxford University Press, 1993.

Woolf, Virginia. *A Room of One's Own.* New York: Harcourt, Brace and Company, 1929.

Wright, George T. *The Poet in the Poem; the Personae of Eliot, Yeats, and Pound.* Berkeley: University of California Press, 1960.

Wright, Louis B. *Middle-Class Culture in Elizabethan England.* Chapel Hill: University of North Carolina Press, 1935.

"The Reading of Renaissance English Women." *Studies in Philology* 28 (1931): 139–56.

Wrightson, Keith. *English Society 1580–1680.* New Brunswick: Rutgers University Press, 1982.

Wrigley, E. A. "Family Limitation in Pre-Industrial England." *Economic History Review* 19 (1966): 82–109.

Wroth, Mary. *The Poems of Lady Mary Wroth.* Josephine A. Roberts (ed.). Baton Rouge: Louisiana State University Press, 1983.

The Countesse of Mountgomeries Urania. London 1621; Women Writers Project, Brown University, 1993.

Wyatt, Thomas. *Sir Thomas Wyatt: The Complete Poems.* Ronald A. Rebholz (ed.). New Haven: Yale University Press, 1981.

Yeats, William Butler. *Selected Poems and Two Plays of William Butler Yeats.* M. L. Rosenthal (ed.). New York: Collier, 1962.

Ziegler, Georgianna. "Penelope and the Politics of Woman's Place in the Renaissance." Cerasano and Wynne-Davies, 25–46.

Index